EPIPHANY
IN THE
WILDERNESS

EPIPHANY
━━ IN THE ━━
WILDERNESS

HUNTING, NATURE, AND PERFORMANCE IN THE NINETEENTH-CENTURY AMERICAN WEST

KAREN R. JONES

UNIVERSITY PRESS OF COLORADO
Boulder

Published by University Press of Colorado
5589 Arapahoe Avenue, Suite 206C
Boulder, Colorado 80303

 The University Press of Colorado is a proud member of
Association of American University Presses.

The University Press of Colorado is a cooperative publishing enterprise supported, in part, by Adams State University, Colorado State University, Fort Lewis College, Metropolitan State University of Denver, Regis University, University of Colorado, University of Northern Colorado, Utah State University, and Western State Colorado University.

∞ This paper meets the requirements of the ANSI / NISO Z39.48-1992 (Permanence of Paper).

ISBN: 978-1-60732-397-6 (cloth)
ISBN: 978-1-60732-398-3 (ebook)

Library of Congress Cataloging-in-Publication Data
Jones, Karen R., 1972–
  Epiphany in the wilderness : hunting, nature, and performance in the nineteenth-century American West / Karen R. Jones.
    pages cm
  Includes bibliographical references.
    ISBN 978-1-60732-397-6 (cloth) — ISBN 978-1-60732-398-3 (ebook)
  1. Hunting—West (U.S.)—History—19th century. 2. Hunting—Social aspects—West (U.S.)—History—19th century. 3. Hunting in literature—West (U.S.)—History—19th century. 4. Hunting in art—West (U.S.)—History—19th century. 5. Hunters—West (U.S.)—History—19th century. I. Title.
  SK45.J73 2015
  639'.10978—dc23
                        2015011285
24   23   22   21   20   19   18   17   16   15   10   9   8   7   6   5   4   3   2   1

The University Press of Colorado gratefully acknowledges the generous support of the Charles Redd Center for Western Studies at Brigham Young University toward the publication of this book.

Cover photograph: "The J.L. Grandin hunting party. #1, Grandin Farm, D.T. (Mrs Grandin and Miss Hague)," 1879, photograph By F. Jay Haynes (H-246, Haynes Foundation Collection, Montana Historical Society Research Center Photograph Archives, Helena, Montana).

For M. R. Jones and C. C. Ditchburn

CONTENTS

ILLUSTRATIONS

ACKNOWLEDGMENTS

My first memories of the hunt are not from North America but Britain, where the woods of my grandmother's home played host to pheasants raised for the local shoot, birds darting across the leafy trails where my brother and I hared around playing out our own wilderness adventures in the bracken. Although born from later wanderings in the landscape and archives of the Rocky Mountains, this project has rekindled such memories and given me fresh insight into the practices, mentalities, and historically valuable contribution of hunting to human culture, socioeconomies, and ecological life. *Epiphany in the Wilderness* took me to great spaces both indoors and out: to the forest, the shooting range, and the taxidermy class (although my mouse, posed on hind legs in attacking grizzly bear-style, remains lost in the post somewhere between London and Kent) as well as animating my "den" with colorful tales and the odd mounted head.

Numerous people and institutions have assisted with this project, starting with the School of History at the University of Kent, which proved endlessly encouraging of my research and awarded financial sponsorship. Particular gratitude is due to Julie Anderson, Jackie Waller, Barbara Bombi, and Mark Connelly, not only for enlivening my working day but also for being such fine friends. The British Academy and the Arts and Humanities Research Council generously funded the project with travel bursaries and sabbatical leave. Thanks are also due to those whom I ran into along the research trail, including specialists at various libraries, museums, and academic institutions. Brian Shovers, Rich Aarstad, Lory Morrow, Molly Holtz, and Charlene Porsild at the Montana Historical Society provided invaluable assistance while I was in Helena as a Bradley Fellow, as did Peter Blodgett and Katrina Denman during my several visits to the Huntington Library, San Marino. A particular debt of gratitude is due to the Autry National Center, Los Angeles, an institution that never fails to bring animation to my research. Thanks are extended to Steve Aron, Liza Posas, Manola Madrid, and especially to Marva Felchlin. There are, additionally, a raft of people who contributed immeasurably to the project by reading drafts and discussing the finer points of the historical hunting trail with me. *Epiphany in the Wilderness* no doubt benefited substantially from the insights of William Beinart, Peter Coates, Jacqueline Fear-Segal, Daniel Herman, John Mackenzie, Neil Pemberton, Colin Samson, and Louis Warren. Thanks also to Darrin Pratt, Jessica d'Arbonne, and the staff at the University Press of Colorado for their patience, professionalism, and enthusiasm for the project.

Heartfelt thanks go out to family and friends who have endured the project and my endless talk of hunting stories and taxidermy trophies, with understanding (mostly) and humor (most certainly). To Mum: I hope you enjoyed wandering over the plains of Wiltshire spying bison herds munching the gentle downland grass as much as I did. And to Neil and Helen: it pleases me greatly that Annabel and Andrew had so much affection for "Fuzz Cody," the Jackalope in my den. My grandmothers, Ismay Jones and Sheila Ditchburn, both instilled in me an appreciation of the land and the power of storytelling, for which I am very grateful. To Clare: I am endlessly appreciative of your love and support, not to mention your enthusiasm for the natural world. Gracie and Gerry, for their part, imparted four-legged wisdoms on performing the hunt as they channeled their inner wolf and mountain lion in contests played out in "the great indoors." Lastly, I'd like to thank my very own hunter heroes: Christopher Coleby Ditchburn, who taught me the joys of wandering in nature and noticing its beautiful intricacies (not to mention how to wrestle imaginary bears), and Michael Jones, whose tales of hunting plastic tigers in the wilds of Wessex no doubt informed this book in a formative way. To Grampy and to Dad: this book is dedicated to you.

EPIPHANY
IN THE
WILDERNESS

THE WEST, STORYTELLING ANIMALS, AND THE HUNT AS PERFORMANCE

One bright winter day in 1873, William "Doc" Carver stepped out onto the plains at Frenchman Creek to defend his credentials as a "hunter hero" of the plains against "Buffalo" Curley. Carver, a dentist and hide hunter, boasted in confident tones how he had killed 30,000 bison and had defended his honor as a sharpshooter many times before. Curley, a known reprobate from Texas, bristled with a competitive edge, egged on by the market hunters he was camped with nearby who were particularly aggrieved at competing with Carver for buffalo hide. It was they who put up the $500 prize for the competition, appointed judges, and ordered ammunition and horses from the Union Pacific. News of the contest provoked significant interest. Amassed were hundreds of onlookers—a curious assemblage of trappers, skin hunters, wolfers, and local Pawnee and Sioux from the White Clay Agency, along with a contingent of soldiers and ladies from Fort McPherson. The crowd waited with bated breath as the bison herd moved into view, their coats glimmering with frost particles, snorts from their nostrils producing clouds of vapor in the cold air. As the shaggy beasts entered the river to drink, Carver, Curley,

DOI: 10.5876/9781607323983.c000

and their entourage of Indian "scorers" (charged with the task of shooting arrows into the fallen, the attached feathers marking each man's kill tally) galloped up the draw. The referee fired a pistol shot, the herd stampeded, and the game was on. Carver, who cut quite a sartorial presence on his favorite steed Surprise, wearing a red shirt and tossing his auburn hair, claimed first blood and soon got ahead. Those watching the melee saw Doc disappear over the bluff, leaving Curley outpaced and his horse spent. As the judges counted Carver's haul, some 160 animals (Curley's score, intriguingly, was not recorded), Doc paused at a buffalo wallow to fill his hat with water and pour it over his wearied horse. As the crowd cheered uproariously, Carver was crowned "Champion buffalo hunter of the plains."[1]

The story of Doc Carver's rifle contest that bracing day in Nebraska presents a classic account of frontier whimsy: gunplay, dueling men, thundering buffalo, and wide prairie vistas. It also illustrates, in colorful style, the centrality of hunting to the western experience as well as its embedded codes of staging and performance. Enacted for reasons of subsistence, for the market, and for sport, hunting left an indelible mark on the mechanics of westward expansion in the nineteenth century, lassoing environments and human communities in a consumptive and cultural bind that was nothing less than transformative. For British traveler Isabella Bird, the West was, quite simply, "the world of big game." Hunting impacted the practical lives of westerners on an everyday level and also emerged as an integral part of the region's mythology. Transmitted by a process of trans-media storytelling that took in oral history, print culture, art, photography, and even taxidermy, the "story" of the hunt, in fact, became a critical device through which frontier experience in the trans-Mississippi was constructed, maintained, and memorialized. As Montana settler Horace Edwards noted in correspondence with a friend, "a letter from me to you would hardly be complete without some hunting sketch would it?" A terrain both literal and figurative, the West was a physical space in which animal capital had tangible economic, political, and social value and an imaginative geography in which the drama of nationhood was played out. Critical players in the performance of the hunt were the masculine hunter hero—"leading man" and exemplar of rugged individualism and all-action bravado; the lady sharpshooter and "wild woman" that subtly subverted his hegemony; and a cast of suitably charismatic beasts waiting in the wings to snarl and stampede, directed at once by biological makeup and the needs of theatrical flourish. A vibrant realm filled with animal and allegorical sign, the nineteenth-century hunting frontier was an animated, expressive, and, at times, contested space. Disentangling the complex relationships between the human actors and the wild things they pursued sits at the heart of *Epiphany in the Wilderness*.[2]

THE NINETEENTH-CENTURY WEST: THE AGE OF THE HUNTER

When Thomas Jefferson sat in the library at Monticello, his gaze flitting from the bucolic confines of the garden to the pile of books on the desk whose subject was the strange lands west of the Mississippi, hunting was probably the last thing on his mind. In common with other political commentators of the late eighteenth and early nineteenth centuries, he believed the highest form of civilization to be an agrarian republic that held society and nature in perfect synchronicity. While cultivating a certain "boldness, enterprise, and independence to the mind," hunting smacked of barbarism and primitive civilization. The future belonged to the yeoman farmer. One hundred years on, things looked a little different. President Theodore Roosevelt was dressing in buckskin to play big game hunter across two continents, "Buffalo Bill" Cody and Annie Oakley, "the first American superstars," wowed audiences on both sides of the Atlantic with their sharpshooting skills, and Frederick Jackson Turner's frontier thesis celebrated the hunting shirt and the pioneer cabin as foundational artifacts of American identity. Hunters were performing everywhere, their collective efforts pointing to a simple conclusion. The nineteenth century was irrevocably shaped by westward expansion, and in that story the hunter stood center stage.[3]

Hunting in the West naturally subscribed to different categories and followed particular chronologies over the span of a century. Hunting for subsistence had long been a feature of indigenous culture, evidenced by the traps, drives, and buffalo jumps (such as the magnificently named Head-Smashed-In-Buffalo-Jump in present-day Alberta) still visible in the contours of the landscape. Dominating the practice and the symbology of the hunt was the bison, a nutritional powerhouse and provider of all manner of goods from rawhide parfleches to skinning knives crafted from scapula bone. The acquisition of horses from Spanish traders in the 1730s saw a mobile and highly effective nomadic hunting culture spread across the plains, reaching its apogee in the early 1800s. For the Lakota, Cheyenne, Blackfeet, and other plains Indians, hunting on horseback was nothing short of revolutionary. According to ethnologist John Ewers, a minute-long chase from two accomplished hunters armed with bow and arrow could yield up to a ton of bison meat. Indigenous hunting was functional and also deeply performative—the dramaturgy of stampeding animals and whirling mounted hunters captivating a legion of observers from Wild Hog of the Cheyenne to plains artist George Catlin.[4]

The first Euro-American explorers and emigrants to the West were beguiled by its faunal complement: nature's performance opened the show in style. From the expedition of Lewis and Clark (1804–6) to the thousands of emigrants traveling the Oregon Trail in the 1840s and 1850s, the sight of a "first" bison, elk, or grizzly bear prompted cries of delight. Writing on a bluff above the Missouri on April 22, 1805, Meriwether Lewis spoke of "immence herds of Buffaloe, Elk, deer, and Antelopes feeding in one common and boundless pasture." Travelers feasted their eyes and filled their cooking pots: wild game was representative of a welcome larder as well as an aspect of wonderment. According to Raymond Burroughs, on its 4,000-mile trek across the West, the Corps of Discovery supplemented rations with 1,001 deer, 375 elk, 227 bison, and 43 grizzly bears (as well as game birds, horses, and more "exotic" western fare including hawk, wolf, and gopher). Emigrants took heed of Lansford Hastings's *Emigrants Guide to Oregon and California* (1845) and brought rifles, pistols, lead, powder, and shot alongside essential supplies of flour, coffee, sugar, salt, and bacon expressly for the purpose of hunting (what Hastings called "making meat").[5]

The settler experience in the West was equally marked by the primacy of the hunt. Jefferson's yeoman farmers eager to claim a slice of prairie sod under the auspices of the Homestead Act (1862) regarded game meat as an invaluable source of sustenance. Cornelius Henderson, who emigrated from Minnesota to Kalispell, Montana, in the 1870s, took to the game trail for a few months every year, finding sage hens welcome culinary relief from his cabbage crop. Hunting for wild game was part of the seasonal cycle of life on the nineteenth-century frontier and also became a key point of cultural reference and social memory. Montana pioneer Nannie Alderson remembered eating buffalo steak in Miles City on her emigrant journey west from Chicago, her first home floored with canvas and animal hide, and plump ranch house cushions stuffed with curly bison hair from one of the last beasts to roam that area. The spoils of the hunt were everywhere, pragmatic and symbolic markers of frontier experience.[6]

More than hunting for the table, the pursuit of wild things in the nineteenth-century West was an issue of market economics. Game meat, skins, and hides were valuable commodities, marking the trans-Mississippi as a resource frontier in which hunting could bring sizeable financial returns. The trade in animal capital connected the West to a global market, enmeshing it in a transnational network that bonded the plains and mountains to the urban metropoles of New York, London, and Paris. As historian George Colpitts notes of the Canadian Northwest, wild meat served as "the first currency" and a means of barter between indigenous tribes and fur traders, attesting to a complex phenomenology of the hunt that spoke of cultural collision and animal exchange. Central to the trade in the early part of the century was the beaver, a critter that had long been of interest to the British crown (sponsor of the Hudson's Bay Company) and in the aftermath of the Lewis and Clark Expedition inspired a procession of free trappers and company men to head to the streams of the Rockies in search of fortune. At the height of the industry during the late 1820s, the American Fur Company (1808–47) was harvesting more than 700,000 furbearers annually.[7]

The beaver population was in serious trouble by the 1830s, but changing fashions for wool and silk hats saved the species from the worst incursions of the market. The bison, however, earned no such reprieve. An archetypal "animal of enterprise," bison were pursued on an industrial scale from the 1860s, facilitated by railroad access, firearms technology, and market demand. The animals were hunted for their meat (notably their tongues, humps, and hindquarters, supplied to army and railroad camps and later, with the development of the refrigerated rail car, to cities on the eastern seaboard) and for their skins (especially after new processes allowed the fashioning of bison hide into soft leather in 1871). The prospect of easy money brought thousands of market hunters to the plains armed with high-powered rifles. Hunting from a "stand" (concealed within range of the herd and firing from rocks or metal supports), buffalo hunters panicked the herd by shooting a lead animal and then fired repeatedly into the resulting melee. When rifles became too hot to use, they were cooled in streams, doused with canteen water, or urinated on. The exercise in butchery ended with packers loading carts and stripping the carcasses, before transit to camp and on by steamer and rail to Chicago. The scale was industrial—a salient indicator of the West as a landscape of appropriation and conquest—and dramatic, captured as it was in the narrative histories of the hide hunters that resonated with paeans to the trans-Mississippi as cornucopian landscape, the "wild and woolly" days of the unbridled frontier, and of the "winning of the West" through a mercantile gaze. By the mid-1880s, however, both the southern and northern herds were gone: some seven million animals were reduced to a few hundred in a matter of decades. A new "story" and a new performance emerged— encapsulated visually in the stark photographs of bloated bison carcasses and bones piled high at railheads (for shipment as lime and fertilizer) by Layton Huffman, Frank Haynes, and other frontier photographers. Three million bison were killed during the 1872–74 period alone, a figure, as commentator William Black noted, equivalent to half the cattle in Great Britain. *Bison bison*, the "monarch of the plains," had been one of the region's most distinctive features and now became the sorrowful symbol of a landscape tamed with extraordinary rapidity. Montana rancher David Hilger, a self-confessed "good shot" and killer of hundreds of buffalo, later lamented, with a conservationist sensibility, his "wanton and ruthless slaughtering of these noble animals."[8]

Alongside subsistence and market hunting, the American West in the nineteenth century saw recreational hunting on a grand scale. The frontier inspired the attentions of a colorful procession of sport hunters throughout the century, and it is this group of hunters in which *Epiphany in the Wilderness* is most interested. Most pronounced during the "golden age" of sport hunting between 1860 and 1890, big game hunters from both sides of the Atlantic flocked to the West to bag its signature trophy animals, play out fantasies of wilderness exploration, and enact a destiny both manifest and (usually) masculine. What made the West distinctive was its monumental scenery, its frontier character, including the prospect of a rub with American Indians, and a fine complement of big game found nowhere else. As Colonel Richard Dodge avowed, "I think that the whole world can be challenged to offer a greater variety of game to the sportsman." These adventurers—in effect the first western tourists—routinely expressed delight at the landscapes of abundance laid out before them: of wide prairies "black" with bison herds, verdant forests abounding with deer, and craggy gulches roamed by grizzly bears—a veritable hunter's paradise born from ecological plenitude as well as the narrative turn of the hunter hero setting the scene for his (and sometimes her) grand entrance.[9]

Sport hunting played a leading role in the development of a leisure economy in the nineteenth-century West while its penchant for what Monica Rico calls "disciplined violence" reflected the exigencies of class, race, gender, and empire. A western tour demanded dedication to the chase, skills with rifle and horse (although that could be practiced), and, first and foremost, financial resources. Being a sport hunter was, fundamentally, an elite activity. Legendary big-spending game hunter George Gore, for instance, spent upward of $500,000 on his three-year shooting spree across Wyoming, Montana, and Dakota in 1854–57. The Irish aristocrat boasted an entourage of forty staff (arranged through the offices of the American Fur Company), including trappers Henry Chatillon and Jim Bridger, fifty greyhounds, a multitude of guns (which took up an entire wagon), a brass bedstead, a bathtub, and a carpet to bring comfort to prairie sod. Totaling some 2,000 bison, 1,600 elk, and 105 grizzlies, Gore's kill tally was nothing short of extraordinary. Jim Bridger described one occasion in which "we shot hundreds o' bufffler for nothin' but the hides, tongues, humps and backstrips and left the rest o' the meat to the coyotes. Seemed like Sir George wanted spec'mens of everythin' that flew or crawled or run—we got 'em all!" Such a comment elucidated the trophy ethos of the big game hunter—of spirited victory and specimen collection—and highlighted an imperial mentality that assumed the right to take resources at will.[10]

The typologies of hunting in the nineteenth-century West—subsistence, market, and sport—volunteered different approaches in terms of tactics, rationales, and ethnographies. Such distinctions were important, not least in terms of target species, environmental engagement, social codes, and ecological impacts. Where, what, when, and how the hunt was prosecuted varied enormously across the vast theater of the trans-Mississippi, validating what Clyde Milner has referred to as "the fragmented unity" of the region and suggesting a legion of microhistories yet to be written on specific communities. Often framed rhetorically in terms of history and honor, subsistence hunters, sport hunters, and marketeers were each keen to assert their own distinct identities that spoke of fraternal camaraderie, cultural mores, and resource entitlements. In each case, the hunt became a frame of reference through which particular groups defined their relationship to the West, both practically and symbolically. Stories spoke of identity politics and territorial claims—marking the testimonial terrain of the game trail as one heavily imprinted with operative meaning. "Performing" their hunting identity by talking about frontier experiences, sport hunters consciously defined themselves against the materialistic marketeer, local western guides lampooned the foppish "tenderfoots" who came for their dose of wilderness adrenaline, and settlers set "their" rights to game against that of the indigene. Rubrics of class, race, gender, and empire shaped the cultural and environmental history of hunting in the nineteenth-century West and rendered the game trail as a place for the construction, articulation, and contestation of social difference. Competing notions of rightful use and ritual code positioned the hunting frontier as a locus of contest—and a deeply performative one at that.[11]

At the same time, however, such distinctions were not always clear-cut. Among the different hunting communities of the nineteenth-century West were cultural exchanges, common visions, and border crossings. For one thing, a significant number of people successfully traversed the boundaries of typology to "perform" the hunt in its various iterations. Henry Bierman, who ventured west in 1880 "to see the country," worked as a Chicago meat-packer and bison hunter before ranching in the Musselshell Valley, Montana. Bierman hunted regularly to supply his family, freighters, and neighbors with meat and fondly recalled sitting down to a Christmas feast, western-style, in 1886 of antelope, rabbit, dried apple pie, and sourdough biscuit. The cryptography of the chase betrayed common ciphers and spheres of interaction, entangling all hunters in a broader "imagined community" based on their quest for game. As historians Thomas Altherr and John Reiger note, "The very act of pursuing prey and perhaps killing an animal propelled every hunter into a comradeship with others." Aside from the structural commonalities of the hunt (quest and pursuit), the hunting experience spoke of a common search for social meaning and embroiled its agents in shared networks of expertise in the trans-Mississippi arena. Subsistence hunters enthused about the thrill of the chase in the fashion of the sport hunters. Sport hunters drew on the economic infrastructure of the fur-trading industry for their western tours and ventured a complicated relationship with frontier guides that both valorized and marginalized the subaltern. Hide hunters may have recorded their bison tally by the dollar quotient, but many traded in the parlance of romantic plains lore. James Mead, hide hunter in Kansas during the 1860s, for instance, spoke zestfully of his "sport" on the prairie and kept buffalo horn as a trophy. The cultural ecology of the hunt was—for all its performative bifurcations—fluid. Moreover, the act of storytelling—of ritually performing the hunt as a way of creating, consolidating, and evoking a frontier identity—was shared by all. The hunting frontier was, at root, a testimonial culture, and stories could be readily shared. Thus, on occasion, "redskins," "game hogs," and "bluebloods" could all be found together around the campfire, a pertinent demonstration of their place in a broader community of performers, bound together not only in the quest for animal capital but also by a need to talk about it.[12]

And what of William "Doc" Carver? The "Champion bison hunter of the plains" himself elucidated the fuzzy boundaries of the hunting frontier. Born in Winslow, Illinois, in 1840, Carver had migrated to Minnesota in 1857 and fallen in with the Santee Sioux. According to the *New York Times*, he became a "thorough Indian, and attained wonderful proficiency in shooting, riding, hunting, and all exercises of the chase." Already skillful at bagging small game (according to biographer Raymond Thorp, he introduced himself to the chief as "a hunter"), Carver grafted an indigenous pedigree onto his frontier education to earn the epithet "Spirit Gun." After three years with the Sioux, he wandered into St Joseph, Missouri, struck an alliance with trapper Charley Bruster, and took up as a hide hunter. During the 1860s and early 1870s, Doc made a tidy profit (using mounted pursuit over the "stand" and winning plaudits from at least one British sport hunter in the process) before working as a hunting guide with "Texas Jack" Omohundro and Buffalo Bill Cody. Hunting with the Earl of Dunraven in Fox Creek, Nebraska, Carver cached a bison head, only to return later and find it badly chewed by a bear. Eager to facilitate a sonorous frontier experience for his client, Doc duly shot another bison, shipped it to England for mounting, and only confessed the deception at a party hosted years later by the earl in his honor. Carver understood the dynamics of the hunt in all its incarnations. But most of all he understood it as performance.[13]

THE STORYTELLING ANIMAL: HUNTING AND PERFORMANCE IN THE WEST

In the *Wilderness Hunter* (1893), a canonical nineteenth-century treatise on the hunting encounter with wild nature and its denizens, Theodore Roosevelt paid homage to the importance of the West in the national sporting imagination. Joining animal and hunter together in a powerful imaginative landscape of wilderness immersion was the materiality of the game trail: the engagement, contest, and hard-fought victory over wild land and its complement of charismatic megafauna. As Roosevelt proclaimed, "No one, but he who has partaken thereof, can understand the keen delight of hunting in lonely lands. For him is the joy of the horse well ridden and the rifle well held; for him the long days of toil and hardship, resolutely endured, and crowned at the end with triumph." Of principal importance in this equation was the story—the remembrance of the chase, its recollection, and its retelling. As Roosevelt explained:

> In after years there shall come forever to his mind the memory of endless prairies shimmering in the bright sun; of vast snow-clad wastes lying desolate under gray skies; of the melancholy marshes; of the rush of mighty rivers; of the breath of the evergreen forest in summer; of the crooning of ice-armored pines at the touch of the winds of winter; of cataracts roaring between hoary mountain masses; of all the innumerable sights and sounds of the wilderness; of its immensity and mystery; and of the silences that brood in its still depths.[14]

Beneath the narrative of communion with the wild was the imprint of the West as a figurative landscape, a panoramic theater in which grand aspirations could be played out.

As Roosevelt's ode demonstrates, the cultural landscape of the hunt was saturated with the language of performance, recital and enactment both intrinsic parts of the game trail experience. *Epiphany in the Wilderness* foregrounds this choreographical gaze, seeing the hunting frontier as an unfolding theater where the roles of hunters and the wild things they chased were rehearsed and replayed for the purposes of personal and social memory. As such, the hunt represented a curated experience, consciously acted out on the game trail and scripted via a range of texts and objects in the hunting "afterlife" that allowed for the exercise of the idealized self of the hunter hero within the sacrosanct space of the trans-Mississippi frontier. Hunters conversed with fellow travelers, published tracts on their adventures, commemorated their journeys in photographic albums, and decorated their homes with artworks and trophies of the chase. These carefully construed totems of the hunt contained what Derrida would call "traces" or even, rather appropriately, "tracks" in the literal translation from French—intensely personal signatures replete with meaning that allowed the staging, recall, and commemoration of moments of intimate and formative experience. At the same time, their significance was thoroughly demonstrative—the hunt was necessarily performed before a series of audiences in order to extrapolate its full importance. From peers on the game trail to the expansive arena of the Wild West Show, hunters broadcast their story through repeat and ritual performance, ratifying the authenticity of their frontier experiences by annunciation. In the process, the discrete trappings of testimonial culture were transmitted to a broader populace eager to imbibe of their "own" frontier drama by reading a story, watching a show, or gazing at a stuffed grizzly bear in a museum case.[15]

From the tracks of the game trail to the Wild West showground, the hunting frontier operated according to various dynamics—both material and abstracted—but looming large was the existence of a narrative framework that laid emphasis on the act of *doing*. Hence the usefulness of performance as an analytical lens through which to explore the nineteenth-century hunting frontier. As such, *Epiphany* assumes the conceptual vocabulary of "actor network theory" as developed by Michael Callon and Bruno Latour to see hunting as a ritually constituted activity in which protagonists construct a sense of meaning around event, place, community, and self by repeating and reinforcing behaviors, rites, and interactions. Both on the game trail itself and in its illustrious afterlife, the hunt was acted out, practiced, and idolized as a site of encounter and epiphany. By interrogating this process in terms of a performance, we can plot the motives and motions of its principal players, deconstruct the nature of their repertory, see how it was received by various audiences, and identify those mechanisms that conferred authority and historical significance. Of critical purchase is the idea that the hunt had to be acted and reenacted in order to establish and consolidate its social meaning. As cultural theorist Judith Butler reminds us, cultural identities have to be "performed" socially in order gain legitimization. Also important is the way in which the vernacular of performance pays heed to the subtle inferences of meaning embedded in testimony, script, and object. As anthropologist Clifford Geertz points out, "The great virtue of the extension of the notion of text beyond things written on paper or carved into stone is that it trains attention on precisely this phenomenon: on how the inscription of action is brought about, what its vehicles are and how they work, and on what the fixation of meaning from the flow of events—history from what happened, thought from thinking, culture from behavior—implies for socio-logical interpretation." A variegated web of relations with its own gestures and interlocutions, the cultural ecology of the hunt is thus usefully under-stood, in the words of Roland Barthes, in terms of its "activity of associa-tions, contiguities, carryings-over," in short, as a site of "playing." Within this methodological framework, the historian's gaze remains critical. As Pearson and Slater note in *Theatre/Archaeology* (2001), a systematic comprehension of performance practice requires interpretation, and this demands understand-ing both the nature of an event and its historical context.[16]

Using performance as its "trail guide," *Epiphany in the Wilderness* explores how the cultural ecology of the hunting frontier was constructed, sustained, and disseminated—in Barthes's terminology, its "play, activity, production, practice." Particularly important is the fact that this conceptual frame of reference allows room for nonhumans, objects, and landscapes to "perform" the hunt as relational participants as well as foregrounding the discursive power of semiotic expression, whereby, as J. L. Austin, asserts, "to say some-thing is to do something." According to Richard Schechner, "Anything and everything can be studied 'as' performance," but the trans-Mississippi West strikes as particularly fertile terrain in which to think about the dynamics of history and illocution. A heady landscape in which the historical grounding of frontier process—political, social, economic, and environmental change—played partner to a powerful mythology, the nineteenth-century West was a both a "stage" for the enacting of individual and national aspirations and an energetic folkloric space. Place and process, "f-word" triumphal and trumped, the richly textured landscape of the nineteenth-century West attests to the power of storytelling to inform historical memory. One is reminded here of Hayden White's assertion that the process by which "story" translates into "history" is imaginative as much as empirical, necessarily rhetorical and poetic in nature, or, more parochially, of the newspaperman's famous adage in *The Man Who Shot Liberty Valance* (1962): "this is the West, Sir. When the legend becomes fact, print the legend." As an operational tool to navigate the com-plex contours of westward expansionism and its mythological reach, perfor-mance, then, has much to recommend it. After all, as Rosemarie Bank points out, Frederick Jackson Turner—grandmaster of western history—chose the "imagined language of the playwright" to describe the frontier as a process in which "'actors' perform history." Equally intriguing was the fact that William F. Cody—another star performer of frontier teleology—relentlessly asserted the *non*-theatrical nature of his productions. Instead, Buffalo Bill's Wild West Show offered history "at play" in a series of apparently unscripted montages, rough and ready, naturally dramatic, and, above all, *authentic*. The implications of this, as Jefferson Slagle points out, were profound. Presented and consumed as unadulterated frontier experience, Cody's all-action West "became history through the act of performance."[17]

If the West represents ideal operative terrain for studying material-semiotic interactions, so too is the landscape of the hunt. In both semantics and structure, hunting seems apt for reading as a performance (after all, it has a start, often a long meandering middle, and a finish). From the outset, scripting and rehearsal was fundamental to those traversing the western game trail. Hunters chose when, what, where, and how to hunt, all with a nod to ritual code and inscribed social meaning. Approached as both travelogue and ontology, many committed significant attention to outfitting (George Gore spent three months selecting guns, dogs, and other sundries) and engaged in reflective musings about their impending experience of the frontier. Once on the trail, the process of introspection continued, demonstrated both in private journal confessions as well as communal display around the campfire, an intimate and deeply performative space described by hunter Grace Gallatin Thompson Seton as the "birthplace of fancy, the cradle of memory." The dramaturgy of the game trail—its repertory—spoke of challenge and triumph, personal edification, historical gravitas, and environmental fellowship. A critical player in performance interlocution, the story "framed" the hunt, allowing protagonists to make sense of their activities, ritually possess events, extract political, social, and ecological meanings, and give them lasting significance. Accordingly, "packing out" meant not only transporting animals and equipment but also a vibrant and powerful mythology for later retelling and ritual ratification. A bust-up with a Fort Union trader led the departing George Gore to unceremoniously burn his outfitting equipment, including carpets, first-edition books, and own hunting journal. The trophies that were shipped out nonetheless provided, in the words of Captain Randolph Marcy, "abundant vouchers for his performances" back home.[18]

Situating the hunter both literally and figuratively, the game trail represented a site of theater, memory, and identity in which performance operated as a vector of knowing and a vehicle for claiming place, past, and process. According to early twentieth-century psychologist John Dewey, this was no coincidence. Instead, he argued, the practical dynamics of the hunt—its implicit sense of action, dramatic pace, and narrative development—helped forge our socially constructed sense of theater: "The interest of the game, the alternate suspense and movement, the strained and alert attention to stimuli always changing always demanding graceful, prompt, strategic and forceful response; the play of emotions along the scale of want, effort, success or failure—this is the very type, psychically speaking, of the drama. The breathless interest with which we hang upon the movement of play or novel are reflexes of the mental attitudes evolved in the hunting vocation." In short, we learned our ideas about theatrics—play, gesture, and practice—from formative experiences as hunter-gatherers.[19]

According to Dewey at least, the structural dynamics of the hunt molded our sense of dramatic code. Perhaps unsurprisingly, the storytelling canon of *Homo sapiens* often returned to the game trail as a site of narrative inspiration. Across the storied expanse of the Anthropocene—from classical legend to twenty-first-century cryptozoology—could be found vibrant and captivating performances of the hunt, confirming novelist Graham Swift's contention that *Homo Sapiens* is a "storytelling animal" and highlighting the fact that, more often than not, those stories were *about* animals. In the trans-Mississippi theater itself, hunting tales galloped across different ethnographic and socio-economic stages, suggesting common structural motifs of identity, instruction, and belonging in the cryptography of the chase. Stories told of how animals coached humans in the ways of the game trail (the Blackfeet's "When Humans and Animals Were Friends"), of unforgiving landscapes and wily foes (Jim Bridger's engagement with an amassed faunal guerilla force of beaver and wolf as he hid in a tree), and of feats of heroism and honor (a grisly encounter with a ferocious bruin became, in the words of writer Clyde Ormond, "as American as a hot dog or apple pie"). For nineteenth-century historian Henry Howe, the performative trappings of the hunting frontier were so pervasive they even struck as a little clichéd. Speaking in a tone that suggested he had perhaps heard one too many stories of the "largest grizzly in the West," he exclaimed: "the whole business of the hunter consists of a series of intrigues."[20]

The sport hunter was arguably the most flamboyant and prolific performer on the nineteenth-century hunting frontier. Possessed with the finances, the artistic erudition, and the cultural networks to transfer experience to typography, their testimony looms largest in the storied landscape of the hunt and the narrative geography of *Epiphany in the Wilderness*. An active consumer of frontier experience, performance was an integral part of the sport hunter's outlook. Many arrived in the trans-Mississippi region already enraptured by a grand narrative of wilderness and wild beasts gleaned from the testimony of other hunters or from the growing mythological imprint of the West on the transnational imagination. Describing their travels, many chose the language of theatrics quite deliberately: positioning the western landscape as a theater in which the drama of hunter's paradise unfolded. A world of exciting stalks, campfire banter, and trophy bags galore, the performance of the sport hunter was whimsical, expansive, and endearing. It also served as an expressive device for the enacting of social difference.

Reading the testimony of the sport hunter as a performance act brings fresh insights into the world of the nineteenth-century frontier, illuminating tropes and referents in the cultural history of hunting as well as pointing to an imaginative encounter between humans and wild things that was just as important as their entanglement in the material world. Aside from their elite authorial vantage, deconstructing the body of material left by sport hunters inevitably raises issues of objectivity, representation, and audience reception. Writers prized themselves as natural historians, geographers, and ethnographers and left an autobiographical trail rich with biotic and cultural flavor: this was part of the authorial script of the hunter hero. At the same time, it is highly likely that hunters embellished their stories for dramatic purchase or teleological convenience (that, after all, was foundational to the performance process). Where did cataloging the flora and fauna end and furnishing the theater of the trail with lively incident and markers of identity begin? Arguably, such distinctions are immaterial if we accept the hunting frontier as a layered landscape of material and metaphysical composition. As historians Eric Hobsbawm and Terence Ranger point out in their analysis of myth, questions of truth or falsehood are less important than the power of an idea to give actions and events particular meaning. Read through the lens of material-semiotic interaction and performance code, it is precisely the *storied* landscape of the hunt that renders it worth a look.[21]

In performing the hunt, hunters created a vibrant mythological landscape that extended far beyond the boundaries of personal reminiscence to encompass social memory. The cultural artifacts of the hunt included hundreds of books on sport, travel, and western adventure, artistic treatments, photographs, and live action shows (presenting the intriguing prospect of hunters "performing" their own performances on the game trail). Even the trophy haul—animal capital in the form of mounted taxidermy and diorama displays—had a tale in the tail, so to speak. This afterlife of the hunt—its material culture—appealed to a broad (and transnational) audience eager to digest the imagined geography of the frontier with its complement of impressive beasts and adventurous characters. Significantly, as Michel Foucault reminds us, the networks at play between performer, audience, and stage resist binary categorization. Thus, as the mythology of the hunting frontier passed from actor to spectator, the process of framing continued. Placed at the nexus of wilderness fantasy and national expansion, the American West had considerable purchase as a metaphorical staging post for armchair adventurers and theatergoers to engage in their own performances of national myth. Frontier experience—a "piece" of the West as imagined landscape of adventure and adrenaline—could be appreciated from afar. As historian Roger Hall notes of the western entertainment "brand" in *Performing the American Frontier* (2001), "citizens could stake their claim to a portion of the frontier simply by purchasing a ticket." The cultural artifacts of the hunt thereby provided an opportunity for "lived experience" to all who shared in its testimony, embedding the game trail not only in codes of personal remembrance but also in national mythologies of westward expansion. Consumed by popular audiences on both sides of the Atlantic as "authentic" frontier experience, the West was duly consummated as a heroic geography, a hunter's paradise of monumental landscapes, charismatic beasts, and a illustrious genealogy of hunter heroes (and, indeed, heroines). Immortalized in trans-media storytelling, the afterlife of the hunt spoke of nature, performance, and the invention of tradition.[22]

Where did this leave Doc Carver? In New York in June 1878, Carver put on a show in which he broke 5,500 glass balls in 500 minutes, earning him the title "Champion Rifle Shot of the World." Prairie showmanship in Nebraska had been a mere prelude to a career as a performing hunter hero. Moving to California in 1876, Carver had taken up as a trick shooter on the exhibition circuit, impressing audiences shooting thousands of glass balls with well-placed aim. In the late 1870s and early 1880s he toured Europe, performing at London's Crystal Palace, for the British royal family at their Sandringham estate, and before landed elites in France, Germany, and Austria. Cementing and communicating Carver's frontier identity, the *Whitehall Review* billed him as "a tall western hunter, riding with the swing of a prairie horseman." Highlighting his segue into the world of western showmanship, Carver published an autobiography—*Life of Dr. Wm. F. Carver of California: Champion Rifle Shot of the World* (1878)—and engaged in negotiations with Buffalo Bill to present "Buffalo Bill and Doc Carver's Wild West, Rocky Mountain and Prairie Exhibition." When it opened in Omaha in May 1883, the program advertised Carver as the "most expert rifleman in the universe," but the pairing of two of the frontier's foremost hunter heroes did not auger well. Following disagreements and litigation, the two men parted company: evidently the stage was too small for them both to satisfactorily perform the hunt. By the end of the decade, Carver was setting sail with another frontier drama, "Wild America," this time with stops in Warsaw, Berlin, Moscow, and Melbourne. The Australian press paid heed to Carver's credentials as performing hunter hero and exemplar of frontier manhood in celebrating a "triumphantly successful actor" and "backwoodsman . . . athlete, and dead shot" whose show (albeit, they argued, short on plot) was full of "hair-breadth escapes, perilous adventures, daring rescues, furious combats, and thrilling situations." Playing frontier guide on a transnational stage, Carver tracked the hunt from ecological experience to entertainment staple.[23]

CONTESTED TERRAINS: MASCULINITY, CONSERVATION, AND ENCOUNTERING THE "WILD"

The performance repertory of the hunting frontier necessarily embroiled its actors in identity politics, contests over natural resources, and engagements with a "wild" both symbolic and real. By exploring such themes, *Epiphany in the Wilderness* positions hunting as a critical marker in the cultural and environmental history of the American West. Often ignored as a ubiquitous presence (as historian Paul Schullery puts it, an "analysis-exempt part of daily life") or hamstrung by moral polemic, the mechanics of power and encounter on the game trail instead highlight important processes of hegemony and subversion in the age of empire as well as the layered cultural meanings of the hunt and its critical relationship to frontier mythology.[24]

As various scholars have illuminated, gender looms large in the identity politics of the game trail. The nineteenth century witnessed a crisis of masculine authority in which vigorous outdoor sports (including hunting) were seen as necessary antidotes for the debilitating trappings of urban industrialism. For a legion of upper- and middle-class men, the West emerged as a savage cornucopia in which to salvage their manhood and make sense of their lives. Performance was an important part of this process, in which the hunting frontier was situated as a landscape that was both inert (a stage of action) and also dripping with mythological purchase as a locus of personal proving. As Monica Rico points out, nature served as a fertile realm in which to "establish, elaborate, and defend masculinity." Using the conceptual language of performance, *Epiphany in the Wilderness* adds to an extant scholarship concerned with the construction of masculinity by exploring how the community of sport hunters corroborated their manhood by encountering the wild, communing together in the homo-social landscape of the game trail, and rehearsing their restorative journey via a variety of cultural forms. Master of the woods in his actions and authorial voice, the sport hunter adhered to a performance code that allowed the full exercise of masculine transformation and the articulation of social prestige. Or, as old-time hunter Eldred Woodcock put it: "if you want to know all about a man, go camping with him." In popular culture, meanwhile, the hunter emerged as a stalwart figure and exemplar of rugged individualism, independence, and physical prowess. This work considers the specifically western attributes of the hunter hero genealogy, finding new configurations of belonging at play. Beyond cultural purchase as an "American native," the figure of the heroic hunter served as a marker of regional identity *and* imperial primacy, enmeshing British and American elites in a transnational colonial fraternity of masculine brotherhood.[25]

The history of hunting in the nineteenth-century West tells a story of masculine hegemony under construction and extrapolation. Significantly, however, it also proposes important qualifications to the monolithic power and reach of the hunter hero. In trudging the game trail of colonial masculinity, sport hunters relied heavily on frontier guides who served as savvy brokers (choreographers, in the parlance of this work) of the wilderness experience. The western game trail was, accordingly, a negotiated space in which other iterations of masculine prowess squared up against the visiting sport. As

Basso, McCall, and Garceau explain, "The real West emerged as a pluralist region where competing notions of manhood played out in encounters among ethnic and racial cultures, classes, and genders." United in the search for animal capital, it was in the performance details of the hunt that such contests were most starkly illuminated. The narrative script—in other words, the *how* and *why* of the game trail—highlights the American West as a rich figurative terrain in which social codes of distinction, legitimization, and hierarchy played out.[26]

Digging further into the realms of storytelling and testimony, *Epiphany in the Wilderness* points to an even greater heresy (and one usefully encapsulated by the image of the J. L. Grandin hunting party [1879] on the front cover). While the "dead white men" of history found in the game trail a place to confirm their social status and quell anxieties about the erosion of hegemonic masculinity, women also took to the hunting trail with gusto, finding their own ways to appropriate the performance of the hunt and, in so doing, venture a challenge to socially proscribed gender roles. For the homesteader, the "lady adventurer," and the "wild woman," the game trail represented a site for personal proving, the rehearsal of woodcraft skills, and the exercise of flamboyant frontier panache. Just as Theodore Roosevelt dressed in buckskin for the purposes of identity confirmation and public show, so too did Calamity Jane. America's "national costume" was not only cut for men.

The contested social meanings of the hunting trail came into relief when the natural resources of the West began to run out. The idea of the trans-Mississippi region as a site of abundant animal capital had animated the performance of hunter's paradise for much of the century and, as faunal populations declined, set the narrative for a new dramatic reading. Witnessing the decline of game stocks, a diverse range of constituencies—from sportsmen-preservationists to camera-hunters and American Indians—proselytized on the imperilment of hunter's paradise and its necessary salvation. Stories attested to the rich social meanings attached to the land—stories of community, biophilia, and belonging and of social difference (race, class, and imperial codes of appropriation and enfranchisement). A complicated territory of appreciation and appropriation, the history of conservation in the West resists reductive treatment. *Epiphany in the Wilderness* acknowledges the material contribution of the sporting elite to the conservationist cause but also positions the hunting trail as a politicized landscape marshaled by power relations. Writing for *Environmental History* in 1995, Thomas Altherr and John F. Reiger called for a thoughtful scholarship that refrained from presenting the hunter as a masculine braggart crashing through the woods or an ecological heir apparent tiptoeing through the timberline, and it is to this memorandum that *Epiphany in the Wilderness* speaks.[27]

This book sits at the intersection between the materiality of the hunt and its storytelling presence—at the nexus of typology, taxonomy, and typography. As Donald Worster reminds us, at the root of any environmental transaction is the materialism of nature, in this case a fecund story of animal capital and its role in processes of westward expansionism. Ever present is an acknowledgment that hunting existed in a physical space and was concerned with an actuality of encounter between people and the wild things that so captivated them. It is in the "material relation with the animal," historian Erica Fudge argues, that our engagement with the nonhuman is fundamentally rooted. At the same time, the constructed nature of our engagement with the "wild" is unassailable. As William Cronon points out in his influential essay "The Trouble with Wilderness," we have created untamed spaces as points of refuge, rescue, and redemption, "the wild" being a "reflection of our own unexamined longings and desires." Equally, it is this cultural inscription that *Epiphany in the Wilderness* addresses. In the storied landscape of the hunt, the quest for game was bound by metaphysics, ritual, and experiential code. For biological anthropologist Matt Cartmill, its importance lay in "symbolism, not its economics." Performance remained a critical coda on, off, and of the game trail, situating the hunt not only as a socioeconomic phenomenon but a dramatic one as well. Visions of paradise, renewal, and redemption enacted a powerful afterlife of the hunt that preserved the memory of the game trail long after the hunter had left and conspired in the creation of an imagined geography. In the words of visual theorist Susan Sontag, there can be "an ecology not only of real things but of images as well."[28]

Taking its cue from dramatic example, *Epiphany in the Wilderness* tracks the performance of the hunt in three acts. Paying respect to the typical chronological (and, as Dewey would have it, innately dramatic) contours of hunting practice, it begins at the western trailhead to examine the actors and agents who collectively encompassed the cultural ecology of the hunt. Act 1 looks at the various players involved in the process: sportsmen crafting their own "perfect" wilderness adventure at every track; the protagonists cast in supporting roles, from fellow travelers and beasts "red in tooth and claw" to firearms loaded with ammunition and expressive meaning; and those women hunters whose presence on the game trail and in performance code destabilized the masculine hegemony of hunter heroism. Act 2 moves on to consider the illustrious afterlife of the hunt as transmitted by a range of cultural artifacts from literature, art, and photography to theater and taxidermy and their role in constructing a national folklore of wilderness and western adventure. Here the hunter moves into position as curator of the hunting "story," the principal producer of the testimonial culture of the hunt and an active agent in disseminating its narrative codes to a broader audience enraptured by the "lived experience" of frontier performers. In the final act, focus shifts to the demise of hunter's paradise and a new roster of conservationist prescriptions for saving the faunal frontier. In the late nineteenth-century the story of the hunt underwent a radical reconstruction in the hands of conservationists, camera-hunters, and Ghost Dancers, each of which constructed a new narrative framework around which to enact political, cultural, and environmental relationships. The performance of the hunt in the nineteenth-century West told a complicated yarn of animal animation and social meaning. Epiphany in the wilderness spoke of environmental encounter and expressive device— an ecology of entanglement between a corporeal world and its allegorical imprint. While all of this was going on, Doc Carver continued to wield his rifle and shoot balls in the air like the frontier heroes of legend.

NOTES

1. The contest is recounted in Chas. R. Nordin, "Dr. W. F. Carver, Wizard Rifle Shot of the World on the Nebraska Plains," *Nebraska History* 10 (October–December 1927): 344–52; Chas. R. Nordin, "Winners of the West," October 30, 1922, Buffalo Folder, Montana Historical Society Research Center, Helena (hereafter cited as MHS); Raymond W. Thorp, *Spirit Gun of the West: The Story of Doc. F. Carver* (Glendale: Arthur H. Clark Co., 1957), 67–76.

2. Isabella Bird, *A Lady's Life in the Rocky Mountains* (Norman: University of Oklahoma Press, 1960 [1879]), 53; Horace Edwards to Henry, Elk Creek, September 21, 1884, Horace Edwards Letters, WA MSS S-1634, Beinecke Rare Book and Manuscript Library, Yale University.

3. Thomas Jefferson to Peter Carr, August 19, 1785, *The Papers of Thomas Jefferson*, vol. 8, ed. Julian Boyd (Princeton: Princeton University Press, 1953), 406–8; Larry

McMurtry, *The Colonel and Little Missie: Buffalo Bill, Annie Oakley and the Beginnings of Superstardom in America* (New York: Simon and Schuster, 2005), 4.

4. John Ewers, *The Horse in Blackfoot Indian Culture* (Washington, DC: Smithsonian Institution Press, 1953), 34. See also Dan Flores, "Bison Ecology and Bison Diplomacy: The Southern Plains from 1800 to 1850," *Journal of American History* 78, no. 2 (September 1991), 465–85; J. Donald Hughes, *American Indian Ecology* (El Paso: Texas Western Press, 1983); Shepard Krech III, ed., *Indians, Animals, and the Fur Trade: A Critique of Keepers of the Game* (Athens: University of Georgia Press, 1981); Calvin Martin, *Keepers of the Game: Indian-Animal Relations in the Fur Trade* (Berkeley: University of California Press, 1979); Christopher Vecsay and Robert W. Venables, eds., *American Indian Environments: Ecological Issues in Native American History* (Syracuse: Syracuse University Press, 1980).

5. Bernard DeVoto, ed., *The Journals of Lewis and Clark* (Boston: Houghton Mifflin, 1953), 98; Raymond Burroughs, *The Natural History of the Lewis and Clark Expedition* (East Lansing: Michigan State University Press, 1995), 283; Lansford Hastings, *The Emigrants' Guide to Oregon and California* (Cincinnati: George Conclin, 1845), 17, 143.

6. Nannie Alderson and Helena Huntington Smith, *A Bride Goes West* (New York: Farrar and Rinehart, 1942), 24–28, 17.

7. George Colpitts, *Game in the Garden: A Human History of Wildlife in Western Canada to 1940* (Vancouver: University of British Columbia Press, 2002), 14. See also Hiram Martin Chittenden, *The American Fur Trade of the Far West: A History of the Pioneer Trading Posts and Early Fur Companies of the Missouri Valley and the Rocky Mountains and the Overland Commerce with Santa Fe*, 2 vols. (Lincoln: University of Nebraska Press, 1986 [1902]); Robert Utley, *A Life Wild and Perilous: Mountain Men and the Paths to the Pacific* (New York: Henry Holt,1997); Richard White, *The Roots of Dependency: Subsistence, Environment, and Social Change among the Choctaws, Pawnees, and Navajos* (Lincoln: University of Nebraska Press, 1983); Elizabeth Vibert, *Trader's Tales: Narratives of Cultural Encounters in the Columbia Plateau, 1807–1846* (Norman: University of Oklahoma Press, 1997); David Wishart, *The Fur Trade of the American West, 1807–1840: A Geographical Synthesis* (Lincoln: University of Nebraska Press, 1979).

8. Richard White, "Animals and Enterprise," in *The Oxford History of the American West*, ed. Clyder Milner, Carol A. O'Connor, and Martha A. Sandweiss (New York: Oxford University Press, 1994), 237–73. Black quoted in the introduction to Richard Irving Dodge, *The Hunting Grounds of the Great West* (London: Chatto and Windus, 1877), xvii–xviii; David Hilger, "Overland Trail," David Hilger Papers, SC854, Box 5, Folder 8, Writings (1907–1935), MHS, 1-6; David Hilger, "Early Days in Dog Creek, Fergus County Montana," David Hilger Papers, SC854, Box 5, Folder

8, Writings (1907–1935), MHS, 31. On the destruction of the bison, see E. Douglas Branch, *The Hunting of the Buffalo* (Lincoln: University of Nebraska Press, 1997); David Dary, *The Buffalo Book: The Saga of an American Symbol* (New York: Avon, 1974); Valerious Geist, *Buffalo Nation: History and Legend of the North American Bison* (Stillwater, MN: Voyageur Press, 1996); Andrew Isenberg, *The Destruction of the Bison: An Environmental History, 1750–1920* (New York: Cambridge University Press, 2000); Tom McHugh, *The Time of the Buffalo* (New York: Alfred Knopf, 1972); Frank Roe, *The North American Buffalo: A Critical Study of the Species in Its Wild State* (Toronto: University of Toronto Press, 1951); Mari Sandoz, *The Buffalo Hunters: The Story of the Hide Men* (New York: Hastings, 1954).

9. Dodge, *Hunting Grounds*, 118.

10. Monica Rico, *Nature's Noblemen: Transatlantic Masculinities and the Nineteenth-Century American West* (New Haven: Yale University Press, 2013), 6; Bridger quoted in Norman B. Wiltsey, "Jim Bridger: He-coon of the Mountain Men," *Montana Magazine* 5, no. 3 (Summer 1955), 14.

11. Clyde Milner, introduction to *A New Significance: Re-envisioning the History of the American West*, ed. Clyde Milner (New York: Oxford University Press, 1996), 2; Benedict Anderson, *Imagined Communities: Reflections on the Origin and Spread of Nationalism* (London: Verso, 1991).

12. Henry Bierman, Reminiscence, SC30: Box 1, Folder 1, MHS, 1–17, 37; Thomas Altherr and John Reiger, "Academic Historians and Hunting: A Call for More and Better Scholarship," *Environmental Review* 19 (1995): 42; James R. Mead, *Hunting and Trading on the Great Plains, 1859–1875*, ed. Schuyler Jones (Norman: University of Oklahoma Press, 1986), 37–40, 73–75.

13. *New York Times*, July 14, 1878; Thorp, *Spirit Gun*, 25; John Mortimer Murphy, *Sporting Adventures in the Far West* (London: Sampson, Low, Marston, Searle & Rivington, 1879), 174–75, 252; "Dr. W. F. Carver—The Evil Spirit of the Plains," *Wild West Buffalo Bill and Dr. Carver's Rocky Mountain and Prairie Exhibition* (Hartford, CT: Calhoun Press, ca. 1883), 5–7.

14. Theodore Roosevelt, *The Wilderness Hunter* (New York: G. P. Putnam's, 1893), 8.

15. Jacques Derrida, *Writing and Difference*, trans. Alan Bass (London: Routledge, 1978).

16. Bruno Latour, *Reassembling the Social: An Introduction to Actor-Network-Theory* (Oxford: Oxford University Press, 2005); Judith Butler, *Gender Trouble: Feminism and the Subversion of Identity* (New York: Routledge, 1999), 24–25; Clifford Geertz, *Local Knowledge: Further Essays in Interpretive Anthropology* (New York: Basic Books, 1983), 31; Roland Barthes, "From Work to Text," in *Image/Music/Text* (New York: Farrar, Straus and Giroux, 1988), 158; Mike Pearson and Michael Slater, *Theatre/Archaeology* (London: Routledge, 2001). On performance studies as a discipline, see W. B.

Worthen, "Disciplines of the Text/Sites of Performance," *TDR* 39, no. 1 (Spring 1995), 13–28; J. Reinelt, ed., *Critical Theory and Performance* (Ann Arbor: University of Michigan Press, 1992); Richard Schechner, *Performance Studies: An Introduction* (New York: Routledge, 2002).

17. Barthes, "From Work to Text," 162; J. L. Austin, *How to Do Things with Words* (Oxford: Oxford University Press, 1962), 94; Schechner, *Performance Studies*, 1–2; Hayden White, *Metahistory: The Historical Imagination in Nineteenth-Century Europe* (Baltimore: Johns Hopkins University Press, 1973), ix; Rosemarie Bank, "Representing History: Performing the Columbia Exposition," in *Critical Theory and Performance*, ed. Reinelt, 234; Jefferson D. Slagle, "America Unscripted: Performing the Wild West," in *A Companion to the Literature and Culture of the American West*, ed. Nicolas Witschi (London: Wiley-Blackwell, 2011), 433. Scholarship that "reads" the West in performance terms is in its infancy but includes precursory works on theatrical production and the mythology of the frontier as a national entertainment staple in the shape of Roger Hall's *Performing the American Frontier, 1870–1906* (Cambridge: Cambridge University Press, 2001); and Jeffrey Mann's *Melodrama and the Myth of America* (Indiana: Indiana University Press, 1993); and as well as scholarship by Banks and Slagle (both cited above) on the performance of frontier mythology at the World's Columbian Exposition and in the Wild West show respectively. Louis S. Warren in *Buffalo Bill's America: William Cody and the Wild West Show* (New York: Alfred Knopf, 2005); and McMurtry in *The Colonel and Little Missie* both explore the question of performance and the celebrity presence of Cody. The question of performativity and the West is, of course, informed by a broad historiography on the myth of the frontier, including Richard Slotkin's trilogy, *The Fatal Environment: The Myth of the Frontier in the Age of Industrialization, 1800–1890* (New York: Atheneum, 1985); *Regeneration through Violence: The Myth of the American Frontier, 1600–1800* (Middletown: Wesleyan University Press, 1973); and *Gunfighter Nation: The Myth of the Frontier in Twentieth-Century America* (Norman: University of Oklahoma Press, 1998); as well as Henry Nash Smith's classic text *Virgin Land: The American West as Symbol and Myth* (Cambridge, MA: Harvard University Press, 1950).

18. Grace Gallatin Thompson Seton, *Nimrod's Wife* (New York: Doubleday, Page & Co., 1907), 177; Randolph Marcy, *Thirty Years of Army Life on the Border* (New York: Harper and Bros., 1866), 402.

19. John Dewey, "Interpretation of Savage Mind," *Psychological Review* 9 (1902): 224.

20. Graham Swift, *Waterland* (New York: Vintage, 1992 [1983]), 62; Clyde Ormond, *Hunting in the Northwest* (New York: Alfred A. Knopf, 1948), 59; H. Howe, *Historical Collections of the Great West: Containing Narratives of the Most Important and Interesting Events in Western History* (New York: George Tuttle, 1857), 120.

21. Eric Hobsbawm and Terence Ranger, eds., *The Invention of Tradition* (Cambridge: Cambridge University Press, 1983), 1–14.

22. Hall, *Performing the American Frontier*, 2; Michel Foucault, "Discipline and Punish, Panopticism," in *Discipline and Punish: The Birth of the Prison*, ed. Alan Sheridan (New York: Vintage Books, 1977), 195–228. On the West and popular entertainment, see Richard Aquila, *Wanted Dead or Alive: The American West in Popular Culture* (Chicago: University of Illinois Press, 1998); James Grossman, ed., *The Frontier in American Culture* (Berkeley: University of California Press, 1994); L. Moses, *Wild West Shows and the Images of American Indians, 1883–1933* (Albuquerque: University of New Mexico Press, 1999).

23. *Whitehall Review*, April 3, 1879; "Dr. W. F. Carver—The Evil Spirit of the Plains," 5–7; *Melbourne Daily Telegraph*, undated clipping in Dr .W. F. Carver Collection, 88.179.52: Scrapbook, Autry Library, Autry National Center, Los Angeles.

24. Paul Schullery, "Theodore Roosevelt: The Scandal of the Hunter as Nature Lover," in *Theodore Roosevelt: Many-Sided American* , ed. Natalie A Naylor et al. (Interlaken, NY: Heart of the Lakes Publishing, 1992), 229. For discussion of hunting and philosophy, animal rights, and ethics, see Simon Bronner, *Killing Tradition: Beyond Hunting and Animal Rights Controversies* (Lexington: University Press of Kentucky, 2008); Jan Dizard, *Going Wild: Hunting, Animal Rights, and the Contested Meaning of Nature* (Amherst: University of Massachusetts Press, 1999); and *Mortal Stakes: Hunters and Hunting in Contemporary America* (Amherst: University of Massachusetts Press, 2003); Ted Kerasote, *Blood Ties: Nature, Culture, and the Hunt* (New York: Random House, 1983); Jose Ortega y Gasset, *Meditations on Hunting* (New York: Charles Scribner's, 1972); David Petersen, *Heartsblood: Hunting, Spirituality, and Wildness in America* (Washington, DC: Island Press, 2000); David Petersen, ed., *A Hunter's Heart: Honest Essays on Blood Sport* (New York: Henry Holt, 1996); Paul Shepard, *The Tender Carnivore and the Sacred Game* (Athens: University of Georgia Press, 1974); James Swan, *In Defense of Hunting: Yesterday and Today* (New York: HarperOne, 1995). In terms of writing on the American West, there are a few "pioneer" surveys. John Merritt's *Baronets and Buffalo: The British Sportsman in the American West, 1833–1881* (Missoula, MT: Mountain Press, 1985) focused on the narrative biography of one of the West's key constituents, as does journalist Peter Pagnamenta's *Prairie Fever: British Aristocrats in the American West, 1830–90* (New York: Norton, 2012), chaps. 1–5. Judith Li's collection *To Harvest, To Hunt: Stories of Resource Use in the American West* (Corvallis: Oregon State University Press, 2007) serves a vital purpose in pointing to the testimonials of ethnic and immigrant groups. Richard Rattenbury's illustrated work for the Boone and Crockett Club, *Hunting the American West: The Pursuit of Big Game for Life, Profit, and Sport, 1800–1900* (Missoula, MT: Boone and Crockett Club, 2008); and Daniel Herman's chapter on the West in *Hunting and the American*

Imagination (Washington, DC: Smithsonian Institution Press, 2003) represent the most comprehensive histories.

25. Rico, *Nature's Noblemen*, 10; Eldred Woodcock, *Fifty Years a Hunter and Trapper* (St. Louis: A. R. Harding, 1913), 226. Coverage of the identity politics of the hunter hero can be found in Herman, *Hunting and the American Imagination*; Stephen Aron, *How the West Was Lost: The Transformation of Kentucky from Daniel Boone to Henry Clay* (Baltimore: Johns Hopkins University Press, 1996); Slotkin, *Regeneration through Violence*; and Smith, *Virgin Land*. For debates on gender and empire, see Greg Gillespie, "'I Was Well Pleased with Our Sport among the Buffalo': Big-Game Hunters, Travel Writing, and Cultural Imperialism in the British North American West, 1847–72," *Canadian Historical Review* 83, no. 4 (2002): 555–84; Greg Gillespie, *Hunting for Empire: Narratives of Sport in Rupert's Land, 1840–1870* (Vancouver: University of British Columbia Press, 2007); Tina Loo, "Of Moose and Men: Hunting for Masculinities in British Columbia, 1880–1939," *Western Historical Quarterly* 32, no. 3 (Autumn 2001): 296–319; Karen Wonders, "Hunting Narratives of the Age of Empire," *Environment and History* 11 (2005): 269–91; John M. Mackenzie, *The Empire of Nature: Hunting, Conservation and British Imperialism* (Manchester: Manchester University Press, 1988). Also valuable for its transnational focus on Anglo settler societies is Thomas Dunlap's *Nature and the English Diaspora: Environment and History in the United States, Canada, Australia and New Zealand* (Cambridge: Cambridge University Press, 1999).

26. Matthew Basso, Lauran McCall, and Dee Garceau, eds., *Across the Great Divide: Cultures of Manhood in the American West* (New York: Routledge, 2001), 6–7. See also Annie Coleman, "Rise of the House of Leisure: Outdoor Guides, Practical Knowledge, and Industrialization," *Western Historical Quarterly* 42, no. 4 (2011): 436–57.

27. Altherr and Reiger, "Academic Historians and Hunting," 39–56. The case for the sport hunter as conservationist is made by John Reiger, *American Sportsmen and the Origins of Conservation* (Corvallis: Oregon State University Press, 2001 [1975]); James B. Trefethen, *An American Crusade for Wildlife* (New York: Winchester Press, 1975); and Thomas Altherr, "The American Hunter-Naturalist and the Development of the Code of Sportsmanship," *Journal of Sport History* 5 (1978): 7–22; and sharply contested by Thomas Dunlap, *Saving America's Wildlife: Ecology and the American Mind, 1850–1990* (New Jersey: Princeton University Press, 1988); Thomas Dunlap, "Sport Hunting and Conservation," *Environmental Review* 12, no. 1 (Spring 1988): 51–59; Lisa Mighetto, "Wildlife Protection and the New Humanitarianism," *Environmental Review* 12, no. 1 (Spring 1988): 37–40; Lisa Mighetto, *Wild Animals and American Environmental Ethics* (Tucson: University of Arizona Press, 1991); and Stephen Fox, *The American Conservation Movement* (Madison: University of Wisconsin

Press, 1981). The case for disenfranchisement of local users is made by Karl Jacoby, *Crimes against Nature: Squatters, Poachers, Thieves, and the Hidden History of American Conservation* (Berkeley: University of California Press, 2001); and Louis S. Warren, *The Hunter's Game: Poachers and Conservationists in Twentieth-Century America* (New Haven: Yale University Press, 1997).

28. Donald Worster, *An Unsettled Country: Changing Landscapes of the American West* (Albuquerque: University of New Mexico Press, 1994), 56–60; Erica Fudge, "A Left-Handed Blow: Writing the History of Animals," in *Representing Animals*, ed. Nigel Rothfels (Bloomington: Indiana University Press, 2002), 3–18; William Cronon, "The Trouble with Wilderness or Getting Back to the Wrong Nature," in *Uncommon Ground: Rethinking the Human Place in Nature*, ed. W. Cronon (New York: W. W. Norton, 1995), 69–70; Matt Cartmill, *A View to a Death in the Morning: Hunting and Nature through History* (Cambridge, MA: Harvard University Press, 1993), 28; Susan Sontag, *On Photography* (New York: Penguin, 1977), 180.

ACTORS AND AGENTS

THE CULTURAL ECOLOGY OF HUNTER'S PARADISE

CHAPTER 1

MASCULINITY, THE "STRENUOUS LIFE," AND THE GENEALOGY OF THE HUNTER HERO

A cheerful fire, a full stomach, after an active and successful day a hunting, lying on a good cowboy bed, your peace
pipe doing fine—a tried and true partner enjoying it all
with you, your pulse beating with the warmth and strength
of a hardy outdoor life; could a man wish for more?

—*Malcolm Mackay, Cow Range and Hunting Trail (1925)*

Born in New Jersey in 1881 and a stockbroker by trade, Malcolm Mackay had
long been enticed by the literary frontier of cowboy and Indian heroes facing
off across the pages of dime novels and popular fiction. Taking inspiration
from the imaginary West, Mackay set out to find his own "inner frontiersman"
in 1901. As he explained: "When I was nineteen years old, I was working in a
banking house in New York, but somehow it in no way satisfied the hunger
of real action and adventure that surged within me." Settling in Red Lodge,
Montana, Mackay struck up a partnership with rancher Charlie Wright and
went on to operate a successful 17,000-acre spread on the East Rosebud River,

DOI: 10.5876/9781607323983.c001

running cattle under the Lazy EL brand. A keen outdoorsman—not least inspired by a duck hunt to Nebraska, aged sixteen, with a group of his father's acquaintances—Mackay regularly left his ranch for the mountains in search of good hunting. The game trail brought muscular adventuring and invigoration for mind and body, so much so that Mackay spoke in quasi-mystical (not to mention Turnerian) terms of "spiritually turning from cowboy to hunter." Wilderness living, the vigor of the rugged frontier, and the homo-social culture of the trail conspired to lend the hunting experience a unique quality and an innately performative timbre. As Mackay mused, "Could a man wish for more?"[1]

The masculine terrain of the Euro-American frontiersman set out in Mackay's *Cow Range and Hunting Trail* was a familiar one. A material agent in the culture of animal capital, the hunter served as defender, provider, and adventurer—killing game to sustain his family—while recreational cultures of the hunt configured the pursuit of game as manly play, gallant sharpshooters trailing game across a theme park wilderness that was equally embedded in a political economy (and ecology) of western conquest. In the idealized terrain of frontier folklore, the hunter strode tall as a leading man, an individual who tamed the wild and transformed himself in the bargain. He was the principal actor in the cultural ecology of the hunt. One need only think of the famous photograph of Theodore Roosevelt (see Figure 1.1), posed in full buckskin regalia and grasping his Winchester, to see the critical purchase of the sporting hunter hero as a signifier of manliness, power, and authority (despite being taken in the less-than-wild setting of a New York studio). Contours of masculinity, conquest, and renewal shaped the hunting experience and, in turn, the environmental history of the West. As a cultural product too, the hunter hero exerted a powerful influence, indicated by such tomes as *Heroes and Hunters of the West* (1860) and its roll call of worthy frontiersmen figuratively led across the Cumberland Gap by Daniel Boone, "father of the West" and a man of "daring, activity and circumspection." If encounters on the game trail said more about the two-legged than the four, then the principal protagonists were white men in particular.[2]

A number of scholars have traced the connections between masculinity, big game hunting, and colonialism. What has been less well observed, though, is the centrality of performance and theater to the cult of the hunter hero, the importance of the West to this typology, and the complex stratifications

FIGURE I.I. Theodore Roosevelt. 1885. Photo by George Grantham Bain. Library of Congress.

in the cultural ecology of hunting on the frontier. Whether expressed in trailside journals, tales around the campfire, or consciously paraded in a range of public forums from photography to staged shows, cultures of theater began on the game trail and extended far beyond the confines of the trans-Mississippi region. Drawing on autobiographical literature, this chapter reconstructs the phenomenology of the hunt as mediated by processes of masculinity in the American West to highlight the importance of the material space of the West (and its animals) as well as cultures of imaginative display. In the construction and dissemination of a heroic pedigree, the hunter hero participated in an encounter between physical space and an idealized "regeneration through violence" that was grounded in frontier geography, faunal exchange, and ritual performance. As Monica Rico notes, "The ritualized killing of wild animals incorporated a rich variety of gestures, objects, sayings, clothing, and images that, when woven together, told a story about masculine triumph over nature." Axioms of self-discovery, proving and renewal, conquering "virgin" land, and competing with faunal "monarchs" graced the autobiographical canon and, critically, broadcast a repertory of ownership, domination, and power over western space. Meanwhile, facing up against the big game hunter, or sport hunter, were a range of alternative (sometimes heretical) models of masculine authority in the shape of the American Indian, the market hunter, and the frontier guide. With their own claims to heroic status, hunting prowess, and codes of regional belonging, these characters played key roles in the fantasy western architecture of masculine affirmation under construction in the "golden age" of sport hunting, often with intriguing results. The beatified hunter hero may have been resolutely western by the end of the 1800s, but his buckskin livery concealed a complex genealogy.[3]

THE CRISIS OF MASCULINITY AND THE WEST AS HUNTER'S PARADISE

The golden age of sport hunting in the West between the Civil War and the closure of the frontier in 1890 drew impetus from Anglo-American cultures of imperial power and racial legitimacy (as historians John Mackenzie, Daniel Herman, and Monica Rico have pointed out), along with the rise of an upper middle class keen to demonstrate their affluence and elite aspirations. Also critical was an intellectual climate on both sides of the Atlantic concerned

with the deleterious effects of modernity and its so-called "crisis of masculinity." As a reaction to many things—war, economic depression, and the
confines of urban industrialism—the latter part of the century witnessed an
outpouring of concern at the apparent overcivilization, feminization, and
degeneration of the Euro-American man. *Hunting Sports of the West* (1865)
bemoaned how "delicate canes and cushioned curricles have taken the place
of rifles and the good old horseback exercises." Solutions to the malaise
were found in various quarters, from muscular Christianity to sport in the
"great outdoors." Frederick Jackson Turner felt that the Boy Scout movement
offered the "foundation of a self-disciplined and virile generation worthy to
follow the trail of the backwoodsman." Hunting, in particular, stirred the
attentions of many as an activity that challenged and channeled masculine
instincts, promised healthy physical exertion and manly camaraderie, and
stimulated vital emotions of duel and subdual. According to Elisha J. Lewis in
The American Sportsman (1906):

> Alone, far away from the busy throngs of selfish men, wandering with some
> favored friend, in sweet communion with the green fields, the stately forests,
> and limpid streams, the mind of the most grave and studious becomes truly
> unbent and freed from its labors. There the heart beats with renewed vigor,
> the blood courses through its usually sluggish channels with a quickened pace,
> and the whole animal as well as intellectual economy becomes sharpened and
> revivified under exciting and healthful influences.[4]

Attention fixed on a number of sacred sites for the execution of cathartic hunting from the Adirondacks to Africa. Looming large in both national
and transnational circles was the American West. John Mortimer Murphy
in *Sporting Adventures in the Far West* (1870) referred to the Rockies and the
Pacific slopes as "without a peer as a recreation-ground for those who love
the ecstatic excitement of the chase," a place of good outfitters, abundant
game, and generally safe from "irritating insects, poisonous serpents or
deadly disease." With the construction of the transcontinental railroad and
an incipient leisure economy tailored to those wishing for a dose of roughing it deluxe, the frontier was both accessible and usefully chaperoned. As
Mortimer added, his hunting camp was always "within a few day's march of
civilization, and the high ways of communication with the outside world."[5]

Long-standing associations of the West as wild terrain free not only from insects or snakes but also from modern strictures—an imaginative space where dreams gained full play—aided in its configuration as a locus of manly renewal. For British hunters seeking sport beyond the confines of (at least in relative terms) a domesticated landscape of deer and fox, and buoyed by an aristocratic colonial modus that saw far-flung reaches of the globe as useful exercise for younger sons suffering financial burden, primogeniture law, and rural change, the trans-Mississippi landscape represented an enticing space of primordial contest. Likewise, in the American national(ist) vernacular, the West had been consistently (and consciously) framed in opposition to the East in a series of turns that reflected both materiality and social construction: culture and nature, civilized and savage, constrained and liberated. Henry David Thoreau famously couched "the tonic of wildness" as an effective antidote to the quiet desperation of encroaching industrialism and encouraged a portentous gaze westward away from Old Europe and to the future, while the popularity of James Fenimore Cooper's *Leatherstocking Tales* suggested developing interest in the national project of wilderness taming, its cultural grounding, and the allure of its principal protagonist: the hunter. When Frederick Jackson Turner articulated his frontier thesis before the Historical Association in 1893, his "West" spoke of many things, but implicit in his vision was the sense of a transformative geography roamed by the iconic pioneer.[6]

The monumental landscapes of the Pacific slope and the Rocky Mountains, the vast expanses of Great Plains, and, most significantly, its full complement of "savage threats" in the shape of charismatic megafauna lent the West salience as the country's foremost wild playground. In that sense, the hunt was irrevocably animal-centered. *Frank Forester's Field Sports* (1864) described western fauna as "the noblest, largest, the fleetest, and, in one instance, the fiercest in the known world." British sportsman William Baillie Grohman called it a "primeval hunting ground" and place of "untrammeled freedom"—a pertinent example of the transnational appeal of the frontier as proving space. Also important was its elemental quality. John Palliser envisaged being "carried backward into some remote and long-past age, as though I were encroaching on the territories of the mammoth and the mastodon." For Frederick Selous, "civilized America" carried no attraction—all cities were alike; instead it was wapiti herds and the bison he wanted to see, namely "wild America." (Selous proved particularly aggrieved at meeting a Chicago journalist in the Bighorn Mountains who "removed him" from his imaginative escapism by quizzing him about travels in Africa.)[7]

Facing off against bears, bison, and bighorn in the frontier amphitheater proved a vital foil to the "sheer dullness of urban-industrial culture" and allowed the performance codes of the hunter hero full rein. "Heclawa" yearned to escape "the monotonous routine of everyday work" while Peregrine Herne sought a more visceral engagement: "My blood was on fire for sterner excitement—I longed to meet death in the face, and look for carnage." As Anthony Rotundo notes, "Men of the late nineteenth century sought to connect themselves to primitive impulses and to define their lives in terms of passionate struggle." Configured as a crucible of personal renewal, the West allowed emasculation anxieties, middle-class ambition, and imperial muscles to be flexed with abandon and romantic flourish. Parker Gillmore extrapolated thus: "I have known a few months of wild Western life do more good informing a character than years passed in cities and continental towns; for here the fop forgets his folly, and the timid and nervous becomes self-reliant." Without the chance to entertain such manly prerogatives, Gillmore felt that "we should become a very unimaginative, unambitious, namby-pamby lot, unfit for wear and tear, bustle and excitement."[8]

Significantly, the pursuit of game in the West promised both escapism *and* prescription. Such precepts were evident in the discourses promoted by Theodore Roosevelt, architect and advocate of the "strenuous life." In *The Wilderness Hunter* (1893), he issued a manifesto of manliness that spoke of the vitality of the game trail and the West as a palliative landscape. Hunting, he asserted, cultivated "that vigorous manliness for the lack of which in a nation, as in an individual, the possession of no other qualities can possibly atone." The Boone and Crockett Club, founded in 1887 by Roosevelt and others, exemplified the cultural turn of the sporting hunter hero in its promotion of "manly sport with the rifle" and a prestigious (and elite) membership earned by bagging three of the large (and, significantly, largely western) species of North American mammals. In the estimation of Roosevelt and his cadre, the overcivilizing influences of urban industrialism had stymied the male spirit. By escaping to the game trail, learning to know and inhabit wild landscapes, wield the rifle, and track and dispatch game, the hunter channeled qualities of "hardihood, self-reliance, and resolution" seemingly lacking in modern life.[9]

Time spent in pursuit of game offered welcome retreat into a past age of action, instinct, and survivalism, but it was not a rejection of modernity entirely. Instead shots fired on the game trail delivered a shot in the arm to industrialism, a salvo for modern society to allow its natural advance. William Murray regarded hunting as a "natural resort for the overworked professional," while the West seemed fit for purpose as "a great national sanatorium" according to the author of *Adventures in the Wilderness* (1869). The search for a trophy promised escapist adventure and staved off atrophy: fresh air, exercise, and exposure to challenging environments encouraged physical and mental wellbeing (a fact corroborated by today's experiments in "green exercise theory" and displayed in the contemporary designs of Frederick Law Olmsted's city parks). As Alfred Mayer extrapolated in *Sport with Gun and Rod* (1883), hunting served as an effective antidote for "artificial pleasures and its mechanical life" in allowing the man to become a "civilized savage . . . finding [his] inner masculinity and returning to the city with a calmed spirit."[10]

Likewise, the complex architecture of hunter heroism promised a retreat into nature *and* into history. Laid out in the introduction to *The Wilderness Hunter,* Roosevelt established the contours of manly sporting culture as one of geographical determinism, of exposure to the wild and its animals and the gains to be had roaming a monumental topography: "The free, self-reliant, adventurous life, with its rugged and stalwart democracy, its wild surroundings, the grand beauty of the scenery, the chance to study the ways and habits of the woodland creatures—all these unite to give to the career of the wilderness hunter its peculiar charms." At the same time, the hunter earned kudos as a *historical* agent, a "natural man" liberated by his vocation, but one possessed with a sense of dynamic virtue and pioneer instinct well suited to his chosen terrain. As Roosevelt explained, the Rocky Mountain trappers and hunters of yore were "men of iron nerve and will . . . skillful shots . . . cool, daring, and resolute to the verge of recklessness." What the American contingent added to British sporting code was, as Thomas Dunlap notes, ideas of woodcraft and frontier education. Cecil Hartley delivered a patriotic litany on the hunter hero thus: "The early pioneers of the West were all hunters. They acquired in the pursuit of the bear, the panther, and the bison, those habits of courage, coolness, presence of mind, and indifference to danger, which made them such formidable enemies to the Indians, and such efficient defenders of the infant settlements." In that sense, the sport hunters of the latter 1800s channeled the frontiersmen of a generation before, celebrating the role of the hunter in the winning of the West and repackaging it for the purposes of macho leisure. As Daniel Herman notes, the idea of a "hunting people" combined the alluring prospect of heritage in a modernizing society with a "cultural authenticity" gleaned through frontier lineage. Hence, where Crevecoeur in *Letters of an American Farmer* (1782) had derided the trans-Appalachian hunting economy as degenerate and uncivilized, rendering its people "little better than carnivorous beasts" and "divided between the toil of the chase, the idleness of repose, or the indulgence of inebriation," a century on the cultural import of the hunter—in the guise of the robust pioneer and the manly sport—looked somewhat different.[11]

What the modern man needed, according to Roosevelt, was "remedial training in barbarism, violence, and appropriation." Such a vision suggested an essentially martial quality to the game trail experience and one well positioned in the colonial context in its advocacy of righteous violence. Certainly the hunter hero gloried in the atavism of the kill, what the British Earl of Dunraven labeled the "savage instinct to shed blood," but by the late 1800s the genealogy was more complicated. As well as frontier bravado and the ability to dispatch game with alacrity, the heroic canon also demanded referents of scientific and explorer acumen, natural history appreciation, self-awareness of the gravitas of the moment, and a performative bent: a full roster of passionate manhood. Also important in the performance of the hunt was the idea of leisured activity across a vibrant frontier playground. Roosevelt's assertion that "the chase is among the best of all national pastimes" thus strikes as significant for its stress on hunting as recreational, an act that nurtured historical pioneering pursuits of subsistence and the frontier progress of "soldiering in the backwoods" but framed it in a contemporary sporting context. The masculine hero did not *need* to hunt for meat—he was, after all, a civilized man—nor did he gain his frontier education from the kill alone. Instead, he was a natural historian and explorer savant, a noble and honorable gent elevated above the materialism of the trigger-happy market hunter in his focus both on game and *the* game itself. As editor Wilbur Parker noted in *American Sportsman* magazine, the hunt appealed for its "vigor, science and manhood displayed, in the difficulty to overcome, in the pleasurable anxiety for success, and the uncertainty of it, and lastly in the true spirit, the style the dash, the handsome use of doing what is to be done, and above all, the unassailable love of fair play, that first thought of the genuine sport." Referents of honor and nobility loomed large in the sporting credentials of the idealized hunter hero (with implicit class and racial demarcations), as did codes of display and storytelling.[12]

Heroic Geography, Virgin Land, and Nature as Theater

Epic masculinity required a suitably heroic setting, and the West provided rugged terrain aplenty. William A. Allen, who arrived in Montana in the late 1870s to farm and raise stock in Billings, wrote in his memoirs, *Adventures with Indians and Game* (1903), of his first encounter with the West in histrionic terms: "From boyhood I had looked forward to this moment. I had longed passionately for a glimpse of these mountains and of the game that inhabits their fastnesseses." Born in Ohio and trained as a dentist, blacksmith, and gunsmith, Allen had been captivated by the frontier from reading dime novels, and now relished setting foot in the Rocky Mountain amphitheater: "As we penetrate the massive openings of the great forests . . . whose towering pines stand like sentinels, we are completely lost persons to the outside world." Later, Allen earned billing as a "capital story teller and a fine actor" around the campfire at close of play. The material West seemed to ooze theatricality in its grandeur and prompted effacement, inspiration, and trenchant displays of masculine valor. As a stage for hunting performance it was unparalleled, expansive, and innately dramatic. For Colonel Richard Irving Dodge, Yellowstone felt "so solitary, so utterly desolate . . . that a glamor of enchantment pervades the place," while the plains—marked by their "vast extent," danger, and romance—encouraged "opportunities for heroism." Sometimes a masculine opponent to be grappled with, at other times a grand setting for the enactment of personal valor, the heroic geography of the West proved vital to the hunter hero.[13]

Apprehended by many as a synonym for survivalist adventure, the West connoted a sense of threat and danger. In such a space, as Dodge observed, "at no time, and under no circumstances, can a man feel so acutely the responsibility of his life, the true grandeur of his manhood, the elation of which his nature is capable, as when his and other lives depend on the quickness of his eye, the firmness of his hand, and the accuracy of his judgment." At the same time, however, the hunter projected another frontier vision that was softer, more charming, and intuitively feminine. Such codes refracted broader binaries of the West as a wasteland/garden and could also be found in the gendered descriptions of animal prey. Hence, the hunter hero played not to a terrestrial opponent to be overcome, but to a landscape both maternal and voluptuous. Dunraven spoke of a landscape of bounty and nurture:

> The comfort of lying flat on your back on the grass, gazing up at the blue sky and the flickering green leaves of the trees . . . You are soothed by the distant chirruping of grasshoppers in the sunshine, the murmur of bees in the tree-tops, and *carillon* of the rushing stream. You are not trespassing and nobody can warn you off. There is plenty of fish in the river, some whiskey left in the bottle, lots of bread in the buggy; and you run no risk of being disturbed, for there is no other human being within miles.

For others, the landscape excited exhortations of romantic affection. William Pickett, veteran of the Mexican campaign and the Civil War, Montana pioneer, and member of the Wyoming legislature, spoke of how his "love for the life of the wilds" brought him to the western game trail every year between 1876 and 1883, while others used a gendered phraseology of the unspoiled and the chaste in speaking of a virgin terrain ripe for conquest by the all-conquering masculine hero. According to Heclawa:

> To live for a season a primitive life, in close contact with Nature's virgin charms; to forget for a time the petty jealousies and quibbles of our effete, selfish world; to climb lofty mountains, descend into the wildest gullies and deepest canyons; to thrust one's way through dense thickets of brush and brier. . . . in short, the absorbing interest of exploration with the excitement of the chase—oh, who can describe the freedom, the exhilaration, the abandon of such an existence.[14]

Roaming across the western theater into the gaze, and the sights, of the hunter hero were its animals. As Dunraven observed, the appeal of the Rocky Mountains lay in its auspicious combination of "excellent game producing country" as well as "gratification of my sight-seeing instincts." In the panorama of nature's show, two elements seemed to impress most: novelty and abundance. As Allen pointed out, "To the student of animal life and of animal history, a hunter's sojourn in the primitive Rockies was a continual delight." The faunal frontier animated hunter's paradise. "Everything was new and interesting, except the mosquitoes," he added. Codes of performance and theater entered the equation here, as hunters spoke in mellifluous tones about their first sightings of the characteristic fauna of the West, projecting a landscape almost cinematographic in its expanse. Spying animals from atop rocky outcrops or across prairie bluffs, the hunter relished his intrusion into a secret kingdom. Pickett recalled the novelty and joy of watching some 5,000 bison on a prairie below, including a resting male he called "Sitting Bull," while Allen recalled how "we let the animals graze, while we sat upon a knoll to feast our eyes." Sportsmen drank in the performance and offered reflections that spoke of natural history, spiritual communion, and an abiding sense of wonder. Some would argue that such interest was pragmatic, founded on knowing the habits of the animal in order to best capture it. As Peregrine Herne noted, the chase and natural history seemed "intimately connected . . . for the reason, perhaps, that both were followed at the same time."[15]

At the same time, florid descriptions of the prairies and mountains suggested more at play. The theater of the West enabled what cultural theorist Laura Mulvey has called scopophilia, the love of looking, a process founded on the aesthetics of the material and also one that conferred power on the seer by virtue of privileged (and often clandestine) vantage. Such was the province of the hunter naturalist, what C. W. Webber called a combination of the primitive and the scientific, a man who "knows nature through the medium of his own sense." Ruminations on the West as a garden of antediluvian wonder allowed the hunter to exercise his masculine authority through not only rifle skills and pugnacious bravado but also displays of scientific erudition, honorable codes of conduct, and lyrical reflection. The hunter hero thus constructed an imaginative landscape with every step, exercising his passionate manhood in scripted descriptions of the great outdoors. Theodore Roosevelt, in *Hunting Trips of a Ranchman* (1885), suggested that immersion in the wilds, appreciation of natural history, and a sense of responsibility was fundamentally rooted in the chase: "Aside from the thrill and tingle that a hunter experiences at the sight of his game, I by degrees grew to feel as if I had a personal interest in the different traits and habits of the wild creatures."[16]

CONTEST WITH THE BEAST: THE EPIPHANY OF ANIMAL
ENCOUNTER AND THE METAPHYSICS OF THE KILL

For all the enjoyment of scoping and sighting, action and contest lay at the center of the masculine terrain of the West, and this was exemplified in the physical and psychological architecture of the hunting quest. Challenge was a vital aspect of the vocation of the hunter hero, the strenuous life implying, in itself, the idea of effort, resolve, and physical endurance. The matrix of game pursuit involved a rehearsal and a rhetoric of movement based on discovery, exploration, tournament, triumph, and ontological reflection. Mortal danger from inclement weather, inhospitable terrain, the catharsis of chase, and a hard-fought contest with ferocious foes seemed necessary parts of the quest and decisive aspects in the regeneration and exhibition of manly codes. Dunraven, for instance, expressed consternation that "I never have an adventure worth a cent; nobody ever scalps me; I don't get 'jumped' by highwaymen. It never occurs to a bear to hug me, and my very appearance insures feelings of dismay or disgust in the breast of the puma or mountain lion." A vigorous pursuit, encounter with dangerous and dynamic faunal enemies, hard work, and a moment of profundity at the kill site represented essential parts of the process of frontier "re-virilization."[17]

As noted by one hunter in Van Dyke's *Flirtation Camp: or, The Rifle, Rod, and Gun in California* (1881), "the chase and its associations are everything; the mere bagging of the game is nothing." Men spoke at length of their sojourns on the stalk, of confronting craggy cliffs and wild streams, trailing across rugged country following tracks and fleeting sightings of prey, of rocky chasms, dismal forests, blinding snowstorms along the way, of the joys of exploration, exhaustion, elation, and of the ferocity of beasts that refused to yield quickly or quietly (especially, it seemed, grizzly bears). Such seemed all part of the repertory of the hunt: in a sense a performance and a practice, a place of display and also of rehearsal. The heuristic value of the game trail drew much from its difficult terrain, steep escarpments, swollen rivers, and freezing temperatures. It was immersive, imaginative, and endorsing, providing occasion for the hunter hero to square up against rugged country and strong-willed game. Peregrine Herne remembered following Rocky Mountain sheep that "led me over paths . . . I learned to leap with them from crag to crag, and to jump down precipices which at other times I would have cautiously avoided." "Buck fever" brought an emotional connection to the trail, the simplicity of survivalism, and single-minded determination. As Mackay summarized of one hunt, "The bear was running for his life. I was running for the bear . . . It seemed I could not go another step; but I was filled with the spirit of the fight and would rather have died than stop."[18]

Notions of danger, failure, and fragile human dominance only served to advance the masculine cause (and the story too). Animals that were hard to find, track, and defeat were particularly prized. As modern hunter Jim Bond notes, the prowess of the sporting trophy rests on a number of variables: the size and impressive nature of the animal itself, but also how the shot was taken, its difficulty, the terrain passed through, the faculty of the animal to escape, and its fierceness. Read as quest, the hunt offered moments of emotional and physical challenge, testing the very soul of the hunter. On the trail of black deer, indefatigable sportsman George Shields detailed an extended foray into "rough country" that tested his mettle as a hunter and a man. Pausing to look into the "awful abyss" into which the deer had fled, his rational-civilized and emotional-primal minds collided: "I looked into the bottom of the canyon and my brain reeled as I thought of the danger and the folly of trying to descend into it." Shields's answer spoke of resolution—"why parley?"—fueled by the sense of an escaping prey and his own capacity for the chase. As he iterated, "A man can go anywhere that a deer can if he (the man) have 'sand' enough." The hunter duly engaged in a "frightful descent" in pursuit of his "antlered fugitive" across rocky country, more ravines and hills, for a full seven and a half hours before dispatching the deer. Shields's oration was deeply performative and action-packed in its storytelling poise. But whatever the reality of the experience, the way he chose to remember it was important. The track was one of hardship and toil. He saw his foe looking back and chiding: "yes, my brave hunter . . . I must now bid you good day. I have been playing with you thus far, but now I have other business to attend to and must leave you." Shields, of course, had other ideas, rhetorically posing to the deer: "I haven't taken this tramp for my health. I'm after that handsome coat of yours, and I'll have it." Not just a preamble to the kill, the chase represented an integral part of the process of capture: the hunt as adjective.[19]

As essential actors in the drama, wild things loomed large in the sporting vernacular. Andrew Williamson spoke of the "new excitement and an interest one hardly ever afterwards feels on his first stalk," a sentiment accentuated considerably by the presence of "such noble animals as were in front of us." The idea of faunal engagement, agency, even *celebrity*, proved integral to the trail experience. After all, the expert hunter needed a suitable nemesis to confirm his triumphant victory at the end of the contest. Sportsmen spoke of "monster" bighorn sheep poised atop rocks in gladiatorial stance, antelope banded together "officiously . . . daring" the hunter to fire at them, and the grizzly bear as a "sanguinary monarch of the wilds." Representations of the animal then served to conjure an opponent of worthy stature and report—of agility, speed, power, and bravado—axioms commonly reserved for the hunter hero himself. The exceptions to this were predators, which were criminalized and categorized as antiheroes in the hunting lexicon as competing takers of quarry and beyond the pale of "game." Wolves were "exceedingly cowardly" according to Dodge, while Edgar Randolph castigated mountain lions as "exceedingly destructive" not only for their dietary needs but also their sense of "wanton-ness." Otherwise, the faunal sparring partners of hunter's paradise often found themselves typecast according to idealized species traits, which served as vital staging grounds for the aspirations of the masculine hero and his narrative quest.[20]

Themes of regality and elegance were commonly used to describe Cervidae—elk, antelope and deer—thus creating a kind of aristocracy of the game trail. This was perhaps no surprise given the popularity of the American West among European sportsmen, but American commentators seemed equally provoked to use the nomenclature of nobility. Making a stand for the exceptional qualities of New World fauna over European antecedents (and those in the West particularly), Henry Howe invited readers of his natural history to "imagine Landseer's 'Monarch of the Glen' magnified to about thrice its size" (Roosevelt called the stag a "pygmy" in comparison). Gendered codes also entered the equation as hunters described vigorous alpha males to match them in legendary stature. Clyde Ormond paid heed to the aural context of the chase as well as its macho airs when he dubbed the elk's bugle call a "high-pitched squeal of masculine rage." For Shields, "the sublimest death-scene I ever witnessed" consisted of an elk playing "fallen hero" in the hunting theater: "The great monster was dead! Talk about great acting." Equally, hunters were prone to characterize Cervidae as submissive female animals wooed by the advance of a two-legged (and armed) paramour. Musing that "an antelope has as much curiosity as a woman," George Shields used calico flags (a common device) to entice the attentions of the herd.

Hutchinson talked of his "flirtation with the most beautiful and coquettish young whitetail deer" that "stood so saucily at gaze"—vernacular evidence of what Mackenzie calls the hunt as "sexual sublimation." Command over the faunal landscape came from contest with masculine foes and conquests of feminized suitors, lending the hunt an air of sexual politics. Van Dyke's hunting memoir seemed pertinently titled *Flirtation Camp*.[21]

Perhaps the greatest accolades of the faunal pantheon were reserved for two species that were uniquely western in their province and symbolic identity. The first of these was the bison. For many hunters (both American and European), the shot at a bison represented the quintessential frontier hunting experience and motivated many a trip on this basis alone (see figure 1.2). Bison were typically described as shaggy, lumbering, sometimes grumpy, stupid even, yet also thunderous in the herd, an effective refraction for the galloping adventure of the masculine hunter hero. As Allen extrapolated, bison were "tearing up the earth with their great hoofs, their tails erect and their large, fiery eyes gleaming, looking like creatures designed to scatter death and destruction." British hunter Grantley Berkeley, who came to the West to "escape from the graceful enjoyment of life" (a common enticement for the aristocratic sportsman keen for greater contest than that provide by the regimented and "tame" dash across the estate), described a dynamic landscape filled with charismatic fauna. Sighting his first bison, he exclaimed: "Oh! What an exciting wild sight . . . thirty rusty black monsters." Overexcited by his first hunt (in which he dispatched three bulls), the flamboyant sportsman retired to his tent for a lie-down. Restored by sherry, Berkeley resumed his errand into the wilderness, glorying in the "savage and robust" qualities of the bison, a "warrior" and "mighty monarch of the desert."[22]

J. S. Campion (a man inspired by meeting George Catlin as a boy and by the romance of becoming a buffalo hunter) exemplified the code of the hunter hero in his description of bison hunting in *On the Frontier: Reminiscences of Wild Sports, Personal Adventures and Strange Scenes* (1878). Journeying to the plains in pursuit of "the free, jolly life," the sportsman subscribed to the conventional codes of the West as a landscape of renewal. "We were full of health, strength and confidence, and voted civilised life to be a nuisance and a bore," he recalled. Conjuring the bison as a martial opponent, Campion spoke of animals amassed "in troops, in squadrons, in divisions, in armies." After a two-hour stalk, he selected a "cantankerous old patriarch buffalo" and

FIGURE 1.2. "A Proud Moment for the Buffalo Hunter," ca. 1902. Library of Congress.

exclaimed with wild abandon: "Now for first blood!" The bison escaped, but Campion was nonetheless "excited by the novelty of the chase, the size of the game, and the pace we are going at." A few days later, Campion conjured the bison as terror incarnate, "his monstrous mane hung round his neck bigger than that of any lion's. His keen, wicked eyes glared at me . . . he suddenly grew and spread, until space became one mass of curling hair, bristling with horns, and glowing with eyes." With a nod to the customary embellishments of the hunting story genre, Campion confessed that afterward he realized the bison "was not as large as the universe."[23]

The grizzly bear, likewise, assumed a prime position in the canon of notorious western critters, particularly for its fierce qualities and the additional drama provided by the fact that bruin conjured the possibility of a reciprocal fight in which the hunter became the hunted. As Allen Jones notes, "The ultimate hunts are those in which the relationship between you and the animal is mutual: you hunt him, he hunts you." In *Sport among the Rockies* (1889), Charles Francis talked about how he and his friends, the "Trojans," "slept in camp dreaming of wrestling bears and Indians." As he noted, "It had frequently occupied the attention of our waking moments; in our dreams we had encountered and overcome many of the brutes, some of them only after a fierce hand-to-hand tussle." It was the ferocity, vigor, and fighting spirit of the grizzly that defined its identity as a prize foe. Captain Randolph Marcy dubbed it "one of the most formidable and savage animals in the universe."

Famed for its ability to evade capture and seemingly absorb hails of bullets without pause, the capture of "Old Ephraim" augured the supreme achievement of the hunter hero. As Marcy pointed out, "The men who would deliberately encounter and kill one of these beasts had performed a signal feat of courage which entitled him to a lofty position among the votaries of Nimrod." Indeed, for Clive Phillips Wolley, bruin's fearsome stature emanated (like that of the hunter hero himself) from his grounding in the West. It was the threat of being mauled in the wilds, "when the lonesomeness of the waste places has fast hold on the man's heart," the prospect of fatigue, camp miles away, and before an "unsympathetic nature" that elevated the grizzly's reputation. Animal personality was a part of the bargain. Bruin's apparently anthropomorphic qualities rendered him a worthy sparring partner. Roosevelt noted the bear's "great, half-human footprints," while Mackay reveled in the prospect of a "hand to hand fight" with a pugnacious grizzly. Pickett thought that the animal's anthropomorphic quality made it entirely plausible that bears and people shared a common lineage, as the Crow thought: "Strip the bear of his winter clothing, hang him up by the chin, put a plug hat on his head, there you have an anatomy, closely resembling that of a man, that noblest work of God." The grizzly was cast as belligerent and highly dangerous, but also, at times, bumbling and humorous. "Place him in an English ploughed field, and I doubt whether he would arouse more fear than ridicule" contended Phillips Wolley. It struck as particularly "annoying" that, despite the fantasy architecture of the chase, bear taxidermy often depicted an "abominably good natured" beast.[24]

Of course, an animal encounter on the game trail was not confined to those species pursued as prey. Domestic animals proved a vital part of the game trail experience, on a practical level and a symbolic one. Horses and mules served as beasts of burden, carrying men and equipment, skins, provisions, and trophies. They were also afforded personalities, stories, and roles in the hunting canon. Often presented as a loyal aide, sometimes feisty or recalcitrant, the horse defined the gentlemanly predilections of the hunter hero and confirmed his passionate manhood in the equestrian connection. According to Owen Wister, the horse was "his foster brother, his ally, his playfellow." Mackay remembered his steeds with affection: Captain, Baldy, Crockett, Prince, Fox, Ginger and Texas. Of Coyote, a stalwart ally on the trail, Mackay noted:

He and I swam icy rivers, crossed treacherous quicksands of the bad-land streams, sweated and thirsted on the alkali plains, enjoyed the beauty of sweet water and tall grasses on the mountain meadows, and through it all we always loved each other, always trusted each other. I hope to meet him again on the starry ranges.

The relationship between horse and rider, in particular, emerged as an important vector through which codes of romance, gallantry, honor, and belonging were translated in the sporting imagination. John Palliser saw buffalo hunting as a "noble sport" in its promise of the chase, horse skills, and the danger of the charge (not least Palliser's proclivity to hold bullets in his mouth and reload on the hoof).[25]

Dogs, likewise, were commonly discussed on the trail and served an equally valuable purpose as worthy domestic subalterns, what *The Complete Sportsman* (1893) called "canine assistants" (see figure 1.3). Grantley Berkeley came to the West, in part, for the chance to run his hounds Druid, Brutus, Chase, and Bar (a signal of the translatable codes not only between American and British codes of masculinity, but also hunting cultures of animal breeding), while A. Pendarves Vivian (the brother-in-law of Dunraven) had taken his hounds to the Nile, Albania, and Greece before coming to the western frontier. Edgar Randolph talked fondly of Major, a bull terrier who howled at the cook's harmonica playing, and Jack, a fox terrier that fought porcupines. Both were, according to Randolph, "sociable companions." For Pickett, meanwhile, canine valor was matched to that of the hunter hero. He described "Pnip," his terrier-collie cross, as "not afraid of any grizly that wore hair, but knew enough of their habits, to keep out of the reach of their teeth or claws and had sufficient activity to do so."[26]

As inferred by the significance of the chase, getting an *easy* bag denied the hunter the full purchase of the experience. Prey had to be fought for and nearly lost to render the hunt of ultimate value. According to Edgar Randolph, "Those hunting incidents which have given me the greatest trouble and exercised my skill the most are the ones I recall with greatest pleasure." In conversation with photographer Laton Huffman (who confessed to not seeing the point of enduring endless tramping over the plains "all for the sake of killing a few deer and bears"), George Shields laid out his philosophy of the hunter's graft as follows:

FIGURE 1.3. "My Dog and I," ca. 1897. Library of Congress.

> Well . . . the game is worth to me at all costs. If we could stand in our front
> door and kill these animals in our yard, we would think it no sport at all, but
> the harder you have to work for your game the more you appreciate it when
> you get it. And if we found no game, the novelty of our mode of travel, the
> grand scenery, the health-giving exercise, the invigorating atmosphere would
> well repay me for all the labor and hardships we endure.

The masculine hunter, then, was a man in possession of a work ethic based
on rugged resolution, self-reliant attributes, and command over rifle and
horse. As Dodge noted, "The Plains hunter must *work*, and he must know
how to work." There was, importantly, a sharp delineation here between
work as vocation and work as play that spoke to a developing division in
the genealogy of the *authentic* hunter hero between the sporting naturalists who upheld codes of gentlemanly fair chase and those who pursued
game for material gain. Dodge explained that "the successful stalking of
a black-tailed buck, even though it involves hours of severe labor; is more
full of pure satisfaction to the thorough sportsman than the murder of
an acre of buffaloes." Such asseverations pointed to the construction of a
vernacular hierarchy of the game trail that afforded the sport provenance
through performed practice. According to W. Webb, who eagerly advised
fellow sportsmen to imbibe of "Buffalo Land," mounted pursuit was the
"only legitimate way" to hunt.[27]

Beyond the exertions of the chase, the kill represented a vital point of contact between the masculine hunter hero and the animal quarry. The kill offered a denouement, a climax, and a historical moment of reflection. According to Dodge, the final showdown represented "the culmination of the pleasure of the pursuit." Chivalrous sportsmen paused to take in the mood before making their first shot, the display of a calm, collected, and philosophical demeanor a confirmation of sporting lineage and proficiency (as well as a way of marking them apart from the trigger-itch of unrefined sportsmen and market hunters). As Dodge pointed out, the "buck fever" led the tenderfoot into "all sorts of absurd situations," whereas the accomplished marksman planned his shot, relaxed, took pause, and assumed control of the fatal environment. With the quarry up close and the conclusion of the quest in sight, the hunter hero faced the ultimate test of his manly valor. As Berkeley recalled, this was the moment when he channeled resolve: "'the time is come' I whispered to the silent air; 'I must kill, or in these realms my power to have done so will be doubted.'" For Allen, the sheer visceral energy of the moment was palpable, as he described his clandestine watching of a white-tailed doe seconds before releasing his weapon in the fashion of a poetic assassin:

> Her great brown eyes glistened like diamonds, her ears moved back and forth as she advanced gracefully and noiselessly, scanning every object. Instinctively I could feel my arm raising slowly and my old Bullard coming into a line with the beautiful neck. In a moment a leaden messenger crashed through the sleek neck and this queen of the wilds was lying bathed in blood.

A successful kill was considered, and then configured, as a moment of epiphany.[28]

Carefully rehearsed and choreographed, the hunting transaction allowed for visceral musings on raw instinct and the nature of the inner man, what Eliza Lewis had called the "animal as well as intellectual economy." Traveling on a hunt in present-day Glacier National Park, Montana, "GWB" offered an insight into the complex (and sometimes competing) sensations that the primordial metaphysics of the game trail inspired:

> There is something rather horrible in the wild and savage excitement that one feels under such circumstances as these; the mingling of exultation over

the apparently successful pursuit, tempered by the doubt about securing the prey, and then the fierce delight, temporary of course, when the capture is assured . . . it seems shocking that a respectable civilized and well-ordered being, such as a person of ordinary civilization living in the nineteenth century may be supposed to be, should, under any circumstances, indulge in such brutal feelings.

An encounter with wild things showed the slim hold of civilization over the human psyche and the brute "character of the animal" within. Such metaphysical ponderings were not unusual. On one occasion, Allen found himself gazing upon the "faultless forms" of a group of deer grazing across a creek and feeling "stung with sorrow at the idea of killing such creatures." Encountering a stag, Andrew Williamson noted, "As he proudly threw up his great wide head and in wonder gazed at our camp . . . I almost felt as if for an hour of such picture, I could have foregone my shot and let him go in peace." Killing was no idle bargain.[29]

Rarely, however, did such remonstrations result in the hunter hanging up his Winchester. Offering a fleeting confessional, Allen wrote, "I raised my rifle and slowly set the hammer at full cock . . . as the sunlight sparkled along the barrel, I pressed the trigger, sending a bullet through the buck's heart." Williamson continued likewise, "A turn of his head in the direction of the forest on his left warned me I had not a moment to lose. Steadily aiming for the heart, I fired." Such reflections were not indicative of an embryonic hunting ethos, but instead allowed the sporting hunter hero to articulate his appreciation for wild nature and the moral economy of the hunt while parading a sense of the power invested in him as well as a dose of storytelling panache. The prize was, in a sense, already in the bag, and the hunter allowed himself a moment to fully absorb the feeling. As Williamson noted on one occasion, "As it was hardly possible anything could occur to prevent his being mine, I lay for some minutes watching him." This epiphany in the wilderness spoke of immersion in nature, metaphysical contemplation, the morality of mortality, and the importance of the confessional in hunting ritual.[30]

Without wishing to take the comparison too far (or, indeed, repudiate the existence of distinct ethnographical and religious traditions infusing human cultures of the hunt), the sacramental attention shown to wild things situated the behavior of sport hunters in a broader milieu of performance and honor rites. Ritual transactions were a foundational part of indigenous hunting practices in which prayers and ceremonial objects thanked the animal for gifting itself to the hunt. When Yakima hunter Sam-A-Lee-Sack brought grizzlies back to the camp, women from the tribe arranged boughs around the animal and memorialized its taking with the following oration:

> Powerful was this bear. Strong and brave was his heart. Strong was his mind. Sharp was his ear. He feared not the enemy. He turned not from the foe. Light was his foot in the forest. Not easy to follow his trail. His step was on the dry rock. His house cunningly concealed. But I found him on the trail. . . . We met; my *tahmahnawis* was strong. I slew him with my power. Other bears will come in his stead . . . When the snows lay deep and cold. There will be meat in the winter tepee. The hungry will be fed. The hunting will be easy. The killing will be plenty.[31]

The metaphysical reflections of the sportsman also resembled what nature writer Barry Lopez has called "the conversation of death" between predatory animals and their prey "in which the animals appear to lock eyes and make a decision . . . It is a ceremonial exchange, the flesh of the hunted in exchange for respect for its spirit." In Lopez's dictum, the shared gaze of wolf and elk suggested an ecological contract, a "sacred order." For the hunter hero, too, the idea of a noble exchange, a charter of complicit predation, satisfied goals of chivalry and masculinity and injected a sense of mutual animality and shared performance code. "GWB" directly referenced how "these feelings seem to be those with which the wolf must have when he is pulling down the exhausted deer." Many hunters spoke of directly of looking into the eyes of their game as if the shared or returned gaze of an animal elicited profound witness. Daniel Barringer spoke of the grizzly with eyes "curiously green" that looked directly at him before the charge, before aiming directly into the animal's left eye to bring it down. Selous waxed lyrical of the buck deer that stared "fixedly down at me . . . its large dark eyes seemed riveted upon me in a gaze expressive both of fear and hope. As I raised my rifle and looked at those appealing eyes, I was for an instant conscious of feelings altogether out of place in a hunter's breast. It seemed a shameful thing to take the life of this trustful brute." Selous recovered his composure, shot the deer in the heart, and duly packed out his nine-point antlers for ceremonial display.[32]

The Transformed Man: Salvation and Belonging in Hunter's Paradise

The mechanics of the game trail—of travel, chase, and the kill—provided a physical and a figurative landscape for the hunter hero to inhabit. On a macro level, the cultural ecology of the hunt created an expansive landscape of transformation in which hunters wrestled not only with bears but their own sense of self. A language of regeneration, discovery, and formative experience provided commonplace. Theodore Roosevelt epitomized the transformative turn of the hunter hero in his rite of passage from effete dandy to cowboy hunter par excellence. A man whom New York contemporaries dubbed "our own Oscar Wilde" and aroused considerable amusement among Dakotans as he came to the Badlands in 1883–84 for "hunting and playing cowboy," Roosevelt engaged in a process of regeneration on the frontier to become what Sarah Watts deemed his era's "most important cultural broker of masculinity." Like many others, Roosevelt had looked to the West for catharsis and escape from urban industrialism, finding in the plains of Dakota a perfect space for the exercise of "excitement, adventure and restless roaming." Paying heed to the appeal of the West among the eastern establishment, the *Dial* noted how the frontier possessed "a special charm for the gilded youth of the Eastern states . . . and Mr. Roosevelt seems to have followed it." Whether they stayed for the length of their safari or put down roots in frontier territory, many hunters found the terrain of the game trail a transformative one. For some, Roosevelt included, part of epiphany in the wilderness meant not only playing games on the frontier but also claiming an identity, both figuratively and literally, that was irrevocably western and also necessarily performative.[33]

Immersing himself in the vigorous landscape of the plains, running horses, trailing game, and facing off the odd desperado, Roosevelt lived the "bully life." He duly emerged from the Dakotas, in the words of Charles Lummis, as a "citizen of the great West." Frontier edification afforded a power and authenticity that Roosevelt convincingly rode to the White House. Lincoln Lang put it succinctly: "Had Theodore Roosevelt never been of the frontier—never known the Badlands of the earlier days—the author does not think he would have been just the man he was." Certainly Roosevelt drew much from his cowboy-soldier credentials, as exemplified in the Rough Rider motif, but the hunting trail was equally instrumental in the metamorphosis. As Teddy put it, "I heartily enjoy this life, with its perfect freedom, for I am very fond of hunting, and there are few sensations I prefer to that of galloping over these rolling, limitless prairies, rifle in hand."[34]

The hunt gave Roosevelt an exercise regimen, a personal coda of transformation, and a script for public pageant. Articulated in such tones as *Hunting Trips of a Ranchman, The Wilderness Hunter,* and *The Winning of the West* (1889–96) and visually represented in the famous photograph taken at Locke's in New York, Teddy consciously traded in the iconography of the hunter, crafting himself as a frontiersman in the mold of those "reckless, dauntless Indian fighters" who led the "white advance throughout all our Western lands." Buckskin was, for him, the "most picturesque of our national dress." Within this masculine swagger there was a fair dose of exhibitionism, as celebrators and critics were wont to note. When the president traveled the West on a two-month tour in 1903, covering some 14,000 miles, he behaved as a veteran hunter in Yellowstone, and in Hugo, California, left the train to breakfast with cowpokes at their grub wagon. Owen Wister (who dedicated *The Virginian* (1902) to his great friend) noted that Teddy was "always in his own limelight, and could not help it."[35]

The idea of the West as a landscape of testosterone and restoration ("testoration," even) proved a common feature of hunting testimony. The adrenaline of success operated in a physiological way to inure hunters from fatigue, as Shields noted of one hunt: "What a marvelous change came over me! I forgot that I was tired; that I was weak; that I was hungry . . . the instincts of the hunter reanimated me and I thought only of killing the grand game before me." As a repetitive exercise, the imprint of many hunting excursions left Shields in no doubt as to "the benefits . . . derived from these expeditions, in the way of health, strength and vigor." For A. W. Dimock, New York banker, meanwhile, the idea of the West as a landscape of renewal prefaced his journey from the outset. Advised by his doctor to take to the hunting trail for healthful restitution, Dimock found the Adirondacks too busy and, inspired by the idea of hunting bison, took to the West bearing letters of introduction from General Sheridan. The imaginative landscape loomed large as he arrived at Fort Sill: "The realization of my boyhood dreams was around me. The spirit of the prairie possessed my soul and shucked off the metropolitan husk that was smothering it." By the time the excursion was over, Dimock confessed how "these wonderful western experiences put new life into me."[36]

Often the story of the restoration of the "inner man" involved a rite of passage, a journey that mirrored geographical wanderings and enacted the metamorphosis of the tenderfoot into towering hunter hero and man of the West. Starting his frontier journey of restoration in July 1882, Canadian lawyer Henry O'Brien accomplished a transformation from greenhorn dandy to seasoned frontiersman as he trudged the game trail itself: the performance quest of the game trail was clearly mapped. In his inaugural diary entry, O'Brien wrote how he dropped his handkerchief and rode back eight miles to find it. The wild terrain appeared less than inviting: "It was a lovely sight this morning to see the sun rising in the clouds and to the right a storm with vivid lightening and rain. I should have preferred to be have been asleep however." On seeing his first bison, O'Brien experienced elation but also a sense of his own isolation: "It is a strange feeling to be absolutely alone on a boundless prairie." The day's hunt brought his first shot, at a rabbit, which he duly missed. On August 4, he mailed a package to his wife and daughters in eastern Canada containing prairie grass, noting how it stuck uncomfortably in clothes and irritated his skin. However, a month of exposure to the masculine proving ground of the West rendered O'Brien a transformed man.[37]

By late August he was explicating on the joys of sleeping under the stars, getting up at 5:00 a.m. to stalk elk, relishing the physical exertions of the hunt and life in the "country of game" and expounding on how his own self-sufficiency—"living off the fat of the land" and grazing a cornucopian larder of grouse, deer, elk, buffalo meat, steaks, beans, bacon, and plum duff without the plum—strengthened the mind by its "freedom from any thought of business" and trained the body "by the reason of having to provide for it." O'Brien, the hardy frontier hunter incarnate, found himself balking at the "tough beef and fixings of semi-civilization," compared with camp-cooked food, and, catching a glimpse of himself in town, saw not a greenhorn lawyer but a feral apparition with "unkempt hair, brown skin and a peeled and still peeling nasal organ and a general frontier aspect." He left for Toronto feeling that his shooting still left something to be desired, but convinced that "this trip seems to me a time for introspection and I think I see something about myself which I did not realize."[38]

James Wilson's account of a trip to the Cascade Mountains in May 1883 explored similar themes. Arriving from San Francisco to Portland, he conjured an image of the hunting party as woefully unprepared: "A genuine back-woodsman would have been greatly amused had he been where he could hear us talk. We were a pretty fresh crowd. A big knife at our side, a pistol in our belt and a magazine gun in our hands, long boots, our pants in the legs, blue shirts and big white straw hats, all new and we ourselves the newest of all." Carried away by the prospect of the hunt, and particularly by animal quarry, Wilson recalled, "I think I can never forget our appearance on that Sunday afternoon, how we did talk about killing deer, cougar and all other varmints. Alas, poor fellows, little did we know what we were talking about. I think we slept but little that night as each one in his dreams was killing bear or being killed by them." Wilson and his crew purchased supplies to stock their wagon in Vancouver, struggled to erect their tent for the first night's camp, and James and a companion walked back to Portland for additional supplies. They got thoroughly lost, but remained thoroughly enticed by playing in the wilderness: "After wandering around to no purpose for about a couple of hours, and feeling tired, we determined to see what we could do for the inward man, and started a fire, unpacked our horses, warmed our beans and had a great feast."[39]

Starting the trail proper, the group set out in sacred silence across Yacolt Prairie, imprinting every step with a sense of gravitas as a proving ground and narrative import. The West was already in place as a sacred (and thoroughly theatrical) geography. "We travelled in single file and never spoke a word for the first four or five miles. We seemed to understand that we wanted all our wind for our boots," Wilson noted. Adventures, mishaps, and trouble with sand flies ensued, and James, in the fashion of the emergent hunter hero, found the isolation and mortal danger of the mountains conducive to personal reflection. Separated from the party for twelve hours and expecting "Mr Bruin" at any moment, he "looked back on my past life from my earliest recollection, and reviewed all my acts and moralized a good deal." Meanwhile, at the end of the trip, Wilson noted his own countenance as a frontiersman fashioned from the trudge of the trail: "We dressed up in white shirts and light boots and went out for a walk, but felt so very uncomfortable." The trip had indeed been one of masculine catharsis in the grand tradition:

> Our trip was taken with the view of ascertaining what real rough life in the mountains was like, and in order to be away from all civilization, to breathe the fresh air and drink pure water, to hunt and prospect . . . We had great

hardships and but little real pleasure but each returned well pleased and with a possible hope of some day going off again. Our health was excellent, and our spirits, as a rule, buoyant. We lost but little flesh and returned much hardier than when we started out.[40]

Frequent in narratives of wilderness transformation were ideas of rena-scence, belonging, and becoming "western." Writing to his sister of a return to the Rockies on an antelope hunting expedition, E. J. Sartain reflected on how it "made me feel like a new man to get back on the prairie after being out east almost a month." The joys of connection with the game trail became a way of practically and psychologically claiming space, as if hunting and regional identity defined and sustained each other. For the colonial adven-turers and aristocrats of the western trails, this sense of frontier association was preserved in stories, trophies, and other cultural artifacts—thus allow-ing the reanimation of hunter's paradise and the claiming of a "borrowed landscape" from far away. On occasion, however, the appeal of the game trail was so strong that it prompted a desire to settle permanently in western climes. William Pickett noted how wistful hankerings for the western game trail brought him back every year during the 1870s on hunting expeditions. In spring 1883, he set up a ranch spread at Grey Bull River, Wyoming, running Hereford cattle. Malcolm Mackay and William Allen, too, came to regard the Rocky Mountain West as home turf. As Sartain pointed out, "A man can get so attached to a country like this that he just can't leave it." So enlivened by the game trail, T. S. Van Dyke moved to California in 1875 and wrote a further eight books on hunting after *Flirtation Camp*, which glorified in Pacific terrain (and firmly cast the author in the role of naturalist hunter hero). Hunting encouraged a connection to place and to people and seem-ingly served as the conduit for "becoming western" in contexts far beyond those of masculine regeneration or a tourist sojourn. Settling in Billings and earning report in *Progressive Men of the State of Montana* (1903) as an "hon-oured pioneer," William Allen proudly labeled himself a "typical old-time westerner." Substantiated by a "loving participation in the hunt, in Indian fighting, and in nature studies," his definition was instructive.[41]

This metamorphosis from greenhorn to indigene (either de facto set-tler or performatively "western man") was played out in trail testimony. Commentators segued between renditions on the wonder of western scen-ery, rugged travails, or the ferocity or curiosity of fauna to issue strident broadcasts of territorial ownership. The theater of the West was one of adventure, transformation, and assimilation. Traveling with market hunter and scout Buffalo Jones, Zane Grey exhorted that "something swelled within my breast at the thought that for the time I was part of that wild scene . . . all was mine . . . mine by right of presence, by right of the eye to see and the mind to keep." The act of killing the charismatic fauna of the West, bison monarchs and sovereign bruins, as Daniel Herman notes, made the hunter feel equally ennobled, a bona fide "American Native." Landscape descriptions, the recounting of the chase, and codes of regeneration and epiphany served, in this framework, to elucidate the provenance of the hunter hero and his symbolic claiming of physical (and imaginative) space. Pickett's journal moved from speaking of "these frontier people" and dreaming of apprehending bison "in a state of nature" to describe elk grazing in "our hunting grounds" (incidentally, one of the tributaries of the Grey Bull River came to be known as Pickett's Creek). The change in tenor was subtle but significant.[42]

Others read the hunt as a vital aspect of frontier acculturalization. Migrating to Montana from Minnesota in 1867, David Hilger, a woolgrower, Lewistown booster, and later librarian of the Montana Historical Society, recalled hunting trips as a youth out of the family ranch at Dog Creek between 1881 and 1884, where mountain sheep, black-tailed deer, and antelope "fell a mark to the deadly aim of my Winchester rifle." For German emigrant and Musselshell rancher Henry Bierman, hunting represented a critical component in the outdoor education of the westerner, part of a process of hardening whereby "a man learns to take care of himself, butting his head against mother nature, and to take what comes his way and say he likes it." Such remarks provided telling evidence on the connections between hunting, identity, and the historical contours of pioneering in the West. Beneath the tales and trails of soulful wanderings and captivating animals, hunters engaged in a process of capture that spoke of the politics of identity, landscape, and memory.[43]

"BROTHER SPORTSMAN" AND THE SOCIAL LANDSCAPE OF THE FRONTIER

In the theater of the game trail, the hunter hero faced not only the rugged western landscape and its faunal complement but also a human audience. For all its prepositions to wilderness immersion, the hunt proved an irrevocably peopled landscape. The company of sportsmen proved the least complicated of these exchanges. Aside from the threat of being shot by a fellow traveler, errant displays of "buck fever," or proclivities for getting lost or needing rescue from angry bears, most sportsmen relished companionship on the trails. The camaraderie of the hunt plugged into a social urge for male bonding, evident in the popularity of fraternal societies, which boasted a US membership of 5.5 million by 1900 (of a male adult population of 19 million) and satisfied the need to perform masculinity in a social context. William Allen admitted, "The pleasures of the hunt are more than half due to the companions who accompany me." The prospect of shared experience represented a key appeal of the game trail. Writing in *Hitting versus Missing with the Shotgun* (1900), "Shadow" advised that "agreeable conversation is a most delightful adjunct to your day's sport, provided your companion knows when to talk as well as the proper time to keep silent." Hunters learned from their partners and tested their own hardihood by comparison, finding civilized manliness in the etiquette, ritual, and conviviality of a masculine group identity. Malcolm Mackay fondly remembered his associate, Horace Mullendore, as "one of the best I ever hunted with, a man of untiring energy, a dead shot, and possessed of an almost supernatural instinct for finding game." The collective encounter of the game trail facilitated a powerful homo-social connection and emerged as a crucible for the testing of frontiering credentials and the enacting of performance code. As Mackay put it, "Our spirits blended in such a manner that no matter what is the nature of the outward circumstance, we each re-acted to it in such a way that brought to the other joy, enthusiasm and quiet content. What a wondrous feeling it is to be out in the wilderness with a man like that! Never a jarring note; absolute dependability each toward the other; in both our hearts a song with the same chord."[44]

The fraternity of the game trail brought validation by testimony and witness. The camp, and particularly the campfire, emerged as a geographic center for the construction of an *experience* with the wild and, most importantly, for the retelling of the quest. The fireside, in particular, served as staging post and center of the mobile community—a practical and psychological site of grounding and repertory. As Pickett explained, "In Mountain Life . . . There is only one living room; that is around the camp fire." The camp was a locating point, a place for gathering. Shields began his hunting day by rising at dawn to sit by the smoldering logs with a strong coffee. Sportsmen actually spent a lot of time in situ (despite the foregrounding of "action" in the testimonial landscape of the hunt), doing very little it would seem beyond playing hunter in a domestic setting. Journals spoke of readying equipment, tending to horses and dogs, cooking, stacking the fire, preparing game, idle chat, and resting up, often waiting for itinerant travelers or for inclement weather to clear. Pickett's Rocky Mountain diary for fall 1876 spent a great deal of time reciting days "in camp" in the Highwood Mountains due to snowstorms, "laying up . . . cooking, eating, and fixing up our guns."[45]

Apparently mundane descriptions of the hunting camp nonetheless obscured its importance as a sacred geography. For Williamson, camp life contained a "wild fascination" that made him feel an "intense longing to be back under canvas." Zane Grey may have described the Colorado trail as "wild and sublime, a thing of wonder, of mystery—beyond all else a place to grip the heart of a man, to unleash his daring spirit," but set against that was a campsite framed by pine woods, wandered by wild horses and slumbering dogs, and centered by its rousing fire, "a picture like that of a hunter's dream." The camp represented a space of masculine corroboration, conviviality, and memorialization. Hunters mustered at the end of the day to ritualistically ruminate and commit the chase to the spiritual wood smoke, collectively choreographing their encounters with wild things. Allen recalled how "stories, wild and improbable" were exchanged over the fire as an integral part of the trail experience: "Every hunter who has been out with a number of others, knows what a pleasant pastime story-telling is after a hard day's march, and how often it is kept up for the greater part of the night." The campfire, then, represented an important locus around which the meaning of the hunt could be chewed over with the grub, constructed and committed to memory. Offering pertinent reflection on the game trail as a landscape of theater in itself, Parker Gillmore pointed out that "among the most ardent Nimrods the retrospect of the day's sport has always caused almost as much pleasure as the actual performance."[46]

AMERICAN INDIANS AND HUNTING GUIDES: ENCOUNTERING THE HOMEGROWN HUNTER HERO

Beyond sporting companions, the encounters of the hunter with other groups on the trail brought to attention alternative models of masculinity. American

Indians represented one such a cadre and were seen by sport hunters in a vein of different and often conflicting modes. Encounters came by traveling with indigenous guides, spending time in tribal encampments, chance meetings on the trail, and, on occasion, as the result of skirmishes. The title of William Allen's autobiography, *Adventures with Indians and Game*, contained an implicit notion of the Indian as an integral part of the landscape of wild excitement on offer in the western theater. Headed west in the late 1840s believing that "human nature can't go on feeding on civilized fixings," British sportsman Edward Ruxton promised his publisher a manuscript on "mountain doins" in the far West, "always supposing my hair is not lifted by Comanche or Pawnee on the scalping route." An encounter with the indigene promised frontier flavor, novelty, and a hint of danger—worthy grist for the storytelling mill.[47]

Some valorized the American Indian as warrior, a fierce and effective hunter, relentlessly savage, and (sometimes gloriously) adversarial. A man in tune with his instinct and the game, an accomplished equestrian, a natural man after Rousseau's tradition, and a first-class assassin, the American Indian represented an alternative model of hunter heroism. For the Earl of Dunraven, the chance to see American Indians "in something like their natural freedom" represented a key part of his hunting sojourn. Assumed to be living in a "state of nature" diametrically opposed to urban industrialism, the American Indian existed in an idealized space beyond the trappings of modernity, in the words of Dunraven, "ignorant but independent, a wild but free man." Travelogues effused with descriptions of thunderous bison charges and the veritable feats of mounted warriors in possession of a skill set that visiting sportsmen sought to emulate. Henry Boller spoke of hunting in the Black Hills with the Mandan White Cow Band and the inestimable dexterity of "the Bear Hunter," while testimonials from the likes of Scottish aristocrat Charles Murray (who traveled in the 1830s to live with the Pawnee), Charles Messiter, and John Palliser described campfire idylls with indigenous hunter heroes, imbibing of the wood smoke and sharing hunting stories. Allen spoke of how the "wily warriors" with their "red blankets lent an additional charm to the view" at the Crow Reservation, before sharing coffee and venison with the "noble red men" and leaving with a hearty handshake.[48]

At other times, commentary on the American Indian took on a more critical flavor. Dunraven lambasted the indigene for his "subtle, twisting and tiny mind" and celebrated guides Bill Cody and Texas Jack as men who "hunt him as a nobler species of game, in whose killing there is infinite credit" (a part of this ire was no doubt due to the fact that Dunraven felt that Indians "interfered considerably with my pleasure and comfort" on the game trail). Others issued pejorative descriptions of western Indians as bloodthirsty, lazy, subhuman, and without redeeming qualities, seeing not a hero in the indigenous tradition but an enemy skulking in the timberline and (especially when game became scarce) a wasteful and dishonorable consumer of wild things and woefully bereft of codes of honor or fair chase. Baille Grohman observed poor marksmanship at play, with implicit racial overtones: "I never heard so much shooting and saw so little hitting as I did in the month we were right among these perfectly wild Indians." Passing critical commentary on the performance codes of the indigenous hunter, he added, "There would be more shouting and waving of arms, and riding at full split up and down the most amazingly steep slopes, than would supply an evening's entertainment at a circus."[49]

Beneath the dramatic flourish of trailside testimony, the hunter's tale spoke a dualistic narrative of idealization and dispossession. On one level, there was a respect and admiration for (or at least intrigue with) American Indian ways and a keen ethnographical bent. At the same time, the recreational whimsies of "playing Indian" saw the powerful and symbolic appropriation of indigenous symbols on behalf of a hegemonic colonial masculinity. When Benedict Revoil glorified the chase as a "wild insensate pastime, in which Maclean and I had taken part as if we hard been genuine Redskins," he figuratively claimed an Indian identity and offered a vivid depiction of his idealized self as expert hunter. By performing "Indianness" on the game trail, hunter heroes found camaraderie, catharsis, and a confirmation of their own racial and national identity, figuratively playing the "other" for the purposes of personal grounding. As Philip Deloria points out, "Disguise calls the notion of fixed identity into question" but also "makes one conscious of a real 'me' underneath." Even the language of empathy and celebration deployed by the hunter hero concealed a subtle process of textual as well as terrestrial conquest at play. The taking of names and practices, not to mention the game itself, provided evidence of an assumed right to the resources of the West. They also established a frontier hierarchy in which the Anglo-Saxon hunter played alpha male and American Indians served as hostile opponents, obsequious subalterns, or primitive hunter heroes affixed firmly to a past age.[50]

Another group encountered on the trail were guides, some of which were American Indians, but many were local Euro-American frontiersmen who eked out a living delivering the hunting experience to increasing numbers of sportsmen from the eastern states and farther afield. Here, too, the relationship was a complicated one. Sport hunters idealized their guides as rugged and hardy characters in possession of exemplary tracking skills and intimate knowledge of the ways of western folk and fauna. Sanctified as authentic westerners, often these men had worked as market hunters or fur trappers and lent a sense of the "real" frontier and local color to the dramatic imprint of the game trail. Texas Jack Omohundro was romanticized accordingly:

> The sight of him in his fringed hunting buckskins, short hunting shirt decorated with patches of red and blue stained leather, pair of delicate white moccasins embroidered by the hand of some aesthetic and loving squaw, with his short, bright brown curls covered by a velvet cap with a broad gold band around it, would play the very mischief with many an eastern girls heart.

Dripping with the qualities that the sport hunter sought to channel, the frontier guide represented a salient masculine role model. Physical vigor, woodcraft skills, a steely countenance, and capable hunting skills marked him as a man apart. Charles Messiter, whose *Adventures among the North American Indians* (1890) described his passage from tenderfoot to hunter hero in the accustomed fashion, recounted an occasion when he emerged from his tent to "find, leaning on his rifle by the camp fire, which he had made up, the best-looking specimen of a frontiersman I had yet seen," a six-foot-tall, tough-talking Indian fighter clad in buckskin. Malcolm Mackay described Ed Van Dyke as "the swiftest and quietest man in the woods it has ever been my good fortune to follow," while Zane Grey saw Buffalo Jones as an exemplar in the finest frontier tradition, "burly-shouldered, bronze-faced . . . great in all these remarkable qualities common to the men who opened up the West. Courage, endurance, determination, and hardihood," and proof of "what a lifetime on the plains could make of a man."[51]

As veteran westerner and cipher to the wilds, the frontier guide functioned as a critical choreographer of the hunt. The game trail was, in that sense, workplace as well as wilderness playground. As an "environmental broker," the guide served as intermediary between the wild and the tourist, providing outfitting equipment, horses, and guns and the benefit of geographical acumen, tracking skills, and hunting advice. Williamson heaped praise on his guide Wilkinson as "an excellent shot and an indefatigable walker . . . passionately fond of the life he led." On sale was the thrill of a chase and a frontier education. Charlie Marble repaired Teddy Roosevelt's famous gun, the "explosive express," after he dropped it on the trail by ingeniously using a strip of his buckskin shirt. Ed Van Dyke, as Mackay admitted, "taught me a lot about woodcraft, trailing, walking, packing and stalking . . . I came home with a wagonload of woods lore if not with a wagonload of grizzlies."[52]

Performance loomed large in this leisure economy of the trail, with guides trading their expertise in terms of entertainment value as well as practical graft. A theatrical countenance was clearly understood by Buffalo Jones as he spread a map of the Colorado Trail out before Zane Grey, advising that "this is virgin ground. No white man or Indian has ever hunted lions there." Grey watched in awe later as Jones lassoed a mountain lion in a tree and "pounced" on him. Storytelling around the campfire, too, proved a notable occasion for collective rehearsal of heroic code. Peregrine Herne, ex–fur trapper, regaled trail companions with tales of his life as a "poor mountaineer" and the "perils and pleasures of a hunter's life," in the process earning the patronage of sportsmen that took him across the world as a hunting guide. Williamson had been resolutely entertained by Wilkinson's talk around the campfire for "many a pleasant and profitable hour." Storytelling was a saleable commodity.[53]

In choreographing the drama of sporting adventure, the frontier guide performed the roles of teacher, scout, and storyteller. Channeling an everyman authenticity, he combined erudition with entertainment and was well versed in the etiquette of performance code—too much showmanship, after all, was a sure sign of fakery. For Murphy, the worthiest guides were "simple and unpretentious men who were as sociable as men could be, and who bore no sort of resemblance either in form, manner, language or expression to Leatherstocking's or any of his ilk. They could not hit an acorn many miles away, nor did they perform heroic feats in hugging a grizzly bear to death or killing every animal they fired at, yet they could give an excellent account of themselves." Baillie Grohman, likewise, lamented time spent on the game trail with "'nobs' and 'snobs'—worshipped lords and those that worship them" and favored the camaraderie of "rough and uncouth champions of the wilds—true men—on whose word you can build, and on whose quiet,

cool-headed though subdued courage you can implicitly depend." Being val-
idated by such men was a sure sign of "becoming western" and thus a genuine badge of honor among the sport hunters. In the company of a "true"
frontier guide, jocular pranks and "theatrical congratulations" represented
welcome signs of a rite of passage from tenderfoot to certified westerner.[54]

At times, however, the theatrics of wilderness adventure made for an
uneasy relationship between the sportsmen and their frontier choreographers. For all their assembled knowledge, the guide was a subaltern whose
job was to facilitate the heroism of the sportsman rather than to upstage
him. In the performance of the hunt there could be only one leading man.
Williamson's testimonial pertinently noted how his guide had served well:
"He had not spared himself in trying to show *me* sport, and to the pains he
took in skinning and marking *my* trophies" (emphasis added). At the point
of the kill, prime metaphysical moment of proving, the scout was expected
to vanish from the scene and allow the sporting hero full rein. Accordingly,
alongside the veneration of the frontier guide existed a competing vernacular of comic gaze, curiosity, and condescension. For Webb, the West
was "infested with charlatans," men without honor who sought to fleece
sportsmen, while Williamson questioned the authority of men he saw as
"notoriously given to romanticizing." Incompetence and laxity were typical
complaints. Messiter lambasted his lily-livered guides who vowed to "give
up the trip and return home" after a band of Sioux appeared at the margins
of camp wielding spears. Others were described as uncouth, eccentric, even
feral. Mackay described Ed Van Dyke as someone who lived in a cabin full of
junk and was prone to drinking tea until three in the morning and working
himself into a trance before the hunt with grunts, groans, and operating by
"hunches." "While he surely was a real hunter, he was a little eccentric, and a
bit slippery," he noted. Such comments allowed the sportsmen to retain an
accomplished vantage as the arbiters of civilized manliness and control over
the game trail on the basis of class, capital, and self-conflated codes of honor.
A failed bag could, of course, be blamed on inadequate auxiliaries. As historian Tina Loo notes, sport hunters "went into the woods with something
even more comforting: a sense of entitlement." After all, the game was theirs
to play.[55]

Local frontiersmen and guides, for their part, were equally ambiguous in
judging their sporting charges, viewing them as capital men and good sports

(in both senses of the word), but also poor shots, pretentious outsiders, and objects of ridicule. William Pickett criticized the way in which "the usual practice of sportsmen coming from the East to the West 'after bear' was to depend on the guide to find the bear, guide the sportsman up to it and allow him to do the shooting. It looked too much like getting the animal tame down enough so that you could 'put salt on his tail,' and then deliver the shot." Pickett's critique offered a fierce indictment of the leisure economy of the trail and its pretensions to hunter heroism and signaled his own claiming of regional identity in the bargain. One hunting guide working out of Midvale, Montana, talked in amused tones of the "pampered darlings of fortune" and took pleasure in molding a frontier drama that allowed the greenhorn to "cherish the pleasing illusion that it was he who fired the fatal shot." As hosts of hunting repertory, guides also asserted their control of the frontier experience by sending patrons on dead-end quests and laughing at their inexpert predilections. One spooked his aristocratic clients by hiding in a thicket and bellowing like a grizzly bear, causing them to flee to camp. The act represented an amusing jape and also an act of gesture politics and resistance (a few moments earlier he had been ordered to retrieve water for a pedigree hound, an "aristocratic breed" worth $5,000, according to its owner). Equally, guides used storytelling to affirm an insider/outside framework of frontier experience. As James Mead, a hunter and rancher who settled in Kansas in the 1860s, noted, "It was the custom in those days along the trail to entertain the 'tenderfoot' with wonderful stories of life on the plains."[56]

In playing the game and sharing the story, then, the genealogy of the hunter hero was a tangled one. According to Horace Edwards, English sportsmen were "natural" to be "nasty." When a group wandered into his camp, bedraggled, wet, and disoriented, however, the "newcomers" were treated with hospitality. Edwards neglected to tell the visitors that his own party had been lost the previous day, despite having a compass. Instead, the group of men sat down at the campfire, sharing food and imbibing a rhetorical digest of all-action adventure and animal contest understandable by all. The next morning, they headed out to the game trail together. The performance landscape of the hunt allowed for amusement, communal ritual, and the consolidation of frontier identity on both sides. In the end, the story was everything. Around the campfire could thus be found fur trappers, market hunters, cowboy soldiers, gentleman sport hunters, and hunter naturalists, each with tales of frontier experience to perform. Such was the semiotic geography of the hunter hero.[57]

NOTES

The epigraph is from Malcolm Mackay, *Cow Range and Hunting Trail* (New York: G. P. Putnam's, 1925), 128.

1. Ibid., 3, 99.

2. John Frost, *Heroes and Hunters of the West* (Philadelphia: H. C. Peck and Theo. Bliss, 1860), 11. On Daniel Boone and the hunter hero in American cultural life, see Stephen Aron, *How the West Was Lost: The Transformation of Kentucky from Daniel Boone to Henry Clay* (Baltimore: Johns Hopkins University Press, 1996); Daniel Herman, *Hunting and the American Imagination* (Washington, DC: Smithsonian Institution Press, 2003), 93–121; Richard Slotkin, *The Fatal Environment: The Myth of the Frontier in the Age of Industrialization, 1800–1890* (New York: Atheneum, 1985); and *Regeneration through Violence: The Myth of the American Frontier, 1600–1800* (Middletown, CT: Wesleyan University Press, 1973).

3. Monica Rico, *Nature's Noblemen: Transatlantic Masculinities and the Nineteenth-Century American West* (New Haven: Yale University Press, 2013), 4. On hunting, masculinity, and empire, see John M. Mackenzie, *The Empire of Nature: Hunting, Conservation and British Imperialism* (Manchester: Manchester University Press, 1988); Greg Gillespie, "'I Was Well Pleased with Our Sport among the Buffalo': Big-Game Hunters, Travel Writing, and Cultural Imperialism in the British North American West, 1847–72," *Canadian Historical Review* 83, no. 4 (2002): 555–84; Greg Gillespie, *Hunting for Empire: Narratives of Sport in Rupert's Land, 1840–1870* (Vancouver: University of British Columbia Press, 2007); Tina Loo, "Of Moose and Men: Hunting for Masculinities in British Columbia, 1880–1939," *Western Historical Quarterly* 32 (Autumn 2001): 296–319; Karen Wonders, "Hunting Narratives of the Age of Empire: A Gender Reading of Their Iconography," *Environment and History* 11 (2005): 269–91; Slotkin, *Regeneration through Violence.*

4. John M. Mackenzie, "The Imperial Pioneer and Hunter and the British Masculine Stereotype in Late Victorian and Edwardian Times," in *Manliness and Morality: Middle Class Masculinity in Britain and America*, ed. J. Mangan and J. Wavin (Manchester: Manchester University Press, 1987), 176–95; Herman, *Hunting*, 122–99; Matt Cartmill, *A View to a Death in the Morning: Hunting and Nature through History* (Cambridge, MA: Harvard University Press, 1993), 134; Cecil Hartley, *Hunting Sports of the West* (Philadelphia: Bradley, 1865), 13; Frederick Jackson Turner, *The Frontier in American History* (New York: Henry Holt, 1920), 358; Sarah Watts, *Rough Rider*

in the White House (Chicago: University of Chicago Press, 2003), 28; Elisha J. Lewis, *The American Sportsman* (Philadelphia: J. B. Lippincott, 1906), 20. On masculinity, see Michael S. Kimmel, *Manhood in America: A Cultural History* (Oxford: Oxford University Press, 2006); Gail Bederman, *Manliness and Civilization: A Cultural History of Gender and Race in the United States, 1880–1917* (Chicago: University of Chicago Press, 1995); Mark C. Carnes and Clyde Griffen, *Meanings for Manhood: Constructions of Masculinity in Victorian America* (Chicago: University of Chicago Press, 1990); Matthew Basso, Laura McCall, and Dee Garceau, *Across the Great Divide: Cultures of Manhood in the American West* (New York: Routledge, 2001).

5. John Mortimer Murphy, *Sporting Adventures in the Far West* (London: Sampson Low, Marston, Searle & Rivington, 1870), 2.

6. On European and British hunting abroad, see Thomas Dunlap, *Nature and the English Diaspora: Environment and History in the United States, Canada, Australia and New Zealand* (Cambridge: Cambridge University Press, 1999), 59–69; Mackenzie, *Empire of Nature*; John Merritt, *Baronets and Buffalo: The British Sportsman in the American West, 1833–1881* (Missoula, MT: Mountain Press, 1985); Harriet Ritvo, *The Animal Estate: The English and Other Creatures in the Victorian Age* (Cambridge, MA: Harvard University Press, 1987). For the relationship between wilderness and the West in an American context, see Roderick Nash, *Wilderness and the American Mind* (New Haven: Yale University Press, 1967); Max Oelschlager, *The Idea of Wilderness* (New Haven: Yale University Press, 1991); Henry Nash Smith, *Virgin Land: The American West as Symbol and Myth* (Cambridge, MA: Harvard University Press, 1950); Slotkin, *The Fatal Environment*.

7. Henry William Herbert, *Frank Forester's Field Sports of the United States and British Provinces of North America* (New York: W. A. Townsend, 1864), 2:147; William Baillie Grohman, *Fifteen Years' Sport and Life in the Hunting Grounds of Western America and British Columbia* (London: Horace Cox, 1900), 2, 4; John Palliser, *The Solitary Hunter or Sporting Adventures in the Prairies* (London: George Routledge, 1856), 630; Frederick Selous, *Sport and Travel: East and West* (London: Longman's Green, 1901), 143–44, 154.

8. John Higham, "The Reorientation of American Culture in the 1890s," in *Writing American History: Essays in Modern Scholarship*, ed. John Higham (Bloomington: Indiana University Press, 1970), 79; Heclawa, *In the Heart of the Bitter-Root Mountains: The Story of the Carlin Hunting Party* (New York, G. P. Putnam's, 1895), xix; Peregrine Herne, *Perils and Pleasures of a Hunter's Life, or the Romance of Hunting* (New York: Evans and Co., 1858), 279; Anthony Rotundo, *American Manhood: Transformations on Masculinity from the Revolution to the Modern Era* (New York, Basic Books, 1993), 232; Parker Gillmore, *Prairie and Forest* (New York: Harper's, 1874), 32–33; Parker Gillmore, *Experiences of a Sportsman in North America* (London: Chapman, 1869), 2–3.

9. Theodore Roosevelt, *The Wilderness Hunter* (New York: G. P. Putnam's, 1893), 8, 29.

10. Murray quoted in Ruth Weidner, "Images of the Hunt in Nineteenth-Century America and Their Sources in British and European Art," PhD diss., University of Delaware, Newark, 1988, 14; Alfred Mayer, *Sport with Gun and Rod* (New York: Century Co.,1883), 11.

11. Roosevelt, *Wilderness Hunter*, 7; Theodore Roosevelt, *Hunting Trips of a Ranchman* (New York: G. P. Putnam's, 1885), 37–38; Dunlap, *Nature*, 63–64; Hartley, *Hunting Sports of the West*, 8–9; Herman, *Hunting*, 2–4; J. Hector St. Jean Crèvecoeur, "What Is an American?" in *Letters from an American Farmer* (New York: Fox, Duffield, 1904 [1782]), 3:69.

12. Roosevelt quoted in Kimmel, *Manhood in America*, 121; Earl of Dunraven, *Hunting in the Yellowstone* (New York: Outing, 1917), 29; Roosevelt, *Wilderness Hunter*, 7–8, 15; Wilbur F. Parker, "What Constitutes an American Sportsman," *American Sportsman* 2 (November 1872): 24.

13. William A. Allen, *Adventures with Indians and Game or Twenty Years in the Rocky Mountains* (Chicago: A. W. Bowen, 1903), 110, 294; George Shields, *Rustlings in the Rockies* (Chicago: Belford Clarke, 1883), 10; Richard Irving Dodge, *The Hunting Grounds of the Great West* (London: Chatto and Windus, 1877), 194.

14. Dodge, *Hunting Grounds*, 3; Dunraven, *Hunting*, 299; William D. Pickett, Diary for 1879 continued, 1, William D. Pickett Diary, SC1436, Montana Historical Society Research Center, Helena (hereafter cited as MHS); Heclawa, *In the Heart of the Bitter-Root Mountains*, xix.

15. Earl of Dunraven, *The Great Divide: Travels in the Upper Yellowstone in the Summer of 1874* (London: Chatto and Windus, 1876), viii; William Pickett, "My First Trip through Yellowstone Park in 1877," 15, William D. Pickett Diary, SC1436, MHS; Allen, *Adventures*, 38, 169; Herne, *Perils and Pleasures*, 298.

16. Laura Mulvey, "Visual Pleasure and Narrative Cinema," *Screen* 16, no. 3 (1975): 6–18; C. W. Webber, *The Hunter Naturalist: Romance of Sporting, or Wild Scenes and Wild Hunters* (Philadelphia: J. B. Lippincott and Co., 1859), 280, 4; Roosevelt, *Hunting Trips*, 290.

17. Dunraven, *Hunting*, 18; Loo, "Of Moose and Men," 305.

18. Theodore S. Van Dyke, *Flirtation Camp: or, The Rifle, Rod, and Gun in California* (New York: Fords, Howard & Hulbert, 1881), 39; Mackay, *Cow Range*, 136; Herne, *Perils and Pleasures*, 22.

19. Jim Bond, *America's Number One Trophy* (Portland: Metropolitan Printing Co., 1950), 6; Shields, *Rustlings*, 95–100.

20. Andrew Williamson, *Sport and Photography in the Rocky Mountains* (Edinburgh: David Douglas, 1880), 14; Allen, *Adventures*, 112; William Pickett, Diary, April 2,

1879–January 1880, 13, William D. Pickett Diary, SC1436, MHS; Herbert, *Frank Forester's Field Sports*, 186; Dodge, *Hunting Grounds*, 209; Edgar Randolph, *Inter-Ocean Hunting Tales* (New York: Forest and Stream, 1908), 48.

21. Henry Howe, *Historical Collections of the Great West Containing Narratives of the Most Important and Interesting Events in Western History* (New York: George Tuttle, 1857), 165–66; Theodore Roosevelt, *Good Hunting in Pursuit of Big Game* (New York: Harper's, 1907), 16; Clyde Ormond, *Hunting in the Northwest* (New York: Alfred A. Knopf, 1948), 3–4; Shields, *Rustlings*, 40–42, 121; Horace Hutchinson, ed., *Big Game Shooting* (New York: Charles Scribner's, 1905), 250; Mackenzie, "Imperial Pioneer," 180.

22. Allen, *Adventures*, 82; Grantley Berkeley, *The English Sportsman in the Western Prairie* (London: Hurst and Blackett, 1861), 18, 244.

23. J. S. Campion, *On the Frontier: Reminiscences of Wild Sports, Personal Adventures and Strange Scenes* (London: Chapman and Hall, 1878), 58, 9, 30–33, 50.

24. Allen Morris Jones, *A Quiet Place of Violence: Hunting and Ethics in the Missouri River Breaks* (Bozeman: Bangtail Press, 1997), 28; Charles Francis, *Sport among the Rockies* (New York: Troy Daily Times Job Printing Establishment, 1889), 59; Randolph Marcy, *Thirty Years of Army Life on the Border* (New York: Harper's, 1866), 318; Malcolm Mackay, "Grizzly Bear Hunting on Snowshoes (1926)," SC1389, Malcolm Mackay Reminiscence, MHS; Mackay, *Cow Range*, 168–69; Roosevelt, *Good Hunting*, 33; William Pickett, Diary 1881, 5–6, William Pickett Diary, SC1436, MHS; Wolley quoted in *Big Game Shooting*, ed. Hutchinson, 246–47.

25. Owen Wister, *Red Man and White* (New York: Harper and Bros., 1895), xxvi; Mackay, *Cow Range*, 78–79; Palliser, *Solitary Hunter*, 80–81.

26. Pickett, Diary for 1876, 25; Howland Gasper, *The Complete Sportsman* (New York: Forest and Stream, 1893), 53; Randolph, *Inter-Ocean*, 110.

27. Randolph, *Inter-Ocean*, 32; Shields, *Rustlings*, 87; Dodge, *Hunting Grounds*, 103; W. Webb, *Buffalo Land* (Cincinnati: E. Hannaford, 1872), 453.

28. Dodge, *Hunting Grounds*, 108–10; Berkeley, *English Sportsman*, 292, 293; Allen, *Adventures*, 249.

29. GWB, "Hunting Wapiti on the Loup," *Forest and Stream*, May 4, 1876, 193. See George Bird Grinnell Papers, Box 31, Folder 156, Yale University Library; Allen, *Adventures*, 110; Williamson, *Sport and Photography*, 23.

30. Allen, *Adventures*, 110; Williamson, *Sport and Photography*, 13.

31. Webber, *Hunter Naturalist*, 280; Donald M. Hines, *Ghost Voices: Yakima Indian Myths, Legends, Humor, Hunting Stories* (Issaquah, WA: Great Eagle, 1992), 252–55.

32. Barry Holstun Lopez, *Of Wolves and Men* (New York: Touchstone Books, 1977), 94–95; GWB, "Hunting Wapiti," 193; Daniel Barringer, "In the Old Rockies,"

in *Hunting at High Altitudes*, ed. George Grinnell (New York: Harper and Bros., 1913) 309–11; Selous, *Sport*, 192.

33. *Badlands Cowboy*, June 19, 1883; Watts, *Rough Rider*, 25–26; Roosevelt, *Wilderness Hunter*, 96; *Dial* 15 (September 16, 1893), 149. On Roosevelt, see also Milton Meltzer, *Theodore Roosevelt and His America* (New York: Franklin Watts, 1994); John A. Garraty, *Theodore Roosevelt: The Strenuous Life* (New York: Harper and Row, 1987); G. Edward White, *The Eastern Establishment and the Western Experience* (New Haven: Yale University Press, 1968).

34. *Los Angeles Express*, May 28, 1903; Lincoln Lang, *Ranching with Roosevelt* (Philadelphia: J. B. Lippincott, 1926), 7; Watts, *Rough Rider*, 131.

35. Theodore Roosevelt, *The Winning of the West*, vol. 1, *From the Alleghenies to the Mississippi, 1769–1776* (New York: G. P. Putnam's, 1889), 29; Watts, *Rough Rider*, 26.

36. George Shields, *Cruising in the Cascades: And Other Hunting Adventures* (Chicago: Rand, McNally & Co., 1889), 25, 176; A. W. Dimock, *Wall Street and the Wild* (New York: Outing, 1915), 248, 309.

37. Henry O'Brien, "Diary of a Trip to the Rocky Mountains," 1882, 1–4, Henry O'Brien Diary, SCIS08: Box 1, Folder 1, MHS.

38. O'Brien, "Diary of a Trip," 10, 22, 28, 35, 36, 38.

39. James Wilson, "A Trip to the Cascade Mountains," 3, 4, MSS p-B 203 vol. 1, Bancroft Library, University of California, Berkeley.

40. Wilson, "Trip to the Cascade Mountains," 17–18, 40–41, 49, 71–72.

41. E. J. Sartain to Grace Fulton, December 6, 1907, E. J. Sartain Letters, 1906–8, 1916, SC1175, MHS; *Progressive Men of the State of Montana*, vol. 1 (Chicago: A. W. Bowen, ca.1903), 5, MHS. The "pioneer" label proved of great significance, and the term was debated at length, for instance, by the Society of Montana Pioneers as to who was deserving of such an epithet. See Clyde Milner, "The Shared Memory of Montana Pioneers," *Montana: The Magazine of Western History* 37 (1973): 2–13; Allen, *Adventures*, 7.

42. George Reiger, ed., *The Best of Zane Grey, Outdoorsman* (Harrisburg, PA: Stackpole Press, 1972), 38–39; Herman, *Hunting*, 201; Pickett, Diary for 1876, 3, 12, 21.

43. David Hilger, "Overland Trail," 1907, 9, David Hilger Papers, SC854, Box 5, Folder 8, Writings (1907–1935), MHS; Henry Bierman Reminiscence, 23, SC30: Box 1, Folder 1, MHS; Pickett, Diary for 1876, 25.

44. Allen, *Adventures*, 185; S. T. Hammond, or "Shadow," *Hitting Versus Missing with the Shotgun* (New York: Forest and Stream, 1900), 82; Mackay, *Cow Range*, 119–21, 33, 147; Bederman, *Manliness and Civilization*, 23.

45. Pickett, Diary for 1876, 18–19, 18–21; Shields, *Rustlings*, 78.

46. Williamson, *Sport and Photography*, 11; Reiger, *Zane Grey*, 22–24; Allen, *Adventures*, 177; Parker Gillmore, *Accessible Field Sports: The Experiences of a Sportsman in North America* (London: Chapman and Hall, 1869), 146.

47. Edward Ruxton, *Ruxton of the Rockies* (Norman: University of Oklahoma Press, 1950), 308.

48. Dunraven, *Hunting*, 26, 124; Henry Boller, *Among the Indians: Eight Years in the Far West, 1858–1866* (Philadelphia: T. Ellwood Zell, 1868), 214–18; see Charles Messiter, *Adventures among the North American Indians* (London: R. H. Porter, 1890); for a typical account, see Allen, *Adventures*, 131.

49. Dunraven, *Hunting*, 8, 125; A. Pendarves Vivian, *Wanderings in the Western Land* (London: Sampson, Low, 1879), 108, 215; William Baillie Grohman, *Camps in the Rockies* (London: Sampson Low, Marston, Searle, & Rivington, 1882), 267.

50. Davenport, *Hunter*, 249; Philip J. Deloria, *Playing Indian* (New Haven: Yale University Press, 1998), 4.

51. Dunraven, *Hunting*, 11; Messiter, *Adventures*, 198; Mackay, *Cow Range*, 124; Reiger, *Zane Grey*, 21–23.

52. Annie Coleman, "Rise of the House of Leisure: Outdoor Guides, Practical Knowledge, and Industrialization," *Western Historical Quarterly* 42, no. 4 (2011): 440; "Charlie and Teddy Pals," news clipping, November 22, 1937, Montana News Association Inserts, MHS; Mackay, *Cow Range*, 33. See also Herman, *Hunting*, 256–61.

53. Reiger, *Zane Grey*, 24–29; Herne, *Perils and Pleasures*, 292, 296–98; Williamson, *Sport and Photography*, 52.

54. Murphy, *Sporting Adventures*, 21, 342–43; Grohman, *Camps in the Rockies*, 30, 16.

55. Williamson, *Sport and Photography*, 52, 3; Webb, *Buffalo Land*, 194; Messiter, *Sport and Adventures*, 114; Mackay, *Cow Range*, 120–22; Loo, "Of Moose and Men," 312.

56. Pickett, Diary of 1880, 14; "The Aristocratic Hunters," news clipping, February 26, 1926, Montana News Association Inserts, MHS; James R. Mead, *Hunting and Trading on the Great Plains, 1859–1875*, ed. Schuyler Jones (Norman: University of Oklahoma Press, 1986), 50, 70. For tricksterism among the indigenous guides in British Columbia, see Loo, "Of Moose and Men," 316–18.

57. Horace Edwards to Henry, Elk Creek, September 21, 1884, Horace Edwards Correspondence, WA MSS S-1634, Folder 6, Western Americana Collection, Beinecke Rare Book and Manuscript Library, Yale University.

CHAPTER 2

THE VOICE OF THE WINCHESTER AND THE
MARTIAL CULTURE OF THE HUNT

The role of the gun in the broader culture and folklore of the American West is well established. Guns, as John Wayne and Gary Cooper informed us in countless Hollywood westerns, won the frontier for civilization. Older iterations of westward expansion from dime novels to Wild West shows issued forth similar praise for firearms as architects of American progress and settlement. According to Bill Cody, along with the Bible, the axe, and the schoolbook, the rifle carried the ideals and practices of Columbia's empire into the West. For trapper Jim Bridger, the power of the deity was less convincing than the mechanical handiwork of a good gunsmith. As he pointed out, "The grace of God won't carry a man through these prairies, it takes powder and ball." Weapons such as the Winchester '73 (a rifle so iconic it played lead character in its own movie alongside James Stewart) and the Colt single shot (dubbed "the Peacemaker" and designated in 2011 by the Arizona legislature as official state gun) gained report as hallowed artifacts of the nineteenth-century frontier.[1]

In the folklore of the "six-gun mystique," the outlaw, the lawman, and the cowboy stand tall as exemplars of American heroic marksmanship. It

DOI: 10.5876/9781607323983.c002

was the movie *Drag Harlan* (1920), as well as writers including Zane Grey and Charles Alden Seltzer, that popularized the term "gunslinger"—thus confirming and embellishing a trope of the West as the domain of the sharpshooter. In recent years, however, historians have cast doubt as to the extent of firearms ownership on the frontier, as well as the intensity and longevity of gun-based interpersonal violence. While Wyatt Earp may indeed have spent more time rounding up hogs than facing off bandits along dusty streets "High Noon" style, it is nonetheless hard to imagine the history of hunting in the West without the Winchester, the Sharps, or the Springfield rifle. The Euro-American hunter relied on the gun as an essential tool for the acquisition of animal capital for the pot, for the market, or for sport. As cattle towns such as Ellsworth and Dodge City eased into a settled existence of gun regulation and civic improvement, firearms and killing continued to predominate in the hunting theater. Guns enabled the harvesting of animals on a grand scale and also gained considerable symbolic portent, becoming trophies in themselves and duly embellishing the performance repertory of the hunter hero. As the program for Buffalo Bill's Wild West and Congress of the Rough Riders of the World noted, Colonel Cody was "a marvelous 'all-round dead shot.' That is, a man of deadly aim in any emergency, with any weapon . . . at any foe, red or white, at any game."[2]

TECHNOLOGY AND THE EVOLUTION OF FIREARMS

The gun facilitated the taking of animal life and thus represented a critical component in the armory of the chase. The arrival of firearms in the West allowed fauna to be killed more easily than ever before. Compare the chasing of bison herds by mounted Lakota armed with bows and arrows and the assembled contingent of railroad sharpshooters wielding breech-loading rifles and able to bring down an animal (usually) with one shot. The Sharps rifle, a weapon sold in both sporting and military versions, earned the moniker "Old Reliable" after buffalo hunter Billy Dixon picked off an American Indian at the Battle of Adobe Walls (1874) at 1,500 yards. The story of hunting in the nineteenth-century American West was thus one of technological inflection: the imprint of new and more deadly weapons on a landscape.

Advances in firearms technology during the nineteenth century allowed the hunter to shoot with greater range, safety, accuracy, power, and mobility.

At the start of the century, hunters typically carried the Kentucky rifle, a smoothbore flintlock, made famous by manufacturers including John Joseph Henry and Henry Leman. These rifles were cumbersome, prone to misfiring, slow to reload, and hard to repair. Firepower and range were limited. They also had a habit of falling to pieces. On his exploration of the Red River in 1806–7, Zebulon Pike found his small-bore rifle no match for the bison. A half century later, Captain Randolph Marcy in *The Prairie Traveler* (1859) advised emigrants to use guns purely as a visual deterrent when faced with Indian attack: "He should halt, turn around and point his gun at the foremost, which will often have the effect of turning them back, but he should never draw a trigger unless he finds that his life depends upon the shot; for, as soon as his shot is delivered, his sole dependence, unless he have time to reload, must be on the speed of his horse."[3]

The demands of the fur trade prompted the first adaptation of the muzzle-loading flintlock rifle. By the 1820s, modified Kentucky rifles with rebored barrels, shorter fore-ends, and percussion ignition systems—so-called plains and mountain rifles—serviced the western fur trading fraternity. By 1842, St. Louis boasted at least twelve gunsmiths, each making in the region of one hundred handmade rifles each year. The foremost of these was a shop established by brothers Jacob and Samuel Hawken in 1825 and famous for its "Rocky Mountain rifles," lightweight percussion half or full stocks of .50 or .53 caliber that were designed specifically for the rigors of the West. As James B. Marsh noted in *Four Years in the Rockies* (1884), "Instinctively does a Rocky mountain trapper, in moments of peril, grab his trusty rifle. It is his companion and his best and truest friend. With a Hawkins [*sic*] rifle in his possession he feels confident and self-reliant."[4]

Further developments in the destructive capacity of firearms came during the antebellum period with the development of breech-loaders, notably the famous Sharps. Patented in 1848, the Sharps could fire four times as fast as the Kentucky muzzle-loader and with greater velocity. The gun found a ready market in the West, and the company produced 2,900 rifles between 1854 and 1859. Many trappers and hunters traded in their old rifles to obtain a better kill ratio. As William Hamilton, a fur trapper in California, surmised, six of his "Mountaineer Miners" crew discarded their Hawkens when they saw Sharps rifles for the first time, as "they were equal in accuracy to our old rifles and far superior in effectiveness." British adventurer Grantley Berkeley was one of the earliest proponents of the breech-loader for sporting activities, bringing a Newcastle-made rifle to test out on the Kansas plains in 1859.[5]

Technical developments and the rise of postbellum mass production techniques revolutionized the American arms industry during the latter half of the nineteenth century. The 1860s saw refinements in breech-loading technology, notably through the use of self-contained metallic cartridges (used in the Springfield 1865 Joslyn rifle) and the development of repeating arms (the Henry, the Spencer, and the Colt revolving rifle). The main player in the repeating rifle industry was the Winchester Repeating Arms Company, founded in 1866 with the production of a rifle based on the Henry repeater, but with a loading gate and a round sealed magazine. The lever action of the 1866 together with its tough build quality won many converts. The company built on the success of its original model with the 1873, a rifle available in carbine, rifle, and musket versions and marked by its iron-coated body.

The West loomed large as a principal market for an industry marked by modern industrial processes and keen to find civilian trade in a postbellum environment. Manufacturers including Colt (1836), Remington (1848), Smith and Wesson (1857), Winchester (1866), and Marlin (1870) courted the attentions of a range of western constituents. Winchester badged its 1866 rifle as ideally suited for "wild country" and altercations with Indians and bandits, while the '73 came in three rifle editions that played to sporting predilections for "the best" weapon. The premier version contained those that delivered the 100 best shots on the testing range and retailed at $100, followed by runs of the best 1,000 at $80 and the standard model at $50. Ordering '73s for himself and for friends, Granville Stuart surmised, "If poor Custer's heroic band had been armed with these rifles they would have covered the earth with dead Indians for 500 yards around."[6]

Implicit in the advertising strategy of the firearms industry was a juxtaposition of industrial fetishism and wilderness iconography. Manufacturers wooed their audience with an essentially modernist pitch, stressing workmanship, reliability, range, accuracy, and often superiority over rival products. Winchester sold the '73 on its strength, simplicity, and rapid fire capabilities. Customers were bombarded with an array of models, variations, and bolt-on customizations including rifles, shotguns, and carbines; different calibers; sights; barrel weights and lengths of sections—at once an indication of the multiple hunting markets that had to be catered to and a canny way of individualizing a purchase. Production techniques may have been Fordist, but firearms manufacturers adeptly understood the multifaceted nature of the gun and its function as both a pragmatic and a symbolic object.

Important in this regard was the iconography of nature "red in tooth and claw," of the glorification of a savage encounter with a primal landscape and the romantic purchase of the gun in that bargain. As Tina Loo notes, the outdoors economy "commodified and circulated anti-modern ideas about the restorative power of the wilderness." Here the West appeared not only as a market but also a marketing device that ably fed the performance of the hunt. Special-edition rifles and decorated plates presented the charismatic game animals of the trans-Mississippi in gleaming metalwork, at once serving a sporting bestiary and richly illustrated document of animal targets, while illustrated exhibit format calendars and prints from the 1870s used new chromolithography techniques to produce striking images of western adventure, charismatic animals, and well-armed hunter heroes. Broadcast in sporting magazines and mail order catalogs and distributed by salesmen to gun traders and clubs, the frontier loomed large as a brand in a colorful (and irrevocably modern) firearms industry. By 1912, the Winchester Repeating Arms Company was selling 324,000 guns a year and turning over a profit of $11 million. As both a practical tool of empire and an ideal type of an imagined landscape, the Winchester '73 truly "won the West."[7]

TECHNOLOGICAL FETISHISM, HUNTING, AND THE FRATERNITY OF THE GUN

George Gibbs, an artist naturalist with an army expedition on the Oregon Trail in 1849, described the emigrant train as a "marching ordnance department." The gun signaled security, civilization, utility, and familiarity, even though possession of firearms sometimes delivered disastrous results among greenhorn travelers. According to A. J. Leach, almost every settler on the frontier had some form of firearm used for hunting small game as well as for the protection of property, family, and livestock. For *Forest and Stream* magazine, the gun was the "constant companion" of the western man. Montana rancher Granville Stuart recalled memories of marksmanship training with his father and two particular guns (a flintlock and a small-bore rifle), elucidating an important connect between firearms and codes of familial and geographical belonging. The community of sport hunters, in particular, devoted much attention to armaments. George Gore brought seventy-five rifles (including a Sharps, along with those manufactured by Purdy and Manton and other famous British marques) and twelve shotguns to the plains in 1855. Among his forty-one-strong entourage one man was employed specifically to look after the weapons, a clear signal of the importance placed on the gun as an artifact of the hunt and a tool of theatrical power. Fur trapper turned hunting guide Jim Bridger remembered Gore's excursion for its array of firearms as well as their collective toll on animal life: "forty guns a-blazin' and a-barkin' from sun up to sundown till the ground wuz fair covered with dead and dyin' critters."[8]

In the contest with the game animals of the West, it seemed that the hunter could count on two advantages, personal proficiency and the wielding of powerful arms. Many certainly felt more at ease with the accouterment of a rifle. As William Pickett asserted, "I had acquired such skill in the use of my rifle and its manipulation, and such confidence in myself, that I did not fear an encounter with any of the wild animals to be met with." The assist was both practical and psychological. William Allen candidly referred to his gun as "my life preserver." The gun cultivated a sense of security and superiority. As Pickett mused, "Deprive man of his destructive inventions, fire arms, the Bear could wipe him from the face of the Earth." Malcolm Mackay expressed similar sentiments. Faced down by an angry grizzly bear, he took solace in his marksmanship and a trusty Winchester: "This time I knew he had to be stopped for good or he would be shaking hands with me and he wasn't a friendly looking animal by a long shot. But I was an old shotgun shooter and the nearer he came the better I liked it, and the safer I felt."[9]

On one level, the increasingly destructive power of firearms suggested a "taming" of the hunting encounter. High-caliber, rapid-fire, telescopic-sighted weapons, along with full metal cartridges and smokeless powder (cordite was invented in 1889), arguably privileged technological advance over frontier dexterity. As H. A. Leveson inferred of a bison hunt, "A well-armed man has but little danger to fear from the animal itself." That said, the wilderness authority of the hunter and the technological allure of the gun worked symbiotically to enhance a sense of frontier drama. According to sporting writer Horace Hutchinson, "Sport, like work, largely depends for its result on the perfection of the tools employed, as well as on the skill and care with which they are used." It was not enough to simply wield a gun. Tactics, marksmanship, proper maintenance of the equipment, and a dash of gall were all needed to succeed.

The hunter required full command over the "machinery of destruction which he holds in his hands." According to Pickett, men without sufficient gun training, survival skills, and steady nerves "better stay at home." For Peregrine Herne, it was such "malicious coolness" that allowed him to feel "comparatively safe" when faced with a charging bruin. The destructive capacity of firearms signaled a mastery over nature, while the ability to use them effectively marked the true hunter hero apart. In fact, the ability to deliver results from a gun represented a potent symbol of masculine supremacy in the wilds. As Theodore Roosevelt concluded, "It is the man behind the rifle that counts after the weapon has reached a certain stage of perfection." Far from taking away the reputation of the hunter hero, the gun only served to enhance it.[10]

Firearms were objects of utility and much more. In the performance of hunting, the gun became an object of veneration and a form of social capital in its own right. Hunters spoke of a visceral connection between themselves and their chosen weapons: the perfect merging of man and machine in the wilderness. After watching a bald eagle and conjuring with the idea he "should gather me in his talons," William Allen seized his rifle and asserted his heroic stature: "The temptation to conquer this proud bird was too strong to be resisted. The power which held him in space was quickly terminated by a ball from my rifle, and he fell to earth with a force that split his body in twain." The six-gun mystique and the savagery of idealized nature connected in the fatal environment of hunter's paradise. Diarists spoke of taking pride in their guns, following maintenance regimens, and keeping them ever ready in case of danger. According to F. A. Wislizenus, author of *A Journey to the Rocky Mountains in 1839* (1912), "During a march the gun lies across the saddle; when one rests it is always close at hand. One never leaves camp without taking it as a cane; and at night it is wrapped in the blanket with the sleeper."[11]

An object of technological fetishism, the gun was celebrated as an icon of industrial artistry. According to the Marble Arms Company, purveyor of outfitting goods as well as the patented "game getter" rifle, "If there is only one thing which warms the cockles of a true sportsman's heart quicker than any other, it is good equipment." Sportsmen spoke enthusiastically of the flight of the bullet, the satisfying echo of the report, and the tactile qualities of a well-manufactured piece. As *The Fireside Book of Guns* (1959) elucidated, "For most men, the gun is an irresistible object . . . the rifle must be raised to the shoulder and sighted, the trigger is squeezed and the hammer, swiftly obedient, clicks sharp, the no nonsense sound of oiled steel on steel. The gun is lowered, examined keenly once more, and returned to rest, the gun handler absorbed for the moment in private visions or longings inexpressible." William Allen paid heed to the intimacy of animal encounter afforded by firearms technology, its destructive potency, and the corporeal power of the human actor in presiding over the fate of a mountain lion: "I could see the platina ball through the rear sight, showing plainly on his throat just over the jugular vein. I was calm now and gave the signal trigger a gentle pull. The report sounded, and his grand attitude of daring, courage and defiance was changed in the twinkling of an eye." The gun appeared as a mesmerizing symbol of industrialism, a product of machined quality and in possession of mortal capacity for destruction. Allen, for one, saw an "innate love" for firearms as a critical part of his sporting interest. As he noted, "The effects produced by a single rifle-shot in an uninhabited region are wonderful . . . While the report was echoing from canyon to canyon, ravens screamed, the mountain thrush chattered in his tree, while the squirrels scampered from branch to branch." In this context, the hunting story fed a broader culture of frontier violence in which the pursuit of game became a sacred act of gunplay, adventure, and survivalism.[12]

The fetishization of the gun translated into a lively firearms culture in which hunters conversed about favored weapons and technical innovations. Theodore Roosevelt expressed something of a truism when he noted, "There is an endless variety of opinion about rifles." Horace Edwards recalled meeting a group of English sport hunters in 1884 near Elk Creek who eagerly discussed their arms haul of a Winchester, two Sharps, and an English Express, while William Allen orated an occasion of masculine posturing between himself and a western guide on the relative merits of Sharps over Winchester (the guide asserting the latter was a "weak" gun not good enough for bison and bruin and, as such, lambasting Allen as a "pilgrim"). Knowledge of firearms thereby emerged as a badge of hunting honor, to the extent that hunters secured prowess on the game trail not only by triumphing over prey but also in flaunting modish gadgetry in front of companions. As one letter to *Shooting and Fishing* magazine attested:

"In . . . 1865 . . . I crossed the plains to the Rockies . . . carrying . . . a Sharps rifle, .52-calibre linen cartridge . . . fitted with a fine Malcolm telescopic sight. The following year found me, with this rifle, camped with a band of hunters and trappers in the Wind River Mountains . . . The rifle itself, as well as the telescopic sight, was something of a novelty . . . Within a year . . . every one of that little company . . . had fittest the best Malcolm telescopic sights to their muzzle-loading rifles. Years afterwards I met members of that little band of hunters. They had discarded their muzzle-loaders and were equipped with Sharps rifles, model 1874, fitted with the best procurable telescopic sight."[13]

Motifs of competitive display and knowledge exchange extended beyond the confines of the hunting trail. Sportsmen compiled detailed renditions on the technical mechanics of gun use in their autobiographies—for instance, British aristocrat William Baillie Grohman's appendices to *Camps in the Rockies* (1910). Horace Edwards wrote to his friend Henry in 1875 extrapolating at length on the merits of the Remington and the Sharps versus the Winchester, the latter which he favored for its light construction and reloading system that allowed it to be carried on the saddle and armed "at a moment's notice." Gunplay peppered guidebooks and manuals such as *Hitting versus Missing with the Shotgun* (1898) and occupied the attentions of the myriad gun clubs that emerged in prospering frontier settlements. Outfits such as the Sacramento Swiss Rifle Club (1852), the Butte Rod and Gun Club (later Rocky Mountain Gun Club) (1880), and the Los Angeles Gun Club (1899) offered target practice, weapons trials, and tournaments aplenty for the regional hunting community. Pickett spoke fondly of long-range target shooting over the winter with gentlemen from Helena, Montana, in 1876, while in 1894, the Denver Rifle Club hosted a demonstration of the Krag-Jorgensen rifle, the disappointing result of which was dutifully reported in *Shooting and Fishing* magazine. "Should a hunter buy a rifle and go out on a trip with it, and find that he must aim several feet to one side and under his game in order to kill it, he would undoubtedly bring the rifle back to the dealer and demand the return of his money, or a rifle with which he could hit something," the editorial railed. Such forums—both textual and organizational—allowed for the discussion of technical information and the performative exercise of codes of masculine erudition. They also served purposes of socioeconomic validation, as Philip Beidler notes, providing "an established fraternity with the opportunity to peruse and savor in a codified, unified fashion, a certain kind of recreational technology that reassures it about the integrity of its values and the permanence of its class status."[14]

With different calibers, technical specifications, and manufacturers (not to mention animal targets), the temptation was to see the West as a locus for weapons testing and experiment. For some, the technical dynamics of gunplay seemed to matter as much as the western environment or its faunal residents (a fact lamented by William Hornaday when he implored hunters to "study the moral principles of your guns, find out exactly what they will do when you put into them"). Selous adapted his Mannlicher elephant gun and brought exploding bullets to see how they would impact (literally) on the faunal frontier, while in the fall of 1878, Pickett took to the game trail to test the "express bullet," a high-velocity shot from Britain that exploded in the body, causing maximum damage. Approaching the Rockies as a de facto firing range, Allen tested "the efficacy of the Express bullet on the deer family," a test duly recorded in graphic detail in his journal for purposes of personal reference and peer review. W. J. Browning recalled buying a special gun from Liddle and Keading gunsmiths in San Francisco and filling it with chilled shot and brass shells to test on game birds. In one shot the monster weapon killed 98, while seven hours of target practice elicited a body count of 811. Such examples presented the West as a tin can alley for mechanical experiment and served to qualify the idea that it was the market hunter alone who participated in an industrial discourse with the faunal frontier.[15]

THE VOICE OF THE WINCHESTER AND THE GUN AS COMMUNICATOR

Debates about the perfect shot demonstrated the importance of the connection between the hunter and his arsenal. Being well-armed and displaying skill with firearms was a foundational aspect of the heroic canon. Unsurprisingly, the storytelling codes of hunter's paradise saw firearms elevated as key elements, even personalities, in possession of some kind of agency of their own. Technical specifications did not fully encompass the romance of the gun. Often incarnated as a reliable friend, the gun became the right-hand man of the hunter hero and an active player in the performance of the hunt. Wislizenus explained how "one gets habituated to his rifle as to a trusty travelling companion." Akin to a loyal subaltern poised to do the hunter's bidding, guns earned kudos for their efficiency, protection, comfort, and company. A. Pendarves Vivian commended his Express rifle for services fulfilled against a grizzly: it had "done its work well." Firearms duly became incorporated into the hunting tale as integral elements to the descriptive process, sometimes even characters in their own right.[16]

Many sportsmen coined nicknames for their weapons or deployed anthropomorphic motifs to suggest familiarity and rapport. Gunmaker Stevens in 1872 played on the intimacy between sportsman and firearm in launching its $18 pocket rifle called the Hunter's Pet, a favorite of Calamity Jane. The nomenclature of the rifle spoke of an intimate relationship between user and product, along with embedded codes of power, gender, race, and conquest. Some titles spoke of destructive capacity, the "explosive express" of Theodore Roosevelt or George Shields's "Old Pill Driver" being examples. Others spoke of historical reputations for violence—Bill Cody's famed .50 Springfield, called Lucretia Borgia—or conveyed a sense of atavistic capacity. Reporting on the common naming of weapons in shooting contests, the Missouri *Intelligencer* of 1825 remarked, "Many of the most distinguished guns acquire names of the most fearful import . . . Blacksnake, Cross Burster, Hair Splitter, Blood Letter, Panther Cooler." For some hunters, the label was humorous or domestically referenced. Edgar Randolph's "Old Meat in the Pot" offered a witty reminder of the role of firearms in sustaining the western hunter nutritionally. Invoking the gun as an architect of justice, Horace Edwards wielded "Old Scrutinizer." Rufus Sage called his rifle "Old Straightener," noting to a hunting companion a relationship of dependence and gendered ownership—"never been known to fail in a case of emergency, I know she will maintain her ancient honor." James Josiah Webb's "Old Blackfoot" and Theodore Roosevelt's 1895 Winchester, called (perhaps apocryphally) "Big Medicine," attested to the seizing of indigenous terminology as marks of colonial takeover.[17]

Allied to the layered linguistics of firearms were the politics of display. Frequently the gun became a trophy all of its own. As items of utility and symbolic import, rifles and shotguns featured highly in hunting photographs and trailside posturing. George Shields recalled coming back from the chase to find Laton Huffman "leaning complacently on his rifle, gazing admiringly on the prostrate form of a monster bull elk that had fallen prey to his deadly aim." The architecture of memorialization in cabins and lodges also allowed for a metamorphosis from tool to trophy. Displayed on racks and walls alongside the fruits of the hunter's labor, the gun represented both instrument and decorative device. It pointed (figuratively) at the prowess of the hunter hero. William Baillie Grohman recalled a visit to a frontier hunter in the 1880s who talked him through the assembled firearms on show in his house. With sporting names such as Uncle Ephraim, Track Maker, Aunt Sally, and Sister Julia, each artifact had "some special degree of merit and long gunning yarns attached to it." Headed home from this own hunting forays west, Grohman hung his faunal spoils and a double express rifle on the walls of his stately home—a salient indicator of the transnational translation of frontier theatrics and the flexibility of the borrowed landscape of the West. Guns took pride of place in the commemoration of the hunt in the great indoors, objects that allowed for ritual retelling of the story and achieved iconographic status as mechanical instruments of the hunter hero.[18]

At times, the gun even became animated to take on voice and its own volition. *The Complete Sportsman* (1893) celebrated the lyrical qualities of firearms as compared to nature's ovations: "the song of the wild bird is sweet from the thorn, but the gun hath more music than these." Such a descriptive spoke to the value of the gun as a powerful totem of industrial pornography but also alluded to a further vocal function and capacity for agency and communication. Sometimes the aural volley of a rifle served a pragmatic purpose. According to one Montana newspaper, buffalo hunters abided by a code of the plains in which the sound of gunfire was used as a kind of prairie telegraph. Two shots signaled presence, heard thereafter, one shot indicated "I'm lost, give me directions," and a second "I'm in trouble." Commonly, however, the orations of the gun expressed power over animal nature. Roaming in Razor Creek, between Bozeman and Miles City, Allen narrated a meeting with a black-tailed deer in which his "Winchester spoke to her, and as the smoke cloud cleared away, I saw her lying on the ground, her neck broken just below the ear." Allen's descriptive offered romanticism and bluntness in equal measure and, critically, afforded the gun a kind of personhood. As a euphemism "spoke to her" served multiple purposes. It offered a retelling of the death of an animal as a gentle and tender moment; translated the trajectory of the bullet from physics to metaphysics; and lent the gun a life, and capacity to take life, all of its own. In such parlance, firearms communicated the objectives of the hunter hero to (a feminized) nature, the act of firing portrayed as a missive of eloquent power.[19]

Allen was not alone in using the terminology. Other hunters, too, chose to articulate their guns as "speaking" to nature through the act of shooting, a literary penchant that only accentuated the sense of the game trail as a performance space. Shields noted how his partner's Express was "belching forth her compliments to the wapiti" and made the hills "echo with her musical voice." On another occasion, Shields himself "turned 'Old Reliable' loose" and her "voice rang out over the mountains"—an oppositional gendered reading that saw the hunter in control of his martial (even marital) firearm. Another rifle, "Old Pill Driver," "spoke to" a bear after "her head" lay pressed "firmly against" his shoulder and "a cloud of smoke arose from her mouth." Shields also spoke of his partner's rifle delivering "lively music" that "quelled the . . . belligerent propensities" of a grizzly. Such choices of words romanticized the hunting moment, conveyed the masculine authority and literary bent of the hunter hero, and deployed a comforting nomenclature of power and passion.[20]

PLAYING WAR: GUNS AND RECREATION

The idea of the gun having voice suggested a theatrical element to the hunting encounter. Also common in the cryptography of the chase was the idea of "playing war." On encountering a group of antelope, George Shields noted a desire to "interview" the herd using an ambush maneuver before unleashing "leaden missiles" into the air. Reveling in the martial connotation, Shields wrote, "The distant hills echoed the music of our artillery" before relating, "Once the smoke of battle cleared away and we looked over the field, we found that we had not burned our powder in vain," with five kills. Military phraseology peppered the linguistic turn of the sporting hunter hero, evident in metaphors of reconnaissance, pursuit, and engagement. As Will Hilger illuminated, "The elk, while I was trying to get around them, got wind of some of us and started off down the mountain . . . I heard them begin to shoot . . . in the basin, surrounded as it was by the mountains, each report echoed and re-echoed until it sounded as there was a hot battle in progress on the mountain."[21]

The practical mechanics of the hunt—scouting terrain, foxing prey, and engaging a faunal foe—meant that military comparison was not hard to muster. In *Hunting at High Altitudes* (1913) William Pickett described a contest between his party and a band of grizzlies as a "battlefield," and even included a map schematic of the terrain showing the movements of different parties akin to a military plan. The fact that many hunting parties in the West contained men with a service background also proved significant (Pickett himself was a veteran of the Mexican and Civil Wars). At the same time, the use of martial metaphor also spoke of the theatrical fixings of the game trail as well as social function. Pickett's descriptions of deer with "flags flying," of roaming mountain ranges, scanning the herd with binoculars, choosing an attack strategy, and charging in for battle exuded a sense of action and suspense that invested the hunting encounter with descriptive drama.[22]

Significantly, for Theodore Roosevelt and his compatriots, aspiring soldiers too young to have seen service in the Civil War but who regarded military culture as affirmingly gung-ho, the hunt provided a valuable outlet for patriotic and masculine exercise. According to Anthony Rotundo, the deployment of "martial ideals and images" represented "a way to focus their vision of a manly life." The broader context of man versus nature, implicit in the hunting quest, thus provided for the unleashing of psychosexual tensions and inclinations for heroic violence. Also appealing was its resolutely amoral character. The West represented a monumental canvas unsullied by historical or geopolitical frames of reference. In the parlance of Henry Nash Smith and Frederick Jackson Turner, here was a territory both "virgin" and "free." Sporting adventures in the West thus carried none of the traumatic connotations of atavism most pertinent in the context of the Civil War. In this battle of the wilderness, violence was honorable and action-packed.[23]

Beneath the frolics and histrionics, of course, the use of a militarized language on the hunting trail revealed material processes of assimilation at play, situating the hunter's game within a broader West of acquisition and conquest. Significant, then, was the fact martial discourse infused the lexicon of the market as well as the sport hunter. Buffalo hunter David Hilger recalled moving and settling in the Judith Basin, motivated largely by "the desire to kill buffalo," and remembered numerous "fierce battles" with "old Mr Bull" who was not "going to surrender his authority without a contest." Complicit in processes of environmental transformation, Hilger noted how the hunting of the "monarch of the plains" "did more to subdue the Indian than all the traps employed by the government in the West." This "battle royal" with the bison enabled the subjugation of the Indian and allowed the annexation of space for the "superior white race and domestic animal." Joined to the Winchester (if not at the hip), the typologies of the hunt stood together to advance Euro-American ambitions for frontier takeover.[24]

The Militarization of the Hunt and the Conspiracy of the Hunter Heroes

Perhaps the most striking example of the relationship between hunting, gun culture, and the construction of the West as a martial ecology was that of the frontier army. While sportsmen "played war" on the game trail, the mechanics of the hunt exerted a profound influence over the military theater. Arguably, in fact, issues of hunting and access to animal capital often dictated the contours on which military operations in the West were navigated. Was the region to remain, in contemporary Euro-American parlance, a "hunting ground of the savage" or was it to be brought into the service of Euro-American civilization? Under the Fort Laramie Treaty (1868), plains tribes, including the Lakota and the Cheyenne, were allotted hunting rights to an area of land between the Black Hills and the Bighorn Mountains, labeled "unceded Indian territory." However, as settlers arrived in greater numbers seeking minerals, skins, and sod, the "hunting reserve" became contested space. Tensions flared as indigene and newcomer grappled over access to the natural resources of the trans-Mississippi region. The hunt became increasingly politicized as indigenous use of the game trail was read as domestic terrorism. Bill Cody noted how the "desperate redskins . . . had made up their mind never to give up that great hunting range" while Elizabeth Custer regarded hunting as synonymous with dissent: the absence of young men from Indian camps "was always executed by the same reason—they were out hunting. We knew how little game there was, and surmised—what we afterward found to be true—that they had joined the hostile tribes."[25]

Curtailing indigenous hunting activities duly emerged as a critical device used by the US Army to subjugate the West. As Lieutenant General John Schofield, commander of the Department of the Missouri (1869–70), railed, "With my cavalry and carbined artillery encamped in front, I wanted no other occupation in life than to ward off the savage and kill off his food until there should no longer be an Indian frontier in our beautiful country." General Miles, architect of the Yellowstone Campaign, a 1,200-mile trek through "Indian country" in 1876, successfully deployed the total war strategy of the Civil War in the western theater. Tribes were resolutely pursued and, most notably, prevented from accessing traditional hunting grounds. As Miles contended, denying the right to hunt presented an efficient way to destabilize the plains economy. As he recalled of the expedition, the Battle of Wolf Mountains (1877), and the consequent surrender of Crazy Horse and his band, "It demonstrated the fact that we could move in any part of the country in the midst of winter and hunt the enemy down wherever they might take refuge."[26]

As well as denying access to indigenous hunting grounds, the military abetted Euro-American hunting for pecuniary and sporting advantage. Complicit in the slaughter of the bison herds, the army issued statements of encouragement to hide hunters as well as offering material assistance in the form of guns, ammunition, supply, and storage. Sheridan reputedly said to John Cook, a buffalo runner, "Let them kill, skin and sell until the buffaloes are exterminated." Military endorsement added a patriotic veneer to the pursuit of animal capital, situating the market hunter as an architect of westward progress. Sport hunters, meanwhile, found the army an impeccable host, lending intelligence, guns, men, and accommodation to their adventurous pursuits on the plains. A party led by Judge Henry Souther of Erie, Pennsylvania, containing George Shields, and guided by Major Bell at the Green River watched bison from a bluff on "reconnoiter"—soaking up the ambiance of a martial encounter—before the troops "with characteristic courtesy" drove the herd back toward their guests for dispatch with military-grade "hard-hitting qualities." Shields fondly recollected the supper of venison and stories from officers "of frontier life, Indian Warfare, hunting yarns" as well as the opportunity to revel in martial codes during "self-imposed duties as a sentry" before hitting the "warpath" against the bison.[27]

With a steady stream of European and American elites eager to bag western trophy animals, significant military resources seemed committed to the cause of chaperoning "sports." Boasting 300 men and sixteen wagons (including "travelling ice-houses" to store game and wine), Cody described his military escort for a group of New York "thoroughbreds" in September 1871 as "the best equipped hunting party I have ever been with." Such activities—from outfitting to carousing—occupied considerable energy on the martial frontier (Elizabeth Custer bemoaned how at times the camp would "tremble at coming dispatches for fear it announces buffalo hunters"). That said, military goals and the recreational performance of "playing war" ably served one another. As Sherman noted to Sheridan, "I think it would be wise to invite all the sportsmen of England and America . . . for a Grand Buffalo hunt, and make one grand sweep of them all." The claiming of the West was advanced by complementary axioms of martial engagement, while the symbolic display of martial power on the plains conjured a potent impression of Euro-American might and right. As Libbie Custer noted, with "jingling spurs, rattling arms, and impatient, stamping horses," the hunting column offered a strident demonstration of martial authority, the "warlike preparations" of the "pleasure party" a signal of deeper processes at work.[28]

SUBSISTENCE, SPORT, AND THE ARISTOCRACY OF THE CHASE

Hunting serviced a multiplicity of functions in the frontier military machine. The first of these was subsistence. Various methods were used to harvest game, including the commissioning of special hunters, the retrieval of meat during forays by visiting sports, and the dispatch of officers and troops in search for quarry. Firearms were instrumental in this engagement. As Elizabeth Custer noted, "The best shots in a company were allowed to leave the column and bring in game for the rest." The eating of game meat proved a vital point of relief for men accustomed to monotonous and meager rations as well as guarding against scurvy and malnutrition. Major A. F. Mulford of the Seventh Cavalry paid heed to the usual tedium of food on the march—"hard tack, bacon and coffee for breakfast, raw bacon and tack for dinner, fried bacon and hard bread for supper"—and added enthusiastically, "If our hunters have good luck . . . we feast on antelope meat." David L. Spotts, a volunteer to the Nineteenth Kansas Cavalry in 1868–69, eager to aid in the pacification of the frontier, fondly recalled the occasion on which he "ate buffalo meat for the first time," noting, "It is much better than army bacon." When rations ran low or harsh winters, ambush, or disease compromised beef herds and supply trains, western game proved particularly important. Winter at Fort Defiance in 1851–52 brought snowstorms, stranded pack trains, dying grass, and the killing of cattle for jerky. With only fifteen days' rations left and a growing sense of alarm, lieutenants were dispatched to muster hunting parties. A second lieutenant with the Third Cavalry, John Gregory Bourke remembered similar concerns at camp in 1873. With supplies running low, hunters secured valuable buffalo, which was "served up on every mess canvas. We find it tough, fibrous and lean, but an excellent substitute for no meat at all."[29]

Lack of provisions represented a serious threat to the integrity of the western army and severely compromised its functionality. As Second Lieutenant Walter Schuyler of the Fifth Cavalry recalled of the Yellowstone expedition, this was an endeavor that tested the mettle of the men physically, psychologically, and nutritionally. In the field, as Schuyler noted, the army needed food to survive. Insufficient supplies prompted insubordination, ill discipline, and lax attention to security. As A. F. Mulford expressed it, "We are now short to rations, but expect a supply today. The teams have been gone two days and as they did not have far to go, there is uneasiness on their account. If they are stuck in the mud, or have been captured by Indians, we will become desperate." Spotts, too, paid heed to problems in the ranks when faced with a lack of food: "Our wagons have to go to the Seventh's supply train for our rations and some of the boys hide in the wagons until outside and then go hunting." In these circumstances, recourse to the game trail denoted an act of rebellion and was punished accordingly. Mulford continued, "Two of our *non-coms* were placed under arrest to-day for going on a hunt for something to eat. They were released and returned to duty a few hours later. Discipline must be maintained."[30]

Alongside subsistence, hunting for sport was common practice in the western army, at least among officers. Leonard Swett recalled a hunting party while stationed at Fort Lincoln in 1875 consisting of twenty-two men, wagons, mules, and 2,200 rounds of ammunition "in case of trouble from the Indians." Their purpose was twofold: supplying the camp with meat and indulging in sporting adventure. Such excursions, often of a lengthy duration and involving a substantial amount of manpower, suggested high levels of captivation with the chase. General Crook spent a month on a hunting expedition in 1886, leaving his second lieutenant in charge of the Department of the Platte with instructions to "act on such cases according to your best judgment without sending [telegrams] to me, unless they involve some important question in which you are in doubt about." One cavalry officer went as far as to contend that the 1867 expedition conducted by General Winfield Scott was an excuse to "visit the Indians and the Rocky mountains, and hunt buffalo on a big scale." While civilians favored "playing war" on the game trail, the officer in the western army took to the hunt for the purposes of recreation, training, and the performance of social difference. According to Manypenny, "In the country surrounding military posts the pursuit of the buffalo and other game is an amusement that the officers engage in."[31]

In the fashion of the civilian sportsmen, military diarists recorded their quests, detailing animals killed, the excitement of pursuit, and jockeying with peers. In letters to his wife, Captain Kinzie Bates of the First Infantry enthused about the West as a theater of boisterous exploring. A missive from Camp Niabara in October 1875 highlighted the centrality of the hunt to the officers' day: "What shall I write about? I get up in the morning at 7 o'clock, breakfast, perhaps Edmunds takes the mounted party on a scout, dinner at 12 o'clock if he gets back, take supper at 5 o'clock, and spend the rest of the evening until dark on a bar in the river waiting for geese and ducks. We come home and settle down in one of the tents with a good fire and talk, talk, talk." Documenting a trip up the Missouri River in 1877, Bates indulged in the conventional axioms of wilderness exoticism, noting a "high state of excitement" and "dancing around the deck" at the sight of deer and, on the Tongue River, locating the West as a cornucopia for game and gaming, "serving with old friends in a superb country, so full of game, including buffalo, that the officers of the 5th and 22nd call it a hunters paradise."[32]

"Buck fever" proved a frequent affliction among officers that sometimes led to frenzied distraction. Elizabeth Custer recalled one occasion in which an officer became so paralyzed by the sight of wild turkeys that "he became incapable of leading, to say nothing of firing his gun: he could do nothing but lie down, great strong man as he was, overcome with excitement." The "Boy General" himself became so enamored by the pursuit of a bison herd on one occasion that he put a bullet through the brain of his own horse and was left wandering the plains undefended with aides for a few hours until spotting the cavalry train. That said, for all the risk of misadventure, hunting among the officer class served a pragmatic function in the martial economy of the West. Roaming territory for quarry involved a de facto reconnoiter, incorporating objectives of mapping and patrol that fitted adeptly into military priorities. As Custer remarked, there was "nothing so nearly resembling a cavalry charge as a buffalo chase." Equally, the game trail fended off tendencies to boredom and listlessness. With the visit of General Smith in spring 1867, Major Andrew Burt recalled excitement among the officers to leave Fort Smith and take part in expeditions to the "wonderful unexplored hunting ground." John Gregory Bourke noted in July 1876, "We have such poor facilities for killing time. Books and newspapers are never to be had," but he pointed to the "many devotees of the chase" at camp. For Burt, "To an officer fond of hunting and fishing, the sport afforded" at Fort Bridger "must in a great measure recompense for the want of society and little inconveniences incident to life at such a remote station." An invigorating pursuit across the plains brought opportunity for practice with firearms and enhanced stamina and physical fitness. Custer indeed saw "no better drill for perfecting men in the use of firearms on horseback" as well as a pleasant way to "break the monotony and give horses and men exercise." His wife concurred: "It was something to occupy every energy, and keep even young and agile men vigilant."[33]

As in civilian circles, the sporting culture of the western army cultivated rivalry and display. Field units engaged in shooting matches that encouraged competition and camaraderie in equal measure (notably a ten-day contest between officers of the Seventh Cavalry and enlisted men from Fort Totten, Dakota) and also pitted their skills against locals (at Fort Bidwell in August 1884 Major Burt successfully faced off against Mr. Brown, a local bookkeeper and expert shot, for a $50 prize). Combining military vectors of inventory with codes of showmanship and performance, officers kept faunal logs of animals killed, named places after their exploits, and paraded their spoils in camp. Custer tallied his season's kill of forty-one antelope, four buffalo, four elk, seven deer, two white wolves, and a fox (taken using a .50 caliber rifle) and wrote up his findings for the *Army and Navy Journal* as an experiment in firearms practice (noting, of course, that his bag was more than that of the whole troop). According to Libbie Custer, the appearance of the camp on return from a sporting expedition "seemed like an animated 'zoo' and each soldier or officer who owned a prize treasure boasted that his was superior to all others." The biotic complement of the West was seemingly reduced to an array of shooting gallery prizes: an illustration of convergence between the leisure economy of sport, competitive masculinity, and martial power in the West.[34]

The Seventh Cavalry's reconnoiter of the Black Hills in July 1874 proved instructive in this regard. A 1,200-mile trek over sixty days to plot opportunities for prospecting, science, and potential sites for army posts, the sojourn proved an occasion for the "Boy General" to play pathfinder, commander, and hunter across delightful game country. The excursion left in a fanfare— played out by the accompanying band to the peals of "Garry Owen,"—and prompted many hunts, champagne picnics, and florid depictions of the fairy-tale West by the cadre of embedded journalists. The trek nurtured frontier ambitions and performance in equal measure. Viewing it as an exercise in mapping and consolidation, First Lieutenant James Calhoun celebrated how "acting as one great pioneer corps," the brigade "paved the way for civilization." The sojourn across uncharted country allowed the general's hunter hero inclinations full scope, netting him figurative ownership over various landmarks—Custer's Peak, Custer's Canyon—as well as his first grizzly. William Illingsworth's photograph of the general, rifle in hand, with Bloody Knife and the vanquished "king of the forest" in the foreground, demonstrated the general's heroic aspirations: "He lay in front of my tent, I, in my buckskins, seated on the ground near his head," noted Custer. The cult of the transformed hunter and the mythology of hunter's paradise can be seen in Libbie Custer's description of the return of the command:

> Many, like the general, had grown heavy beards. All were sun-burnt, their hair faded, and their clothes so patched that the original blue of the uniform was scarcely visible . . . By and by the long wagon train appeared. Many of the covers had elk horns strapped to them, until they looked like strange bristling animals as they drew near. Some of the antlers were brought to us as presents. Besides them we had skins, specimens of gold and mica, and petrified shells of iridescent colors, snake rattles, pressed flowers, and petrified wood.[35]

According to army wife Katherine Fougera, the hunt brought "a glamor to army life that nothing ever quite equaled." Like European noblemen, officers approached and appropriated the animals of the West, crafting an aristocracy of the chase in which they strode through preeminent. The politics of display touted rubrics of class, social status, and masculine affectation. A marker of the hierarchies of military life, the "best shot" was reserved for the commanding officer. James Calhoun recalled how "Custer was about to shoot an antelope when several of the Indian scouts shot it. Custer promptly fired several shots over their heads as a reminder that they were trespassing, they quickly emptied their saddles on flattening themselves to the ground." Elite pretensions such as the keeping of hounds, extravagant carousing at camp, and the veneration of equestrianism added to the patina of nobility. General Crook maintained a famous fondness for hunting the plains with setters and pointers, while Elizabeth Custer spoke of the "endless delight" her husband gained from his forty loyal stag and foxhounds (in *Boots and Saddles* she devoted more pages to talking about dogs than enlisted troops).[36]

Meanwhile, with so many western commanders harboring a hankering for sport—Crook, Custer, Sheridan, and Miles, to name a few—the conflation of the military leader with the hunter hero archetype was a common tendency in both self-promotions and hagiographic treatments. Under the pen name "Nomad," Custer wrote for *Turf, Field and Farm*, touting his own credentials as plainsman as well as the "true, manly sport" to be had on the prairies, while Elizabeth Custer celebrated her husband's sporting personality with aplomb: "I never tired of watching the start for the hunt. The General was a figure that would have fixed attention anywhere. He had marked individuality of appearance, and a certain unstudied carelessness in the wearing of his costume that gave a picturesque effect, not the least out of place on the frontier." According to his wife, Custer's manly horsemanship and his intuitive connection (and command over) his steed and the land around marked him a knight of the plains:

> Horse and man seemed one when the general vaulted into the saddle. His body was so lightly poised and so full of swinging, undulating motion, it almost seemed that the wind moved him as it blew over the plain. Yet every nerve was alert and like finely tempered steel, for the muscles and sinews that seemed so pliable were equal to the curbing of the most fiery animal . . . With his own horses he needed neither spur nor whip. They were such friends of his, and his voice seemed so attuned to their natures . . . By the merest inclination on the general's part, they either sped on the wings of the wind or adapted their spirited steps to the slow movement of the march.[37]

Reflexive display reigned supreme in the code of the soldier hunter hero. So too did the syntactic alignment of hunting skills with martial prowess.

A Frontier Education in the Ranks and Indians as "Bucks"

Among the lower ranks, the issue of hunting betrayed different codes. The elite dynamics of the game trail and the priorities of military discipline meant that the right to hunt was typically confined to officers and VIPs. Troops went along as loyal subalterns to look after horses, carry equipment, and maintain rifles. As Kevin Adams notes, "In a sense, officers used contemporary military customs and beliefs to re-create a form of aristocracy on the frontier, with enlisted men serving as their retainers." While Elizabeth Custer was keen to present her husband as an everyman of the frontier, presiding over a democratic band of brothers, others spoke of a martial hierarchy of the hunt and the firm boundaries of social category. As A. F. Mulford remarked, "We have strict orders not to fire without orders from the commanding officer," adding, "It is enough to provoke a Deacon to see so much game on every hand, and not be allowed to take a shot at it." Such regulations were there to save ammunition; preserve discipline, focus, and the integrity of the column; minimize chances of ambush or accident; and uphold the hierarchical structures of military life. James Calhoun recalled the following incident: "Some of the soldiers are very careless in shooting across the column. Antelope were plentiful. Some came within 25 yards of the command, and the soldiers were firing in all directions. The excitements at one time became so great as to cause a stampede with one of the artillery carriages . . . this caused a circular to be issued prohibiting shooting at game." On another occasion, an errant teamster left the column with a Gatlin gun in pursuit of antelope, only to be mired in mud. He was ordered to walk for the rest of the march. At Grand River, Calhoun pointed out that "if any shot were fired as a signal of danger I fear very little attention would be paid it."[38]

The requirements of military security and discipline meant that hunting among the troops remained contingent on gaining a hunting pass. Some commanders granted permissions freely in order to gain meat for the camp or to deploy troops to aid officers on sporting forays. Others—especially in hostile locations—proved more reticent. The hunt often emerged as part of a reward system for good behavior or, in particular, good marksmanship. To his delight, David Spotts obtained his inaugural pass to join a party on January 27, 1869. The joy was short-lived: sightings of American Indians near camp the next day caused the permit to be revoked. Frustrations were evident as the hunters looked to smaller-scale faunal contests for their amusement: "Now that we cannot go outside we will have to do something in camp to get us some excitements. The boys are bringing in centipedes, horned toads and tarantulas, and trying to get up a scrap with them."[39]

When they were allowed out, meanwhile, troops enjoyed the roaming culture of the trail, banter with peers, and the excitement of game sport. Hunting promised entertainment, target practice, and an escape from the

confines of military authority. As one recruit noted of a hunting detach-
ment in Arizona, "Good times ahead . . . we will go hunting and do just
about as we please." Sent out to create a chopping camp to build huts for
the commander, McConnell enthused, "The three weeks we spent in the
woods, during most of which the weather was delightful, was like a 'picnic,'
no military duty to perform, our time at our disposal, after the quota of logs
were cut, which was generally completed by noon, and in the afternoon and
evening we hunted."[40]

Set against the exigencies of military discipline was the issue of troop
training. David Spotts recalled the first encounter of his column with a bison
herd in 1868 in which the animals passed fifty feet away, wandering past for
half an hour, and the regiment still missed most of them: "In their excitement the men forgot to use the rear sight on their guns, so shot too high."
The inauguration of drill training and riding exercises duly sought to develop
the skill set of the hunter hero within the ranks, albeit within the confines
of camp and under strict regimental authority. Army General Orders nos. 8
and 9 (April 2, 1867) mandated drill and target training, while no.10 (April 16,
1867) required practice with the Springfield rifle daily at ten and two o'clock.
A. F. Mulford recalled bareback riding at camp with the Seventh Cavalry near
Bismarck, designed "to give you confidence in your ability to ride," as well as
mounted training with hard tack targets to "see how many bullets they can
put through the tack man."[41]

Some, however, saw no substitute for full immersion in the western
landscape armed with a gun and a charge to find game. Major William A.
Thornton, for one, suggested to Colonel H. K. Craig in 1856 that, in addition to ten ball cartridges every week for drill (with rewards of whiskey for
top scores), the men be taken out on hunting duty. Exposure to the hunting trail—the martial ecology of the West—would make the perfect soldier,
staving off the debilitating influence of urban and industrial life that had
proved such a powerful referent for the sport hunters. Captain Randolph
Marcy issued a strident manifesto in favor of the hunting trail as military
boot camp in *Thirty Years of Army Life on the Border* (1866). Presenting camp
life as monotonous and "detrimental" to the "physical and moral" well-being
of troops, he recommended that troops take readily to the game trail. An
"army of well-disciplined hunters will be the most efficient of all others
against the only enemy we have to encounter," he asserted. The western

theater seemed a perfect landscape for encouraging a vigorous constitution and a model soldier based on the hunting genealogy of the frontiersman. According to Marcy:

> I know of no better school of practice for perfecting men in target-firing, and the use of firearms generally, than that in which the frontier hunter receives his education. One of the first and most important lessons that he is taught impresses him with the conviction that, unless his gun is in good order and steadily directed upon the game, he must go without his supper . . . The man who is afraid to place the butt of his piece firmly against his shoulder, or who turns away his head at the instant of pulling trigger (as soldiers often do before they have been drilled at target-practice), will not be likely to bag much game or to contribute materially toward the result of a battle.

The skills of the hunting trail—knowledge of terrain, woodcraft, a healthy disposition, and gun skills—ably translated to the needs of the military. As Marcy urged, all of these skills "will be found serviceable in border warfare."[42]

Beyond translatable skills, scouts and army officers in the western theater referred to their adversaries using the lexicon of the game trail. Custer, for one, adopted a hunting metaphor to describe the pursuit of Indians as akin to "shooting swallows in the wing, so rapid were they in their movements." That indigenous warriors often imitated bird and animal calls and took naturalistic names aided the translation. As they trailed the plains, the Seventh saw Lakota brave Running Antelope and antelope herds as targets in their sights, common quarry for the taking in the martial ecology of the West. In an article for *Galaxy* magazine, Custer described a pursuit of "prowling" Sioux on the Yellowstone as akin to one of his sporting sojourns, with a passing nod to the provenance of the gun. He spoke of striking for the trail, admiring the scenery, sleeping close to his "trusty Remington," and leading the "leaden messages" of carbine fire, which "went whistling on its deadly errand" toward the "wily Redskins." At times even, American Indians were directly referenced as "game." Ambushed by a hostile plains party, General Custer remembered "my men pouring in their rifle-balls by hundreds, yet none bringing down the game" while Major A. H. Nickerson wrote of the Arizona campaign, "Once on the trail, neither trailers nor troops took any more rest than was absolutely necessary to enable them to move again; but doggedly, persistently, untiringly, they followed on like sleuth-hounds until the game was run down." During a scouting mission from Camp Verde in winter 1873–74, Schuyler offered a detailed description of the pursuit of a band of Apache. His narrative spoke of tracking the prey, stalking, surveillance, strategies of capture, and a firefight in which two "bucks" escaped and eight were killed.[43]

The corollary was also true: military vernacular on occasion conjured the frontier army as "prey" rather than "predator." This was informed by practical experience of ambush. Schuyler, for instance, recalled an occasion in which an army hunter was found by scouts on the confines of camp after being scalped by Apaches who were looking to steal horses. It was also a product of the long-standing construction of the savage Indian in the Euro-American mindset. Lieutenant Thomas Sweeny, member of the Second Infantry during the Sioux campaign, wrote of the "desolate spot" of Yuma Camp in 1851, expecting "at some unguarded moment, for nature cannot watch forever, I shall be surprised I suppose, cut off, massacred, minced sans remorse, by wretches." Much like the civilian hunter heroes who drew resolution and alertness from the mettle of their quarry, the use of the "prey" analogy seemed to encourage a state of perpetual readiness and resolve. Major Burt at Fort Smith spoke of his march from Fort Kearny to Fort Smith in 1867 accordingly: "The country through which we are now passing was valued by the Indians as their most precious hunting grounds. . . . we feasted upon game . . . our scouts were constantly on the alert." It also offered a self-inverted view of conquest that justified attack as defense and confirmed the status of the American West as a war zone. For B. Randolph Keim, maneuvers in the "heart of the chosen hunting-grounds of the hostile bands" brought into relief the contest between hunter's paradise and the "red man's paradise." Put simply, the battle for game was the battle for the West.[44]

GUNS, HUNTING, AND THE MARTIAL ECOLOGY OF THE WEST

It is perhaps no surprise that, occupied by hunting as a modus of subsistence, sport, or training and embedded in a performative culture of the game trail, many described military engagements in terms of a hunting vernacular. While the sport hunters played war, the military played with the iconography of the game trail. The juxtaposition was important: both spoke of the conjuring of the West as a martial ecology, a space in which military language and behaviors communicated axioms of power. In many ways, hunting defined the contours of this engagement. The beatification of General Crook—described as "a graceful rider, a noted hunter, and a dead-shot, skilled in all the secrets of wood-craft and Indian warfare," a martial Daniel Boone who when "not chasing Indians during the heyday of the great Indian wars . . . was chasing wild animals"—highlighted a common terrain of sport and land seizure. As they blazed game trails armed with Winchesters, Sharps, and Springfields, hunters in the West collectively (and sometimes self-consciously) advanced goals of colonial conquest. Firearms proved vital in this equation as technological agents of transformation and as communication devices. A colorful tool of empire, the gun spoke of contested space, the political economy of land appropriation, and the performance codes of the hunt.[45]

NOTES

1. "Buffalo Bill's Wild West and Congress of Rough Riders of the World," n.d., 90.253.85, 22, Autry Library, Autry National Center, Los Angeles (hereafter cited as Autry); Bridger quoted in Charles G. Worman, *Gunsmoke and Saddle Leather: Firearms in the Nineteenth-Century American West* (Albuquerque: University of New Mexico Press, 2005), 59.

2. John Cawelti, *The Six-Gun Mystique* (Bowling Green, OH: Bowling Green State University Popular Press, 1984 [1970]); "Buffalo Bill's Wild West and Congress of Rough Riders of the World," 14. For qualifications on the nature of violence and extent of gun use in the West, see Robert Dykstra, *The Cattle Towns* (New York: Alfred A. Knopf, 1968); and Robert Dykstra, "Body Counts and Murder Rates: The Contested Statistics of Western Violence," *Reviews in American History* 31, no. 4 (December 2003): 554–63; Michael Bellesiles, *Arming America: The Origins of a National Gun Culture* (New York: Alfred A. Knopf, 2000); Roger D. McGrath, *Gunfighters, Highwaymen & Vigilantes: Violence on the Frontier* (Berkeley: University of California Press, 1984); Richard Maxwell Brown, *Strain of Violence: Historical Studies of American Violence and Vigilantism* (New York, Oxford University Press, 1975).

3. Randolph Marcy, *The Prairie Traveler, A Handbook for Overland Expeditions* (New York: Harper and Brothers, 1859), 188.

4. Jacob Hawken moved to St. Louis in 1818 and established himself as a gunsmith, brother Samuel arrived four years later, notably fashioning a rifle for trapper William Ashley in 1823. The brothers formally began trading together in 1825 under the J and S Hawken brand. James B. Marsh, *Four Years in the Rockies* (Newcastle, PA: W. B. Thomas, 1884), 41.

5. W. T. Hamilton, *My Sixty Years on the Plains* (New York: Forest and Stream, 1905), 217.

6. Stuart quoted in Worman, *Gunsmoke*, 387.

7. Tina Loo, "Of Moose and Men: Hunting for Masculinities in British Columbia, 1880–1939," *Western Historical Quarterly* 32, no. 3 (Autumn 2001): 301.

8. Gibbs quoted in Worman, *Gunsmoke*, 62; A. J. Leach, *Early Day Stories* (Norfolk, NE: Huse, 1916), 94; "Dr. George Bird Grinnell, Buffalo Hunter," *Rod and Gun News*, ca.1876, clipping, Box 35, Folder 198, George Bird Grinnell Papers, HM223, Manuscripts and Archives, Yale University Library; Granville Stuart, *Forty Years on the Frontier* (Cleveland: Arthur Clark Co., 1925), 1:33; Norman B. Wiltsey, "Jim Bridger: He-Coon of the Mountain Men," *Montana* 6, no. 1 (Winter 1956): 14.

9. William D. Pickett, Diary of 1880, 13, William Pickett Diary, SC1436, Montana Historical Society Research Center, Helena (hereafter cited as MHS); William Allen, *Adventures with Indians and Game, or Twenty Years in the Rocky Mountains* (Chicago: A. W. Bowen, 1903), 108; William Pickett, Diary for 1881, 6, William Pickett Diary, SC1436, MHS; Malcolm Mackay, *Cow Range and Hunting Trail* (New York: G. P. Putnam's, 1925), 167.

10. H. A. Leveson, *Sport in Many Lands* (London: Chapman and Hall, 1877), 2:236; Horace Hutchinson, *Big Game Shooting* (New York: Charles Scribner's, 1905), 3; Pickett, Diary for 1880, 13; Peregrine Herne, *Perils and Pleasures of a Hunter's Life* (Philadelphia: John E. Potter, 1855), 14; Theodore Roosevelt, *The Wilderness Hunter* (New York: Charles Scribner's, 1926), 370–72.

11. Allen, *Adventures*, 186; F. A. Wislizenus, *A Journey to the Rocky Mountains in the Year 1839* (St. Louis: Missouri Historical Society, 1912), 122–23.

12. Marble Arms Company, catalog no. 18, 1911, 95.235.8, Autry; Larry Koller, *The Fireside Book of Guns* (New York: Ridge Press, 1959), 10; Allen, *Adventures*, 108, 19.

13. Roosevelt, *Wilderness Hunter*, 370–72; Horace Edwards to Henry, December 28, 1875, Horace Edwards Correspondence, WA MSS S-1634, Folder 6, Western Americana Collection, Beinecke Rare Book and Manuscript Library, Yale University (hereafter cited as Beinecke); Allen, *Adventures*, 136–68; *Shooting and Fishing*, quoted in Worman, *Gunsmoke*, 399.

14. Edwards to Henry, December 28, 1875; *Shooting and Fishing*, July 18, 1894; Beidler quoted in Jonathan J. Hooper, *Rod and Gun* (Tuscaloosa: University of Alabama Press, 1992), ix–x.

15. William Hornaday, *Taxidermy and Zoological Collecting* (New York: Charles Scribner's, 1894), 13; William D. Pickett, Diary for 1878, 10–13, William Pickett Diary, SC1436, MHS; W. J. Browning and F. F. Flournay, "Hunting Big Game in Early Days," MS982, Braun Research Library Collection, Autry National Center, Los Angeles.

16. Wislizenus, *Journey*, 122; A. Pendarves Vivian, *Wanderings in the Western Land* (London: Sampson, Low, Marston, Searle & Rivington, 1879), 153.

17. Roosevelt quoted in "Charlie Marble and Teddy Pals," November 22, 1937, Montana News Association Inserts, MHS; George Shields, *Hunting in the Great West* (Chicago: Belford, Clarke & Co., 1888), 39; *Intelligencer* (Missouri) quoted in Worman, *Gunsmoke*, 11; Edgar F. Randolph, *Inter-Ocean Hunting Tales* (New York: Forest and Stream, 1908), 8; Horace Edwards to Henry, September 21, 1884, Horace Edwards Correspondence, WA MSS S-1634, Folder 8, Beinecke; Rufus B. Sage, *Rocky Mountain Life, or Startling Scenes and Perilous Adventures in the Far West* (Boston: Wentworth, 1857), 320; James Josiah Webb, *Adventures in the Santa Fe Trade, 1844–47* (Philadelphia: Ralph Biber, 1974), 116–17.

18. Shields, *Hunting in the Great West*, 78; William A. Baillie Grohman, *Camps in the Rockies* (New York: Charles Scribner's, 1910), 142; and *Fifteen Years' Sport and Life in the Hunting Grounds of Western America and British Columbia* (London: Horace Cox, 1900), frontisplate.

19. Howland Gasper, *The Complete Sportsman* (New York: Forest and Stream, 1893), 1; *Anaconda Standard*, December 13, 1925; Allen, *Adventures*, 135.

20. Shields, *Hunting in the Great West*, 34, 39, 106, 74.

21. Shields, *Hunting in the Great West*, 124–25; *Helena Independent Record*, October 18, 2001.

22. Grinnell, *Hunting at High Altitudes* (New York: Harper and Bros., 1913), 239; Pickett, Diary April 2, 1879–January 1880, 13.

23. Anthony Rotundo, *American Manhood: Transformations in Masculinity from the Revolution to the Modern Era* (New York: Basic Books, 1993), 232.

24. David Hilger, "The Last of the Buffalo," 6, David Hilger Papers, SC854: Box 5, MHS.

25. William Cody, "Famous Hunting Parties of the Plains," *Cosmopolitan* 17, no. 2 (June 1894): 137; Mary Burt, ed., *The Boy General: Story of the Life of Major General George A. Custer as told by Elizabeth Custer* (New York: Charles Scribner's, 1901), 115.

26. John Schofield, *Forty-Six Years in the Army* (New York: Century Co., 1897), 428. For General Nelson Miles and the Yellowstone campaign, see Jeffrey V. Pearson, "Nelson A. Miles, Crazy Horse, and the Battle of Wolf Mountains," *Montana: The Magazine of Western History* 51 (Winter 2001): 53–67.

27. John Cook, *The Border and the Buffalo* (Topeka: Crane and Company, 1907), 663–64; Shields, *Hunting in the Great West*, 145–52, 140–41.

28. Sherman quoted in David D. Smits, "The Frontier Army and the Destruction of the Buffalo: 1865–1883," *Western Historical Quarterly* 25, no. 3 (Autumn 1994): 314; Cody, "Famous Hunting Parties," 137–39; Elizabeth Custer, *Following the Guidon* (New York: Harper and Bros., 1898), 264, 195.

29. Custer, *Following*, 34; A. F. Mulford, *Fighting Indians in the 7th United States Cavalry* (Corning, NY: Paul Lindsley Mulford, 1878), 79; David L. Spotts, *Campaigning with Custer and the Nineteenth Kansas Volunteer Cavalry*, ed. E. A. Brininstool (Los Angeles: Wetzel, 1928), 53; Diary of Electus Backus, 1851–52, mssHM 66248, Huntington Library, San Marino (hereafter cited as Huntington); Charles Robinson, ed., *Diaries of John Gregory Bourke*, vol. 1, *November 20, 1872–July 28, 1873* (Denton: University of North Texas Press, 2003), 240.

30. Walter Scribner Schuyler to George Schuyler, November 1, 1876, Fort Laramie, Wyoming, Papers of Walter Scribner Schuyler, MSS WS87, Huntington; Mulford, *Fighting Indians*, 87; Spotts, *Campaigning with Custer*, 110.

31. Leonard Swett to Laura Swett, June 14, 1875, Fort Lincoln, Papers of Leonard Swett, mssHM 68244–68272, Huntington; References to Crook and Scott quoted in Kevin Adams, *Class and Race in the Frontier Army: Military Life in the West, 1870–1890* (Norman: University of Oklahoma Press, 2009), 85; George W. Manypenny, *Our Indian Wards* (New York: Da Capo Press, 1880), 149.

32. Kinzie Bates to wife, October 8, 1875, May 16, 1877, and May 29, 1877, Papers of Kinzie Bates (1863–1929), mssHM 60325–60354, Huntington.

33. Custer, *Following*, 33, 208; Merrill J. Mattes, ed., *Indians, Infantry, and Infants: Andrew and Elizabeth Burt of the Frontier* (Denver: Old West Publishing Co., 1960), 158, 62, 248; Robinson, *Diaries of John Gregory Bourke*, 1:355; George Armstrong Custer, *My Life on the Plains* (New York: Sheldon and Co., 1874), 47; "Nomad" (George Armstrong Custer), "On the Plains," *Turf, Field and Farm*, October 12, 1867.

34. Custer, *Following*, 33, 120, 217; Custer, "On the Plains."

35. Lawrence A. Frost, ed., *With Custer in '74: James Calhoun's Diary* (Provo, UT: Brigham Young University Press, 1979), 15–16; Elizabeth Custer, *Boots and Saddles* (New York: Harper and Bros., 1885), 192–93.

36. Katherine Gibson Fougera, *With Custer's Cavalry* (Caxton, ID: N.p., 1942), 78; Frost, *With Custer in '74*, 25; Burt, *Boy General*, 141, 144.

37. Custer, *Boots and Saddles*, 106–8.

38. Adams, *Class and Race in the Frontier Army*, 60; Custer, *Following*, 33, 241; Mulford, *Fighting Indians*, 80; Frost, *With Custer in '74*, 25, 29.

39. Spotts, *Campaigning with Custer*, 114.

40. H. H. McConnell, *Five Years a Cavalryman, or Sketches of Regular Army Life on the Texas Frontier, 1866–1875* (Norman: University of Oklahoma Press, 1996), 55.

41. Spotts, *Campaigning with Custer*, 53; Mulford, *Fighting Indians*, 92.

42. Randolph Marcy, *Thirty Years of Army Life on the Border* (New York: Harper and Bros., 1866), 283–85.

43. Custer, *Following*, 7; George A. Custer, "Battling with the Sioux on the Yellowstone," *Galaxy* 22 (July 1876): 94–97; A. H. Nickerson, "Major General Crook

and the Indians: A Sketch," 1890, 17, Papers of Walter Scribner Schuyler, MSS WS58, Huntington; Walter Schuyler, "Notes of a Scout from Camp Verde to McDowell and Return," December 1, 1873–January 26, 1874, Papers of Walter Scribner Schuyler, MSS WS68, Huntington.

44. B. Randolph Keim, *Sheridan's Troops on the Border: A Winter Campaign on the Plains* (Philadelphia: David McKay, 1881), 59, 101; Schuyler to George Schuyler, November 1, 1876, Papers of Walter Scribner Schuyler MSS WS87, Huntington; Mattes, *Indians, Infantry, and Infants*, 99; Arthur Woodward, ed., *The Journal of Lt. Thomas W. Sweeny, 1849–1853* (Los Angeles: Westernlake Press, 1956), 57–58.

45. Robinson, *Diaries of John Gregory Bourke*, 1:243.

CHAPTER 3

LADY ADVENTURERS AND CRACK SHOTS

Hunter Heroines in the Nineteenth-Century American West

> There was an old and rather brutal saying out west,
> to the effect that this was great country for men
> and horses, but hell on women and cattle.
>
> —*Nannie Alderson, Montana homesteader*

Drawing on codes of Victorian manhood, hunting narratives of the nineteenth-century West typically broadcast a monolithic vision of hunter heroes armed with sharpshooting skills and a penchant for adventuring. Exemplars such as Buffalo Bill Cody, Theodore Roosevelt, and George Armstrong Custer collectively advanced the expansionist ambitions of the American nation in assimilating landscapes and animals while maintaining a gentlemanly moral code, a sporting attitude, and a charismatic swagger to boot. John Frost's *Heroes and Hunters of the West* (1855) eulogized "the exploits of the Heroes of the West," men in possession of "the bolder and rougher features of human nature in their noblest light, softened and directed by virtues that have appeared in the

DOI: 10.5876/9781607323983.c003

really heroic deeds of every age, and form pages in the history of this country destined to be read and admired when much that is now deemed more
important is forgotten." Such was the performance genealogy of the hunter
hero as outlined in the last two chapters.[1]

The role of women in this noble parade was typically confined to that of
observers, watching with trembling admiration as their men won the frontier
for American nationhood and manliness. As Elizabeth Custer recounted in
Following the Guidon (1890), a typical hunt involved the men riding heroically
in pursuit of game while the women chatted, had a picnic, and viewed the
performance through opera glasses. Traditional writing on the West, what
Susan Armitage has called a "hisland," only served to cement this polarized
narrative of masculine heroics and feminine subservience. Wallace Stegner
dubbed the West a tale of "male freedom and aspiration versus female
domesticity," while in *Virgin Land* (1950) Henry Nash Smith heralded the pioneer woodsman as a critical pillar of the mythic West and a heroic archetype,
"one of the fixtures of American mythology." Traditional writings assumed
women to be reluctant pioneers and gentle tamers who left the job of exploration and assimilation to the menfolk while revisionist treatments continued to position domesticity and domestic space as the principal frames of reference for discourses on the female frontier. According to Larry McMurtry,
"The frontier was not feminine, it was masculine." Corralled to the homestead by gender norms, poverty, and isolation, women, according to Julie Roy
Jeffrey, "tried to maintain the standards of domesticity . . . with which they
had been familiar before emigration," while Annette Kolodny argued that
women steered clear of subduing the virgin wilderness to focus on creating
a home and a garden of earthly (and earthy) delight. Such readings suggest
that women apprehended their geographies of contact on the frontier as a
"potential sanctuary for idealized domesticity."[2]

This was, however, not always the story. Alongside the masculine hunter
hero of the plains and mountains, women emerged as willing and competent participants in the hunt. For a number of educated upper-class women
the prospect of independent travel, sport, and adventure elucidated opportunities for gender empowerment and the transgression of societal norms.
The lure of the frontier and its associations with strenuous activity, simple
living, and escapism held cross-gender appeal. For pioneer women, meanwhile, hunting served multifarious purposes within the context of a domestic

frontier economy that encompassed the realms of subsistence necessity and codes of ownership and belonging. The "lady adventurer" and the "armed western woman" represent important qualifications to the hegemonic narrative of masculine heroics and point to a discreet "woman's way of knowing" and a new performance on the game trail.[3]

THE LADY SPORTSMAN: THE HUNT AS ADVENTURE NARRATIVE AND EXCURSION TO EMPOWERMENT

The opportunity to travel in the American West, to encounter its animals and wander its monumental landscapes, proved a powerful lure for the educated Euro-American elite in the 1800s. In *Impressions of a Tenderfoot during a Journey in Search of Sport in the Far West* (1890), the Duchess of Somerset recalled how she relished the prospect of the "unknown lands" of the Rockies and the chance of "health, sport and pleasure." Idealized in society chat, newspapers, and literature and made accessible by the transcontinental railroad and the services of local outfitters, the West presented a grand tour of wilderness exoticism and healthy exuberance. Women proved as enticed by the prospect of hunter's paradise in the West (with its strenuous life and invigorating airs) as Theodore Roosevelt and his breed of sportsmen adventurers. As the *St. Louis Globe Democrat* noted in a 1905 editorial entitled "Bear Hunting as a Sport for Women: Strenuous and Dangerous Forms of Recreation Appeals to many Dianas," "Women have turned to bear hunting in the Rocky Mountains as the most fascinating and health-giving of sports." In that sense, the refrains of the hunter hero and the hunter heroine were analogous.[4]

A visit to the West as a paradise for the female hunter hero implied, as it did for their male cohorts, a class and a racial vantage. The promise of a sporting expedition to the Rockies in pursuit of game spoke of an aristocratic pedigree, or at least the aspirations of one (both in terms of the necessary finances required for such as endeavor as well as training in the vocation of hunting for pleasure). The craze for outdoor sports common among educated eastern elites was not confined to men, so much so that prominent sporting publications such as *Outdoor Life* and *Forest and Stream* dedicated columns to what they called "the lady sportsman." *Forest and Stream* included a letter "to the ladies" in 1873 and, by the following year, boasted six female contributors. This relaxing of the hypermasculine entrance requirements of the hunting fraternity reflected the creation of a sporting naturalist hunter hero tradition. Elite women who loved the chase thus gained entry into this club by virtue of their socioeconomic status and respectable femininity, in the process advancing the sanctification of hunting rights on the basis of leisured gentility, class, and pursuits both imperial and empirical. As Andrea Smalley notes, "While men represented the long human history of hunting, women symbolized those qualities of recreational hunting that elevated the sport above all other forms of wildlife use."[5]

The popularity of the western tour among foreign travelers (notably the British) often reflected a colonial gaze that saw travelers take in far-flung reaches of the globe in the interests of self-development, wilderness adventure, and natural history. For the lady adventurer, the West afforded the same benefits of healthful recreation that attracted her male cohorts with the added enticement of vaulting conventional gender boundaries. Isabella Bird, the forty-two-year-old daughter of a Yorkshire clergyman, visited the American West in 1872–73 seeking in its remote scenery and adventuring prospect a relief from the chattering confinement of English society. *A Lady's Life in the Rocky Mountains* (1879) saw her gleefully report on an intrepid 800-mile trek across the "unprofaned freshness" of a Rocky Mountain landscape that was "no region for tourists or women." Speaking with an imperial and a romantic voice, she claimed grand landscapes "by right of love, appropriation and appreciation" and relished her flight from the Victorian cult of womanhood into a world of "grandeur, cheerfulness, health, enjoyment, novelty, freedom, etc." As Joyce Kelley has noted, for the educated woman of independent means, a trip to the wilderness offered escapist pleasure and a route toward affirming the duties of empire while extending her reach far beyond the domestic. Consumed by a passion for exotic travel, Bird went on to visit Malaysia, China, Vietnam, Tibet, and India, becoming the first female member of the Royal Geographical Society in 1892.[6]

Isabella Bird encountered a frontier economy saturated with the economic and social trappings of the hunt. She met emigrants armed with rifles in case they "fell in with game" as well as Welsh settlers who divided their time between stalking game and stock raising; she also spent time in the mountains with fur trappers, including Mountain Jim, a one-eyed "ruffian" whom she encountered while overwintering with a neighboring family. Denver seemed literally awash with creatures of the chase: "hunters and trappers in buckskin suits, men of the Plains in huge blue cloaks with belts and revolvers, teamsters in leather suits, horsemen in fur coats, and caps and buffalo hide boots . . . brooding dandies, rich English tourists." Bird eagerly imbibed of this hunter's paradise, waxing lyrical on the "intoxicating" qualities of an outdoors life, sleeping under the pines, and spending time on horseback (especially riding astride on a Mexican saddle, which cured the backache she had suffered from since childhood). In a letter to the *London Times* she described her errand into the wilderness in language every budding hunter hero would recognize: "I spent weeks in the depth of winter in a mountain cabin with a couple of young sportsmen for company, a bare larder, and a temperature considerably below zero." The frontier represented a landscape of rejuvenation, resort, and epiphany, for Bird "the very place I have been seeking, but in everything it exceeds all my dreams."[7]

Significantly, Bird herself was no hunter. She balked at the "kill" and demonstrated a genteel antipathy toward firearms, reluctantly stowing a pistol under her pillow when traveling solo in the Rockies, though she couldn't "conceive of any circumstances in which I could feel it right to make any use of it." At the same time, she seemed entirely comfortable with the theatrics of the game quest. The power of the hunt as melodrama seemingly became so great that the actual modus of the hunt (the kill) assumed subsidiary significance. Letters to her sister (which were published in the British magazine *Leisure Hour* and formed the basis for *A Lady's Life in the Rocky Mountains*) found her robustly embracing a sense of frontier adventure, enmeshed in ideas of proving and renewal in the "Eden" of Colorado and (figuratively at least) "eating and sleeping like a hunter."[8]

Born in Sacramento, California, in 1872, Grace Gallatin Thompson Seton was a classic example of the lady adventurer. Heralding from an affluent family with interests in minerals and hardware, she had a comfortable yet unconventional upbringing living in hotels and friends' houses following her parents' divorce. In the 1880s she worked on a San Francisco newspaper as a writer and book artist under the non-de-plume "Dorothy Dodge." A trip to Paris brought an encounter with naturalist Ernest Thompson Seton. The two married in 1896 and lived as New York socialites before moving to a rustic mansion in the Connecticut backwoods. Running a house with seven servants and attending garden parties thrown by the Queen of England, Seton might be perceived as a genteel creature, a supporting wife of an outdoors hero famed for his writings and animal art. However, she showed herself to be far more than "Nimrod's wife." Co-founder of the Girl Pioneers and president of the Connecticut Women's Suffrage Association, Seton was an independent and accomplished woman and author of seven books based on her own expeditions. These ranged from the tentative admissions of a green-horn sportswoman in *A Woman Tenderfoot* (1900) to the assured countenance of a seasoned lady adventurer in *The Log of the "Look See"* (1932). A record of her travels in Paraguay, *The Log* contained a photograph of Seton in rid-ing boots and jodhpurs, wielding a rifle and ruminating on the benefits of solo travel in the time-honored fashion of the hunter hero: "And to be alone! An expedition, like matrimony, entails much adjustment of personal habits and predilections. In the Look-See business he travels furthest who proceeds under his own steam."[9]

Seton's first book, *A Woman Tenderfoot*, described an 1897 trip taken by her and her husband in search of game in Yellowstone and the Tetons. Written in the first person, it clearly communicated the performance codes of the game trail and established the author as expert witness to a landscape both intimate and dramatic. Much like her male counterparts, Seton positioned herself as actuary and chronicler of the hunt, as Lucinda MacKethan notes, maintaining "the narrator's voice—that of a cool, charming, confident hunter determined to witness and record all that was 'out there,' wherever she was." Describing her entry into the wilds as a pioneering white woman, Seton deployed the idea of the greenhorn to show her own narrative devel-opment and map the practical mechanics of the game quest. She presented her husband as the great hunter hero while confirming her own sporting cre-dentials and vociferating a feminine-empathetic connection with game. The rhetoric of transformation situated the hunter heroine firmly in the sporting canon while her expressions of passivity and empowerment pointed to the tensions and transgressions of gender boundaries on the hunting trail.[10]

Seton spent the first part of *A Woman Tenderfoot* imparting practical advice, a device that alluded to her own journey from untried traveler to accomplished adventurer and also highlighted the importance of prepara-tion, inventory, and catalogue to women and men hunters alike. Taking leave from female hunting manuals, including *Women in the Hunting Field* (1913) and *Ladies in the Field* (1894), she compiled a list of must-have supplies along with advice on "how to ride, how to dress for it, how to shoot, and how to philosophise." Notably, the "woman-who-goes-hunting-with-her-husband" was encouraged to avoid all domestic duties, suggesting a certain irony to the implied codes of subservience in such a moniker. The mantle of domestic responsibility, according to Seton, was "the reason women so often dislike camping out . . . You cannot be care free, camp-life's greatest charm, when you have on your mind the boiling of prunes and beans, or when tears are starting from your smoke-inflamed eyes as you broil the elk for dinner." Such a rubric highlighted Seton's vantage as a hunter heroine in her own right, seeing in the wilderness trail freedom from the domestic sphere, courtesy of a spirited mind and the benefits of a privileged lifestyle.[11]

As Seton described life on the game trail, the empowering potential of her position as a female hunter heroine became clearer. The West facilitated a stalwart challenge of gender conventions, and this she performed as literary rendition. Henceforth, we find her exalting the beauties of the sporting life in language befitting the masculine hunter hero. She applauded the "spell of the West" in comparison to "the dim and frivolous East!," relished the joy of treading where "none but the four-footed had been before," and extolled the joys of "robust" activity and "the fascination of the wild life." Her musings illuminated the disruptive aspects of the hunting experience on the conventional contours of Victorian gender identity. Seton transcended the role of helpmate to stalk and shoot, becoming captured by the desire to bag her own antelope and thus claim ownership over the animal by the possessive voice ("it is," as she notes, "a Western abbreviation in great favour"). Refusing to see her gender as a limitation, Seton railed against charges of vulnerability or weakness, admonishing herself during a bear hunt with the words: "You little fool, stop your whimpering. The others are made of flesh and blood too . . . brace up." Codes of female decorum were discarded as she galloped when "a trot is more proper" and adopted a divided skirt for riding astride, "the only way" to ride in the West. At the end of *A Woman Tenderfoot*—with the typical affectations of the hunter hero autobiographer—Seton described her journey as one of exploration and personal catharsis to become an accomplished woman of the wilds forged by the performance of frontier experience, what she called "the joy of the living and of the doing."[12]

Dorcas Miller dubbed *A Woman Tenderfoot* "a primer for women's independence." Nevertheless, Grace Seton's travelogue account of female proving on the hunting trail was not an unabashed liberationist manifesto. Although keen to demonstrate the loss of her tenderfoot status, she pointed out, "I am still a woman and may be tender." An identity as a refined outdoorswoman seemingly demanded comportment and feminine identity as well as a hankering for the wilderness—themes remarkably similar to the hunter hero in his lofting of gentlemanly ways and restrained acts of violence. Such a tendency was evident in the performance repertory of other lady adventurers. Isabella Bird expressed similar ambiguities of revilement and revelry at nature's savagery in *A Lady's Life in the Rocky Mountains*. For all Seton's demonstrations of competence in the wilds, articulations of desolation and anxiety took hold at various moments and were articulated in gendered binaries—a pertinent signal of the limitations to a fully liberated voice for women hunters. Based on "a woman's dread of the unknown and untried," she feared the "hundred dangers . . . which seemed made to annihilate me." Nimrod, by contrast, was "blithe and unconcerned," maintaining his patriarchal power as ever-watchful guardian, hunter-instructor, and monarch of the trail. Even nature seemed to obey him: "Nimrod held up his finger as a warning for silence. We listened. We were so still that the whole world seemed to be holding its breath."[13]

Riding astride also seemed to precipitate a certain amount of discomposure, a signal that the hunter heroine was not entirely free from the constraints of social judgment even in the midst of Rocky Mountain wilderness. Seton proved keen to explain how her patented design (illustrated in the book) allowed the "woman-who-hunts-with-her-husband" to ride astride while appearing to remain sidesaddle. Issues of visibility and etiquette had also bothered Isabella Bird, who, despite her wholehearted advocacy of riding astride, dismounted outside Colorado Springs to ride into the town in a socially appropriate fashion. Such badges of femininity allowed outdoorswomen to hoist their respectability as lady adventurers and contrasted them with the boisterous (and socially deviant) frontier "wild woman." Isabella Bird took particular umbrage with an article in the *Times* that remarked on her "masculine habiliments." Isabella wrote to her editor noting that her attire was commensurate with that worn by *"ladies* at Mountain resorts in America" (her emphasis). "My indignation and disgust have not cooled down yet. I can imagine a lady who 'dons masculine habiliments' quite capable of thrashing an editor on less provocation," she railed. Seton, too, proved keen to assert her status as refined lady. After participating in the ruckus of a cattle roundup, she drew a sharp distinction between her approach to the game trail and that of one of the West's most famous cross-dressing frontier "wild women": "I . . . only wanted . . . to make an honorable dismount and go somewhere by myself where a little brook babbled nothings, and the forget-me-nots placidly slept. Rough riding and adventures of the Calamity Jane order tempted me no more."[14]

Seton offered a blend of heroics and delicacy in the classic mold of the lady adventurer. As such, the title of a *Good Housekeeping* article summed up well her public articulation of the female hunter hero: "Feminine Charms of the Woman Militant." This motif came through strongly in discussions of the kill. Narrating a utopia of domestic bliss in the Tetons, she described a herd of "sportive mermaids" drinking in the lake and watched over by their "lordly master." Seemingly racked by a conflict between her thirst for western excitement and sentimental attachment to animals, she urged Nimrod to "shoot, shoot" before recoiling at the sight of animal suffering. The thrill of the chase and its wilderness exoticism—the wild—and the mechanics of feminine sensibilities—the civilized—seemingly collided. As Seton noted, "My woman's soul revolted, and yet I was out West for all the experiences that life could give me." As the previous chapter indicated, metaphysical musings on life, death, and the conversation between hunter and prey were part of the vernacular of the gentleman sportsman in the late nineteenth century. Seton's viewpoint, nevertheless, issued a particular perspective on the sporting vocation by virtue of its consciously invoked gender codes. She defined her response to the kill—empathetic concern for animal welfare—as irrevocably feminine, a recourse that signaled not only her compassion as a sporting sort but also her intrinsic womanhood in a gender binary governed by expressive versus instrumental reactions. Having demonstrated a woman's sense of sentiment at the suffering of brute creations, Seton resumed the sporting quest and the descriptive turn of the hunter hero: "the deadly quiet of but one idea—to creep upon that elk and kill him—possessed me." The thrill of the moment, the report of the gun, and the falling of the animal conformed to typical descriptors of the kill as enshrined in the masculine tradition. Standing over her quarry, Seton mused: "I had no regret. I had no triumph—just a sort of wonder at what I had done." Days later, having orchestrated a kill of a "powerful buck with royal horns" watched over by his "peaceful family" of antelope does, she experienced a similarly emotive moment, this time pondering the brutalization of self and the execution of western fauna to satisfy the sportsman's "vanity." Seton decided that "hunting does not make one wholly a brute, crying Kill, kill!," but for her at least, the kill had lost its luster in favor of "seeing the creature at home amid his glorious surroundings . . . and feeling . . . the gleeful sense of joy and love in nature, both within and without." Such musings paid heed to the complicated gender codes of hunting, morality, and conservation in the naturalist tradition for women as well as men.[15]

HUNTING FOR THE POT AND FOR SPORT: THE HOMESTEAD ECONOMY AND THE GAME TRAIL

If Isabella Bird and Grace Seton represented classic examples of the lady adventurer, then western homesteaders such as Evelyn Cameron, Agnes Morley Cleaveland, and Elinore Pruitt Stewart were part of a female hunting culture that appeared more utilitarian and domestic. Hunting represented part of the subsistence cycle of pioneer culture and became part of the domestic mythology of the resilient female pioneer as depicted in August Leimbach's *Madonna of the Trail* sculpture series (1928), which featured a ten-foot-high frontierswoman clutching her son and a rifle modeled on Daniel Boone's own. Hunting from the homestead emerged as a vector through which frontier identity was secured and often involved the renegotiation of gender norms, thereby suggesting a place for the frontierswoman alongside the lady adventurer in the roster of female hunter heroes.

Evelyn Cameron's interaction with sport in the West began in the mold of lady adventurer. Born in 1868 to an aristocratic family in England, Evelyn traveled to Montana in 1889, on honeymoon with new husband Ewen, in search of game with one of Custer's old scouts. Discovering a veritable sporting feast of deer, mountain sheep, and grizzly bears, Ewen labeled the eastern Badlands of Montana as "a regular sportsman's paradise." Back in England, the well-to-do couple pined for the wild charms of the American West, its mountain landscapes, abundant game, and undulating prairies. After a year in England, they returned to the West as permanent settlers, hoping to raise polo ponies on a ranching spread near the town of Terry.[16]

In the years that followed, hunting remained an integral part of settler edification. Both Ewen and Evelyn shot grouse and deer for the table, which Evelyn then butchered, dressed, and cooked. Her diary entry for February

15, 1893, noted, "put on 'bockers' and shot out with Ewen." Tales of sport proved common around the kitchen table and gave Cameron a topic of conversation to enliven exchanges between her and the visitors who came through. As she remarked of local rancher Henry Tusler, "He is an awful bore to entertain . . . I gave him some hunting reminisces." Meanwhile, the yearly cycle of ranch life (which soon switched from polo ponies to raising cattle, horses, and chickens) involved an extended hunting trip lasting a few months at a time every year through to the 1899–1900 season, each one pains-takingly recorded in Cameron's frontier journal. The couple relished their annual excursions to the Badlands for all kinds of reasons. On a purely sport-ing level, the game trail afforded the chance to shoot a greater variety of fauna than the coyotes and grouse that the couple routinely took pot shots at or loosed hounds on (a vestige of their aristocratic vocations hunting fox in Britain). As avid amateur naturalists, Evelyn and Ewen eagerly anticipated the opportunity to study nature in the field, while, on an emotional plane, interacting with the great outdoors seemed to bring them closer together. As she noted in an article for the *New York Sun* entitled "A Woman's Big Game Hunting," "I consider a hunting expedition one of the most desirable ways for a couple to spend a holiday." Lastly, but no less vital, the trip secured a stock of meat for the ranch.[17]

Cameron's diary indicated a substantial overlap between her chores at the ranch and on the hunting trail. Back home, she catalogued her duties on a daily basis, from cooking and cleaning to washing and wood gathering. At the hunting camp, similar patterns applied. Cameron packed provisions, tended the fire, darned, did laundry, cooked, and skinned animals. Living in an abandoned cabin on November 12, 1894, she described a litany of house-hold duties: "I washed 5 handtowels, 2 napkins, 1 dish cloth, 2 pillow cases. Did even graze my knuckles. I swept out the shack, under the bunks, full of green brush carried in by a skunk I think." Diary entries conveyed a life of toil, seemingly substantiating Grace Seton's antipathy toward serving as camp maid. When she did hit the trail, Evelyn Cameron typically served in a support capacity. Sometimes she acted as scout or game driver, but mostly minded the horses, having instructions "not to show up" until Ewen returned or "a shot was heard." She waited for hours while her husband stalked game, spending her solitary moments observing nature and flicking though *Titbits* magazine. The mechanics of the hunt betrayed gender hierarchies common

in wider society. Cameron, like Seton, described her husband as central protagonist and the Nimrod of the trail. While agreeing that Evelyn served as
excellent aide-de-camp, he mentions her in his diary entries only as incidental
witness to sporting activity and the habits of prey.[18]

Yet, in common with most frontierswomen of the West and the other
hunter heroines discussed here, Evelyn Cameron was not a reluctant pioneer
or a helpless servant. She proved resourceful, vigorous, and played a critical
role in the subsistence economy of the ranch and on the game trail. Diary
entries find her using condensed milk and snow in the absence of cream,
treating a cut on her hand with a homemade remedy of water, salt, and
bacon fat, and running the camp single-handedly. When the ranch business
faltered, she earned money as a roving photographer, capturing members of
the local community keen to record their frontier identities. A curious photograph of Evelyn Cameron standing on the saddle of a horse illuminated
her riding skills, eye for theatrics, and adventurous spirit. Like Grace Seton
and Isabella Bird, she adopted the practice of riding astride, wearing a parti-
tioned skirt of her own design or a pair of Ewen's trousers on the trail. Citing
reasons of practicality as well as notably improved agility and endurance,
she regarded a "stride-legged" stance as "the only safe way for a woman to
ride." As a committed sportswoman, Cameron grasped any available chance
to join the hunt as an active participant and proved easily as good a shot
as her male compatriots. One January morning in 1897 she awoke to find
the temperature at thirty below, but still "put on comforter woollen jacket
and jacket knickers, combi, sealskin cap" and hiked three miles at 7:00 a.m.
to seek out game. In winter 1894–95, she repeatedly rebuked fellow hunters
Alec and Mr. C for their callow temperaments and inaccurate marksmanship:
"Having these kind of young men to take out spoils all our pleasure. Mr C's
terribly green and too fond of his ease to care about hunting much." Ever
the lady adventurer, Cameron betrayed scant concern about traveling solo
in the wilderness. On the 1899 trip, she camped unaccompanied north of
the Yellowstone River while her husband restocked provisions. On his return,
Ewen remarked that the folk of Terry thought it "dreadful that I could be left
here alone." Meanwhile, during the 1898 sojourn, Evelyn Cameron's prowess
as outdoorswoman contrasted sharply with female companion Effie, who
demanded tea in a china cup, dropped her "lucky stone," and occupied her
time on the trail confined to the tent with headaches. With Effie desperate

to get a "bag" but proficient only at scaring away game, Ewen expedited her departure by killing an antelope, which she promptly packed off to a taxidermist and packed out herself.[19]

Such entries convey an impression of Evelyn Cameron as an able outdoorswoman at ease in the wilds. Her aptitude with horse and rifle suggest entry into a domain usually reserved for men and, in fact, won her status as a regional luminary. On the way home from their 1895 hunt, the Camerons resided at the MacQueen House hotel in Miles City, where Evelyn received a billing suitable for a female hunter hero: "A lady Mrs Malone introduced me to in [the] sitting room said it was like talking to some character out of a book to talk to me!! The hunting trip seems to make them think the woman who hunts a wonder." Like Calamity Jane and other "wild women," Evelyn Cameron seemed to represent a living artifact of frontier whimsy and cut a radical presence in her articulations of sporting prowess. Locals talked in astonished tones of her predilection for "roughing it" when gathered at the Terry Post Office. Occasionally, her unabashed rejection of conventional gender binaries caused friction, notably in Miles City, where Cameron recalled that "a warning was given to me to abstain from riding on the streets . . . lest I might be arrested!" At the same time, however, Cameron managed to retain authority and decorum despite the tongue-wagging. A fusion of class, racial, and regional codes of identity help to explain such a process. Although Cameron transgressed gender boundaries, her educated aristocratic upbringing together with her settled life as a "rural masculine woman" allowed her to retain respect. She symbolized what historian Laura Browder has labeled "a powerful archetype of the armed western woman . . . skilled at using firearms, yet not violent, exotically different in her western attire, yet emphatically white and domestic." The ability to shelter children with one hand while shooting varmints in the other, ably celebrated in Leimbach's *Madonna of the Trail*, required a flexible approach to gender norms for the purposes of subsistence. As such, the skills required for life on the game trail by the female hunter hero—resilience, independence, woodcraft—seemed vital to the functioning of a successful homestead and emerged as integral parts of the frontierswoman's identity. Moreover, the experiences of hunting, the challenges, adventures, and routines of the great outdoors, fostered a sense of belonging and advanced a sense of selfhood for many frontierswomen. As Evelyn Cameron attested, "To the woman with outdoor propensities and a taste for roughing it there is no life more congenial than that of the saddle and rifle, as it may still be lived in parts of the Western states."[20]

In common with Evelyn Cameron, the hunting experiences of Agnes Morley Cleaveland highlighted codes of subsistence and belonging, adventuring in the wilderness, and female adaptability. Cleaveland was born in New Mexico and grew up on a ranch in Socorro in the 1880s where riding and shooting were part of a frontier education. After her father died from an accidental gunshot wound, she strayed into masculine domains for the purposes of necessity, maintaining a sense of femininity by riding sidesaddle yet working "side by side with the men, receiving the same praise or same censure for my undertakings." Offering pertinent commentary on the mythology of the masculine western hero and the subtle adjustments to gender norms invoked by circumstance, she noted that "men walked in a sort of perpetual adventure, but women waited—until perhaps lightning struck." Her experiences working on the ranch, like that of many frontier women, seemed representative of "a passive, unspectacular heroism." The title of Cleaveland's autobiography itself, *No Life for a Lady* (1941), hinted at the complex message of gender politics offered by the frontierswoman hunter. Where Isabella Bird stressed her feminine deportment and credo as a literary outdoorswoman in labeling her 1879 book *A Lady's Life in the Rocky Mountains*, Cleaveland played on customary ideas of the West as too wild and demanding for the gentler sex. Perhaps she did so for artistic flourish, to conform to literary tropes (evident in Elizabeth Custer's account of culture on the plains in *Following the Guidon*) or to stress her own femininity in a rough and ready frontier landscape demanding frequent renegotiations of so-called masculine and feminine pursuits.[21]

Cleaveland's hunting experiences highlighted the complex navigation of sexual categories undertaken by the frontierswoman on the game trail. Recalling a bear hunt in New Mexico, she spoke of the arrival of Montague Stephens, renowned hunter hero and author of *Meet Mr. Grizzly* (1890), at the ranch en route to meet General Miles for a ten-day sporting expedition. Learning that the general was otherwise indisposed, Agnes Cleaveland volunteered to take his place, a bold move that met the following retort from Stephens: "Hunting grizzlies isn't exactly a chivalrous pursuit. It could be extremely inconvenient to have a young lady along." Undeterred by Stephens's misogynistic banter, Cleaveland remonstrated as to her own prowess as a stalker of game and noted the presence of a large bear track not far from the ranch. Stephens relented and the hunt began. Making a satirical poke at gender binaries, Cleaveland noted that "male hunters will probably scoff at the impressions which were uppermost in a girl's mind" before offering details on the hounds and guns taken by the party, a detail, she explained, that was a "concession to the male viewpoint." This hunter heroine knew her own mind and was well versed in the social conventions of the game trail. Further navigations of gender etiquette emerged as her horse went lame and the party fretted about leaving Cleaveland alone. Encouraging them to proceed, she duly reminded Stephens of the "unchivalrous" culture expected of men on the trail. In any case, Cleaveland was familiar with the terrain, had a knife and matches, took confidence in the fact that all dangerous animals had been scared off by the less than stealthy stomping of her hunting partners, and betrayed "no terror" about spending the night in solitude. Like Cameron, Cleaveland knew the hinterlands around the ranch. This was *her* territory, a known and claimed space.[22]

Returning to camp, Agnes Cleaveland found the hunting party corralled together celebrating their killing of a bruin. Once more juxtaposing her matter-of-fact frontierswoman vantage with a feminine sensibility befitting of the model lady adventurer, she wrote, "I wanted to feel sorry for the bear, until I remembered what the carcass of one of our milk-pen calves looked like when we found it one morning, too far from home, with bear tracks all around it." Sympathy for the beast was further eroded when Agnes found herself sharing a horse with the bear's odorous hide. As the hunting excursion continued, Cleaveland was invited to shoot a bear for herself. Lured by campmate Dan's comment that "'tain't every girl can say she's killed a grizzly," she climbed a tree with gun poised while Stephens entered the den to look for bear sign. As the animal emerged from its cave, Cleaveland pulled the trigger only to imagine that she had actually shot Stephens, an illusion supported by his falling over a log at that precise moment. She spoke of a "spasm of agony" in thinking of her crime, panicked at finding her gun empty of cartridges, and entertained visions of the disgruntled bear returning to maul her. In the melee of the sporting moment, Cleaveland found herself reverting to "a badly scared girl in an awesome setting," her capable frontierswoman persona seemingly replaced by that of a helpless female out of place in the wilds. Cleaveland's multifarious activities on and around the ranch had necessitated frequent crossings of accustomed gender boundaries. With the domestic sphere extended for the purposes of household economics, she could track bear sign from the ranch, wander the game trail, and even appreciate the bear's perspective (and its destructive potential). However, the prospect of a direct showdown with an animal imbued with such symbolic import—a four-legged nemesis of the masculine hunter hero and a bellowing manifestation of nature red in tooth and claw—raised the specter of sexual stigma and an "unwomanly" identity.[23]

A glance at the experience of Elinore Pruitt Stewart suggests that such cultural tensions were commonplace for the hunter heroine. Born in 1876 in Fort Arkansas, Elinore grew up in Oklahoma before forging an itinerant existence following railroad crews after the death of her parents. She married a civil engineer and moved to Kansas, only to resettle in Denver with her daughter following the death of her husband in an industrial accident. Answering an advertisement for a housekeeper lodged by Scottish rancher Clyde Stewart, Elinore took up residence at the ranch at Burntfork, Wyoming, in April 1909. A profligate writer, Elinore used her correspondence with Mrs. Coney (for whom she worked as a laundrywoman in Denver) to chew over her daily activities, assuage the loneliness and drudgery of homestead life, and, pertinently, to "share adventures." Lively documents of the trials, routines, and vibrant eccentricities of frontier life at the turn of the nineteenth century, the letters were later serialized in the *Atlantic Monthly* and published in book form as *Letters of a Woman Homesteader* (1914) and *Letters on an Elk Hunt* (1915), both to considerable public and critical acclaim.[24]

Stewart's authorial voice was that of a strong pioneering woman striding forth, a widowed economic migrant making her way in a West of opportunity, socialization, and agrarian self-sufficiency. A work of historical fiction not without its fair share of self-invention—biographer Susanne K. George described Stewart's catalogue of her routines as "adventures"—the narrative nonetheless offered an appealing celebration of rural life, Anglo-Saxon folk tradition, and upward mobility on the frontier. It also alluded to what Janet Floyd has called "feminized frontier individualism," namely the matter-of-fact tenacity of the pioneer woman who found in the West "a separate sphere of activity and fulfillment that matched the masculine ideal." Stewart vividly described her running of the household economy (one letter talked of a day spent cutting hay, milking seven calves, and making thirty jars of jam and jelly), filing claim on her own homestead adjacent to the ranch, and having four children in as many years (Elinore and Clyde married eight weeks after her arrival at Burnt Fork). At the same time, her stories highlighted frictions regarding gendered space and work norms. Aware of the shortage of male labor, on one occasion Stewart took the horses out of the barn and mowed the field herself. Her responses proved intriguing, ranging from anxiety (fearing discovery by her husband) to confessional (that she enjoyed the experience) to pride at infringing on gender rules ("adding feathers in my cap in a surprising way"), yet she only gained final validation from a male audience (her husband said she had "almost as much sense as a 'mon'").[25]

Much of Stewart's writing in *Letters of a Woman Homesteader* concerned the domestic and the pastoral, a nod to Annette Kolodny's depiction of the frontierswoman taming the West from the hearth and the garden. However, her autobiographical voice also channeled that of the hunter heroine. One notable story in *Letters* described the occasion of a "most charming adventure," undertaken with her young daughter, camping and hunting in the mountain hinterlands. The idea sprang from an expedition undertaken by a group of local women who traveled across the Uinta Mountains to Utah, some hundred miles away, to buy fruit. Clyde forbade Elinore from attending out of concern for their toddler Jennie, a point that she understood, but she "continued to look abused lest he gets it into his head that he can boss me." A few days later, with the men away from camp on the roundup, Stewart decided the spell of the wild was too strong and planned her own camping trip. Following a track into the mountains, the mother and daughter set up camp and shot jackrabbits. Consciously invoking the specter of the hunter hero, she mused, "I felt very like Leather-stocking." A meal of bacon and coffee around a campfire and a serenade of coyotes sent them to sleep, while the glorious scenery of the trail prompted Stewart to compare the riches of an outdoors vocation with the recreational mores of her urban sisters: "I kept thinking how superior I was since I dared to take such an outing when so many poor women down in Denver were bent on making their twenty cents per hour in order that they could spare a quarter to go to the 'show.' I went to bed with a powerfully self-satisfied feeling." The next morning the pair awoke to find fifteen feet of snow and a blizzard, which Elinore Stewart greeted with Evelyn Cameron's resilience rather than Agnes Cleaveland's panic. She turned the horse loose to wander home (some thirty to forty

miles) to raise the alarm, stoked the fire, counted her ammunition (calcu-
lating that sixteen rounds meant food for thirty-two days), left her daughter
with a "baby" (a wrapped-up towel) to amuse her, and went off in search of
food. Returning to a conventional gender trope, the narrative from here on
centered on the motif of the vulnerable female rescued by the rugged outdoorsman, with Elinore and Jennie seeking refuge in a cabin frequented by
a southern trapper. Faced with two women knocking at the door, Zebulon
Pike Parker accused the visitors of spying for the game warden, but Elinore
assured him she was "no more than a foolish woman lost in the snow."[26]

Elinore Stewart's second compendium, *Letters on an Elk Hunt* (1915),
described a two-month camping expedition in the Green River in pursuit
of game. Stewart's testimony (like that of Cameron's) illuminated the critical location of the hunting trail in the mental and geographic landscape of
the pioneer woman. At the same time, the work was consciously framed
with publication in mind, thus revealing that connections between hunting,
storytelling, and performance were not confined to the masculine hunter
hero (or to lady adventurers or "wild women"). Throughout the trip, she
corresponded with an editor at the *Atlantic Monthly,* Ellery Sedgwick, who
followed her travels with interest (writing four days in, "I wonder how many
elk skins you are sleeping on at night") and offered advice on writing on the
move (advising her to give in to "the blind madness of writing . . . whether
an elk is sighted or not"). Like other self-conscious hunter heroines, Stewart
proved keen to assert the authenticity of her frontier credentials while playing to normative gender codes that defined her love of the outdoors as somewhat unusual. While the author was "powerfully glad" to be headed off
on an expedition she felt would be a "heap of fun," German neighbor Mrs.
Louderer failed to fathom the appeal of "roughing it" in the wilds: "For why
should I go? Vat? Iss it to freeze? I can sleep out on some rocks here and with
a stick I can beat the sage-brush, which will give me the smell of the outside.
And for the game I can have a beef kill which is better to eat as elk."[27]

Half of Stewart's *Letters* detailed the party's trek to the hunting grounds,
paying heed to the role of the quest in the descriptive paradigm of the hunter
hero, along with conventions of relating the charms of the country and the
pioneer personalities encountered on the way. On reaching the trailhead,
Stewart described wild land, beautiful animals, and rugged scenery in the
customary style. She noted the difficulty of climbing with a gun and, like

Agnes Cleaveland, found different codes of etiquette in play: "Men who are most gallant elsewhere are absolutely heartless on a hunt." Stewart presented herself as a rough and ready frontierswoman hunter heroine, noting that the women of the party were equally gripped by "a little of the hunter's enthusiasm." Despite paying lip service to the ideal of the female tenderfoot (both women injured themselves firing weapons), they were determined to make their own kills. Elinore Stewart vowed to remain on the game trail until she had bagged "her" elk (the privilege of which she had bought a license for, unlike the barbaric and destructive "tooth-hunters"), while Mrs. O'Shaughnessy shot two elk that were packed out to provide "many a meal . . . for little hungry mouths." Back home and sitting in her rocking chair, Stewart confessed a new appreciation for the domestic comforts of the homestead, her family, garden pansies, and animals, but maintained a fond recollection of the hunting trail nonetheless, a fantasy adventure that seemed enriching to both spirit and stomach. Conjuring a transformative landscape common in the canonical tradition of the hunter hero, she noted: "Our experiences on our trip seem almost unreal, but the wagonload of meat to be attended to is a reminder of realities. I have had a fine trip; I have experienced about all human emotions."[28]

Stewart presented an erudite exercise in the codes of the frontierswoman hunter heroine, a voyage of adventure, and a cast of lively frontier characters, captivating animals, and charming landscapes. As Susanne George notes, the descriptive turn of the elk hunt also represented an exercise in "social documentation," of confirming a process of belonging and of frontier socialization. A disconnect between the plucky hunter heroine schooled in the descriptive turn of the chase and Stewart's moral views of hunting nonetheless emerged in her private correspondence. As she wrote in a letter to friend, "I am a rank fraud. I *hate* guns." Believing it a prerequisite of frontier life, Stewart explained that she had tried to learn to acquit herself with a rifle by firing rounds at sage chickens, "to make believe I liked to shoot," yet ultimately found herself uneasy over the kill and the inevitable encounter with "dying agony." In *Letters*, however, the voice of the "trembly kneed coward when it comes to shooting the wild creatures just for the name of doing so" was subsumed before the countenance of the robust hunter heroine. "Of course the publishers suppose me to have a little courage and valor," she noted, but "if in any letters it seems as if I enjoyed *hunting* you will know that is humbug." Such remarks suggest a need for caution in reading the "truths" of nineteenth-century trail testimony, and, perhaps more interestingly, they elucidate the centrality of performance on the hunting trail itself. For women as well as men, a penchant for the chase seemed part of the normative codes of frontier life.[29]

BUCKSKIN SUIT OR SIDESADDLE?: GENDER POLITICS AND THE NEGOTIATIONS OF THE FEMALE HUNTER HERO

In a review of Annette Kolodny's *The Land Before Her* (1984), geographer Jeanne Kay writes, "The American pioneer: male or female? Clad in a buckskin hunting shirt or a gingham dress? Subduing a virgin wilderness or nurturing a garden?" Such commentary suggested that the game trail was no place for a woman. However, a glance at the nineteenth-century female hunter hero suggests a different reading. Hunting became part of the subsistence culture of the female pioneer and a recreational pastime for lady adventurers. The game trail promised exhilaration, an encounter with wild nature and settler culture and the chance to cultivate independence, a sense of belonging and personal edification. It also emerged as a critical performance space around which women told stories about the West and ruminated on their place in landscapes both material and fantastical.[30]

With its narratives of personal endurance, romantic affectations, catalogue of animal habits, and musings on etiquette and social custom, the testimony of the hunter heroine pointed toward a new performance on the hunting frontier that challenged the masculine hegemony. In the noted article "A Woman's Big Game Hunting," the *New York Sun* marveled at Evelyn Cameron's journey from tenderfoot to accomplished frontierswoman, telling stories of sharpshooting women, wilderness adventure, and animal contest to rival that of any frontiersman: "I've spent January and February in a tiny Indian tent . . . with the mercury 40 degrees below zero, and our noses and chins were all blistered with the cold. And I've had my hair frizzled by lightning so that it made a cracking sound." The mantra of the hunter hero and the hunter heroine were eminently translatable.[31]

The female hunter hero cut a radical presence in challenging the boundaries of women's work and play—contesting the stereotype of women as feeble, pedestrian, and dependent on men while pointing to a new angle on the "female frontier" in terms of the gender dynamics of westward conquest. The game trail elucidated the ways in which, for purposes of adventure as well as economic need, women operated beyond the cult of true woman-hood. Ernest Thompson Seton, for instance, issued firm praise of his wife: she was "a dead shot with a rifle, often far ahead of the guides, and met all kinds of danger with unflinching nerve." Straying beyond the domestic confines of hearth and garden, women found in the landscape of the hunt a place for the loosening of cultural norms. Not all walked the path of Grace Seton, who strode from the game trail to become an activist for equal voting rights, but successful hunting endeavors undoubtedly fostered the idea of women as strong, resilient, and competent in realms typically seen as the preserve of men. Determining firm linkages between the hunting cultures in the West and the adoption of female suffrage (Wyoming granted women the vote in 1869, followed by nine other western states before 1916) may well be difficult, but the notion that women could hold their own with a gun and a horse demonstrated possession of a skill set held in high regard. As historian Daniel Herman notes, "If women were strong enough to hunt they were strong enough to enter politics and business."[32]

The women discussed in this chapter found in the West an opportunity to expand into spheres considered the domain of men and eagerly embraced the mantle of hunter heroism and its associated performance staples. Yet one might still ponder whether their hunting activities facilitated decisive social change in the status of women. The lady adventurer and the frontierswoman apprehended the game trail with delight and devotion, but many of these women proved marginal, atypical, even deviant figures. The majority of hunting narratives continued to subscribe to the dominant paradigm of the male hero pitted against a suitably virile (and masculinized) animal neme-sis, with women relegated to bystanders at the main performance. Elizabeth Custer's *Following the Guidon* proved emblematic in its elevation of military heroism and simpering female sycophancy. Those women who sought to capture the trophy of hunter heroine for themselves faced the possibility of enervating social commentary, accusations of deviance, and sexual stigma based on their supposedly "manly" traits and success on the game trail. It was socially acceptable to celebrate a sense of adventurous spirit or pioneer resourcefulness when tied to a sense of imperial progress or robust domes-ticity, but when hunter heroines beat the masculine hero at his own game, that was potentially more problematic. When commentator W. Davenport Adams cheered Isabella Bird for "never wanting in courage or resolution," he celebrated her resolve. His verdict that she "carried in her bosom a man's heart" nonetheless raised more complicated questions about normative gender traits and their transgression. Whether to wear buckskin or calico, to ride astride or adopt the sidesaddle, embroiled the hunter heroine in a complicated sociopolitical topography of socially constructed "male" and "female" behaviorisms and pertained to sporting practicality as well. Some women stridently espoused their affection for hunting, reclaiming the (albeit limited) territory of gender renegotiation by riding roughshod over criticism with well-placed acerbic retorts and a preference for solitary travel. Others qualified their orations by playing submissive helpmate or sentimental traveler, grounding themselves in the comforting shroud of gender conventions. For some, this was a self-directed mechanism to protect and proclaim their feminine identity, for others, a conscious tactic to secure social acceptability while skillfully negotiating the limits of gender heterodoxy. As Glenda Riley observed, "A significant number of western women . . . kept going, finding ways to appear domestic while doing what they wanted to do." Outfoxing the dichotomies of a gender binary, like prey, seemed a matter of reconnaissance, subtlety, and noticing the right moment to strike—rather like Evelyn Cameron, who, after sweeping clean the floor of the hunting shack, assumed the modal stance of the hunter hero by adorning its walls with trophy illustrations taken from her Winchester cartridge packets.[33]

NOTES

The epigraph is from Nannie Alderson and Helena Huntington Smith, *A Bride Goes West* (Lincoln: University of Nebraska Press, 1942), 221.

1. John Frost, *Heroes and Hunters of the West* (Philadelphia: Peck and Bliss, 1855), vii.

2. Elizabeth Custer, *Following the Guidon* (New York: Harper and Bros., 1890), 194–212; Glenda Riley, *The Female Frontier: A Comparative View of Women on the Prairie and the Plains* (Lawrence: University Press of Kansas, 1988), 4; Wallace Stegner, *The Sound of Mountain Water* (New York: Dutton, 1980), 195; Henry Nash Smith, *Virgin Land: The American West as Symbol and Myth* (Cambridge, MA: Harvard University Press, 1978), 12; Larry McMurtry, *In a Narrow Grave: Essays on Texas* (Albuquerque: University of New Mexico Press, 1968), 44; Julie Roy Jeffrey, *Frontier Women:*

The Trans-Mississippi West (New York: Hill and Wang, 1979), 73; Annette Kolodny, *The Lay of the Land: Metaphor as Experience and History in American Life and Letters* (Chapel Hill: University of North Carolina Press, 1975), xiii.

3. M. F. Belenky, B. M. Clinchy, N. R. Goldberger, and J. M. Tarule, *Women's Ways of Knowing: The Development of Self, Voice, and Mind* (New York: Basic Books, 1986); Laura Browder, *Her Best Shot: Women and Guns in America* (Chapel Hill: University of North Carolina Press, 2006), 76–77.

4. Susan Margaret McKinnon St. Maur, *Impressions of a Tenderfoot during a Journey in Search of Sport in the Far West* (London: J. Murray, 1890), vii; *St. Louis Globe Democrat*, April 30, 1905.

5. "Our Lady Sportsmen," *Forest and Stream* 1 (January 15, 1874): 361; Andrea L. Smalley, "'Our Lady Sportsmen': Gender, Class, and Conservation in Sport Hunting Magazines, 1873–1920," *Journal of the Gilded Age and Progressive Era* 4 (October 2005): 377. See also Carolyn Merchant, "George Bird Grinnell's Audubon Society: Bridging the Gender Divide in Conservation," *Environmental History* 15 (January 2010): 3–30.

6. Isabella Bird, *A Lady's Life in the Rocky Mountains* (Norman: University of Oklahoma Press, 1960 [1879]), 54, 104; Joyce Kelley, "Increasingly 'Imaginative Geographies': Excursions into Otherness, Fantasy, and Modernism in Early Twentieth-Century Women's Travel Writing," *Journal of Narrative Technique* 35, no. 3 (2005): 357.

7. Bird, *Lady's Life*, 34, 78, 73, 102; Kay Chubbuck, ed., *Letters to Henrietta* (Boston: Northeastern, 2003), 148.

8. Bird, *Lady's Life*, 177, 52; Chubbuck, *Letters to Henrietta*, 154.

9. Grace Gallatin Thompson Seton, *A Woman Tenderfoot* (New York: Doubleday, Page & Co., 1905 [1900]); Grace Gallatin Thompson Seton, *The Log of the "Look See": A Half-Year in the Wilds of Matto Grosso and the Paraguayan Forest, over the Andes to Peru* (London: Hurst and Blackett, 1932), 133.

10. Lucinda MacKethan, "Grace Gallatin Thompson Seton: Excerpt from *A Woman Tenderfoot*," *Legacy: A Journal of American Women Writers* 27, no. 1 (2010): 195–97.

11. Seton, *Woman Tenderfoot*, 7, 15, 16, 17–58; Mrs. Stuart Menzies, *Women in the Hunting Field* (London: Vinton, 1913); Lady Violet Greville, *Ladies in the Field* (New York: D. Appleton, 1894).

12. Seton, *Woman Tenderfoot*, 21, 82, 357, 22, 79, 145, 32, 196, 361.

13. Dorcas Miller, *Adventurous Women: The Inspiring Lives of Nine Early Outdoorswomen* (Boulder, CO: Pruett Publishing, 2000), 83; Seton, *Woman Tenderfoot*, 361, 283, 102, 105, 83.

14. Seton, *Woman Tenderfoot*, 25, 284; *London Times*, November 21, 1879, 3; Pat Barr, *A Curious Life for a Lady: The Story of Isabella Bird, Traveller Extraordinary* (Middlesex: Penguin, 1970), 184.

15. *Good Housekeeping*, February 25, 1912, cited in MacKethan, "Grace Gallatin Thompson Seton," 195; Seton, *Woman Tenderfoot*, 84–87, 92–94, 172–81.

16. Ewen Cameron quoted in Donna M. Lucey, *Photographing Montana, 1894–1928: The Life and Work of Evelyn Cameron* (Missoula, MT: Mountain Press Publishing, 2001), 10.

17. For detail on the Camerons' lives, notably Evelyn's journals from 1893 to 1900, see Evelyn J. and Ewen S. Papers, MC226, Montana Historical Society Research Center, Helena (hereafter cited as MHS); Evelyn Cameron, Diary for 1893, Box 1, Folder 4, Diaries 1893–94, Evelyn J. and Ewen Cameron Papers, MC226, MHS; "A Woman's Big Game Hunting," *New York Sun*, November 4, 1900.

18. Cameron, Diary for 1893; Ewen Cameron, "Sport in the Badlands of Montana, USA," Box 6, Folder 13, Evelyn J. and Ewen Cameron Papers, MC226, MHS.

19. Evelyn Cameron, Diary for 1899, Box 2, Folder 1, Diaries 1899–1900, Evelyn J. and Ewen Cameron Papers, MC226, MHS; Evelyn Cameron, Diary for 1898, Box 1, Folder 6, Diaries 1897–98, Evelyn J. and Ewen Cameron Papers, MC226, MHS.

20. Evelyn Cameron, Diary for 1895, Box 1, Folder 5, Diaries 1895–96, Evelyn J. and Ewen Cameron Papers, MC226, MHS; Evelyn Cameron, Diary for 1893 and Diary for 1894, Box 1, Folder 4, Diaries, 1893–94, MC226, MHS; Evelyn Cameron, Diary for 1898; Evelyn Cameron, "'The Cowgirl' in Montana," *Country Life*, June 16, 1914; Judith Halberstam, *Female Masculinity* (Durham, NC: Duke University Press, 1998), 58; Laura Browder, *Women and Guns in America* (Chapel Hill: University of North Carolina Press, 2006), 75; "A Woman's Big Game Hunting."

21. Agnes Morley Cleaveland, *No Life for a Lady* (Boston: Houghton Mifflin, 1941), 127, 156, 157.

22. Ibid., 204, 205, 208.

23. Ibid., 210, 216–18.

24. Elinore Pruitt Stewart, *Letters on an Elk Hunt by a Woman Homesteader* (Lincoln: University of Nebraska Press, 1979 [1915]), vi.

25. Elinore Pruitt Stewart, *Letters of a Woman Homesteader* (Boston: Houghton Mifflin, 1914), 17–18, 15–17; Janet Floyd, *Writing: The Pioneer Women* (Columbia: University of Missouri Press, 2002), 25; Susanne K. George, *The Adventures of the Woman Homesteader: The Life and Letters of Elinore Pruitt Stewart* (Lincoln: University of Nebraska Press, 1992), xiii.

26. Stewart, *Letters of a Woman*, 23–44.

27. Stewart, *Letters on an Elk Hunt*, 13, 14.

28. Ibid., 99, 100, 104–5, 161.

29. George, *Adventures*, 30–31, 199.

30. Jeanne Kay, "Review of Annette Kolodny, *The Land before Her* (1984)," *Annals of the Association of American Geographers* 75, no. 3 (September 1985): 459.

31. "A Woman's Big Game Hunting."

32. Ernest Thompson Seton, *Trail of an Artist-Naturalist: The Autobiography of Ernest Thompson Seton* (New York: Charles Scribner's Sons, 1940), 343. The absence of a female Daniel Boone figure is noted in Annette Kolodny's *The Land before Her: Fantasy and Experience of the American Frontiers, 1630–1860* (Chapel Hill: University of North Carolina Press), 4; Daniel Herman, *Hunting and the American Imagination* (Washington, DC: Smithsonian Institution Press), 231.

33. W. H. Davenport Adams, *Celebrated Women Travellers of the Nineteenth Century* (New York: E. P. Dutton, 1903), 433; Glenda Riley, *Confronting Race: Women and Indians on the Frontier* (Albuquerque: University of New Mexico Press, 2004), 28.

THE "AFTERLIFE" OF THE HUNT

STORY, IMAGE, AND TROPHY

LANDSCAPES OF TESTIMONY

Performing the Game Trail in Literature, Art, and Photography

In *Hunting Trips of a Ranchman* (1885), Theodore Roosevelt described a candlelight scene at his "home-ranch" in the Badlands. Casting his gaze from the broad prairies to the cabin's interior with its deer antlers over the fireplace, stacked rifles, sporting writings, and cowboy chatter, Roosevelt offered at once a celebration of the western environment and its material culture. In this idealized space, hunting represented the habitual activity of the sporting rancher (of which Roosevelt represented an archetype). As he effused, "No rancher who loves sport can afford to be without Van Dyke's *Still Hunter*, Dodge's *Plains of the Great West* or Caton's *Deer and Antelope of America*; and Coues's *Birds of the North-west.*" The rough-hewn bookshelves of the log cabin represented an important locus of translation between the game trail and its imprint in literary and visual culture, from the hunting encounter to a new performance in its "afterlife."[1]

The frontier West provided the sporting fraternity with a vivid landscape of monumental nature, pioneer spirit, gunplay, and the sacred stalk, earning it the moniker of game utopia in the mind's eye of many a hunter. However,

DOI: 10.5876/9781607323983.c004

this experience ended on the hunting trail unless hunters could find a way of recording their endeavors, of capturing the essence of the chase and preserving its memory. "Packing out" meant not only hauling equipment and trophies but also transmitting the stories of the trail. In order to ensure its continued relevance, the performance of the hunt demanded a retelling for the men (and, indeed, the women) who roamed western haunts. Joining *Hunting Trips of a Ranchman*, then, were a legion of testimonials that kept the spirit of the chase alive and collectively broadcast a rich narrative landscape of hunter's paradise.

Intimate tales of the trail allowed the hunter to articulate the significance of the hunting moment—the epiphany in the wilderness—for the purposes of memorialization, identity politics, and environmental claim. Communication of experience seemed an important part of performance code, especially for the "sports" that visited the West to claim its signature animals, and this was manifested in a rich testimonial culture spanning visual and literary media. As Peregrine Herne lyricized in *Perils and Pleasures of a Hunter's Life, or the Romance of Hunting* (1858), "I love to paint those scenes with words." The curatorial gaze of the hunter hero was introspective—the urge to "write" the hunt a scripted affirmation of heroic endeavors, communing with nature and emerging victorious from the timberline with story and trophy in tow. At the same time, the formative frontier experiences of the embodied hunter hero required an audience, and this was found in the hunting community as well as a broader public whose principal engagement with the frontier came secondhand. The hunt, it seemed, could be performed as "lived experience" and also enjoyed by proxy. Exuding themes of wilderness exoticism, civilized saber rattling, and all-action histrionics, the easily translatable "story" of the game trail as depicted by the hunter's repertory allowed the testimonial culture of the hunting fraternity to feed into the broader folklore of the West that was under construction in the latter years of the nineteenth century. "Hunter's paradise" thus became an intrinsic part of the collective mythology of the frontier, acted and reenacted to form a transnational "community of memory" that encompassed both personal reminiscence and popular digest. Told and retold in print and image, the imagined frontier was enshrined as a landscape of great portent—ritual and repeated performance ensuring its commitment to posterity. As Richard Slotkin notes, "Preserved in the form of narrative . . . through periodic retellings those narratives become traditionalized." Played out by hunter actors and consumed and embellished in equal measure by a cadre of readers enraptured by the idea of a western landscape brimming with hunting adventure, the performance dynamics of the hunting frontier West were multilayered.[2]

PERFORMING THE HUNT AS STORIED LANDSCAPE

When Euro-Americans described hunting exploits in the West, they were only the latest witnesses to an imaginative geography. American Indian communities had crafted a storytelling tradition around the hunt for centuries. The Crow told how "Old Man Coyote" taught the tribe about the merits of the buffalo jump by challenging people and bison to a race, while the Yakima exchanged tales about the Phantom Buck, a huge animal with white spots that had the power to repel arms. For the Kutenai, "story" itself carried such power that hunters refused to tell anyone if they were going after bear, because the animals would hear and thus be forewarned. A richly storied landscape, the western hunting trail was a site of environmental encounter and cultural communication long in the making.[3]

In Euro-American tradition, the performance of the hunt in story began at the campfire, where the hunting fraternity gathered at the close of day to trade stories of wild things. George Shields fondly recalled sitting around the fire engaged in "the recital of the day's adventures and triumphs." The smoldering fire provided a hub around which the hunt could be teased out, chewed over, and memorialized. It was a space set aside for performance (alongside subsistence functions of warmth, food, and security). In a process of narrative map making, hunters here shared trailside intimacies and gave first airing to their stories of wilderness exploration, contest, and camaraderie. Such conversations extended well beyond the game trail, suggesting few geographical boundaries to the transmission of a testimonial landscape. William Kingston, a British sport hunter who visited Missouri, Kansas, and the Rockies, recalled that his peers "frequently afterwards met in old England . . . where many a long yarn was spun about our adventures in the wild regions of the 'far West.'"[4]

Print culture continued and extended the story of the hunt, with the imaginative space of the West unfolding on every page. Literary media spanned various genres, including sporting press, fiction, nonfiction and autobiography, each of which delivered its own take on hunting dynamics. From inauspicious beginnings in *The Sports Man's Companion* (1783), the sporting manual by the 1840s had become a buoyant industry, expressed in the fascination surrounding the woods lore of Frank Forester as well as numerous hunting guides, including New York–based *Spirit of the Times* (1831), with a circulation of 22,000. Such publications offered technical guidance to the sporting community and also narrated the conquest of the West in journal form. *American Turf Register and Sporting Magazine*, for instance, reprinted the letters of George Catlin, while *Spirit of the Times* had a regular column entitled "occidental reminiscences, farther West" in 1845–46. Such tomes stressed, in the words of David Cartwright's *Natural History of Western Wild Animals and Guide for Hunters, Trappers and Sportsmen* (1875), "practical knowledge" as well as "narratives of personal adventure" that communicated the colonization of the frontier as well as the inculcation of hunter's paradise as a trope. With the 1870s came further iterations of sporting print culture in the form of the magazine *Forest and Stream* as well as book runs from the Boone and Crockett Club. In these publications the West loomed large as a trophy of the sporting imagination. Part of *Forest and Stream's* objective was to serve as gazetteer for a specialist community seeking what and where to hunt within a wider remit of "entertainment, instruction and information." As editor George Grinnell wrote to a potential advertising customer in the shape of the Denver and Rio Grande Railroad, "It is not random firing. Every copy goes into the hands of a sportsman."[5]

Adventure fiction, expressed in books, newspapers such as New York's *Herald* and *Tribune*, and high-circulation magazines, including the *Atlantic, Harper's Weekly,* and *Frank Leslie's Illustrated,* abetted in the creation of a cult of the frontier based on conquest, Indian attack, rugged individualism, and glorified violence. Here, too, the hunt was performed in all its dynamic glory, offering chronology, characters, and choreography to the western story. The dime novel, in particular, broadcast the figure of the hunter hero and the heroic geography of the trans-Mississippi. According to Philip Durham, three-quarters of all Beadle and Adams dime novels related to "the various forms, problems and attitudes of life on the frontier." "The Young Trail Hunters: or New York Boys in Grizzly Land," written by T. C. Harbaugh for *Beadle's Boys Library of Sport, Story and Adventure* in 1900, aggrandized the Rockies as "one of the grandest hunting-grounds on the face of the globe," an ideal location for the eastern boys (and some girls) raised on a diet of frontier fantasy to exercise their ambitions as hunter heroes in the making. Armed with brand new Winchester rifles, the trio in Harbaugh's story braved bison hunting, unknown trails, and Indian attacks to find their inner Nimrod. George Lasalle's "Burt Bunker, the Trapper—A Tale of the North West Hunting Grounds," a title in *Beadle's Half Dime Library* (1878), swapped the tenderfoot imagery for the "grizzled old prairie veteran" in telling the story of Burt, "the hero of many a thrilling adventure." With his "herculean frame" and his rifle "Betsy Jane," Burt strode forth as an exemplar of American pioneer masculinity in the canonical tradition.[6]

Alongside sporting press and adventure fiction, the story of the West as hunter's paradise gained broadcast in hagiographical accounts. Accounts of the lives of notable frontier folk attested to popular interest in the winning of the West and in the lives of "great men" (and sometimes women). This literature gloried in exceptional feats and the larger-than-life personalities that roamed a wild terrain, ably illuminated in such texts as *Famous Frontiersmen, Pioneers and Scouts: The Vanguards of American Civilization* (1880). Significantly, the frontier hero was more often than not dressed in the garb (both literally and figuratively) of the hunter. Such a label proved important, first, in highlighting the game trail as a locus of national renewal and socio-economic portent and, second, in situating the hunter as a heroic figure and an archetype of patriotic strength. Available for public digest and mental vivification were a roster of (usually male) performers, including Daniel Boone (the pathfinder), George Armstrong Custer (technically a soldier hero, but his writings were full of hunting stories), Theodore Roosevelt (the hunter naturalist), Buffalo Bill (sharpshooting scout and showman extraordinaire), James "Grizzly" Adams (wild man and theatrical tamer of the wilds), and Calamity Jane (hard-drinking "wild woman," scout, and all-round raconteur). The antics of the frontier hunter was equal parts enthralling and instructive. B. Hartley, author of *Hunting Sports of the West* (1865), saw his book as of dual cultural value: first, in providing entertainment for "a large class of readers who are always delighted with the narratives which abound in wild adventures, thrilling incidents and hair breadth escapes" and, second, of "positive utility" in depicting individuals whose qualities of "perseverance, presence of mind in danger, endurance, enterprise . . . are not unworthy of study and imitation." Codes of renewal and vigor translated from game trail to the pages of fiction, suggesting a blurring of boundaries between an experience "lived" and "read" as well as the application of Frederick Jackson Turner's frontier thesis to print culture. Lofting the hunter hero as a paragon of American masculinity, Hartley issued forth a striking and evocative picture of a man wrapped in the codes and colors of the game trail:

> His dress, you observe, consists of a leather hunting shirt, and a pair of trousers of the same material. His feet are well Moccasoned. He wears a belt round his waist, his heavy rifle is resting on his brawny shoulder; on one side hangs his ball pouch, surmounted by the horn of an ancient buffalo, once the terror of the herd, now containing a pound of the best gunpowder; his butcher-knife is scabbarded in the same strap, and behind is a tomahawk, the handle of which has been thrust through his girdle. He walks with so rapid a step, that probably few men could follow him, unless for a short distance, in their anxiety to witness his ruthless deeds. He stops, looks at the flint of his gun, its priming, and the leather cover of the lock, then glances his eye towards the sky, to judge the course most likely to lead him to the game.

A "monumental figure" standing before the game and the reading public, Hartley's beatitude to the hunter encompassed a list of core traits: dependable explorer, trophy-adorned indigene, brave sharpshooter, and witness to the West, all bound up in a mantle of adventuring swagger that was eminently theatrical. The impression was iconic, visual, and, significantly for the purposes of storytelling, one of resolute action. As Hartley advised, "His rifle is raised, the report follows, and he runs. Let us run also."[7]

AUTHENTICITY AND AUTOBIOGRAPHY

Resonant in the storied performance of the hunt was a sense of true-life adventure. As *Heroes and Hunters of the West* (1869) advised, "The exploits of the heroes of the West, need but a simple narration to give them an irresistible charm." In that sense, the literary landscape of the hunter hero represented a worthy heir to the campfire story and the trailside journal. Reviewing *Letters on an Elk Hunt* (1915), the *Boston Transcript* applauded Elinore Stewart's account of the "little daily occurrences" on the trail and essentialized its appeal as the "natural recital" of "an ordinary woman." Translated from the tracks of the West to popular literature, Stewart's personal story allowed readers to take to the game trail for themselves—in the words of the *Transcript,* "we feel with her the zest and the pathos of the chase." As she trudged the trail, so did the reader: the performance was shared through the transmission of testimony. As such, the most expansive articulation (and dissemination) of hunter's paradise lay in autobiographical literature. Here the afterlife of the hunt was allowed its full historical, mimetic, and metaphysical denouement, seemingly unadulterated and as raw as the lands it purported to describe.[8]

Hunting autobiographies proliferated on both sides of the Atlantic during the 1800s to become a recognizable genre. Often these narratives offered a metropolitan gaze, from the vantage of the civilized viewing a landscape of otherness. The hunting story crafted the West as an exotic space set apart from "real life" in the parlance of Edgar Randolph. Hunting stories were typically written by tourists, wealthy sportsmen heralding from the East and from Europe, and often bore the imprint of New York and London publishing houses. In this sense, tales of the game trail formed part of an elite Anglo-American imperial discourse, of the claiming of space as well as story through the recollection of frontier experience. Significantly, however, the hunting testimonial also emerged as a product authored by westerners. Here, too, the notion of claiming territory (and indeed regional identity) through the hunting tale proved important. In *Memoirs of a Hunter: Fifty-Eight Years of Hunting and Fishing* (1948), Charles Myers—who moved to Wallula, Washington, in 1860 in pursuit of good hunting—stressed the down-to-earth quality of his testimony:

> The character sketches of my pioneer neighbors, hunting and fishing trips
> told of in the following chapters, are set forth with no pretense of any literary
> style, but in an offhand way as I remember them. Many of the hunting and
> fishing trips are carbon copies of letters written almost immediately after the
> excursions in out-door recreations. I have religiously avoided any attempt to
> dramatize any of the incidents of the stories of rod and gun, but have endeav-
> oured to hold high the noble art of hunting and fishing, since it begets health,
> prolongs life and makes enduring friendships.

As a label, hunter's paradise was etched on the West from outsiders and insiders, tourists and settlers alike. Titles from prominent Montanans William Pickett and Malcolm Mackay gainfully promoted their home as a game utopia. Mackay himself became an eager collector of Charlie Russell prints, judging the rugged West on canvas as a timely reminder of a landscape that had now passed. Russell in turn drew the illustrations for Mackay's memoir. William Pickett, meanwhile, authored pieces for the sporting press while his published diary appeared in the Boone and Crockett Club's homage to the game trail, *Hunting at High Altitudes* (1913). These texts spoke of thrilling encounters, adventuring in the wilderness in the genre mold, but also charted a process of exploration, ownership, and identity formation.[9]

Also important to note was the fact that the hunting autobiography encompassed both women and men writers. The imperial tour of the lady adventurer (and attendant travelogue), chronicles of pioneer homesteading, and the broadcast of tales of "wild women" such as Calamity Jane provided a crop of literary hunter heroines to match tales of masculine adventuring in the wilds, at least in terms of scope if not in print quantity. Intimate recollections of wilderness exploration and hunting escapades included Marianne North's *Recollections of a Happy Life* (1892), Theodora Guest's *Round Trip in North America* (1895), and Courtney Borden's *Adventures in a Man's World: The Initiation of a Sportsman's Wife* (1933) as well as those works discussed in the previous chapter from the likes of Grace Gallatin Thompson Seton, Elinore Stewart, and Agnes Cleaveland. In common with their male counterparts, women travelers and pioneers saw the autobiography as a critical locus of reflection, proving, and literary erudition, constructing in the process their corollary reputation as hunter heroines.[10]

The writer "Heclawa" noted the plethora of published hunting autobiographies in the preface to *In the Heart of the Bitter-Root Mountains* (1895): "The author is fully conscious of the fact that he is adding another to the vast number of books on hunting and kindred subjects with which the bookstores are already flooded." Why did so many hunters choose to publish their memoirs? Justifications (often included in book prefaces) often centered on ideas of personal and nostalgic record. By performing the hunt in print, it was cemented for posterity. Indeed, one might argue that the hunt was only completed by the appearance of a published tome, a trophy to signal the provenance of the hunter hero (and heroine) over both story and landscape. As such, the hunting autobiography was an artifact heavily imprinted with operative meaning, a curated object that laid out the idealized self of the hunter hero. This was, however, often a somewhat clandestine performance. Clothed in the discourse of chronicle, the testimonial literature of the game trail typically stressed freshness and factual report. Thus, while authors often remarked on the fact that they were writing in (and sometimes for) a specific "genre," the existence of narrative formulae was obscured by an insistence on the individuality of an experience that was unscripted and as "raw" as the landscape it purported to describe. Lincoln Ellsworth, writing of his book *The Last Buffalo Hunt*, noted: "The story (if such it can be called) was all written on the day following my return from the hunt in my room in a little frontier hotel. It is little more than a diary account of facts, written before the glow from the good outdoors had worn off and intended as a memory in after years."[11]

Memorialization dominated the autobiographical landscape of the hunt. *Gun and Palette in the High Rockies* (1914) by William Wroe was conceived "as a little souvenir and record of the trip for distribution among our friends," while Henry Bannon hoped that by writing his hunting story down it might spare him the tedium of repeating it to countless friends back home. In general, testimonial culture resonated with the idea of recording the historical moment and allowing the author to "relive" it via ritual rendition. This was a performance in and of itself. According to Vermont writer and illustrator Rowland Robinson, the replaying of the hunt via literary reportage allowed for the vaulting of geographical and temporal boundaries and thus permitted the "imprisoned sportsman" to travel "to the freedom of outdoors."[12]

Also frequent in justifications for writing was reference to historical portent and an era now vanished. The performance of the hunt was timely, above all else. William Allen in *Adventures with Indians and Game* (1903) offered memories of a region "wrested from savage domination for the establishment of civilization by that class of timeless, brave and heroic pioneers, of which the author is a notable example." R. B. Marcy described his *Thirty Years of Army Life on the Border* (1866) as a document of a "fast vanishing race" and wild animals destined to disappear in a "world fast filling up" as well as his "experience in the life of a frontiersman." In a sense, the narrative of a "lost age" imparted a degree of gravitas, attaching the personal testimony of the author to a distinct "epoch" and contributing to a broader discourse on the "vanishing frontier" that effectively subsumed history and theater in a grand narrative of westward expansion.[13]

In a performance sense, the written word allowed the authors to confirm their hunting credentials and adopt the trappings (and associated kudos) of trusted narrator. The dramatic purchase of the hunt, after all, depended on a convincing actor as well as captivating script. Authenticity was absolutely integral to the provenance of the writing project. As *The Spectator* said of Isabella Bird's *A Lady's Life in the Rocky Mountains* (1879), here was "spontaneous and unadorned narrative." Common in autobiographical literature, then, was a conscious positioning of the author as expert witness. John Mortimer Murphy's *Sporting Adventures in the Far West* (1870) was typical of many texts in promising to communicate the tenor (if not the full transcript) of actual conversations from "around the campfire or in the Indian's wigwam."[14]

Cast as erudite chroniclers of the frontier (by themselves and their readers), the hunter heroes of popular literature often strayed into the realms of instruction, not only narrating frontier exploits but also offering advice for others. Performing the hunt, in this context, meant assuming the guise of hunting guide—a label of great substance for those who had trailed the West and imbibed the teachings of local scouts. George Shields published *Rustlings in the Rockies* (1883) hoping to inculcate in the reading public a sense of the benefits of "healthy outdoor sports" as well as "a desire to participate in such scenes and pleasures." A follow-up book, *Cruising in the Cascades: And Other Hunting Adventures* (1889), articulated similar goals (as well as a more cynical admission that *Rustlings* had been financially lucrative). For Grantley Berkeley, correspondent for *The Field* and author of *The English Sportsman in the Western Prairies* (1861), the written performance of his western trip was consciously undertaken to "tell Englishmen in what ways they should proceed on a visit . . . what adventures they would most likely encounter, what would be the costs of their journey, and how they best fit themselves out and at the least expense." Berkeley hoped that the bison he had shipped home, stuffed and exhibited in the window of the London offices of *The Field*, would offer additional inducement based on material proof: "My brother sportsmen will be able to judge of the game the plains afford."[15]

Female authors offered specific guidance on how to perform the hunt as a woman. Offering tuition for trailing spouses or solo adventurers as to the "proper" navigation of geographical and gender boundaries, their testimonials pointed to the complex cultural codes at play on the game trail as well as the function of popular literature in upholding and challenging gender heterodoxy. Grace Seton's *A Woman Tenderfoot* (1900) began with an invocation that stressed her authenticity as narrator and the value of a female perspective on the game trail. Such introductions proved common in the vernacular of the literary outdoorswoman. As Seton explained, "This book is a tribute to the West . . . the events related really happened . . . and this is why, being a woman, I wanted to tell you about them, in the hope that some going-to-Europe-in-the-summer-woman may be tempted to go West instead." Her husband, named "Nimrod" after the elite hunter of classical legend, was established early as "alpha male" with the authoress as "helpmate." It was he who succumbed to the "mountain madness" while she played reluctant traveler forced to tuck "my summer-watering-and-Europe-flying-trip-mind away (not without regret, I confess)." An accompanying illustration depicted Grace in feminine attire—a flowing skirt, tailored riding jacket, and jaunty hat—far from press images of Calamity Jane in buckskin and also very different from the photographic record of Grace in slacks and safari hat taken later for *The Log of the Look-See*.[16]

In general, hunting autobiography typically paired an introspective gaze with an abiding wish to share the story. Far from offering a schizophrenic performance on the page, this combination of intimacy and oration found a convincing voice in testimonial culture of the late nineteenth-century West. An obvious extension to the performance codes of the game trail, the literary landscape offered a new chance for ritual enactment and the conscious display of power, scientific knowledge, and literary verve via carefully crafted script. As Tina Loo notes, for many hunters, the act of writing served as a form of "rhetorical revirilization." Most significantly, the tales of hunter's paradise as set out in sporting literature and autobiography garnered wide popular appeal. The story was, in that sense, a leveler—a performance of the hunting quest that could be participated in by all. Isabella Bird's *A Lady's Life in the Rocky Mountains* struck a chord with its deeply personal voice: one commentator noted that "while reading it one seems to feel the pure, keen, mountain air around one," and it had gone through eight editions by 1912. Readers eagerly imbibed of the restorative smoke and banter of the campfire glow as if taking to the trail themselves. Edgar Randolph pertinently saw his *Inter-Ocean Hunting Tales* (1908) of interest to anyone "whoever feels the sportsman's ardor." For Montague Stevens, the allusion was even conscious. As he advised in *Meet Mr. Grizzly* (1943), readers should approach the book as if a campfire yarn. Incorporated into the intimacies of the trail through the literary landscape, the hunting story encouraged its audience to suspend constraints of time and space and participate in the performance of the hunt by proxy. In this fashion, the oral testimonies of hunting literature extended the context of the campfire to an "imagined community" that stretched from the local to the transnational.[17]

WRITING HUNTER'S PARADISE: THE CRYPTOGRAPHY OF THE CHASE DECONSTRUCTED

Print culture ably communicated the dramatic contours of hunter's paradise from trailside testimonial to collective refrain, but what *exactly* was the story that was told? In its simplest sense, the repertory of the hunt in print mimicked that of the enacted performance on the game trail. Set within the confines of the journey, the story typically bore the hallmarks of a travelogue or a quest in which the geography of game pursuit and the scribbled notes of the trail journal gave structural guidance. The document typically began on the steamer, railroad, wagon, or trailhead—the start of the errand into the wilderness—and ended with packing out. As such, the readers performed the hunt as they read the choreography of quest, figuratively treading the game trail as they turned each page. Inflections of writing styles, meanwhile, including Romanticism, adventure fiction, folk tradition, and natural history writing, fed into the autobiographical coda, lending the hunting story a kind of "fictionalized reality" that narrated the conquest of the West through the lens of frontier mythology, established literary devices, and personal engagement.

Most significantly in the content of the story was the invocation of the West as hunter's paradise—a metanarrative that provided shape and substance to the autobiographical imagination. Dillon Wallace described a "sportsman's Eden" in *Saddle and Camp in the Rockies* (1911) while Emerson Hough deemed the mountain West quite simply "best outdoor country and the best big game country the world ever saw." The trans-Mississippi theater was consciously and consistently presented as a magical space unrivaled for sport. Murphy decreed it "without a peer as a recreation-ground for those who love the ecstatic excitement of the chase," while the Pacific slope offered a "veritable paradise" in the eyes of William Baillie Grohman. Assertions of pastoral and pristine quality abounded. In a chapter of his autobiography entitled "hunter's paradise," James Mead described a hybrid landscape of Old

World scenery and raw frontier life: "The whole country had the appearance of a well-kept park belonging to some English nobleman . . . here and there scattered among the buffalo were herds of antelope feeding, playing, travelling about, and adding variety to the landscape." Likewise, in *Prairie and Forest* (1874), Parker Gillmore described a peaceable kingdom, in the fashion of Edward Hicks's canvas (1848), where buffalo, deer, beaver, and the like "pass their lives in peaceful, happy contentment."[18]

Writers reveled in the trans-Mississippi theater as red in tooth and claw, primitive and vibrant, a cornucopia of game in a broader imagined West of abundance. Themes of contest and challenge proliferated. Allen summed up his autobiography thus: "Many personal accidents, hazardous undertakings, conflicts with savages and wild beasts in a strange land, loom up large as I recall my past days." Like most "tall tales," the literary reading of the chase contained a tendency toward embellishment. Fearsome and charismatic beasts loomed large in the monumental landscape of the hunting story, often with associated motifs of metaphysical encounter and personal edification. As Kent Stockmesser notes, "There is a complete American bestiary in frontier narratives and hand-to-hand combats with buffalos, bears and mountain lions are a standard fixture." Tussles with wild nature brought excitement, elation, adversity, sometimes humor, even disaster, all enacted within the narrative framework of a quest.[19]

Onto this sensational stage of primal action strode the figure of the all-conquering hunter hero (and sometimes heroine) in various roles—eyewitness and guide, outfoxed by canny prey and humbled to metaphysical reflection by nature's grandeur and finally emerging as fully seasoned inductee into the frontier hall of wilderness fame by the end of the story. In *Perils and Pleasures of a Hunter's Life, or the Romance of Hunting*, Peregrine Herne promised readers a dramatic montage of hunting performance, a show of "what a man is capable of daring and doing, even for the mere love of adventure." The compendium *Hunting at High Altitudes* typified the format in its offerings of heroic testimonial. "In the Old Rockies," by Daniel Barringer, combined literary affectation with martial power in a "bear story" featuring shock-and-awe violence, the performance codes of a "dancing bear," steely resolution and "glorious excitement" at the mortal contest, and a comic aside where Barringer bolted during his ritual claiming of the carcass upon hearing bruin let out a final groan (the true hunter hero could laugh at himself). In *Historical*

Collections of the Great West (1857), Henry Howe favored axioms of solitude, wilderness renewal, and self-discovery in the heroic canon: "With no friend near me more faithful than my rifle, and no companions more sociable than my horse and mules, or the attendant coyote . . . which mightily serenaded me, with a plentiful supply of dry logs on the fire, and its cheerful blaze streaming far up into the sky . . . I would sit cross legged enjoying the genial warmth . . . Scarcely did I ever want to change such hours of freedom for all the luxuries of civilized life." Fantasies of escapism and epiphany completed the semiotic landscape of hunter's paradise.[20]

Performed as story, the hunt allowed for discourses on strenuous rejuvenation, savage encounter, philosophical reflection, and trailside banter, all within the quixotic narrative of animal pursuit. This highly attractive fusion of authenticity and adventuring found an eager market in postbellum industrial society. Just as the West provided meat for the tables of the industrial east, so too did it serve up digestible tales of hunter's paradise for an eager public. The game trails of the West offered an escape from the confines of capitalist markets, city grime, labor strife, and mechanized regimentation. Hunter's paradise also allowed for the reading of western history in leisure-format guise, the overarching narrative of westward conquest framed as travelogue (accessible yet exotic, informative yet diverting). Violence in the West—exercised against the animal and the indigene—provided a benign, uniformly patriotic, and relatively uncomplicated tale of colonial power and territorial acquisition. Hunter's paradise thus configured history as adventure tourism, while the gun politics of the chase offered not atavism but entertainment. It proved a successful formula. Rufus Sage's *Scenes in the Rocky Mountains* (1846) ran to a 1,500-copy run in its first edition, all of which sold, as did several further editions. Literature satisfied curiosity in the West and sometimes inspired a visit. Big game hunter Frederick Selous in *Sport and Travel: East and West* (1901) noted how "as a boy I used to devour ravenously the works of Ballantyne, Mayne Reid, Catlin and other writers of fact and fiction concerning the wonders of the great continent of North America, and from that time onwards had always nourished a strong desire to visit that country." Others, meanwhile, chose to conjure "their" West in the safety of the great indoors. Hartley confessed that "hunting adventures with bears, panthers, wild cats and other animals of a similar description, are, on the whole, enjoyed much better as one reads them in a book by a quiet fireside." Whether they inspired literal or imaginative journeys, the storytelling landscape of hunter's paradise constructed a powerful tradition of the West that persists to this day.[21]

Painting the Hunt as Scene: Art, Photography, and the Visual Rendering of Hunter's Paradise

If literature served up a rich textual geography of hunting and hagiography, then art and photography provided its corollary: a pictorial compendium on which the public could feast their gaze. Visual culture represented an important aspect of the hunting afterlife and eased the passage of hunter's paradise from personal to social memory. Hunting, of course, had long been a subject for artistic expression in the West, notably in American Indian pictographs and petroglyphs illuminating aspects of the chase and its cosmological significance. Performed in art, the physical and cultural contours of the hunt were implicitly bound together. As Linea Sundstrom notes, rock art was "purposely located within the larger landscape" to signpost places of sacred import (Ludlow Cave in the Black Hills, where images commemorated the birthing place of bison from their subterranean origins), historic hunting sites (Ulm Pishkun, Montana), and even to conjure up prey populations with embedded "hunting magic."[22]

A brief glance at nineteenth-century "ledger art" (accounting books from traders and government agents that American Indian artists recycled as sketchbooks) also highlights the fact that testimonial landscapes of the hunt were not that different across artistic media and, indeed, ethnic traditions. Howling Wolf of the Cheyenne commemorated the human and animal actors of the game trail in snapshots of hunters following animal tracks as well as a cornucopian "who's who" of prey (turkeys, bear, deer, antelope, raven, rabbit, skunk, wolf, and coyote). In *The Life of the Red Man*, by Kiowa artist Zo-Tom, meanwhile, the importance of performance code in the immediate afterlife of the hunt was illuminated in a series of montages: a large group assembled for a feast; meat from prey animals hanging on poles over the fire; two warriors returning single file from a hunting expedition; and a collection of four bison pursued at full gallop by mounted hunters armed with bows and rifles. And, finally, in the visual feast provided by plains artist "Katse" was encapsulated the full dramaturgy of the hunt: blood gushing from a mortally wounded ten-point buck, a startled deer fixing the gaze of the hunter after hearing the report of his shotgun, a ferocious grizzly with open jaws and lolling tongue, and a crafty skunk poised to squirt musky scent into the eyes of his pursuer. Populated with swaggering hunter heroes, formidable animal actors, dramatic action, and a dose of humor, the indigenous landscape of hunting art ably communicated the narrative codes of hunter's paradise.[23]

Hunting in European art was commonly associated with Arcadian and aristocratic scenes (perhaps most famously Edwin Landseer's iconic portrait of a stag in *Monarch of the Glen* [1851]). American artists worked largely within this tradition, celebrating companionship and gentlemanly chase without geographical specificity in such works as John Ritts Penniman's *Hunter and His Dog* (1805) and William Ranney's *On the Wing* (1850). It was, arguably, the American West that gave national sporting art its distinctive creative voice. A fresh and dynamic canvas with potential expositions on monumental wilderness, charismatic species, and the frontiersman hero, the western theater inspired dramatic rendition in artistic form just as it had done in the literary arena. Here, too, were oppositional paradigms of man versus nature as well as explication on the heroic geography of frontier takeover. Grounded in material encounter and laden with imaginative portent, the visual culture of the game trail was perforated by themes of adventure, quest, sacred violence, and epiphany. As Richard Rattenbury points out, hunting art was dominated by the traditions of Romanticism and Realism, thereby complementing the "fictionalized reality" that marked the literary rendering of hunter's paradise. While the story gave narrative thrust to the hunt in its afterlife, art allowed its aesthetic expression in panoramic style.[24]

Scientific illustrator Titan Ramsey Peale and landscape artist Samuel Seymour accompanied Stephen Long's expedition (1819–20), highlighting a synergy between frontier exploration, visual culture, and the popular communication of natural history. The hunt figured highly in this enterprise. Not only did Peale work as a subsistence hunter for the party, but also, in common with John James Audubon, killed his animals before memorializing them on canvas. Works by the two artists featured sparsely in Long's report on the "Great American Desert," although Peale's sketches of Indians, bison hunts, landscapes, and western animals were placed on display in father Charles's Natural History Museum in Philadelphia as well as in the Academy of Natural Sciences.

Of immense significance in early western hunting art was George Catlin, whose *Hunting Scenes and Amusements of the Rocky Mountains and Prairies of America* (1845) provided a pictorial and ethnographic study of Indian life and, in particular, the bison hunt. Images of Lakota hunters adorned with wolf skins and creeping up on wandering herds, ceremonial rituals, and undulating prairies foregrounded the West as a panoramic hunter's paradise. Catlin's works—totaling more than 600 western-themed paintings—captured the popular imagination and appeared in exhibits in London, Paris, and New York as "the Indian Gallery."

Expositions on the hunt also came from Karl Bodmer and Alfred Jacob Miller, both of whom traveled at the behest of private sponsors. Bodmer journeyed up the Missouri in 1833–34 with German prince Maximilian of Wied, charged with documenting the natural history of the frontier for inclusion in Wied's own *Travels in the Interior of North America* (1843). Significantly, visual record was seen as a vital aid to autobiographical reportage. Miller, meanwhile, accompanied Scottish aristocrat Captain William Drummond Stewart, compiling more than a hundred sketches on his travels through the Rockies and Oregon in 1837. Reviewing an exhibition of his work in New York, the *Mirror* exclaimed: "The different buffalo hunts, the encounter with the grisly bear, the hunter's camp, and all the wild scenes of peril and adventure through which his pencil has followed his gallant friend, are depicted with a life-like force and reality." After a sojourn in Europe, Miller plied his trade from a studio in Baltimore, creating canvasses—such as the series of 200 watercolors on western subjects for patron William Walters in the 1850s— that gloried in the excitement of the faunal frontier and combined a sense of authentic encounter with a patina of imaginative storytelling.[25]

The second half of the nineteenth century saw the western hunting trail firmly installed as a staple of frontier art. As Brian Dippie notes, the visual West revolved around "representational paintings, drawings, and sculptures showing men (and it is essentially an art by and about men) and animals in unspoiled natural settings." Wilderness landscapes, the fraternal culture of the mountain man and the cowboy, American Indians, historical epics, and ruminations on western animals dominated the annals of western art. Significantly, hunter's paradise proved a common motif invoked across visual terrain. Works by William Jacob Hays, including *Herd on the Move* (1861) and *The Stampede* (1862), gloried in the cornucopian mass of the thundering bison herd, while Charles Russell broadcast the West as a rugged and savage game utopia in such pieces as *Bear Fight* (1899) and *Whose Meat* (1914), both of which favored a realist style while at the same time communicating imaginative motifs of action, suspense, and contest. Albert Bierstadt's *Wind River Country* (1860) presented a romantic landscape in the foreground of which a bruin gnawed hungrily on an antelope carcass—nature grand and dreadful in equal measure. An enraged bear, emerging from a cave strewn with bones to face a mounted hunter, also provided the subject for William de la Montagne Cary's *A Bare Chance* (1870). The hunter hero came in for visual commemoration in R. LaBarre Goodwin's *Cabin Door Still Life* (1889) and Frederic Remington's *The Hunter's Supper or Hunter's Camp in the Bighorns* (1900). In a testament to the power of a heroic geography to incite artistic display, Arthur Fitzwilliam Tait depicted hunting culture and the oral homo-social world of the campfire in *The Buffalo Hunt* (1862) and *A Good Time Coming* (1862) without ever having ventured to the West. Entranced by sport in the Adirondacks and keen to cast himself in the role of frontier hunter hero, Tait himself had posed in buckskin garb for the photograph *On the Warpath* (1851).[26]

Pictorial depictions of the game trail found a receptive audience among a public captivated by the enigmatic echelons of the frontier. Currier and Ives, the principal lithographers of the age, listed some 140 works for sale with trapping, hunting, animals, and nature as their subject matter. As Elliott West has demonstrated, the West represented a powerful advertising motif and sold all manner of goods and services—from prunes to Marlboro cigarettes. Hunter's paradise, in fact, presented a recognizable "brand" that paid heed to the vigor and vibrancy of "nature's nation," the patriotic codes of westward conquest, and the idealized traits of frontier folk. The capital power (both cultural and pecuniary) of hunting iconography was starkly evident in the advertising strategies of firearms manufacturers. Leader in the field was Samuel Colt, who commissioned George Catlin to produce twelve scenes of hunting adventure in the 1850s, loosely based on his sketches of the Dakotas twenty years previous but with Colt pistols and rifles added to the frontier panorama (weapons that were not even invented at the time of his visit). Lavishly decorated prints and calendars produced by the likes of Remington and Winchester from the 1870s, meanwhile, sold shotguns and rifles on the back of hunter's paradise using designs from artists including Frederic Remington, Carl Rungius and Arthur Burdett Frost and playing on genre tropes of savage terrain, animal contest, western bravado, and (of course) the dramatic purchase of the gun. Of thirty-four high-quality color calendars produced by Winchester between 1887 and 1930, twelve boasted a definitively western theme. The 1891 calendar designed by Remington featured a stock of western figures—cowboys, Indians—as montages and for the main scene, entitled *Shoot or You'll Lose Him*, a man in a forested landscape poised to shoot an elk as his companion and dog looked on. Four years on, Frost's calendar centered on "success," with two men smoking beside a log on which their trusty rifles leaned. A giant grizzly lay dead in the foreground, its blood on the snow. Calendar images were vivid, action-packed, and painted with an attention to dynamic realism, a visual celebration of the hunter's game in the West.[27]

PHOTOGRAPHY AND THE LEXICON OF CAPTURE

Stories and art allowed for the telling of the hunt in a textual and graphic testimonial culture. Photography, however, offered the prospect of a different kind of commemoration: the visual actualization of the game trail. For Susan Sontag, the camera promised a different engagement with the world: "A photograph is not only an image (as a painting is an image), an interpretation of the real; it is also a trace, something directly stenciled off the real, like a footprint, or a death mask." Pioneered by William Henry Fox Talbot at Lacock Abbey, near Chippenham, Wiltshire, in 1839, as well as by contemporary Frenchmen Niepce and Daguerre, the photograph represented the new medium of the nineteenth century. It allowed for occasions to be solemnized, for historical and genealogical document, and even for the conjuring of immortality through visual encapsulation. According to Daguerre, the photographic image was "not merely an instrument which serves to draw nature . . . [it] gives her the power to reproduce herself." This modish technology, resonant with industrial wizardry and seemingly able to preserve a moment for time immemorial, captivated the public's attention. In the famous essay "The Stereoscope and the Stereograph" (1859), Oliver Wendell Holmes marveled at how "shadows" within the photograph offered a permanent imprint while "their originals fade away." Commentators pondered the revolutionary impact of the new invention, its imprint on the collective imagination, and its relationship to print culture and narrative tradition.

Blurring the boundaries between original and representation, past and present, the camera lens provided a fresh way of apprehending space and culture. According to Walt Whitman, photography heralded a "new world—a peopled world, though mute as a grave. . . . we could spend days in that collection, and find enough enjoyment in the thousand human histories, . . . Time, space, both are annihilated, and we identify the semblance with the reality." The photographic gaze intimated a novel way of "seeing" and the possibility of a new cryptography of the chase.[28]

For the sport hunter in particular, photography represented a valuable medium of memorial and a new site of performance. As Susan Sontag notes, the photograph offered the enticing possibility of "experience captured." With a number of sportsmen keen to document their travels, the camera emerged as a useful tool of the trail. As L. W. Brownell noted in *Photography for the Sportsman Naturalist* (1904), the camera gaze and its embodied image memento allowed the hunter to be taken "back in memory, away from the haunts of men, to the woods; and he can, while looking over them, relive the moment." Alongside the sketchbook and the journal, the photograph served as a device of record and reflection for those looking to celebrate their errand into the wilderness and its moments of epiphany. According to Oliver Wendell Holmes the camera enticed with its prospect of a "mirror with a memory." Where Maximilian of Wied and William Drummond Stewart had taken along illustrators to graphically record and recall their western adventures, a slew of hunting parties in the late 1800s deployed the camera for similar processes of visual capture and commemoration. The prominent sporting magazine *Forest and Stream* ran an article on the use of the camera in the field in 1892, while writer L. W. Brownell heralded the opportunity the camera brought for a new "epoch" in performances on (and of) the game trail: "Heretofore, in our nature works and sportsman's books we have had to be content with drawings, always inaccurate, often ludicrous, and sometimes even grotesque in their untruthfulness to nature." In contrast to the reminiscence culture that graced literary, artistic, and oral iterations of the afterlife of the hunt, photography appeared more immediate and present. Evoking a new kind of precision and directness, it took place "at" a moment rather than recalling it. As Roland Barthes related, the photograph provided "never anything but an antiphon of 'look,' 'see,' 'there it is.'" This "superimposition . . . of reality and the past" spoke of authenticity and autobiography, both codes common to other renderings of hunter's paradise, but photography suggested an extra layer of realism and visual potency. The camera provided hunters with a material fragment of the hunting encounter, a conduit to a particular moment that bridged the gap between the mental recollections and imaginings of the game trail in print and visual media and the object-artifact culture of taxidermy.[29]

That hunters deployed the camera to record their encounter with the West suggested a curiosity with the aesthetic and technological parameters of photography. It also betrayed an interest in catalogue and witness. In that sense, the hunting photograph drew from a wider cultural proclivity to document the histrionics of westward expansion for posterity. As Megan Williams extrapolates, "Its instantaneous ability to transform the present into the past makes the photograph the quintessential mirror of the 'new' American experience and of our desire for an immediately useable past." This possibility of rendering the "now" as historical record had particular application in the context of westward expansion. For emerging frontier communities, photography offered an opportunity of claiming space and identity, of conjoining geography and portraiture into a visual record of autobiography for broadcast to family and friends. The camera highlighted processes of settlement, transformation, and identity formulation and elucidated on the exotic wonders of a "vanishing" landscape as well. Shooting parties were similarly captivated by a desire to record their engagement with the West as a form of "portrait chronicle." Here the function of the camera was multifaceted. Hunters sought to memorialize an encounter with the frontier, record their achievements as wilderness heroes, document the trophy haul, and take home a souvenir for framing. On a deeper level, the desire for visual record demonstrated a claim to ownership of both geography and history. As Susan Sontag notes, "Faced with the awesome spread and alien-ness of a newly settled continent, people wielded cameras as a way of taking possession of the places they visited." Moreover, the hunting photograph allowed for the projection of a certain kind of belonging that cemented a connection between hunter and the landscape of capture just as storytelling had done. As Barthes reminds us, "Every photograph is a certificate of presence."[30]

Some hunters duly became budding amateur photographers. Andrew Williamson, a Scottish hunter, brought a camera on his 1878 trip to the Rockies out of a desire to provide "an amusement at the time" and to create images for perusal later to "recall many a pleasing incident." Others engaged the services of professionals. Frank Jay Haynes and his $13,000 custom Palace Studio railroad car (complete with darkroom and diorama) ran a brisk trade in photographing sporting visitors and their collective trophy hauls. Between 1885 and 1905, Haynes ran the rails across the West at a price of thirty-five cents a day, payable to the Northern Pacific. Railroad, rifle, and camera colluded to present hunter's paradise as a materiality and a visual montage for consumption in the colonial marketplace. The Northern Pacific even produced a specially designed hunting car for elite sporting tourists, complete with a porter and a cook, which traveled the prairie as a mobile shooting range, pausing for up to several weeks to allow for hunting excursions. Haynes photographed the Houghton-Marble party in 1876, documenting Massachusetts industrialists Henry and Jerome together with their families and an amassed trophy haul of birds strung up on a custom-built Worcester Excursion railcar (see Figure 4.1).[31]

The career of frontier photographer Laton A. Huffman highlighted networks of empire in the West as well as storytelling codes of co-production. Born in Iowa in 1854, Huffman moved to Fort Keogh in 1878 as an itinerant photographer before establishing his own studio in Miles City, Montana, in 1881, from where he recorded scenes of ranch life, prairie landscapes, and American Indians and duly reproduced them as postcards, prints, albums, brochures, envelopes, and collotypes for sale and mail order. An example of the recycling of capital from the western hunting exchange, timber for his studio came from the *Bachelor*, an old buffalo steamer. Meanwhile, as supplement to his photographic business, Huffman worked as both buffalo hunter and game guide, facilitating the material as well as the aesthetic consumption of the West. Themes of nostalgia, abundance, rugged masculinity, and the "vanishing" frontier loomed large in Huffman's photographic presentations. Casting himself as the visual chronicler of a disappearing landscape, he mused: "It was worth while, despite the attendant and ungodly smells of that old process . . . there *was* no more West after that."[32]

The mythology of hunter's paradise graced many of Huffman's photographs. He depicted hunters posing with their spoils at his studio, and, on occasion, he served as roving photographer for hire on the game trail itself. Commissioned by George Shields, Huffman accompanied the sportsman during his field trip to the West in 1880, his photographs adapted as line

FIGURE 4.1. Mrs. Henry Houghton and Mrs. Jerome Marble pose with game birds from a hunt in Dakota Territory, 1876. Photograph by F. Jay Haynes (H-29, Haynes Foundation Collection, Montana Historical Society Research Center Photograph Archives, Helena, MT).

drawings for *Rustlings in the Rockies* (a common translation between different visual storytelling media). Following a mention by Shields and the reproduction of the photographs in *American Field*, Huffman received a warm response from a sporting community eager to document their experiences visually. As he noted, "I think I have been personally and by letter had forty propositions to go during the summer coming." In addition, Huffman sold stock images to a national audience eager to possess their own souvenir of the western panorama. An 1883 catalogue entitled "Latest Yellowstone National Park Views, Indian Portraits, Miscellaneous Montana Views and the Only Choice Hunting Scenes Published" thus included twenty-five images of the chase alongside landscape shots and portraits of Custer. In that sense, photography allowed for a vicarious living of the game trail from afar, an imbibing of frontier fixings through the act of purchase—what Barthes dubbed adventure by animation.[33]

The connection between photography, memory, and the frontier was of particular fascination to Evelyn Cameron, who found in the mechanics of the camera a way to supplement her income from ranching and document the key moments of settler life in Montana. Cameron developed an interest in photography in the early 1890s, when she and husband Ewen settled at the Eve Ranch on the Powder River. When the ranching business faltered in the early days, the pair had nurtured the idea of returning to the Orkney Islands where Ewen planned to author a book on ornithology with Evelyn supplying accompanying illustrations. In the end, they decided to remain in Montana to raise polo ponies (a less than successful venture), but Cameron continued her photographic vocation, studying the art "after the house hold has retired to rest." Learning from mail order brochures, boarders at the ranch, and her own experience (for each image that Cameron took, she recorded the aperture size, exposure time, and developing process), she acquired keen skills as a frontier photographer and established a thriving business through the echelons of the post office in Terry and a rented room at the local hotel on Wednesday afternoons. Customers were various, ranging from cowboys, sheepherders, and homesteaders to British expatriates, all of whom looked to Cameron to chronicle their place in the western landscape. An Oxford-educated professor and local rancher, J. H. Price, noted in a letter of thanks for a photo album, "I am charmed with it—and in my old age I shall be able to look through it and recall incidents of my Montana life."[34]

Cameron's successful photographic outfit was, as biographer Donna Lucey points out, not that unusual on the frontier, where a number of women prospered as proprietors of photographic studios, often moving up from jobs as assistants when their husband-proprietors died or left home. The

US Census of 1890 duly recorded some 2,201 female photographers nation-wide, although many found it difficult to gain recognition in an exclusive and male-dominated industry (when it was founded in 1866, the San Francisco Photographic Association barred women from entry). Cameron, though, presided single-handed over the photographic enterprise and won decisive plaudits. Witness to the entire process, she traveled to photographic sites, took the shots, developed the images using dry plates, finished sample prints with gold chloride and burnishing, and delivered them to her clients with an order form attached. Her work impressed with its aesthetic sensibility, capturing local flavor and the harshness of the landscape in a way that reflected personal closeness as well as a "woman's way of knowing," translated to the image culture of the West (according to one photographic commentator of the 1920s, women were in possession of quicker perceptions, a greater eye for color, and a refined sense of beauty in depicting natural scenes). Cameron was particularly proud to receive correspondence from Laton Huffman, who remarked that of all the photographs he had seen, both professional and amateur, "none had pleased him better than hers."[35]

As an adjunct to her professional role as frontier chronicler, Cameron also saw in the camera a way to satisfy personal interests as hunter and natural historian. Native fauna as well as people caught her photographic gaze, and the camera became a trusty companion on the game trail. Keen to capture the variety and wonder of local bird life in particular, she took intimate photographs of eyries and hawk roosts, climbing thousands of feet to secure a close-up view and even poking birds with her tripod to elicit a suitable pose. In fact, the willingness of hunters to embrace photography implied that the cultures of the rifle and of the camera were analogous, even symbiotic at times. L. W. Brownell contended that the photographer needed to "learn all there is to know about still hunting and then double every precaution," while Huffman's hunting background served him well when he took to western trails with a camera. Dressed in buckskin and hiding in hollow logs for hours awaiting game, the preamble to capturing an animal on camera used the same skill set as the "sport" armed with a gun. Meanwhile, the broader nomenclature of photography often referenced the language of the hunt. Cameras were aimed and loaded, subjects shot, and images lofted as trophies. The phrase "snapshot" (itself derived from hunting terminology) had already entered the popular photographic vernacular by 1860. Both technologies shared an imperial genealogy of appropriation, logistics, and linguistics—a colonial gaze directed through gun sights or camera lens. For Sontag, the camera even served as a sublimation of the gun, both being "fantasy machines whose use is addictive."[36]

The technological bind between gun and camera saw a trade in novelty items such as the 1889 Bean's Breech-Loading Gun Cane, a device that allowed the gentleman hunter a genteel stroll with the ladies, with a concealed weapon for occasions of manly target practice. In fact, various patents were lodged for camera weapons that used the gun body as a vehicle for photographic technology in the mid- to late 1800s. London inventor Thomas Skaife produced his pistol camera, later called "pistolgraph," in 1859 for the princely sum of a guinea. As he explained, the product was "in size and shape not unlike a pistol . . . held in the hand, and manipulated by means of a trigger, like a pistol: one being constructed to take life, the other likenesses." Keen to photograph his hunting haunts in the White Mountains, Massachusetts-based photographer and inventor B. W. Kilburn devised a contraption that melded the shotgun and the camera together in a curious hybrid technology, "used like an ordinary shotgun . . . when a bird rises it must be brought to the shoulder, a dead aim taken at the feathered object, and the trigger pulled." Placing a standard four-by-five-inch compact picture camera on a stock to create the "gun camera" (1883), Kilburn combined the maneuverability of the firearm with the functionality of image capture, thereby allowing for the taking of pictures in rugged places where a tripod would be impractical. The camera could be detached and folded for ease of travel, while gunsights and trigger made its mechanism efficient and direct. Kilburn's patent was manufactured until 1886, having received popular plaudits at its inaugural demonstration on New York's Broadway.[37]

The mechanics of the hunt and chronographic innovation sat comfortably together, as evidenced in the work of pioneering cinematographer Edward Marey, collaborator with Eadward Muybridge, who developed the "fusil photographique" (1882), a photo gun with sights and a long barrel that allowed multiple shots at moving avian targets at the rate of 120 a minute, while Kodak entered the market in 1915 with the Eastman gun camera. Significantly, however, such devices never extended their market share beyond gimmicks. The British Photographical Society balked at Skaife's "hideous and unscientific" invention and its use of "cacophonous photographic slang." Kilburn himself favored a standard setup for his photo tours of Colorado (ca. 1890) and Yosemite (1872), from which he produced stereographs of mountain scenes, deer hunts, prospecting, and frontier communities for the popular market to become the largest producer in the country and the sole distributor of stereoscopic images from the Columbian Exposition. That said, patents for "gun cameras" did highlight a common technical imperative at work. Although the connections between the technologies of killing and image capture might be overstated (not least in the environmental and ethical ramifications of consumptive versus nonconsumptive hunting of animals), both proved integral agents in the communication and memorial of hunter's paradise.[38]

The limits of technology placed constraints on the ability of the camera to provide a "snapshot" to rival the speed and impact of the Winchester. Only with Eastman's Kodak No. 1 (1888), a fast-exposure, portable camera with the capacity to record a hundred images on a single roll of film, was the true possibility of a "rapid-fire camera" realized. Early developments in photography, the collotype and daguerreotype, by contrast, involved complicated and necessarily sedentary processes of exposure, confining the limits of the technology to the studio context. With the invention of wet plates and glass negatives in the 1850s and gelatin dry plates in the 1880s, the prospect of outdoor photography proved more realistic. Hauling a camera into the nineteenth-century West thus meant a serious logistical undertaking. Williamson had been advised by friends not to take cameras into the "trackless wastes" of the Rockies. Once there, he spent a full three weeks unpacking equipment carefully packed in felt-lined boxes. Photography on the game trail meant navigating rugged and sometimes dangerous terrain and staking out game in inclement conditions. The *San Francisco Examiner* reported on the wanderings of California photographer Mary Winslow, whose "only arms are a revolver and a man's hat." A testament to the vocation of the spirited female traveler, Winslow took her buggy "wherever she pleases." Equipment was heavy and fragile, too: slides, glasses, focusing screens, chemicals, cloths, plates, tripod, photographic tent, bottles, sponges, acids, and related accouterments weighed in at as much as 120 pounds. Huffman's self-made camera with a Perry lens (1884) weighed 50 pounds alone, while Shields wrote of the photographer's "frantic" stance when the mule carrying his precious exposed dry plates and other photographic materials waded into a swollen river of its own volition.[39]

In actual fact, the complexity of the photographic process rendered taking a picture a performance itself. Equipment took a long time to assemble, while wet plates had to be coated with chemicals, dipped in silver nitrate prior to shooting, and then developed within an hour. Even with the use of dry plates, the photographic experience proved an arduous process often demanding improvisation. California photographer Eliza Withington took to using her skirts as a darkroom while Edward Buxton favored sewn-up blankets as a de facto darkroom on a Rocky Mountain trip in the 1890s. As Buxton confessed, some of the results struck as rather "strange." On occasion, just setting the stage created real logistical problems. Having shot a nine-foot stag on a precipice, Williamson decided the power of the scenery warranted a photograph in situ, "overlooking a great gulch, with the Piney Range and distant mountains in the direction of the Mount of the Holy Cross fading away into the far distance." The decision meant outfitting a donkey the following day, cutting a trail through the brush to the ridge, carrying equipment and water, balancing the tripod on a windy escarpment, and sheltering the camera with blankets. Delighted with the results, Williamson included the image in his photographic journal.[40]

Story and Stage: The Practice and Performance of Hunting Photography

Storytelling remained at the heart of the culture of visual reproduction, unsurprisingly perhaps, given the literal translation of "photography" as writing with light. John McIntire's "Photographic Album of a Rocky Mountain Hunting Trip" (1898) elucidated the way in which sportsmen used the camera to craft visual autobiographies: narrative chronologies of the hunt from trailhead to trophy display. An inaugural picture presented the party next to the railcar at Sheridan, Wyoming, before moving on to show the pack team en route to the Stillwater Valley and the first camp at Slough Creek. Further images conveyed a sense of the camp on the move, trailing up the ridge and packing in and out; others document McIntire's first kill, scenes of horses and horseplay; and a gradually accruing trophy haul of antlers and bodies in each camp shot. McIntire felt the need to include only minimal captions, suggesting that the images were transparent enough without textual accompaniment. The private album provided the hunter with a visual architecture of recollection, its images sufficient to allow for "on-going continuity" between an individual and the act of remembrance.[41]

Similar themes could also be found in the commercial albums sold by photographers, implying that hunter's paradise as a referent was installed enough in the minds of the viewing public to require little narration. In *Sports, Pastimes and Pursuits of Canada* (n.d.)—a scrapbook of images sold for popular consumption as picture books, prints, or stereographs—photographer William Norman paired wilderness mythology with the realism of the camera gaze in billing his scenes (taken, incidentally, in a Montreal studio) as "photographed from nature." Images (complete with Norman's internationally renowned staged "winter" shot) referenced the genre staples of the hunt: "the chance shot," "game in sight," "the guide," "the hunter," "hunters resting," "Returning," "Sunday in the Bush," and "going out." *Life in the Backwoods* (n.d.), produced by the London Stereoscopic Company, subscribed to a similar model. It consisted of a selection of Rocky Mountain scenes taken from the hunting trip of J. W. Turner; the price of a guinea bought a wilderness chronicle featuring shots of landscape, animals, the stalk, and a large grizzly guarding a deer carcass. The last image, captioned "two hours later," depicted a man sitting on a log and looking down at the vanquished bear. The power of the image was paramount, a panorama of the ocular assembled through visual clues. In this fashion, photographic culture suggested a new aspect to hunting memory: that of biotic realism. According to Laton Huffman, photographs were "in a class by themselves . . . they tell their own story."[42]

At the same time, the photograph remained a "hybrid text" that required a textual contest to fully extrapolate its meaning. *Life in the Backwoods* offered a visual version of a story J. W. Turner had already recounted in literary form in *Three Years Hunting and Trapping in America and the Great Northwest* (1888). Even the images of *Life in the Backwoods* relied on captions for contextualization after the fashion of a silent film. An inchoate art form, early photography perhaps inevitably drew from other media, notably print culture, for its messages. For Charles Millard, photography sprang from an "essentially literary tradition." Viewers decoded and digested the visual image of the chase with reference to a preexisting performance code that framed its meanings as well as its aesthetic conceits. As Victor Burgin explains, "Objects present to the camera are *already in use* in the production of meanings, and photography has no choice but to operate upon such meanings."[43]

Although some nineteenth-century commentators decried the camera as a disruptive technology, the visual culture of the hunt only served to embellish literary renditions. Both shared a similar predilection for presenting "fictionalized realities" and adventurous autobiographical takes on the West. Often they worked to frame one another. George Grinnell, editor of *Forest and Stream*, noted of a striking picture of a moose hunt submitted for publication: "It would be interesting if there were a story of the killing of this moose to go with the picture." George Harrison, meanwhile, wrote to Grinnell of a manuscript in which he felt photographs "help make up for defects in the text." This process of narrative symbiosis was evident in Williamson's photographic journal. Here the image remained the core medium of communication. Plates of camp life, the stalk, the "happy hunting grounds," and a slew of trophy "heads" offered a strident iconography of hunter's paradise. Alongside these Williamson offered textual detail, "a few notes, explanatory of the photographs taken, and a short account of the excellent sport obtained." The West as hunter's paradise was communicated by a sophisticated process of trans-media storytelling.[44]

The camera advertised itself as a device for framing reality, with photographer situated as both oracle and witness. Despite its pretensions to authenticity and the necromancy of "freezing a moment in time," photographic depictions of the hunt were nonetheless almost entirely staged. The portrait chronicle necessitated a performance. For one thing, the assembly and exposure times required by early cameras stripped the technology of any great sense of immediacy. Beyond that, the photographic image compartmentalized its creations into discreet boxes, straight-edged boundaries effectively corralling ecological and social realities according to the limits of the film plate. As Burgin notes, "Compressed against the viewing screen into a single plane, chopped by the viewfinder into neat rectangles . . . the naturalness of the world ostensibly open before the camera is a deceit." Subjects were posed and scenes staged to create a particular impression. Even the fact that sitters had to remain still for several seconds lent the images a patina of rigidity and design. As historian Martha Sandweiss reminds us, "It was difficult for a subject to be caught off guard by a process that required a sitter to hold still for up to several seconds." In that sense, the photograph illuminated the willful idealization of hunter's paradise as much as its facsimile. Beneath the veneer of realism lay the invention of a tradition in which sportsmen and photographers served as co-producers in an imaginative and inherently performative process.[45]

Sandweiss pertinently observes the difficulty of reading a photograph, not least for its "capacity . . . to evoke rather than tell." That said, in terms mythological or folkloric imprint, the visual narrative of hunting was fairly straightforward to decode. Trophy photographs imparted a powerful collective memory that was decidedly homogenous in its thematic configuration. Whether taken in the studio or on the trail, as stock images or for private clients, the photographic game trail subscribed to a number of common referents, aesthetic conventions, and performance motifs. The visual story "told" of wilderness action, rugged scenery, armed masculinity, faunal abundance, and primal contest. Hunting photography assumed the aspect of a discernible genre, one fully compatible with extant literary and artistic media of memorial, but with the added imperatives of biotic realism. Nature loomed large as a framing device, the mountains, trees, and meadows of the West a glorious visual stage for the hunt. At times resplendently rugged, elsewhere peacefully pastoral, the western landscape exuded a sense of raw serenity commensurate with the story of the chase and the dynamics of game trail performance. In the foreground, the mobile community of the hunt, the camp, provided a common focal point. Tents frequently appeared as framing devices in the mid-range. Strewn packing boxes, mess tins, ropes, and whittled timber provided evident signs of life on the trail and served as vital emblems of camaraderie and woodcraft. The fire, sometimes smoking, provided a visual locus of gathering. At the center of the composition, as core subject, stood the hunter hero, either alone or with peers in a celebration of strenuous living and robust adventuring. This juxtaposition of the western landscape and the hunting community elevated the campsite as a sacred space in which the civilized and the savage were honored in equal measure.[46]

The photograph substantiated at once the plenitude of the natural West and the province of the hunter hero (see figure 4.2). Sportsmen (and sometimes women) looked proudly at the camera, their gaze signaling ownership, vitality, and control over the space around them. Few hunters subscribed to the performance codes of Theodore Roosevelt or Calamity Jane in donning themselves head to toe in buckskin, but for some a sense of occasion demanded a certain attention to detail. Some depictions cast their subjects

FIGURE 4.2. "Our Camp in Indian Territory," ca. 1899. Library of Congress.

self-consciously in "Sunday Best" to suit the dramatic portent of the hunt and the process of historical record. For the majority, though, the photographic gaze demanded realism, and thus the utilitarian threads of camp dress predominated. Standing before the splendor of their custom-fitted Worcester Excursion car, the wives of Jerome Marble and Henry Houghton paid heed to the translatable (and androgynous) codes of hunter heroism in posing before the camera in trousers and jackets, guns gripped masterfully. Firearms completed the "look" of the hunter and represented critical visual artifacts in the photographic canon. Propped up on boxes and trees, slung over hunter's shoulders, or brandished in combat readiness, they "spoke," like William Allen's Winchester, of hunting prowess and expert witness (see Figure 4.3). Command over the landscape was clear.[47]

The presentation of animal bodies, meanwhile, fell into paradigms of the living-domestic and the dead-wild. Dogs and horses looked on in the manner of loyal subalterns, standing near their masters with an air of docility and obedience. In sharp contrast, prey animals were almost always featured as vanquished forms, either displayed as individual trophies or hung in multitudes as testament to the bounty of the West and the expertise of the hunter. Heavily stylized for the camera, the image culture of the hunt juxtaposed an animate intimacy between hunter and his four-legged aides and assembled body of butchered trophies. Corpses on display, game animals were posed

FIGURE 4.3. "A Prairie Exhibition in Dakota," ca. 1890. Library of Congress.

for the camera gaze and claimed in a visual pageant of conquest (see figure 4.4). In this sense, taxidermy and photography represented artifacts of
co-production and were often complicit in each other's creation. As Brownell
exclaimed, the hunter "can bring home with him not only trophies in the
way of antlers and skins, but also pictures of the game he was seeking, taken
in their native haunts."[48]

The trophy shot cast hunters and wild things as dual focus subjects, locked
together in the act of capture (at least figuratively). A visual signifier of the
sexual politics of empire, victorious hunters claimed their prey in symbolic
displays of domination. Some held the antlers aloft in an affirmation of mastery, as in a photograph of Malcolm Mackay that portrayed the author holding a huge antler rack under the caption "It was a Dandy Head." Others paid
heed to the performance of the hunting contest with pithy captions that celebrated an impressive trophy haul (one photograph of a wall full of trophy
shields was entitled "Just a few of the best") or indulged in the sacramental
violence of the hunt, as in one image in Shields's *Cruising in the Cascades*
(1889) that juxtaposed a dead grizzly and rifle with the strap line: "death and

FIGURE 4.4. "Seven and One Hanging—Team in the Woods for More," ca. 1903. Library of Congress.

the cause of it." Laid out on the ground or presented as faunal fragments in the form of heads, skins, or antlers, the photograph allowed the hunter to ritualistically "own" the trophy on camera by standing over (or sometimes on) wild things. Such images sanctified the implicit violence of the kill, effectively denaturalized the animal, and privileged the corpse in a way that other literary and artistic afterlives of the hunt had not done. The animal was claimed, repackaged, and disembodied in photographic performance.[49]

This visual glorification of dismemberment analogized the hunting trophy shot to another genre of nineteenth-century visual record: that of lynching photography. In both scenarios, victims were typically strung up in branches or roped to timber frames, surrounded by a crowd, and often photographed in relation to trees, water, and other natural points of reference. Comparison might also be drawn between the masculine camaraderie of the hunting party and the vigilante posse, the photographic depictions of assisting horse and dog teams, the ceremonial display of the prey, and the selling of postcard mementoes. Themes of racial hatred, justice, and retribution (which marked the practice of lynching) were far less evident on the game trail where the tendency was to glamorize quarry as noble foes (aside from predatory animals that were often criminalized), although one might argue that the crusading ethos of westward expansion lent the hunt a certain sense of mission. Notably, Selma Congressman John Lewis remembered how the "citizen posse" of the town in the 1960s were know as "squirrel shooters" in his memoir *Walking with the Wind* (1998).[50]

Thinking of further frames of reference, we might compare the nineteenth-century trophy photograph with images of prisoner abuse at the hands of US military personnel in Abu Ghraib (2004) and Zabul Province, Afghanistan (2012). Such analysis must be tentative given the perforation (also true of lynching photographs) of a human-animal binary as well as the imprint of a modern digital culture and institutional (military) context. Themes of mutilation, martial masculinity, and the symbolic claiming of the "enemy" on camera warrant a closer reading than is possible here, but suffice it to say that some commentators have made a connection. According to the *New York Times*, infractions at Abu Ghraib and Zabul bespoke a frontier mentality, of a "self-reliance required in isolation" that bred "heroic camaraderie" and a tendency toward "tribal violence." Sociologist Philip Zimbardo ventured the following assessment: "Indeed, recall from another era, media images of big game hunters and sports fisherman standing beside their prey . . . Trophy photos are exemplars of power and mastery, of how mighty beasts can be overpowered by skill and technology. The same is true of the Abu Ghraib trophy photos." Certainly, the nineteenth-century hunt subscribed to the idea of a savage wilderness and the conquest of the animal body, courtesy of imperial power and photographic culture. In some photographs, hunters aimed rifles at their already dead foes or used taxidermy animals to "stage" an all-action wilderness encounter, introducing a black humor to the tableaux that depicted the theatrical codes of the hunter hero, an apparent inurement to violence, and (some argue) a kind of psychological release. Zimbardo badged the "war pornography" of Abu Ghraib and Zabul as an essentially modern phenomenon, a signal of military-industrial power and digital media. The western experience suggests at least a qualification.[51]

Set against such comparisons was the tendency of the hunting photograph to favor a view of the hunt that was almost entirely bloodless. Even in the most striking assemblies of necrogeography—landscapes of death—visions of butchery, skinning, and animal entrails (practical aspects of turning prey into trophy) rarely made it into the photographic record. A shot of hunters near Magpie Gulch, MT (1889) paralleled the standing human protagonists with a row of strung-up ungulates and rifles offering vertical symmetry to the piece. A mountain lion lay in the foreground, eyes closed and paws

FIGURE 4.5. "The Perils of Frontier Life—A Fierce Encounter with a Giant of the Forest," ca. 1905. Library of Congress.

stretched out as if asleep. In part, this focus on the peaceful endgame of the hunt reflected technological barriers to encapsulating the chase and the kill on camera. Freeze-framing a grizzly charge or a bison stampede challenged the prerogatives of visual capture in a way that art or literature—imaginative media of recollection—did not have to grapple with (hence the use of the taxidermy animal in a photo titled "The Perils of Frontier Life," Figure 4.5). More than that was an attention to an idealized landscape of hunter's paradise and a complement of charismatic beasts framed to highlight physical beauty, romanticism, and animation even as rigor mortis set in.[52]

Quixotic visions of the hunter's game as a pavilion of grand adventuring effectively disengaged the hunt from its more gory (and complicated) aspects, a process that drew some analogy with Civil War photography. At Antietam (1862), bodies were, for the first time, subject to visual depiction on the battlefield. A co-production of the gun and the rifle, images of wounded and dead soldiers broadcast a message of industrialism, fraternal strife, and national bloodletting. As historian Megan Williams argues, photography transformed the theater of war into a landscape of pastoralism, using aesthetic codes and ecological aspect to soften the battlefield into a space of redemption. As she notes, photography professed the "triumph of the American landscape over the specter of national division." Likewise, the image culture of the hunt used the frame of rugged nature to construct a heroic geography of recreation, adventure, and wholesome encounter that sanctified and sanitized hunting as a form of "disciplined violence." Photography, in turn, allowed the viewer to share the hunter's gaze over a peaceable kingdom.[53]

In actual fact, the juxtaposition of the dead and the pristine in the trophy shot paid heed to a longstanding fascination of nineteenth-century photographic culture with death and memorialization. As Barthes reminds us, the camera allows us to get up close and personal with mortality. In this sense, the camera offered its own distinct conduit to the afterlife of the hunt as a specific genre form. As evident in contemporary interest in funereal images of child corpses, spiritualism, and ghost photography, the camera seemingly held the power to abet, document, and even fend off death and decay. From Navaho storytellers to the gothic novellas of Edgar Allen Poe, cameras were invested with the power to "steal" souls. Creatively toyed with by writer Ernest Hornung, the detective fiction pulp novel *The Camera Fiend* (1911) featured a crazed scientist using a camera to conceal a gun, thereby shooting and shooting his victims simultaneously. Others read in photography a means to record death and commit it to history. William Fox Talbot had seen his invention as a way to mark "the injuries of time"—a metaphor with obvious applicability to visual capture on the game trail. The camera elucidated the fleeting nature of life, but also preserved it forever—this made it an idea medium to convey the visual paradox of the hunt and its associations with a nature, both alive and assassinated. As Sontag notes, photography professed a tendency to both "consecrate and desecrate." For Barthes, photographic processing seemed analogous to that of a mortician, a visual production saturated with "funereal immobility" and its subjects "anesthetized and fastened down." According to critic John Berger, the "saving of image from nothing" involved a "certain act of redemption." Read as eulogy, photography represented a complicated artifact of the hunt.[54]

Broadcast in private scrapbooks and frames, depicted in galleries, the press, and literature, or sold as lithographs, stereographs, and prints for public consumption, photography satisfied what Sandweiss calls "Americans' sense of self" and impressed on "broader cultural imaginings." Its market reach was substantial and its audience an eager one. Huffman had already produced 83,000 prints by 1883, a mark of the mass production abilities of the new technology and of the mass appeal of the West as an aesthetic and historical subject. Stock images of the frontier included prairie homesteads, shop fronts and main streets, western characters in the shape of cowboys, miners, and outlaws, military sites and encounters, landscape shots, and American Indians. Joining those was a presentation of hunter's paradise. Part ecological realism and part idealization, it presented monumental and cornucopian nature, the adventure of the hunter hero, and the capture of charismatic animal foes. The image culture of the camera brought a new angle to the performance of the hunt that carried its broadcast further. A medium of communication and memorial, photography transformed the moment to history and created a usable past, allowing the incorporation of hunter's paradise as national autobiography. As Williams notes, "The experience *of* the photograph is equated with *living* the scene it depicts."[55]

THE TESTIMONIAL CULTURE OF THE HUNT: SI(GH)TING AND MEMORY

As they wandered the game trails of the West, hunters viewed the environment first and foremost through an ocular gaze. In concert with storytelling and journaling, art and photography conspired to commit the hunting experience to memory. Each exerted a powerful impression on the afterlife of the game trail as media of personal reminiscence and social record. The testimonial culture of the hunt was multifaceted and enabled acts of performance across a variety of media. Returning to the eastern seaboard in 1908 after ranching in Montana, Malcolm Mackay crafted a bespoke room with log-clad walls, Indian rugs, cattle skull ornaments, and a haul of Charles Russell's artworks. The so-called Russell Room reassembled hunter's paradise in a new geography, a "borrowed landscape" of the frontier preserved for posterity in the great indoors. Attending a soiree to dedicate the room, Helen Mackay recalled:

> We sat around the fireplace, which as yet had had no fire, to dedicate it. The squaw of the Medicine Man [Nancy] sat far left, then the Medicine Man [Charlie], then two Braves [family friends], then the owner of the teepee [Malcolm], and finally his squaw [Helen] next to the fireplace on the right. With great ceremony the squaw of the owner of the teepee made a fire and lighted it. Then the Medicine Man talked to us for over two hours in Indian sign language, with his squaw interpreting. I can never forget the pleasure and the magic of that evening. We were completely transported into the past.[56]

Aside from its unapologetic appropriation of Indian symbology, the occasion pointed to the power of hunter's paradise as a landscape of performance. Gathered in an act of consecration, guests engaged in a communal worship of the West through its signature artifacts, a kind of séance for the national Self enacted through trans-media storytelling. Even without fire, the sacred embers of the campfire ignited the telling of stories and the ritual performing of frontier identity by returning to the heroic geography of the hunting trail. Secured through a testimonial culture that was both intimate and inclusive and communicated through the repertory of frontier experience, the West was firmly installed as a consecrated space.

NOTES

1. Theodore Roosevelt, *Hunting Trips of a Ranchman* (New York: G. P. Putnam's, 1885), 13–14.

2. Peregrine Herne, *Perils and Pleasures of a Hunter's Life, or the Romance of Hunting* (New York: Evans and Co., 1858), 279; William Kingston, *Adventures in the Far West* (London: Routledge, n.d.), 8, 192; Robert Bellah, *Habits of the Heart: Individualism and Commitment in American Life* (Berkeley: University of California Press, 1985), 153–54; Richard Slotkin, *The Fatal Environment: The Myth of the Frontier in the Age of Industrialization, 1800–1890* (Middletown, CT: Wesleyan University Press, 1985), 16.

3. Cary Ziter, *The Moon of Falling Leaves* (New York: Franklin Watts, 1988), 40; Donald M. Hines, *Ghost Voices: Yakima Indian Myths, Legends, Humor, and Hunting Stories* (Issaquah, WA: Great Eagle, 1992), 227–30, 269.

4. George Shields, *Rustlings in the Rockies* (Chicago: Belford Clarke and Co., 1883), 10; William Kingston, *Adventures in the Far West* (London: Routledge, 1881), 192.

5. David Cartwright, *Natural History of Western Wild Animals and Guide for Hunters, Trappers, and Sportsmen* (Toledo: Blade Printing and Paper Co., 1875), vi; *Forest and Stream*, December 10, 1885, Papers of George Bird Grinnell, HM223, Box 36, Folder 209, Yale University Library; George Grinnell to S. K. Hooper, Denver and Rio Grande Railroad, September 20, 1895, Papers of George Bird Grinnell, HM223, Box 23, Folder 36, Yale University Library.

6. Daryl Jones, *The Dime Novel Western* (Bowling Green, OH: Bowling Green State University, 1978), 8; T. C. Harbaugh, "The Young Trail Hunters: or New York Boys in Grizzly Land," *Beadle's Boys Library of Sport, Story, and Adventure* 60, no. 5 (Feb 25, 1900), 89.141.184, Autry Library, Autry National Center, Los Angeles (hereafter cited as Autry); George Lasalle, "Burt Bunker, the Trapper—A Tale of the

North West Hunting Grounds," *Beadle's Half Dime Library* 2, no. 50 (1878), 89.102.11, Autry.

7. E. G. Cattermole, *Famous Frontiersmen, Pioneers, and Scouts: The Vanguards of American Civilization* (Chicago: M. A. Donohue and Co., 1880); B. Hartley, *Hunting Sports of the West, Adventures of the Most Celebrated Hunters and Trappers* (Philadelphia: Bradley and Co., 1865), 7–8, 252–54.

8. John Frost, *Heroes and Hunters of the West* (Philadelphia: Theodore Bliss, 1869), vii; *Boston Transcript*, October 13, 1915.

9. Edgar Randolph, *Inter-Ocean Hunting Tales* (New York: Forest and Stream, 1908), 2; Charles E. Myers, *Memoirs of a Hunter: Fifty-Eight Years of Hunting and Fishing* (Davenport, WA: Shaw and Borden, 1948), i; see Allen's autobiography, *Adventures with Indians and Game, or Twenty Years in the Rocky Mountains* (Chicago: A. W. Bowen, 1903); as well as his edited Montana diary in *Hunting at High Altitudes: The Book of the Boone and Crockett Club*, ed. George Bird Grinnell (New York: Harper and Bros., 1913), 15–241; Malcolm Mackay, *Cow Range and Hunting Trail* (New York: G. P. Putnam's, 1925).

10. Constance Gordon Cumming, *Granite Crags of California* (Edinburgh: William Blackwood, 1886 [1884]); Marianne North, *Recollections of a Happy Life* (New York: Macmillan, 1892); Theodora Guest, *Round Trip in North America* (London: E. Stanford, 1895). Courtney Borden, *Adventures in a Man's World: The Initiation of a Sportsman's Wife* (New York: Macmillan, 1933).

11. Heclawa, *In the Heart of the Bitter-Root Mountains: The Story of the Carlin Hunting Party* (New York, G. P. Putnam's 1895), v; Lincoln Ellsworth to Charles Sheldon, March 5, 1916, Garvan Sheldon Collection, MS232, Box 1, Folder 2, Yale University Library.

12. William Wroe to Charles Sheldon, April 10, 1917, Garvan Sheldon Collection, MS232, Box 2, Folder 48, Yale University Library; Henry Bannon to Charles Sheldon January 15, 1920, Garvan Sheldon Collection, MS232, Box 1, Folder 2, Yale University Library; Rowland Robinson, *Hunting without a Gun and Other Stories* (New York: Forest and Stream, 1905), 356.

13. Allen, *Adventures*, 7–8; Randolph Marcy, *Thirty Years of Army Life on the Border* (New York: Harper and Bros., 1866), x–xi.

14. *Spectator* quoted in Pat Barr, *A Curious Life for a Lady: The Story of Isabella Bird, Traveller Extraordinary* (Middlesex: Penguin, 1970), 184; John Mortimer Murphy, *Sporting Adventures in the Far West* (London: Sampson Low, Marston, Searle & Rivington, 1870), 1.

15. Shields, *Rustlings in the Rockies*, v; George O. Shields, *Cruising in the Cascades: And Other Hunting Adventures* (Chicago, Rand, McNally & Co., 1889), 7, 25; Grantley

F. Berkeley, *The English Sportsman in the Western Prairies* (London: Hurst and Blackett, 1861), 294; Berkeley quoted in *The Field*, May 12, 1860, 354.

16. Grace Gallatin Thompson Seton, *A Woman Tenderfoot* (New York: Doubleday, Page & Co., 1905 [1900]), 7, 15, 16.

17. Tina Loo, "Of Moose and Men: Hunting for Masculinities in British Columbia, 1880–1939," *Western Historical Quarterly* 32, no. 3 (Autumn 2001): 305; W. H. Davenport Adams, *Celebrated Women Travellers of the Nineteenth Century* (New York: E. P. Dutton, 1903), 430; Randolph, *Inter-Ocean Hunting Tales*, iii; Montague Stevens, *Meet Mr. Grizzly: A Saga on the Passing of the Grizzly* (Albuquerque: University of New Mexico Press, 1943), 1.

18. Dillon Wallace, *Saddle and Camp in the Rockies* (New York: Outing Publishers, 1911), 38; Emerson Hough, *Let Us Go Afield* (New York: D. Appleton, 1916), 104; Murphy, *Sporting Adventures in the Far West*, 2; W. A. Baillie Grohman, *Fifteen Years Sport and Life in the Hunting Grounds of Western America and British Columbia* (London: Horace Cox, 1900), 1; James R. Mead, *Hunting and Trading on the Great Plains, 1859–1875*, ed. Schuyler Jones (Norman: University of Oklahoma Press, 1986), 56; Allen, *Adventures*, 11; Parker Gillmore, *Prairie and Forest* (New York: Harper's, 1874).

19. Allen, *Adventures*, 11; Kent Stockmesser, *The Western Hero in History and Legend* (Norman: University of Oklahoma Press, 1965), 244.

20. Herne, *Perils and Pleasures of a Hunter's Life*, vi; Daniel Barringer, "In the Old Rockies," in *Hunting at High Altitudes*, 309–11; Henry Howe, *Historical Collections of the Great West Containing Narratives of the Most Important and Interesting Events in Western History—Remarkable Individual Adventures—Sketches of Frontier Life—Descriptions of Natural Curiosities* (New York: George Tuttle, 1857), 290; Jan Dizard, *Mortal Stakes: Hunters and Hunting in Contemporary America* (Amherst: University of Massachusetts Press, 2003), 83.

21. Rufus Sage, *Rufus B. Sage: His Letters and Papers, 1836–1847, and Scenes in the Rocky Mountains; with an annotated reprint of "Scenes in the Rocky Mountains and in Oregon, California, New Mexico, Texas, and the Grand Prairies,"* vol. 1 (Glendale, CA: Arthur Clark, 1956), 22, 26–27; Frederick Selous, *Sport and Travel: East and West* (London: Longmans, Green & Co., 1901), 143; Hartley, *Hunting Sports of the West*, 7–8.

22. Linea Sundstrom, *Storied Stone: Indian Rock Art in the Black Hills* (Norman: University of Oklahoma Press, 2004), 201.

23. Zo-Tom Ledger Book, 4100G.1, Howling Wolf Ledger Book, 4100.G.2, and Southern Plains Ledger Book, 491.P.3441, Braun Research Library, Autry National Center, Los Angeles (hereafter cited as Braun).

24. Richard Rattenbury, *Hunting the American West: The Pursuit of Big Game for Life, Profit, and Sport, 1800–1900* (Missoula, MT: Boone and Crockett Club, 2008), 247. Also see William H. Goetzmann and William N. Goetzmann, *The West of the Imagination*

(New York: Norton, 1988), for a discussion of image culture and the imperial gaze in the West.

25. Quoted in Rattenbury, *Hunting the American West*, 253–54.

26. Quoted in Clyde A. Milner, Carol A. O'Connor, and Martha A. Sandweiss, eds., *The Oxford History of the American West* (Oxford: Oxford University Press, 1994), 675.

27. Elliott West, "Selling the Myth: Western Images in Advertising," in *Wanted Dead or Alive: The American West in Popular Culture*, ed. Richard Aquila (Urbana: University of Illinois Press, 1996), 269–91. For depictions and analysis of Catlin's work for Samuel Colt, see Herbert G. Houze, Carolyn C. Cooper, and Elizabeth Mankin Kornhauser, *Samuel Colt: Arms, Art, and Invention* (New Haven: Yale University Press, 2006), 203–45. Calendars illustrated in Richard Rattenbury, *The Art of American Arms Makers* (Oklahoma City: National Cowboy and Western Heritage Museum, 2004).

28. Daguerre quoted in Susan Sontag, *On Photography* (New York: Penguin, 1977), 188; Oliver Wendell Holmes, "The Stereoscope and the Stereograph" *Atlantic Monthly*, 3 (June 1859): 738–48; Whitman quoted in Jane Rabb, ed., *Literature and Photography: Interactions, 1840–1990* (Albuquerque: New Mexico University Press, 1995), 21.

29. Sontag, *On Photography*, 3; Holmes, "The Stereoscope and the Stereograph"; George Bird Grinnell, "Hunting with a Camera," *Forest and Stream*, May 5, 1892, 427; L. W. Brownell, *Photography for the Sportsman Naturalist* (New York: Macmillan, 1904), 25–26, 3; Roland Barthes, *Camera Lucida: Reflections on Photography* (London: Vintage, 1993), 5, 76, 84, 115.

30. Megan Rowley Williams, *Through the Negative: The Photographic Image and the Written Word in Nineteenth-Century America* (New York: Routledge, 2003), 3; Sontag, *On Photography*, 8, 65; Brownell, *Photography for the Sportsman Naturalist*, 25; Barthes, *Camera Lucida*, 87.

31. Andrew Williamson, *Sport and Photography in the Rocky Mountains* (Edinburgh: David Douglas, 1880), 1, 1993 Folio 3, Beinecke Rare Book and Manuscripts Library, Yale University (hereafter cited as Beinecke); "Mrs. Houghton and Mrs. Marble of Worcester, Mass. with NP observation car," 1876, photograph by F. Jay Haynes (H-29, Haynes Foundation Collection, Montana Historical Society Research Center Photograph Archives, Helena, MT) (hereafter cited as MHSP).

32. L. A. Huffman to George Bird Grinnell, n.d. (ca. May 1912), Papers of George Bird Grinnell Box 25, Folder 42, Yale University Library.

33. Larry Len Peterson, *L. A. Huffman: Photographer of the American West* (Missoula, MT: Mountain Press, 2003), 58, 60–61; Barthes, *Camera Lucida*, 20.

34. Donna Lucey, *Photographing Montana: The Life and Work of Evelyn Cameron, 1894–1928* (Missoula, MT: Mountain Press, 2001), 122, 152. See also Kristi Hager, *Evelyn Cameron: Montana's Frontier Photographer* (Helena, MT: Farcountry Press, 1997).

35. Peter Palmquist, ed., *Photography in the West* (Manhattan, KS: Sunflower University Press, 1989), 124; Ira W. Martin, "Women in Photography," *Pictorial Photography in America* vol. 5 (1929): n.p.; Huffman quoted in Lucey, *Photographing Montana*, 184.

36. Brownell, *Photography for the Sportsman Naturalist*, 108; Sontag, *On Photography*, 14–15.

37. Kilburn's patent was manufactured between 1882 and 1886 for a niche market. An advertisement for the device appeared in Scovill's Manufacturing Co., *Scovill's Photo Series No.20, Dry Plate Making for Americans* (New York: N.p., 1886), 22; Skaife quoted from his talk to the North London Photographic Association, November 28, 1860 and quoted in *Photographic News* 4 (November 30, 1860): 370; Promotional piece for Kilburn's gun camera in M. Butcus, *Photographic Advertising A–Z* (N.p., n.d.), 82. See also Linda McShane, *"When I Wanted the Sun to Shine": Kilburn and Other Littleton, New Hampshire, Stereographers* (Littleton, NH: Sherwin Dodge Publisher, 1993).

38. *British Journal of Photography*, December 15, 1860, 968, and May 1, 1860, 138.

39. *San Francisco Examiner*, March 14, 1895; Shields, *Rustling in the Rockies*, 82–86.

40. Eliza Withington, "How Women Make Landscape Photographs," *Philadelphia Photographer* 13 (1876): 357–79; Edward Buxton, *Short Stalks, or Hunting Camps, North, South, East, and West* (New York: G. P. Putnam's, 1892), 96; Williamson, *Sport and Photography*, 1, 24.

41. John McIntire, "Photographic Album of a Rocky Mountain Hunting Trip, 1898," WA photos 37, Beinecke; John Berger, *About Looking* (London: Bloomsbury, 1980), 60.

42. William Norman, "Sports, Pastimes, and Pursuits of Canada," n.d., WA Photos 242, Beinecke; *Life in the Backwoods* (London: London Stereoscopic and Photographic Company, n.d.), Beinecke; Huffman to Grinnell, n.d. (ca. May 1912).

43. Williams, *Through the Negative*, 10; Charles Millard, "Images of Nature, a Photo Essay," in *Nature and the Victorian Imagination*, ed. U. C. Knoepflmacher and G. B. Tennyson (Berkeley: University of California Press, 1977), 24; Victor Burgin, ed., *Thinking Photography* (London: Macmillan, 1982), 47.

44. George Bird Grinnell to H. C. Pierce, October 31, 1895, Papers of George Bird Grinnell, HM223, Box 23, Folder 36, Yale University Library; George Harrison to George Bird Grinnell, March 12, 1910, George Bird Grinnell Papers, HM223, Box 31, Folder 151, Yale University Library; Williamson, *Sport and Photography*, 5.

45. Burgin, *Thinking Photography*, 47; Martha Sandweiss, *Print the Legend: Photography and the American West* (New Haven: Yale University Press, 2002), 225.

46. Sandweiss, *Print the Legend*, 330.

47. "Mrs. Houghton and Mrs. Marble of Worcester, Mass. with NP observation car."

48. Brownell, *Photography for the Sportsman Naturalist*, 25.

49. Malcolm Mackay, *Cow Range and Hunting Trail* (New York: G. P. Putnam's, 1925), 114 opp.; "Just a Few of the Best," Photo 948-590, MHSP; Shields, *Cruising*, 66.

50. John Lewis, *Walking with the Wind: A Memoir of the Movement* (San Diego: Harvest, 1998); James Allen, ed., *Without Sanctuary: Lynching in America* (Santa Fe: Twin Palms, 2000).

51. Seymour M. Hersh, "Torture at Abu Ghraib," *New Yorker*, May 10, 2004 at http://www.newyorker.com/magazine/2004/05/10/torture-at-abu-ghraib; "US Troops Posed with Body Parts of Afghan Bombers," *Los Angeles Times* April 18, 2012; "Images of GIs and Remains Fuel Fears of Ebbing Discipline," *New York Times*, April 19, 2012; Philip Zimbardo, "The 'Trophy Photos': Abu Ghraib's Horrors and Worse," Op-ed, October 25, 2005, http://www.zimbardo.com/downloads/Trophy%20 Photos%20OP%20ED%20.pdf; Marita Gronnvoll, "Gender (In)Visibility at Abu Ghraib," *Rhetoric and Public Affairs* 10, no. 3 (2007): 371–99.

52. "Hunting Party, 1889, at Magpie Gulch," Photo 948-552, MHSP.

53. Williams, *Through the Negative*, 6; Monica Rico, *Nature's Noblemen: Transatlantic Masculinities and the Nineteenth-Century American West* (New Haven: Yale University Press, 2013), 6.

54. Barthes, *Camera Lucida*, 5–6, 9, 14, 57, 92, 115; Talbot quoted in Sontag, *On Photography*, 69; John Berger, *On Looking* (London: Bloomsbury, 1980), 58.

55. Sandweiss, *Print the Legend*, 6; Williams, *Through the Negative*, 11; Monica Rico, *Nature's Noblemen: Transatlantic Masculinities and the Nineteenth-Century American West* (New Haven: Yale University Press, 2013), 6.

56. Helen Raynor Mackay, "Good Medicine: A Gracious Lady Remembers CMR in Her New Jersey Home," *Montana: The Magazine of Western History* 7 (Winter 1957): 37–38.

CHAPTER 5

STAGING THE GAME TRAIL

The Theatrical Wild

Storytelling cultures of the textual and illustrated variety provided the opportunity to construct hunter's paradise for the purposes of personal recollection, social translation, and commercial transaction. Further renditions of the western hunt came courtesy of other mediums and incorporated new artistic and technological directions. One of these, theater, allowed for the hunt to reach a new stage of realism and immersion, repackaging the plot formulas of print and visual culture with added dramatic purchase. Performed on stage, the hunt could be reenacted as well as retold, incorporating the elements of testimonial culture and offering the audience the possibility of intimate experience through live-action encounter. The performed hunt was played out in a variety of popular entertainments in the late 1800s, of which the most influential, arguably, was Buffalo Bill's Wild West Show. As Frederic Remington recalled of Cody's pitch in London's Hyde Park: "At present everyone knows where it is, from the gentleman on Piccadilly to the dirtiest cooler in the remotest slum of Whitechapel . . . One should no longer ride the deserts of Texas or the rugged uplands of Wyoming to see

DOI: 10.5876/9781607323983.c005

the Indians and the pioneers, but should go to London." Choreographed for public broadcast across a transnational geography, "the West" made an easy transition from dramatic locale for hunting adventure to a performance subject of its own. The key tenets of hunter's paradise—the thrill of the chase, animal antics, wilderness danger, and gunplay—eagerly translated to a theatrical context. Armed with a penchant for storytelling and flamboyant gesture, the hunter hero trod from the timberline to the stage with ease, reprising a role as orator and guide that he (and indeed she) had already performed on the game trail.[1]

FRONTIER GENEALOGY AND RITUAL PERFORMANCE

Performance had long been a feature of indigenous hunting in the West for the purposes of ritual affirmation, cultural bonding, and environmental explanation. Blackfeet warriors adorned with horns and hooves conjured herds of blacktail deer with their whirling invocations, while the Hunkpapa Sioux commemorated the life cycle of the bison in their ritual dances. Implicit in the hunt were the "raw elements of narrative," as Charles Jenkins called them—chronology, choreography, and characters—each ready to take their place in the performative landscape. Ritual demonstration was an important part of hunting preparations, a way of auguring good fortune and binding subsistence and symbolic dynamics together. The Kutenai practiced a three-day ceremony with songs, dance, and offerings to the grizzly on its spring emergence (which was also said to dance to the new season). Feasting and celebration also took place at the end of a hunt, designed to pay thanks to the provident animal and homage to the hunter's skill. According to the Yakima, performance was also part of the hunting lore of the bruin. As Listening Coyote noted, "In my dream I saw him dancing his war dance, heard him singing his war song . . . I have heard him tell in song how he will string your entrails on the growing bushes, how he will scatter your limbs and fragments of your body along the trail." The bind between hunting and performance in (and, indeed, of) the West sported a distinguished genealogy.[2]

In the Euro-American vernacular, hunter's paradise made the conceptual leap from a flat medium to a live performance through various media that collectively conspired to take the drama of the West to a national and international stage. Prominent among these were exhibitions and world's fairs, Wild West shows, and other staged entertainments, including public lectures, animal acts, and variety arts. Roland Barthes read the photograph as a "primitive theater, a kind of *Tableaux Vivant*, a figuration of the motionless," but the stage went one better. Theater and shows provided a different kind of snapshot of the hunt, more flamboyant and fluid than other iterations. Although photography offered a *kind* of movement across several images, it did not emerge from the chemical imprint. The stage, however, allowed the performance codes of hunter's paradise full sensory reign, adding the drama and high jinks of live action to the storytelling canon that spanned print and image culture. The 1885 program for Buffalo Bill's Wild West Show summed it up perfectly: here were "pictures of western life" rendered in glorious 3-D, with the smell of gunpowder, the sound of thundering bison, and the effusive presence of the hunter hero as ringmaster, orator, and lead. As with other storytelling modes, here was a flavorsome "fictionalized reality" that stressed authenticity of encounter, of real people and events alongside an adventuring narrative that spoke of playful tales of game pursuit and the power politics of westward expansionism.[3]

As Michael Steiner reminds us, expos and world's fairs denoted "'shock cities' embodying the hopes and fears of their times." In the nineteenth-century imagination the allure of the West was palpable, with expositions in Philadelphia, Chicago, and St. Louis each making determined attempts to narrate the frontier experience. The Centennial Exposition in Philadelphia (1876), the first world's fair in the United States, attracted some 10 million people, meaning that an astonishing one in five US citizens attended. Attendees to Fairmont Park strolled the two and a half acres, taking in new inventions including the Corliss stream engine, Bell's first telephone, and Heinz's ketchup. Most significantly, visitors to Philadelphia had the chance to come face to face with hunter's paradise, rendered in the form of a frontier cabin adorned with pioneer sundries and populated with "real-life" hunters.[4]

Sponsored by *Forest and Stream*, the exhibit highlighted the way in which the frontier and the mechanics of the hunt had become embedded in the sporting imagination as iconic foundations of American character. Depictions of the cabin were faithfully reproduced in magazines such as *Harper's*, *Leslie's*, and *New York Weekly*. The commemorative booklet *The Masterpieces of the International Centennial Exhibition* (1876) ran a piece on the cabin with its game birds, guns, and bubbling steam, noting, "As we saunter down the walks into the deepest and darkest part of the ravine, we suddenly come upon a hunter's camp, perfect in all its details, and we are transported for a moment far away from the busy scenes around us to the distant western country, to the aboriginal forests." In common with the storytelling modus operandi of hunter's paradise, the exhibit allowed for a temporal reassignment, a virtual reality escape to the imagined West that protected the essence of national identity: "Here is a phase of American life that must be new and interesting not only to most of our foreign friends, but also to many of our own people from the eastern States, where civilization is rapidly crowding out all traces of colonial life." *Forest and Stream* agreed, presenting the cabin as an artifact of American primitivism, pastoralism, superabundance, and conservation ethics: "The hunter's camp is life at the beginning. It shows the chosen home of the race when it had half emerged from the savage and brutish, but its senses were not yet blunted to the flavor of the woods and fields. It is a reminder of the world's youth when it was content to play and be happy. Then the streams were for pleasure and not for power; the savannas were for strolling and not for killing; the forests were storehouses of game and nuts." Read as a stage of human development, the hunt was, put simply, right at the start, the West a crucible in which civilization developed in dynamic, invigorating, and irrevocably American ways. It was also layered with romantic allusion, a picture of catharsis, cogitation, and artistic osmosis ripe for the imprint of the naturalist hunter hero. According to *Forest and Stream*, "The whole scene is one for quiet, rest and contemplation. It is poetic and picturesque."[5]

At the Columbian Exposition of 1893 the motif of the hunter's cabin retained currency as a marker of the American experience. The popularity of sport hunting as a gentlemanly vocation in the interim years, together with pronouncements on the saliency of the frontier as a repository of American values from historian Frederick Jackson Turner, only added to its kudos as an artifact invested with auspicious meanings. Thirty million visited the expo at Chicago's Jackson Park during its six-month existence, wowed by the 633-acre site and its fusion of entertainment spectacle in the Midway, technological fetishism in the White City, and ode to bucolic nature in the wooded "orderly oasis." Dedicated to the memory of Daniel Boone and Davy Crockett, the hunter's cabin sat on a small island surrounded by woods and guarded by animal sculptures of the grizzly "Old Ephraim" and a bison "prairie king." Sponsored by the Boone and Crockett Club, the cabin was laden with hunting gear and memorabilia. "Woolen blankets, skins, saddles, and lassos are strewn carelessly over rude tables, bunks, and chairs, field glasses and weapons lean against the rough walls," wrote Herbert Howe Bancroft in his *Book of the Fair* (1895). Animation came in the form of resident woodsman Elwood Hofer, a buckskin-clad hunter on sabbatical from hunting for the Smithsonian in Yellowstone National Park, who "guided" visitors through the camp and entertained them with tales of the chase. Commentator Halsey Ives recalled, "Wearing fringed buckskins and sporting long hair and a wide-brimmed felt hat," Hofer performed as hunter hero exemplar, spinning yarns, listening to reminiscences from old "pioneers loving to re-call the vanished days," and answering questions of "younger inquirers pleased to see before them . . . this chapter of their romances."[6]

Surrounded by a "dead zoo" of trophies and infused with the evocative woodsmoke of the campfire, the hunter-actors of the exhibition circuit performed the hunt to a mass audience, their oratory and accouterments servicing the creation of the West as a national landscape—a "performed" frontier experience promising nostalgia for the wilderness of yore and a bright future for a nation founded on pioneer virtue. Just as Turner used the figurative landscape of the "stage" to explain his frontier theory, so too did the exhibition culture of the late nineteenth-century blur the boundaries of history and theater in crafting metanarratives on the past and the present. Underneath the assertions of realism and authenticity were implicit codes of dramaturgy: believability, it seemed, came from a convincing act. As Rosemarie K. Bank observes of the Indian actors playing "other" Indians at the Columbia Exhibition, the "interactions and interrelationships among these roles helped turn the fair's intellectual and pedagogical intentions into a performance." The frontier fixings of hunter's paradise told a similar story.[7]

HUNTER'S PARADISE TAKES TO THE STAGE: WILLIAM CODY AND THE WILD WEST SHOW

Across the road from Jackson Park in May 1893, William F. Cody took to the stage with his Congress of Rough Riders of the World. Famed for its boisterous broadcast of frontier iconography, Buffalo Bill's Wild West Show represented the pinnacle of western-themed entertainment in the late 1800s. On its opening night in Chicago, 18,000 people packed the auditorium, while some 2 million witnessed the show during its six-month run. Since hosting his inaugural exhibition in Omaha, Nebraska, in May 1883, Cody had successfully entertained audiences with set piece historical reenactments and displays of frontier flourish in the eastern United States and across the Atlantic. Crowds gathered at Earls Court on May 9, 1887, to witness the premiere of Cody's Wild West Show in London in an event that the *London Illustrated News* heralded as "an exact reproduction of daily scenes in frontier life." For the next five months, the "Drama of Civilization" played twice a day to crowds averaging 30,000 people and, on two occasions, to Queen Victoria.[8]

According to Cody himself, a critical function of his Wild West Show lay in "bringing the West to the East" via a series of colorful montages. Authenticity represented a critical tenet, presenting an autobiographical and instructional bent that reprised the function of historical text. In fact, Cody was keen to stress that this was not a show or a performance but a reenactment—educational and realistic. The presence of rip-roaring spectacle merely reflected the historic qualities of frontier life as performed by those who were simply "acting" themselves. As manager Nate Salsbury said of the 1893 program, the show was intended to make the public "acquainted with the manners and customs of the daily life of the dweller in the far west." As such, Cody's pitch consciously sidestepped the world of frontier performance, positioning itself apart from productions of folklore and melodrama and instead foregrounded an authorial voice and a historical frame of reference analogous to an exhibition or a "living" museum. This sleight of hand allowed Cody's troupe to indulge in the full gamut of melodramatics without audiences buying into the felicities and fictions of theater. As the *Illustrated London News* put it, "It is not a circus, nor indeed is it acting at all." Instead, the acts offered in Cody's ensemble were the stuff of history—"an exact reproduction"—told by expert witnesses and *not* the work of artistes. That said, flourishes of dramatic purchase were everywhere to be seen and played a critical part in the show's appeal. Importing the canonical stories of the game trail and injecting a sense of populism as well as animation, Cody's Wild West attracted widespread public fanfare. Part reenactment, part historical drama, and part travelogue, it laid bare the contours of the West in three hours of performance entertainment. From Pittsburgh to Paris, Barcelona to Baltimore, the all-action histrionics of the frontier were faithfully reproduced and firmly positioned, figuratively if not physically, in the West. *Il Corriere* thought the attempt to cheat geography an "awkward caricature," but the *Liverpool Mercury* spoke for many in praising the verisimilitude of Cody's presentation: "a piece of the Wild West . . . bodily transported to our midst." Also impressed was Mark Twain, who noted in a letter to Cody, "I have seen your Wild West show two days in succession and have enjoyed it thoroughly. It brought vividly back the breezy, wild life of the Great Plains, and the Rocky Mountains, and stirred me like a war cry."[9]

Of course, Buffalo Bill was no stranger to the world of frontier dramaturgy when he unveiled his inaugural Wild West ensemble in Omaha. In fact, his career as "plains celebrity" was an object lesson in the entanglements of hunting as performance and the complicated bind of sport, storytelling, and conquest that cartwheeled across the late nineteenth-century plains like storm-blown tumbleweed. Born in Iowa in 1846, Cody moved with his family to Fort Leavenworth and in his adult life cultivated a reputation as polymath frontiersman—wagon master, freighter, hunter, army scout, and raconteur. The sobriquet "Buffalo Bill" came directly from the hunting trail and an eighteen-month stint hunting bison for the Kansas Pacific Railroad, during which he killed 4,862 animals—and set the tone for his emerging fame as "hero of the plains." From the world of market hunting and its trade in animal capital, Cody moved seamlessly into the western tourist industry as a hunting guide for the legion of well-to-do sportsmen seeking a fantasy frontier "experience." As choreographer of the chase, Buffalo Bill offered daring hunts, Indian encounters, camp banter, buffalo steaks and champagne, with the stories and trophies of the game trail framed for purchase and posterity as artifacts of memory. Accordingly, when General Sheridan and a group of New York sporting "thoroughbreds" arrived at Fort McPherson for a hunt in September 1871, they found sixteen assembled wagons, two military companies as escort, and a buckskin-clad Cody brandishing rifle and sombrero, ready to enact the script of hunter's paradise in all its flamboyant glory. He noted that "as it was a nobby and high-toned outfit . . . I determined to put on a little style myself." Galloping across a western terrain that was both workplace and theater, Cody played the performing hunter hero with flourish. According to journalist Henry Davies's account in *Ten Days on the Plains* (1871), Cody "realized to perfection the bold hunter and gallant sportsman of the plains."[10]

As a hunting guide, Buffalo Bill showed himself to be a shrewd manipulator of frontier mythology. An awareness of the West as a landscape of performance (and one in which the provenance of the hunt loomed large) proved invaluable as Cody went on to colonize the world of popular entertainment. The subject of more than 1,700 dime novels commencing with Ned Buntline's *Buffalo Bill: The King of the Border Men* (1869), countless biographies, and various iterations of his memoir *The Life of Buffalo Bill* (1879), his literary imprint was extensive. Throughout, Cody was presented as frontier witness, "western man of the best type," whose life experiences had been "of almost continuous excitement." The performance codes of the hunter hero peppered hagiographic treatments, the hero of the piece identified as a "tireless rider, hunter, and scout," "gallant cavalier," and "a dead shot, a splendid horseman, and an absolutely fearless fighter." From the early 1870s, meanwhile, Buffalo Bill appeared in a series of frontier melodramas, beginning with *Scouts of the Prairie* (1872–73). In these animated dime novels of action, revenge, justice, and Indian attack, the game trail furnished discursive repertoire. Floored by an attack of stage fright on the opening night of *Scouts of the Prairie* at Nixon's Amphitheater, Chicago, Buffalo Bill resorted to an improvised quip about a hunting trip with local magnate Milligan (who was present). Laughter rippled through the crowd, and costar Ned Buntline followed up by saying, "Well, Bill, tell us about your hunt." Cody's soliloquy on the chase attested to his natural sense of showmanship and, importantly, pointed to the important role of the hunt in providing him with a performance routine that was well practiced. According to the man himself, "I told the story in a very funny way, and it took like wild-fire with the audience."[11]

As various scholars have illumined, Cody's Wild West Show functioned as a vector through which ideas of nationhood, progress, technology, gender, and empire were communicated. In Buffalo Bill's telling of the western story, the dueling, and dualistic, figures of the cowboy and the Indian stood center stage as carriers for the mythic frontier and for the sociopolitical prevarications of modern America itself. Running beneath, too, was the imprint of the West as hunter's paradise, a heroic geography that provided script, lead characters, and action scenes. A glance at the program serves to highlight the importance of hunting as a core theme in Cody's landscape of reenactment and reverie. The 1893 Chicago season promised firearms fetishism and the glorification of western martial cultures in the shape of sharpshooting by Johnny Baker and Colonel Cody, horse racing and riding contests by Euro-Americans and American Indians, and storming displays of buffalo and elk hunts. Guns, all-action movement, and the prospect of savage encounter with four- and two-legged foes denoted staple elements in the storytelling architecture of hunter's paradise and, accordingly, worthy grist for the Wild West performance. When Cody's ship docked in Gravesend, Kent, en route to London, his entourage included 121 passengers, 97 Indians, 180 horses, 18 buffalo, 10 elk, 5 Texas steers, 4 donkeys, and 2 deer. As *Punch* noted of his arrival, the "Coming Centaur" had crossed the Atlantic "In quest of new game, / With horses half frantic, / And riders the same."[12]

The hunt provided choreography and chronology to Cody's Wild West Show, sometimes the two so entangled that it was hard to separate them. In an oft-repeated show finale, "The Attack on the Settler's Cabin," hunting served as both situational context and adjective for action. The scene began with a pioneer returning to his homely stead from a successful hunt (complete with deer slung over his horse) to find his wife crying hysterically as whooping Indians descended on the clearing. In rode a deus ex machina in the form of Cody and his cowboy band, dispatching the invaders with a hail of gunfire and restoring order to the clearing. Beyond proscriptions on the sanctity of the family and the western code of "no duty to retreat," the set piece positioned the hunting economy as a primary stage in frontier development, cast the West as a provident yet savage wilderness, and valorized the Euro-American hunter hero as both provider and soldier savior. The hunt thereby provided a cohesive structure in which the "Drama of Civilization" could be played out. In this animated frontier of gunplay, exotic animals, and colorful action, historical epochs fitted neatly into theatrical acts. Cody's great contribution to the formula of hunter's paradise was live action, a rhetorical flamboyance, and the prospect of widespread broadcast. The synthesis of material and imagined geography, already a feature of the memory architecture of the game trail, gained a further, resolutely histrionic twist. Past and performance conjoined in the landscape inhabited and projected by Buffalo Bill. As one of his celebrators, William A. Annin, observed, Cody's frontier country "was nothing but a huge Wild Western Show."[13]

Aside from its chase scenes and flourishes of western (read hunting) skills, Cody's major contribution to the staging of hunter's paradise lay in his sanctification of westward conquest. "Attack on the Settler's Cabin" grounded heroism in the patina of subsistence and soldiering, while the 1893 program celebrated frontier resolve in the "vanguard pioneers . . . keen of eye, sturdy of build, inured to hardship, experienced in the knowledge of Indian habits and language, familiar with the hunt, and trustworthy in the hour of extremest danger." In Cody's genealogy of the hunter hero, meanwhile, Indian warriors from Sitting Bull to Black Elk provided indigenous renditions in displays of riding, bison hunting, and weapons proficiency. A critical reading of the Wild West Show might view such an enactment in negative terms, the American Indian as dastardly foil to the honorable agents of settlement to square up against (and prevail over) in what Richard White has dubbed "inverted conquest." At the same time, demonstrations of indigenous pursuits could also be read in a less monolithic, more salutary (or, at least, sympathetic) way, as heretical avatars of hunter heroism, albeit draped in contemporary axioms of vanishing race and noble primitivism.[14]

Historical reenactments of "Custer's Last Rally" and "The Battle of San Juan Hill" issued forth a less complicated (at least at the time) celebration in exalting two of the West's foremost exemplars of the manly canon—Custer and Roosevelt—in stylized soldier form. Pertinently, of the "Rough Riders" in Cody's troupe (a band historically designed to recruit the cowboy, miner, hunter breed of western frontier machismo), none were *actual* hunters. Authenticity came both from the story—the triumph of the hunt as drama— and also from the provenance of the leading man. Buffalo Bill's hunting credentials were uncontested, and it was Cody, of course, who played both Custer and Roosevelt in these montages. Preeminent hunter hero and alpha male of the theatrical frontier, in his Wild West Show Buffalo Bill led from the front. According to promotional literature, he was a "genuine specimen of western manhood." "An extraordinary hunter," Cody presented a model of heroic identity forged on the frontier: "Tall beyond the lot of ordinary mortals, straight as an arrow, not an ounce of useless flesh upon his limbs, but every muscle firm and hard as the sinews of a stag, with the frank, kindly eye of a devoted friend, and a natural courtly grace of manner . . . from spur to sombrero one of the finest types of manhood this continent has ever produced." A career as a hunter had given him "an eagle eye and iron nerves—to think quick, to resolve, to fire, to kill," and, according to the 1893 program, it was those "gifts" that "rendered him famous."[15]

In addition to the stylized hunter hero archetype, the Wild West Show gave center stage to animal actors. Bison, in particular, were an important part of the spectacle, providing a sense of animate action as well as subjects for a story (and a hunt) to be built around. After all, what was "Buffalo Bill" without his faunal namesakes? In common with Cody's literary landscape of memory, a disjuncture existed between the mechanics of bison hunting as used by the typical market hunter *and* the idealized bison hunting enacted by Buffalo Bill as polymath hunter hero. In the Wild West Show performance, horseback riders galloped around the arena felling the encircled herd with well-positioned bullets (blanks, in this case—by the 1880s, bison were far less expendable). It was thus the sporting hunter hero who earned full performing expression in Cody's theater. In part, the choice was one of choreography. Watching sequestered hunters lying on the ground at the stands and strafing animals with gunfire hardly struck as entertaining as the horse-bound antics of rifle wielding "knights of the plains." In conversation with Zane Grey, Cody noted that the use of the "stand" was "not [so] much hunting as it was railroad building"—far less alluring. As in the textual "afterlife" of the hunt, the chase injected a vital sense of contest and anticipation (even though the roundup spoke more of spotted bison than wild monarchs of the plains). And while the physical limits of the arena circumscribed the possibility of reenactment (in a way that textual reminiscence avoided), there was a great deal more showmanship afforded by the roving pursuit over the firing squad. Of his London show, Cody noted how "we gave them a buffalo hunt, in which I had a hand, and did a little fancy shooting." The preference was also ideological, one that spoke to the myth of the frontier and the narrative function of the Wild West Show. When the curtain went up, the West had to be won, and won with conviction, honor, and aplomb. This "storied past" bespoke American power, democracy, and progress in action; hence the 1893 program was perfunctory in its assertions of Cody as a "practical marksman" who claimed 4,862 bison in eighteen months.[16]

At the same time, the staged bison hunt traded in a romantic conquest of the frontier, one in which victory with honor was best secured by the sport hunters and their recreational displays of gentlemanly masculinity. In this reenactment, Cody was selective rather than disingenuous. Firm connections existed between the economies of leisure, politics, and militarism in the West. And true to form, he put on an excellent show as cavalier of the prairie. As the London *Era* noted: "No one I ever saw so adequately fulfills to the eye all the conditions of picturesque beauty, absolute grace and perfect identity with his animal . . . He is the only man I ever saw who rides as if he couldn't help it and the sculptor and the soldier had jointly come together in his act." Moreover, in translating the leisure economy of the hunt from plains to showground, Cody communicated an important continuity in the performance codes of hunter's paradise. He also showed himself to be a master at traversing the boundaries of hunter heroism for the purposes of popular entertainment and patriotic masculinity. To some extent these distinctions were liminal—as hunting guide and, indeed, Wild West showman, Cody continued to make money from animal capital (or, at least, some)—but his choice of hunting style remained instructive.[17]

The ultimate test of the hunter-performer, then, rested in an ability not only to catch the game, but also to play it. Jobbing actor, scriptwriter, and director of the western story, William F. Cody led the hunter's gaze and reshaped the hunt and its meaning in western mythology. From market hunter to marketeer of the frontier myth, he skillfully navigated the landscapes of hunting and performance before a series of different audiences, playing trail guide and leading man before an adoring crowd. As Joy Kasson points out, "Cody played the part of a real frontiersman playing the part of an actor playing the part of a frontiersman." Reanimating the fantasy architecture of the West in a series of acts, the frontier was brought to life wherever Buffalo Bill's troupe pitched their tents. In the process, "the past according to William F. Cody" was committed to national entertainment and historical memory. As Jefferson Slagle points out, the act of performance itself—dramatic communication—proved integral to the blurring of boundaries between frontier mythology and historical truth. As he notes, "Buffalo Bill's Wild West was a significant participant in the writing, speaking, singing, dancing and acting of popular western history . . . the incidents performed by wild westers became history via the act of performance." The people were authentic, the places too, so why not the script, especially as construed by a "representative man of the frontiersmen of the past." It was, then, as a hunting scout writ large—complete with authentic western voice and embodied expertise—that best encapsulated Buffalo Bill as "America's first megastar" (as Larry McMurtry has described him). As the *New York Herald* reported, "It is not every day that one can see on the stage a real border scout fighting over again his battles." Even the fact that he presented himself as an "old scout" who had never been to more than twenty or thirty theatrical shows played to a storytelling trope of the rough and ready westerner set against the cultural

affectations of the urban East. When Buffalo Bill traveled east on the invitation of Sheridan, he dressed in full buckskin regalia. "Something told me that
some of the people I had met in New York might want to know just how a
scout looked in his business clothes," Cody noted, and he was right. Buffalo
Bill wowed high society with the homegrown exoticism of the hunter aesthetic and went down a storm (though his attempts at "artistic dancing" fell
flat). Those who had hunted with Cody on the plains were transported back
to the game trail while those who knew him from dime novel adventures
immediately recognized the unmistakable garb of the western action hero.
Cody's sartorial choice, then, elucidated many things: the showman's awareness of the power of frontier performance; the fact that his celebrity identity
was rooted in a western geography; and the multiple uses of animal capital.
From the testimonial culture of the game trail came provenance as a theatrical performer. As W. E. Webb put it adroitly in *Buffalo Land* (1872), he was
"altogether the best guide I ever saw. The mysterious plain is a book that he
knows by heart."[18]

"GRIZZLY" ADAMS: LIVE ANIMAL COLLECTION
AND THE CARNIVAL OF THE CHASE

Also navigating the borderlands of game trail authenticity and the public
choreography of hunter's paradise was James "Grizzly" Adams. Born in
Massachusetts around 1807, Adams grew up fired with the joys of the game
trail, and as a young man he roved the forests of Maine, Vermont, and New
Hampshire trapping wild animals for the circus trade (on one occasion even
apprehending a Bengal tiger that had escaped from his employers). After a
short-lived apprenticeship in the family shoemaking business and an ill-fated
investment in St. Louis in which his wares went up in smoke, Adams resolved,
like so many others, to find his fortune in the California goldfields. Again,
like so many others, his various attempts at making it on the Pacific shore—
prospecting, ranching, trading—faltered, and he decided in 1852 to head into
the mountains to escape from "the civilized world," armed with a wagon, a
bedraggled oxen team, and two rifles.[19]

At first glance, Adams's errand into the wilderness bore a familiar hue,
of the retreat from civilization and the hunting trail as possessing a form
of innate catharsis in its raw truth and harsh simplicity. He set out for "the

wildest and most unfrequented parts of the Sierra Nevada, resolved thence-
forth to make the wilderness my home and wild beasts my companions."
Setting up the stage for primitive heroics in the tradition of hunter's paradise, his autobiography crafted the West as grand and romantic, a provident
landscape where "game never failed" and he found "health excellent; my
time pleasantly and continuously occupied." A heroic geography lent itself
to the storytelling codes of the hunt. To Adams, the trees were "giants in
themselves," and the grandeur of "new and romantic scenes . . . enchanted
my imagination, and seemed to inspire me with a new life." That new life
was as a trapper, hunter, and broker of animal capital, although Adams's
rendition of the western skin trade had a twist: capturing live beasts for
the show market. Adams bartered skins, sold meat to emigrant trains, and
also made a "rich harvest" from captive animals acquired on expeditions in
the Sierra Nevada, Humboldt Mountains, Rockies, and Cascades through
the mid-1850s. As British hunter Frank Marryat recorded in *Mountains and
Molehills* (1855), his charges were often shipped to mining towns, where "on
the Sunday following, the famous grizzly bear of America, would fight a wild
bull." In spring 1853 Adams himself stepped into the ring for a bruin wrestling contest in Mariposa, a victory that netted him $800 and a contract from
Messrs. McShee and Robinson for fresh grizzlies to ship to South America for
the ring. In sum, Grizzly Adams ran the full gamut of western animal capital;
as Marryat noted, he was a "bear hunter, a bear trapper, and bear fighter."[20]

Like Buffalo Bill Cody, Grizzly Adams gained his nom de plume from animal association and hunting, lending him a kind of feral presence and connection to the wild frontier. Also in common with Cody, Adams's hunter
hero was resolutely theatrical and embedded in a culture of performance first
exercised on the game trail. To the public gaze, he presented himself as "a
kind of demigod in the glorious and magnificent creation," a man of "roving
and adventurous disposition" and "resolute spirit and indomitable energies."
Visually, too, the "Old Hunter" (as he called himself) cut quite a presence in
a buckskin suit and deer skin hat adorned with a fox brush. Once more, the
storytelling codes of the hunt appeared to demand a patina of demonstrative
(inter)action with the primeval landscape, of a wrestling with the wild that
was both figurative and literal in Adams's case. The hunter thus found himself "seized with an insatiable desire to make myself master of the untamed,
but I believed not untameable, denizens of the mountain ranges," and he

described his encounter with the West as a series of daring episodes full of formidable animal opponents and flourishing displays of enacted bravado. *The Adventures of James Capen Adams: Mountaineer and Grizzly Bear Hunter of California* (1860), which duly regurgitated Adams's trailside stories for popular consumption, courtesy of San Francisco journalist Theodore Hittell (who was for Adams what Ned Buntline was for Cody), pictured its subject as a stalwart frontier hero facing off against the wilderness. One illustration showed the hunter pitted against a giant elk, about to plunge a knife into the heart of an adversary that was anthropomorphically posed rearing on its hind legs.[21]

It was, however, the bruin that was consistently framed as Adams's faunal hunter hero opponent and necessary foil, a beast that "in the consciousness of his strength and magnanimity of courage, alone of all animals, stands appalled in the face of any enemy, and turns not from the sight of man." Perhaps the greatest of game trail performances lay in the capture of "Samson," a 1,500-pound grizzly, a "terrible animal" and "monarch of the forest" prone to "unearthly bellowings." Referencing his authorship as a hunter hero and personal take on hierarchy in the economies of western animal capital, Adams noted: *This* winter, thought I, colossal as he may be, he shall be my prize. I did not wish to kill him for his hide, tallow, and meat. If he was an animal of the magnitude I suspected, he was too superb a creature for such a sacrifice. I wanted him alive—I wanted him for exhibition—I wanted to show him as a monster specimen of such of his species as inhabited that quarter of America." Adams lured the bruin into a log trap, where the performance continued, with actions that make for rather uncomfortable reading today, but were well within the confines of contemporary animal welfare practices. Adams beat the bear with a stick, threw dirt at him, and pacified him using fire and red-hot pokers, tension maintained by the idea that at any moment the surly bruin might break free. He didn't, and Adams and his compatriots fashioned a wooden crate and wagon to transport Samson to camp. The capture of the cubs Ben Franklin and Lady Washington, meanwhile, injected camaraderie and comedy into the perfomative hunt—projecting the alternate identity of bruin as cuddly comic and of the hunter hero as upended. Proof of his everyman status (like Cody, able to laugh at himself), Adams described how "a hunter of great bears was thus besieged by little ones" and forced to hide in a tree as they scurried beneath. Lady Washington, in particular, offered a total (and irrevocably gendered) contrast to Samson in her "pleasing, so child-like" countenance and status as a "companion and friend" and "the prettiest little animal in all the country." Franklin, Adams's favorite, protected him against the incursions of other grizzlies (becoming severely injured in the process) while the "Old Hunter" fashioned him moccasins to alleviate sore feet acquired from traversing the Great Basin. Both roamed with Adams on the game trail, sometimes on collar and chain, carrying game and other loads. As he explained, if tutored from an early age (and not spared the rod), the bruin could be acculturated into a "pet" and "a most affectionate and faithful servant."[22]

Running through Adams's game trail performance, then, was a characteristic epistemology of the hunter hero: of the man "wilded" and renewed, but wilderness duly tamed by his masculine presence. Also representative of the narrative canon was a juxtaposition of epiphany in solitude, matched with the need for an audience. As Adams elucidated, after killing a sow bear in Yosemite, "My feelings, as she thus lay dead at my feet, it would be difficult to describe. I looked at the hills around, to see if any eye had beheld my success; but all was silence. I looked to the heavens; but all was quiet, only a vulture was circling like a speck in the distant ether. I was alone in the gorge, and, as I looked upon the dead monster, felt like Alexander sated with victory, and wishing another foe to engage, worthy of my prowess."[23]

Adams got his audience before too long. As the "Old Hunter" packed out his wares from the mountains, communities on the way stopped to gawk at the traveling entourage. It must have presented quite a sight. Headed for Portland after an expedition in fall 1853, Adams described a western ark of faunal capital both dead and alive: horses, a wagon of buffalo robes, skins, skulls, dried meat, and a "herd" of six bears, four wolves, four deer, four antelope, two elk, and an Indian dog. The fruit of one season's hunt, the beasts were set for shipment to Boston for the museum and traveling show trade. What marked Adams apart as a hunter hero was his connection not only to the dead but also to the live trophy. As acolyte William Wright noted, Grizzly was not only "an uncouth Knight-errant of the mountains" but an animal tamer in possession of an esoteric understanding of the ways of wild things. Put simply, he "dealt in live grizzlies as well as dead ones." At Stockton "a large crowd" gathered around the "stores of curiosities" awaiting transit to Lima, while a trip to Sonora provoked similar interest in the feral Adams and his bizarre entourage, their attention "equally divided between me and the animals—they doubtless thinking me the queerest one of the lot . . . I suppose I appeared somewhat grotesque, if not savage, with my long beard and Indian hunting suit." On another occasion, at the wharf in San Francisco one over zealous voyeur got too close to the bear cage and received a cuff, "the want of which probably interferes with his comfort, while sitting, to this day." Adams, roused to the grizzly's defense, drew his pistol and exclaimed it was a "justifiable assault." The man backed down, an excited crowd chanted "hurrah for the wild Yankee," and Adams duly bought them drinks. Such encounters suggested live animal performance as an end point to the game trail, "living prizes" in Adams's own parlance to match the trophies taken by sporting parties as markers of their experience in the wilderness.[24]

Adams's culture of performance extended far beyond titillated glances at the feral frontiersman in the entrepots of the Pacific shore. Instead Grizzly's command of animal capital, performative storytelling, and roster of faunal accomplices took him to a professional stage. From a series of traveling shows at San Jose and San Francisco in 1855–56 (notably presiding over "pony races" with the bears at Colonel Joe Rowe's Pioneer Circus at the San Francisco Union Theater), Adams established his Mountaineer Museum at 143 Clay Street in San Francisco (later, at Clay and Kearney as the Pacific Museum), complete with live animals (bears chained to bolts in the floor, caged cougars and bruins, and corralled elk, antelope, and later a sea lion and baboon) as well as taxidermy. Watching over the "happy family" was a buckskin-clad Adams, who, ever the performing hunter hero, slept at the exhibit on a bison robe.[25]

The collection attracted sizeable public interest as an artifact of hunter's paradise reconstructed, somewhat incongruously, in an urban basement. The *Daily Alta California* commented on the museum as a place of "wild charms but all conducted with decorum." It offered a perfect blend of frontier romance—the hunter hero incarnate who "has been some years in the mountains and encountered many hardships and dangers in capturing the monsters now in his collection"—and his charges, literally wrestled from the savage wilderness. Ben Franklin, in particular, offered comic explication on the equestrian hunter and the pursuit of game: "A perfect wonder in his way. His keeper mounts him and gives him an invitation to shake him off. Bruin stands on three legs and rolls like an elephant but when this method fails he throws back his paws and claws his rider down. He stands up on his hind legs and his keeper gives him a gentle shove and over and over and over he goes as if impelled by an irresistible force. This animal weighs 800 pounds and, in the mountains, hunts with his master and is very eager for game." At the same time, the museum earned plaudits for its reasonable price and educational function. As the *Daily Alta California* noted, "The rooms have been very conveniently fitted up, and, as the price of admission is fixed at only 25 cents, there is no doubt that crowds will be attracted to witness so great and so many rare specimens of Natural History."[26]

Most important to Adams's cult of celebrity was his association with the press. The man himself took out advertisements in local papers, walked his bruin pets down the streets for publicity, and gained particular purchase from an association with journalist Theodore Hittell, later editor of the *San Francisco Evening Bulletin* and keen Adams biographer. As Storer and Tevis noted, the *Bulletin* printed more than a hundred "news notes" on Adams through 1857, making Hittell his "unofficial public-relations officer." In a slew of articles for the *Bulletin* in October 1856, Hittell waxed lyrical about the Mountaineer Museum, its display of animal capital, and its formidable host. In the "Great Show of Animals: Mountaineer Museum" Adams's menagerie earned top billing as a veritable cornucopia—"the *largest collection of wild animals* ever exhibited on the Pacific Coast"—and offered readers biographies of its faunal personalities, Samson, Lady Washington, and Benjamin Franklin. A second article hailed the exhibit for its demonstration of frontier taming, "one of the most complete examples of the power of man over the ordinarily savage and ferocious denizens of the forests," while the third in the series, entitled "Great Show of Animals," focused particularly on the "happy family" of bruins. Ben was "as playful as a kitten when he feels lively and gets a huge log chain over his back. He rears, pitches, jumps, shakes his head, tumbles and rattles his chain with a sort of terrific playfulness," and Funny Joe was "clumsy and ludicrous" in his anthropomorphic gait—"He will sit and stand, dance, take a gentleman's arm, and walk about, swinging his body like a lady, or chew tobacco and smoke cigars, like a gentleman of the first stamp." In its animal displays, the museum offered an important conduit to the world of hunter's paradise, both material and imagined. It channeled the storytelling codes of the game trail—Adams himself was "reminded of the freshness and freedom of the forests," claiming to "live over again in imagination the golden days when I trod, in pleasure and in joy, upon the mountain side."

He noted how each animal "recalls its own special adventure"—and offered instruction on the organic quality of "bear-ness." When Franklin died in January 1858, the *Bulletin* ran an article called "Death of a Distinguished Native Californian." Rumor had it that one of Adams's grizzlies served as a model for the artist Charles Nahl, who designed the California flag, while *Spirit of the Times* mentioned Adams's collection in lobbying for zoological collections in New York City. Depicted on 1858 commemorative handbills for the laying of the Atlantic Telegraph, at the very least, Grizzly and his parading bruins cut a presence as artifacts of the theatrical frontier. As James Madison Grover noted, the bears went down a storm, "even in the land where grizzly bears were common."[27]

On April 1860, Grizzly Adams opened his California Menagerie in a tent at the corner of Thirteenth Street and Fourth Avenue in New York City for a six-week show (and subsequent tour), under the sponsorship of P. T. Barnum. The performing hunter hero and the theatrics of the game trail made an easy transition to the stage. According to the *Spirit of the Times*, it was "the most curious, unique, and interesting museum of animated nature ever presented to the public." A trans-media exercise in the promotion of hunter's paradise (and some two decades before Cody's extrapolation), the celebrity of Adams and his bruins was secured by parade, show, and literary explication. In a carnival atmosphere on opening day, Adams traveled along Broadway on a float, bedecked in his hunting attire and marshaling three grizzly bears. Under the heading "Wild Sports in the Far West," the *New York Weekly* ran fifteen articles on the "California hunter, and 'wild man'" for public digest. Meanwhile, the pamphlet *Life of J. C. Adams, Old Adams, Old Grizzly Adams, Containing a Truthful Account of His Bear Hunts, Fights with Grizzly Bears, Hairbreadth Escapes, in the Rocky and Nevada Mountains and the Wilds of the Pacific Coast* (1860), produced to accompany the exhibit, narrated the trail backstory to the California Menagerie. In the preface to the ten-cent booklet, Adams confirmed his credentials as plain-talking frontier storyteller, seeking no validation beyond the Rocky Mountain hunters who knew he spoke the truth. Hunting was celebrated in various iterations—as employment, sport, for the prospect of hand-to-hand contests, daring escapades, and comic asides. It was an ideal existence: to Adams, "a hunter's life has always been my delight, and I know of nothing so exciting, to my taste, as the pursuit of wild animals, and the varied adventures that accompany an ardent and enterprising spirit engaged in such pastime" (in an intriguing reference to Cody's later presentations, he also noted bison hunting to be an "admirable mixture of the agreeable and remunerative; but there is a monotonous sameness in all such expeditions").[28]

The exhibit contained 150 live animals, over which Grizzly Adams presided as master of ceremonies. The abundant West, the savage wilderness tamed, and the provenance of the hunter represented critical axioms of the performance. Barnum valorized his business partner as frontier hero extraordinaire, his profession lending him "a recklessness which, added to his natural invincible courage, rendered him truly one of the most striking men of the age." This feral countenance, somewhat out of place on the streets of the Big Apple, rendered Grizzly "quite as much a show as his bears." He was a feral artifact, shaggy coated and half-animal, a creature of the primal forest, and a keen artifact of the exotic frontier. As Barnum recalled, dressed in hunter's buckskin with wolf pelt draped around his shoulders, Adams appeared a "rough, fierce-looking, powerful, demi-savage." At the same time, the show's main purchase lay in its displays of domestication, the subaltern grizzly rendered as "docile as kittens" courtesy of superior human authority and a whimsical message on the project of wilderness taming. Barnum described the typical show scene in which Adams performed "firm as adamant and as resolute as a lion" before the "thousands who saw him dressed in his grotesque hunter's suit, and witnessed the apparent vigor with which he 'performed' the savage monsters, beating and whipping them into apparently the most perfect docility." An advertisement for the show thus presented a frontier that gloried in its wilderness identity but kept it comfortably corralled: "DANCING BEARS, SINGING BEARS, CLIMBING BEARS, BEARS that TURN SOMERSAULTS, BEARS that have SERVED as PACK HORSES for Adams, and have slept with him for many years in the Mountains, etc. There are also bears that are dressed and perform as SOLDIERS; Bears that appear in LADIES COSTUME, Hoops, Crinoline, etc. The exhibition also includes hundreds of preserved specimens of Natural History, which have fallen before the deadly rifle of Adams."[29]

The pairing of Adams and Barnum was telling. Both men were not averse to telling a yarn, and both had a keen sense of showmanship. On his deathbed, Adams confessed to a clergyman that he had "told some pretty large stories about his bears." As Barnum recalled of his partner, "In fact, according to his story, California contained specimens of all things, animate and inanimate, to be found in any part of the globe" (Adams reputedly sold him a golden California pigeon, a rare acquisition until its paint wore off). Meanwhile, as narrator of the frontier and theatrical hunter hero, Adams became a fixture of the New York scene. One newspaper noted, "Few of our city readers have not seen the strange old man taking a morning airing with a bear or two, accompanied by a limited but noisy band, composed of a bass drum and a piccolo flute. He had frequent personal encounters with his bears and, after a time, people began to feel a want of something in their daily paper if the chronicle narrated not how Old Adams had lost a leg, an arm or part of his head on the day before, through the petulance of his chief grizzly." As narrator of the West, Adams performed an important broadcast of hunter's paradise. His recollections—a mixture of material encounter and storytelling license—were irrevocably truthful in their depiction of the culture of the hunt. In this he was an exemplary guide. On his death on October 25, 1860 (the result of many bruin-inflicted injuries), Grizzly Adams was buried in Charlton, Massachusetts. Chiseled on his gravestone was the impression of a man, rifle in hand, walking with a bear. The inscription read:

> And silent now the hunter lays,
> Sleep on, brave tenant of the wild!
> Great Nature owns her simple child
> And Nature's God to whom alone
> The secret of the heart is known
> In silence whispers that his work is done.[30]

Adams's identity as performing hunter hero continued into his afterlife. Hittell's biography, published in both San Francisco and Boston in 1860, ran to further editions in 1911, 1912, and 1926. *Beadle's Boys Library of Sport, Story and Adventure* ran a story by Frank Powell titled "Old Grizzly Adams: The Bear Tamer, or the Monarch of the Mountains" (1899) in typical dime novel formula, depicting Adams as a grizzled veteran of the trail, "wild beast hunter" clad in buckskin and living with his "family" in the "deepest recesses of the mountains" roaming across print copy to fight Indians, duel with gamblers and road agents, even ride a bear through a mining camp. *Captain "Bruin" Adams, The Bear Tamer: Old Grizzly* (c. 1880), produced for the London pulp market, traded similar themes of the feral frontiersmen wrestling with the wilderness in its depictions of the bear-riding hunter with a rifle named "fire fangs," mysterious encounters with "the Wild Huntress" and "the Avenger," and Indian kidnap plots on the savage frontier. Like Cody, Adams became the subject of "border dramas," his performing hunter hero further sensationalized in such productions as "Grizzly Adams, Hunter of Sierra Nevadas." Based on a play of the same name written in the 1880s by E. T. Goodrich, the show promised entertainment and instruction on a *"historical personage,* bringing out vividly all those noble traits of character, which makes him an *ideal creation.* The *action of the play* abounds in *active* life, yet devoid of *Gunpowder or Yelling Indians*, while it possesses strong dramatic interest, sparkling and interesting dialogue, Startling situations and brilliant tableaux." An animated hunter's paradise for the stage, the *Ann Arbor Argus* commended the cast and scenery as "most elaborate and realistic." By the time William Wright wrote his own homage to the bruin, *The Grizzly Bear* (1909), he was crediting Adams as inspiration to go West, as well as ennobling him as the "prince of all hunters." Significantly, by the time Adams made it onto the big screen courtesy of Disney's *Life and Times of Grizzly Adams* (1973), based on Charles Sellier's biography of the same name, he had made the full journey from performing hunter hero to ennobled conservationist: "The incredible story of a man who is adopted by the animals of the forest and blessed with the ability to live in harmony with the wilderness. His fear of animals turned to respect. His respect turned to love. He discovered man and animal can work together to survive."[31]

THE CAMPFIRE RESTORED: WALTER McCLINTOCK AND THE CONTEMPLATIVE GAZE

The showmanship of Cody and Adams offered theatrics, flourish, and the West as a melee of action, a tableau of animated color. Other performative carriers of hunter's paradise, meanwhile, more consciously referenced the intimate storytelling codes of campfire oratory on the lecture circuit. Walter McClintock, hunter and writer, figuratively invited the public to join a gathering around the embers of the fire pit and imbibe of its woodsmoke in his talks. Based on McClintock's experiences as part of a government forestry expedition to Montana (1896) and his subsequent adoption into the Blackfeet tribe by Chief Mad Wolf, his lecture "The Blackfeet Indians and the Plains and Rocky Mountains" offered up exotic tales of Indian customs, practices, and legends. The idea of the West as a hunter's paradise also loomed large in the narrative landscape configured for a public audience in the early 1900s. As the *New York Herald* vociferated, "He gave time to incidents of the chase." McClintock introduced the Rockies as "game country" before talking about the hunting adventures of indigenous and Euro-American travelers. An inveterate storyteller, McClintock crafted an evocative scene of primal utopia: "You can distinguish the heavy hoar from the willows and the snow clinging to the branches of the pines . . . A fire burns beneath a tripod in front of the lodge," in a region of abundant game and trails "traversed only by hunters, trappers and Indians." The power of the Winchester, the grandeur of the mountains, the howling of wolves, the habits of the outdoor kitchen, and the action-packed prospect of a grizzly bear in camp one night offered genre staples of panoramic wilderness scenery, savage and dangerous animals, gun lore, and trail culture. As with many hunters, McClintock cast himself as the hero woodsman, in communion with the ways of nature, the freedoms and rejuvenating attributes of the West, and nostalgia for a life since past: "I felt in accord with the world, as though I belonged to the forest. My heart was light, I was as free as the air . . . Now I look back on those days of hard work and simple living in that prairie wilderness as the happiest days of my life. Then every part of me in mind and body seemed sound and sane. On those broad prairies were no worries nor pessimists: no taxes, laws, no creeds—nothing but a wonderful freedom and contentment."[32]

McClintock lectured at Carnegie Hall and various venues on the eastern seaboard and took his lecture tour to Europe as well. He spoke before the Berlin Society of Anthropology, Ethnology and History; the Royal Institute of Great Britain, the Royal Dublin Society, at Oxford and Cambridge Universities, and before the Crown Prince and Princess at Potsdam. The power of oral testimonial and autobiographical authenticity proved integral to his repertoire, lending a sense of authority and ethnographic exactitude to his narrations. Audiences warmed to the use of specific incidents of adventure. *Oxford Magazine*, for one, was enthralled by the tale of a "thrilling grizzly." Ideas of fantasy as well as literary pedigree set the scene, as the *Berliner Lokal-Anzeiger* explained how McClintock "gave us a wonderful insight into that fairy world of beauty reminding us of the days when we read the Leatherstocking Tales." The speaker gained plaudits for his authentic voice and adventuring style. Auditoriums were packed with interested folk, who were, according to the *Deutsche Warte*, "delighted with the wild romance and splendor of the scenery which the explorer reproduced." Yale University's *Gazette* praised the tales of "real life" and also attested to the communication and reception of the hunter's paradise motif. The magazine summarized McClintock's story as one of "into the wild and unfrequented country of now Montana, then a paradise for hunting and fishing." In a sense, public oratory allowed the listener to experience the game trail by proxy, the West and its spirit brought to life by a good story. As Alfred Hayes, secretary of the Birmingham and Midland Institute, explained: "He made the audience feel almost the same sensations which he himself had experienced in the romantic life he lived." For Wilhelm, ex–crown prince of Germany, listening to tales of the West prompted his own desires for travel and escapism: "I do hope the day may come when I myself can ride a pony along 'old Indian Trails.' You know my love of nature, outdoor life and hunting . . . One gets a <u>longing for the wilds</u>, being fed up with all civilization (so called civilization)."[33]

Apart from the power of the autobiographical gaze, McClintock communicated his story using visual material. Colored slides added to the oratory, highlighting the way in which the mythology of the West was sold using compatible, and mutually referential, trans-media mediums. Alfred Hayes found the images mesmerizing: "The coloured lantern slides were of astonishing beauty, quite beyond anything I had thought possible." Visual artifacts aided the sense of immersion, and allowed the audience to capture an image of the region. *Riget* applauded the use of slides, noting how "his marvelously beautiful pictures, of which each one could be called a work of art, helped people to understand what McClintock told . . . and one had a feeling of making oneself the journey which he described." Some among the scientific community saw the visual quotient as too lowbrow, detracting from the ethnographic credentials of the talk. In a somewhat acerbic review, the Berlin *Taegliche Rundschau* berated the "contemptible (base) joy" the general public " took in the picture" but confessed to the power of the images to impress, "sinfully beautiful in their coloring." The image complemented and embellished McClintock's testimony, his fluent prose and engaging slides communicating an evocative scene. Adeptly summed up by Arthur Tait from the Leeds Institute of Science, Art, and Literature, McClintock's public oratory allowed his audiences to be in "living touch with the poetry of nature."[34]

Leading Ladies of the Chase: Hunter Heroines and the Contestation of Masculine Hegemony

In the reenactment of hunter's paradise, the wilderness hero came in many guises (as the likes of Cody, Adams, and McClintock illuminate). Significantly, *he* was not always a *he*. Just as women patrolled the contours of the game trail in the form of plucky pioneers and lady adventurers, so too did they inhabit the theatrical landscape of the frontier. Women in western melodrama often played the role of demure subservients or damsels in distress—homesteaders attacked by Indians, naïve travelers tricked by villainous ne'er-do-wells, and such like—but there were notable deviations from the script. With its privileging of testimonial culture and the oratory of the expert witness, the performance codes of the hunt allowed room for other voices to emerge: notably in the form of the gun-toting heroine. More commonly known by her nom de plume Calamity Jane, Martha Canary (or Cannary) trod the boards as a buckskin-clad scout and raconteur whose exploits on the hunting trail mediated the myth of female passivity on the frontier and confirmed the "wild woman" as a key character in the staging of the West in national folklore. Equally important in the show(wo)manship of the female frontier was Annie Oakley, "armed western woman" and staple in Cody's Wild West Show with her twirling guns and sharpshooting routine. On one level, these new renditions inhabited the territory of whimsical entertainment, but they also raised the specter of an alternative reading of frontier experience and a destabilization of the position of the masculine hunter hero through performance practice. As Rosemarie Bank reminds us, "Performers complicate unitary readings and performance resists binary interpretations." In the "live action" repertory of the hunt, the leading man did not always get the best lines or, indeed, the best shot.[35]

Born in Princeton, Missouri, on May 1, 1852, Martha Jane was the eldest of six children born to farmer Robert W. Canary and his wife Charlotte. In 1864 the family set out for Montana, seeking prosperity and fortune in the mineral boom, setting the stage for the emergence of Calamity Jane as a frontier heroine. In her eight-page autobiography, *Life and Adventures of Calamity Jane, By Herself* (1896), Martha presented the journey west as a formative one. The vernacular of the hunt was lofted early on as she confirmed her credentials as a female hunter and all-round thrill-seeker: "The greater portion of my time was spent in hunting along with the men and hunters of the party, in fact I was at all times with the men when there was excitement and adventure to be had." Having already depicted the life of a hunter as one of dynamism and action, Jane spoke of her abilities as a "fearless rider" and a good shot before offering comment on the collective identity of the traveling party: "As the pioneers of those days had plenty of courage we overcame all obstacles." Adventuring and exhilaration, riding and gun skills, frontier resilience and bravado—these all represented essential attributes of the hunter hero of the West. Pertinently, all were qualities claimed by Calamity Jane as she (and others) constructed her place in the canon of western folklore.[36]

At Virginia City, the Canarys eked out an existence in the rough and ready prospecting community. Her mother did laundry and ran a bordello. Her father gambled. Both died in 1866–67, leaving Martha and her siblings orphaned and destitute. She drifted between forts, mining towns, and railroad camps working as a mule skinner, construction worker, and teamster before traveling for several years with the US Army (1870–76). In her autobiography, Canary spoke of thousands of scouting missions and daredevil military escapades, wowing readers with news that she had been only "minutes" away from the Little Big Horn and thus setting a hypothetical premise of the saving of one of the West's foremost hunter heroes by his female equal (riding in, all guns blazing, in a style Custer would have seen, no doubt, as his own). Canary indeed appeared on the army payroll at Fort Saunders in 1872, but most likely she served as itinerant cook, teamster, laundress, prostitute, comic foil, and all-round good sport rather than pathfinder (see figure 5.1). One traveler recalled her working at Coffee's Ranch on the Platte River in 1874 as an "entertainer—dancing, drinking much bad whisky and in various ways relieving her victims of their coin, which she spent with a free and willing hand." In any case, Jane was operating far beyond the conventional boundaries of female domestic behavior and, in the process, gaining a reputation as a rambunctious character known for her driving skills, coarse language, drinking exploits, and, of course, masculine dress. General Dodge considered her a "regimental mascot" and "a queer combination" of cook, nurse, and adventurer, while journalist Thomas Macmillan noted that "she had the reputation of being a better horse-back rider [and] mule and bull whacker (driver), and a more unctuous coiner of English, and not the Queen's pure, either, than any (other) man in the command." Macmillan's words implied that, by effectively

FIGURE 5.1. Martha "Calamity Jane" Canary, ca. 1800–1900. Autry National Center.

demonstrating her masculine dexterity, Calamity had gained acceptance into the company of men.[37]

In July 1876, Calamity Jane rode into Deadwood on a wagon train from Fort Laramie. The *Black Hills Pioneer* announced with interest that "'Calamity Jane' has arrived"—a testament to growing local interest in her as a frontier whimsy. Wearing a suit of fringed buckskin and brandishing a rifle, Calamity cut a pictorial presence as the archetypal hunter hero. That Jane was traveling with a bona fide example of such, namely Wild Bill Hickok, aided the impression. Keen to dress their arrival in the prospecting camp with pomp and fanfare, the entourage "rode the entire length of Main Street mounted on good horses and clad in complete suits of buckskin" before pitching their tents—frontier heroes in the making clearly understood the dynamics of performance code in stoking the cult of celebrity. In subsequent months, Jane frequented the Gem Saloon and other venues working as a dance-hall girl. The demands of town life required a sartorial adjustment and camp mate Joseph "White-Eye" Anderson recalled that Calamity asked to borrow money for female fixings, noting, "I can't do business in these old buckskins." Jane, nonetheless, ensured the perpetuation of her hunter hero persona by hard drinking, regaling folk with tales of her wilderness exploits in the saloon (described by Anderson as "some of the toughest stories ever heard"), howling at the top of her voice when riding along Main Street, and displaying a general tendency for trigger-itch. When she rode into Cheyenne in 1877, the *Daily Sun* paid heed to a character renowned for her typical pioneer resolve and unconventionally mannish survivalism in an editorial announcing the arrival of "the well-known frontierswoman."[38]

Calamity Jane the hunter heroine took hold of popular consciousness in the landscape of frontier mythology under construction in the 1870s. In Horatio Maguire's locally distributed pamphlet *The Black Hills and American Wonderland* (1877), she was billed as a raven-haired buckskin-clad "dare-devil boy . . . giving as good an imitation of a Sioux war-whoop as a feminine voice is capable of" while his bellicose celebration of westward expansion, *The Coming Empire* (1878), presented her galloping through a valley in trademark buckskin with pistol firing aloft. Meanwhile, Calamity Jane the "female scout" gained a national stage courtesy of the dime novel. Edward Wheeler presented Calamity as a principal character in *Deadwood Dick: Prince of the Road* (1877), and she subsequently appeared in around twenty novels.

Wheeler's Calamity was deployed with artistic license in mind, her name used to invoke the idea of the cross-dressing "wild woman" and to strike an authentically western pose without undue attention to historical accuracy. A boisterous female foil to Deadwood Dick, Calamity cursed, smoked cigars, engaged in riding and shooting escapades and saved her hero from risky scenarios. Presented as "a boyish figure . . . dressed in a carefully tanned costume of buckskin," she remained ambiguous as a gender model. Her masculine affectations were situated as aberrant (the result of a traumatic romantic tryst), and her ultimate aspiration was revealed to be settling down with Dick, while underneath the buckskin bluster and weatherworn countenance, Wheeler continued to assert her pretty complexion. She did, though, represent a transgressive figure as a hunter heroine and was keen to point out her ability to fill the boots of frontier masculinity. As she noted in *Deadwood Dick on Deck, or Calamity Jane, the Heroine of Whoop Up* (1878), "I'm as big a gun among the men as any of 'em." The image of Calamity as a "sport"— both hunter heroine and wild western woman archetype—remained a staple through the series. In *Deadwood Dick on Deck*, she appeared on the cover and earned top billing. Early in the story, two prospectors encounter the "strange girl of the hills" galloping past, rifle in hand, after hearing her singing from afar about the "life of the scout, gay and free." Offering a frontier litany on the skills possessed by the hunter hero (adventurousness, knowledge of the wilds, gun skills, integrity, and tenacity), one Argonaut praised Calamity as "the most recklass buchario in ther Hills," who "kin drink whisky, shute, play keerds, or sw'ar . . . the gal's got honor lef wi' her grit" and "knows every krook an' hoel in ther hull Black Hills."[39]

After roaming the Dakotas, Montana, and Wyoming, Martha Jane Canary came back to Deadwood in October 1895. It had been a decade and a half since the camp last witnessed her presence, and in that time she had become nationally recognized as a dime novel star and performing hunter heroine. The *Black Hills Daily Times* chose to foreground a folkloric frontier presence rather than her reputation as an alcoholic drifter in announcing her as "Calamity Jane! The fearless Indian fighter and rover of the western plains." The fanfare surrounding Jane's return highlighted a community grappling with its own history as well as the politics and psychology of frontier closure. As the *Rapid City Journal* noted, Calamity served as "the prickly cactus symbol of the pioneer days at the heart of their depravity." Local boosters and

Calamity Jane alike saw the financial potential of the female hunter motif as Deadwood segued into an era of settled respectability. Calamity posed in full buckskin regalia at H. R. Locke's photographic studio in 1895 and sold the prints to tourists headed west for a slice of the wild life of the dime novel. In 1896 she trod the boards as a frontier hellcat as part of the Kohl and Middleton dime museum tour. Hailed as "The Famous Woman scout of the Wild West!," Calamity stirred the audience with tales of hunting, riding, and shooting exploits while brandishing a shiny Winchester. Copies of her freshly launched autobiography, *Life and Adventures of Calamity Jane*, offered punters a take-home saga of hunting on the literary frontier. A litany of authentic narration in the fine tradition of the hunting yarn, it was, according to the *Daily Times*, "one of the most interesting and thrilling stories of western life ever put in type." Canary garnered sizeable public interest as a personification of frontier dramatics; as biographer J. Leonard Jennewein remarked, she combined "flair, with exuberance, with a native sense of showmanship." Like Buffalo Bill, she was able to see the entrepreneurial opportunities of tapping the West of the popular imagination, although she never seemed to be able to make the adjustment from "wild woman" on the stage to everyday life. Beset by a string of failed relationships, problems with alcoholism, and a capricious personality, Canary struggled to live up to her legend or to escape from it, unable, as Richard Etulain points out, "to bridge the gap between experience and performance."[40]

When Martha Canary died in Dakota on August 1, 1903, the *Princeton Press* praised her as "one of the most picturesque and daring characters that has ever roamed the Western plains." William Allen reminisced in *Adventures with Indians and Game* (1903) about an encounter on a game trail near Custer City with "a white woman riding towards us at full gallop" with "daring intrepidity . . . rapidity of movement and . . . deadly skill with firearms." Eulogies spoke endearingly of her wildness, freedom, and dynamism. The feral ways of the "female scout"—a heretical model of the performing hunter hero—matched the idea of a West brimming with gunplay and gumption. With her penchant for manly garb and hunting vernacular, Calamity Jane flouted codes of propriety and ventured a firm (and publicly displayed) challenge to the masculine hegemony of the hunter hero. When she appeared at Frederick T. Cummins's Pan-Indian Exposition in 1901, the *Buffalo Morning Express* duly reported on the entrance of "the heroine who wears a hero's garb"—a significant endorsement of the rights of women to tread (and in convincing style) the hallowed grounds of frontier machismo. The Chicago *Inter Ocean* hailed Calamity Jane as an exemplar of the new western woman by enticing readers with tales of the "most interesting woman" who "wears buckskin trousers and is not afraid of a mouse." For her part, Canary admonished the "new women" of Chicago, who were "way behind the times," and threatened, in suitably dramatic prose, to show them the measure of a *real* western woman by riding the boulevards "astride her broncho" armed with a rifle in search of suburban coyotes.[41]

At the same time, Calamity Jane never achieved recognition beyond that of a flamboyant eccentric. Lady adventurers and resourceful homesteaders tested the limits of public acceptability in their negotiations of gender roles on the game trail, but Canary's cross-dressing antics and supposedly "manly" airs posed a greater challenge to normative codes. A sense of "grotesque wildness" may have suited the stage story of hunter's paradise, but society was not yet willing to renegotiate the terms of gender socialization. Accordingly, Calamity Jane was typically confined to the role of oddity, an aberration of the "wild and woolly" West. In the words of biographer Duncan Aikman, she was "a delectable novelty, a vivid and genial allegory of an era's hearty rowdiness." Others were far less generous, seeing in Canary a deviant woman and "disreputable old harridan" who "dressed like a man" and "drank whiskey in saloons with men." Hardly a paragon of virtue herself, famous Deadwood madam Dora Dufran called Calamity Jane a "parody on womanhood, shorn of all decency and most womanly attributes." As a buckskin-clad hunter heroine, Calamity Jane enthralled the reading public with her tales of sharpshooting and trailside revelry. Appreciation of hunting performance, however, did not bring social acceptability for a rough and ready woman living an unorthodox existence.[42]

Neither "wild woman" nor "lady adventurer," Annie Oakley's take on the performing hunter heroine spoke of a frontier upbringing, the world of the competition shooting circuit, and the choreography of the Wild West show. In common with those of Calamity Jane, the precise details of her upbringing and entry into the world of theater remain sketchy. Born to Quaker parents in Darke County, Ohio, in August 1860, we know that Phoebe Ann Moses grew up in an environment of backwoods poverty. When her father Jacob died of pneumonia, the seven-year-old Annie built traps from cornstalks to secure grouse, quail, and squirrel for the family table—a youthful example of the adaptability of the female pioneer as well as a signal of the nutritional importance of game meat to settler society. Recalling these years, Oakley described (in model show(wo)man style) how she rejected the disapproval of her mother and her insistence on schooling to take to the woods as a place of adventure, finding solace in quail hunting and collecting wild flowers. She talked gleefully of the first time she took down her father's Kentucky rifle from above the mantle, filled it with enough powder to kill a bison, and set it to work on local squirrels. As she told the *Nashville Barrier,* "I guess the love of a gun must have been born in me." This was her "creation story"—of formative moments finding power and poise in the company of firearms—and one faithfully reproduced in the programs for Cody's Wild West Show. *The Rifle Queen: Annie Oakley* (1884) spun an ostentatious yarn of a young Annie shooting bears and apprehending outlaws and Indian "red devils" in classic dime novel style, noting how the huntress "intuitively stole away over the fields with her brother's shotgun, and before her parents knew she had conquered the inborn fear of all girls for firearms." Produced for the British market, the booklet's cover image clearly showed the importance of the game trail in Oakley's celebrity persona. On either side of a picture of Oakley gripping her shotgun were the words "life feats, exploits, adventures, hunting" and "wonderful dead shot on the wing and run."[43]

After two years drudgery in service for a couple she called "the wolves," Annie ran away and returned to her mother (now on husband number three). Minded to capitalize on her skills as a hunter, she spent her youth stalking local game birds and rabbits to supply Charles Katzenberger's grocery in Greenville and the hotels of Cincinnati. Evidently proficient, Oakley built up a lucrative business and was even able to pay off the mortgage on the family farm. Providing for the family table represented a foundational part of her emerging frontier folklore, but market hunting had become rather inglorious as a boast. Reluctant to talk about her bag, she noted in *Powders I Have Used* (1914), "I won't say how much, as I might be called a game hog." In a recital far more befitting the mantle of a hunter naturalist, Oakley pointed out how she never shot a stationary animal, wanting to give it fair chase and render herself "quick of eye and hand." According to Oakley, grocery clients favored her as a hunter principally because she always aimed for the head, thereby securing a quick death and minimizing the amount of buckshot that made it to the dinner plate.[44]

The legendary story of the rifle competition between the young Ohio farm girl and a trick shooter may well be apocryphal, but it swiftly became an integral part of the Annie Oakley legend as performed for public digest. According to the popular account, Frank Butler was working as a trick shooter for the show circuit and killing time before the start of the season in Cincinnati. Boasting that he could beat all comers at a rifle match, local hotelier Jack Frost arranged a competition at the Oakley showgrounds, with a $50 prize (some say $100). Butler, who was billed with his partner Sam Baughman as "champion sharp-shooters and most illustrious dead-shots . . . the sportsmen's famous hunter heroes," boasted that he could beat "anything then living"—apart from Doc Carver or his arch-nemesis Captain Bogardus—and thought there was nothing to fear when a young woman accepted the challenge. Butler was yet more surprised when a youthful Annie Moses (who had never shot birds from a trap before) beat him fair and square, twenty-five to twenty-four. A romance developed, and the two got married (either in 1876, as Annie claims, or in 1882, according to Frank, the latter being the more likely date as Annie was in the habit of subtracting six years from her age) and traveled together on the vaudeville circuit. When Butler's then partner, John Graham, fell ill, Annie stepped in and stole the show. She had competed on-and-off in regional shooting matches and was now vaulted to celebrity. By 1882, Annie had taken Oakley as her stage name and played top billing in a husband-and-wife shooting act for the Sells Brothers Circus that showcased rifle skills, horse(wo)manship, and the whimsical antics of the couple's pet poodle.[45]

An Irish immigrant and an Ohio farm girl may have strained the limits of credulity as "The Great Far West Rifle Shots," but they were eminently compatible with Buffalo Bill's Wild West Show in its focus on family-friendly, all-action entertainment. William Cody and Nate Salsbury encountered Annie Oakley and Frank Butler in 1884 in New Orleans but were initially reluctant to add another shooting act to their bill. Then, when Captain Bogardus and his sons left the show early the following year, Oakley got in touch asking for a job. Cody was less than keen on the idea at first, worried that a petite 110-pound woman would not be able to step into the shoes of the hunter hero superstar (not to mention deal with the recoil from a twelve-bore shotgun) but decided to give her a trial run at the 1885 season opener in Louisville, Kentucky. While the Wild West showmen prepared their entourage for the next round of "America's National Entertainment," Annie plunged herself into vigorous preparations at the Cincinnati shooting range, including an exhibition event in which she shot 4,772 out of 5,000 balls in nine hours. Arriving early for the April 24 premier show, Oakley set about a quick practice in the arena, firing her shotguns from both hands and hitting everything that came out of the traps. Nate Salsbury, who had been watching in the wings, reputedly hired her on the spot and lost no time in spending $7,000 on lithograph prints depicting "Little Sure Shot" (as Sitting Bull had named her when he encountered Oakley at a revue in St. Paul in March 1884) in her shooting regalia. What Buffalo Bill's all-action fanfare of gunplay, patriotism, and masculine authority needed was a hunter heroine.

Annie Oakley's gun-slinging gentility was a winning formula that saw her through sixteen seasons with the Wild West Show. As the 1893 program noted, "In dress, style, and execution, she was as *original* as she is attractive." A female "Buffalo Bill," she rode into the arena with a sense of flair in her fringed skirt, sombrero, and embroidered jacket, greeting the audience with waves and kisses—the picture of homespun domesticity. As Butler set up the guns and clay traps, cowboys brought in a kitchen table well stocked with firearms. Oakley started slow, easing the audience into her mesmerizing firearms master class, and slowly racked up the tension and the difficulty factor. Press agent Dexter Fellows noted how "the first few shots brought forth a few screams of fright from the women, but they were soon lost in round after round of applause." Butler threw balls in the air and swung them from cords, set off clays from traps, held playing cards aloft as targets, and, in the piece de resistance, invited Oakley to shoot a burning cigarette from between his lips. "The peerless lady-shot" hit her targets from standing, from looking through a mirror (or sometimes the polished blade of a table knife) with the gun across her shoulder, and aimed backward from a chair, all of which were performed without sleight of hand. The performance was genuinely remarkable. One trick that Oakley performed to perfection was, of course, selling herself as a western girl. Her attire, firearms skills, and frontier storytelling as "armed western woman" sat comfortably in Cody's histrionics and won plaudits as a "slender yet muscular Diana of the northwest" and "a Western girl with quiet, expressive eyes and a voice as soft and silvery as the rustling of a summer's breeze among the trees."[46]

At the end of the ten-minute revue, the audience was left hypnotized by the remarkable display of shooting from the agile and girlish four-foot-eleven woman who ended her routine with a sassy leg kick. She was, according to the *London Evening News,* "the most interesting item on Buffalo Bill's programme . . . far and away the best." From her initial stint in the 1886 season as a novelty act, the "champion markswoman" grew to become one of the show's principal stars. By 1892, she was getting second billing, at once a signal of her allure and a calculated decision, according to Nate Salsbury, to calm the crowd before the salvo of a show full of careening wagons, cracking rifles, and whirling horses. As he pointed out, "Women and children see a harmless woman there, and they do not get worried."[47]

Oakley was a curious breed of star that, in her complex navigation of gender codes, ably exemplified the ambiguities of the hunter heroine. She was, quite simply, thrilled to be "the first white woman to stand and travel with what society might then have thought impossible." As a shot she was superlative, better arguably than Cody (she used live rounds when he fired blanks and steered clear of horseback shooting for fear of showing him up). Facing the possibility of a three-way contest at the Wimbledon shooting club during the London tour of 1887 with female stars Oakley and Lillian Smith ("the California huntress" who joined Cody's troupe in 1886 on the back of Oakley's success), Cody politely declined. Smith earned criticism for wearing a plug hat and shooting the haunch of an iron deer target (a cardinal sin for any ethical "sport"), but Oakley excelled. The unwillingness of Cody to show up was, according to the *Glasgow Evening News,* tantamount to a concession of defeat.[48]

Oakley's expertise at shooting spoke of a new technological age of firearms, matching industrial age acumen with Wild West show(wo)manship and a new take on hunting as sport, courtesy of the trap shoot circuit. Her biographical entry for the Wild West Show program related records, matches, and tournaments in meticulous detail (thousands of balls hit, weapons used) alongside a frontier yarn that spoke of her "inherent love for firearms and hunting." Oakley approached her vocation with an instrumental gaze, channeling an accuracy and athleticism typically identified with men. The *New York Tribune* thought her "wonderfully quick" and her shots "swift and true." Meanwhile, her take on the metaphysical connection between gun and marks(wo)man harkened back to the descriptions of the "hunting moment" on the western game trail from the masculine hunter hero: "You must have your mind, your nerve and everything in harmony."[49]

Oakley's performing hunter heroine cut a heretical presence in its presentation of gender empowerment on the frontier, the new womanhood, and the freedoms and opportunities for the 1890s "Gibson Girl." Skills with a gun brought security and independence for the woman living alone, as Oakley explained—for "the woman living in the lonely farmhouse, and for the business woman returning home late at night from work, the knowledge of how to use a pistol is a Godsend." According to historian Glenda Riley, Oakley served as a "prototype" for a new generation of women entering the arena of competitive sports, particularly rodeo. Much like Calamity Jane, Annie Oakley was viewed by posthumous biographers through the lens of twentieth-century feminism, as in the case of Courtney Cooper, author of *Annie Oakley: Woman at Arms* (1927), who saw her eponymous gun-toting heroine as an ideal role model for an "outdoor feminine organization" seeking a mascot of the ilk of Buffalo Bill or Kit Carson.[50]

As a performing sharpshooter, Annie Oakley acted out a rip-roaring exercise in hunter hero heresy. Literally calling the shots, she picked off cigar targets from the mouths of various male "props" (including her own husband and the future kaiser, Wilhelm II) and played the men at their own game in the world of competitive trick shooting. On one occasion, she faced off against Grand Duke Michael, missing three out of fifty shots to his fourteen. He left, according to one London newspaper, "abashed, but firmly convinced of the superiority of American markswomen over Russian amateur sharp-shooters." Outside the arena, Oakley too promoted the usefulness of the "armed western woman" in offering President McKinley fifty "lady sharpshooters" for service during the Spanish American War, a pertinent match to Theodore Roosevelt's regiment of hunter heroes in the shape of the Rough Riders. In her shooting acumen and flamboyant frontier fixings, Oakley unreservedly contested the hegemony of the male hunter hero. As *The Rifle Queen* pointed out to its readers, "with natural ability and a little encouragement . . . courage and perseverance" some women "can do what any man can do." The *Springfield Republican* read her performance as equal parts impressive and mutinous: "She handles a shotgun with an easy familiarity that causes the men to marvel and the women to assume airs of contended superiority."[51]

And yet Oakley offered a safe, socially conservative take on the "woman at arms." A petite, respectable woman who worked with her husband, dressed in feminine attire (which she designed and made), and performed always in sidesaddle, Oakley did not present an all-guns-blazing challenge to gender orthodoxy in her preference for homespun domesticity. As Tracey Davis notes of her act, "There is an implicit questioning of order in this design but not a radical agenda for reordering." Oakley may have been shooting "at" her husband, but ultimately she was not aiming at him. Visitors to her show tent, meanwhile, found her sewing clothes, brewing tea, or baking cakes. The artifacts of her trade (and the ephemera of any good hunter hero) were present—guns, trophies, and skins—but they were strewn between pillows, trinkets, and domestic adornments. The arrangement remained, as actress Amy Leslie noted, "a bower of comfort and taste." Part sharpshooter and part homemaker, Oakley saw herself as a model of the virtuous Victorian lady. Calamity Jane she was not. As circus performer Fred Stone pointed out, "There was never a sweeter, more lovable woman than Annie Oakley. It was always amusing to watch people who were meeting her for the first time. They expected to see a big masculine blustering sort of person and then the woman with the quiet voice took them by surprise." *The Rifle Queen*, for one, exhibited some relief that Oakley's "mannish quality" was confined to her gun skills: "For when the rifle or shotgun is laid aside, she is acknowledged to be an affable, natural and womanly 'American girl' who has by her unusual skill and pleasant, quiet ways made friends with all the sportsmen who have met her." Society endorsed the idea of the performing hunter heroine, but preferred it safely corralled in domesticity. Oakley, for her part, took refuge from the dramatics of the Wild West Show by taking to the field, noting, in classic hunter heroine style how "any woman who does not thoroughly enjoy tramping across the country on a clear frosty morning with a good gun and a pair of dogs does not know how to enjoy life. God intended women to be outside as well as men, and they do not know what they are missing when they stay cooped up in the house enjoying themselves with a novel."[52]

Trans-Media Storytelling and the Broadcasting of the Hunt

Oral testimony, literature, art, photography, and theater collectively promoted the West as a hunter's paradise of adventuring and animation. Each artifact, visual, oral, and textual, represented a hybrid text that communicated, sometimes deliberately, with the other mediums of memorial. Print, visual, and performance culture served up a rich and evocative diorama of the chase, resulting in a cultural architecture of the hunt that proved remarkably homogenous. Autobiography loomed large in the genre, rendering hunter's paradise a kind of testimonial culture that privileged the western landscape and its animals, hunters, and game trails through personal encounter. Asseverations of individual experience, authenticity, and identity resonated, giving hunter's paradise provenance as, in Baudrillard's parlance, a "reflection of a profound reality." A sense of history, of personal epiphany and cultural seismology, also prevailed in the performative canon. Commentators seemed palpably aware that the West was party to unbridled social, ecological, and political change, a world in the making that demanded an actuarial gaze. Hunters, then, saw their endeavors through the lens of histrionics, betraying a need to push the moment from present into past even before it happened. Documentation lay at the heart of the functionality of memory and identity, committing the moment to posterity and freezing a grand narrative in time from the trailhead to the trophy shot. This was, rather like the camera, an exercise in lifelike illusion. The storytelling of hunter's paradise effectively obscured the mechanics of staging, exaggeration, and reimagining embedded in the process. Hunters and commentators cultivated an invented tradition that combined authenticity and experience with fantasy, self-imagining, and a nostalgic glance—a "fictionalized reality" and ecology of entanglement.[53]

When Frederick Jackson Turner stood before the American Historical Association to deliver his frontier thesis in 1893, he confirmed the passage of hunter's paradise from personal memory to a canonical lexicon of national autobiography. In the social imagination, the West served as a crucible of imperial triumph won by contest with the wilderness. The hunter hero gained special report as an archetype of patriotism and vigor: "The wilderness masters the colonist . . . It strips off the garments of civilization, and arrays him in the hunting shirt and the moccasin . . . Little by little he transforms the wilderness, but the outcome is not the old Europe . . . The fact is, that here is a product that is American." Confirmed through reenactment, publication, and oratory, the West had been firmly installed as a game utopia, while the character of the hunter hero, so beloved of the American psyche, was truly westernized. At the behest of hunters themselves as well as their

associate producers of memory, the mythology of the West as game utopia had become idealized and immortalized as an integral part of frontier
experience. This powerful mythology of wilderness adventuring offered a
potent "discourse of civilization" that satisfied individual needs and attracted
a wide audience to boot. To paraphrase Clyde Milner's classifiers of memory,
it served as a space of personal testimony, a regional identity, and a national
epic. A useable past for an assertive nation, the story of the hunt allowed for
the articulation of westward conquest as a heroic yarn. The taking of animals for sport, market, and food represented an intensely ideological act—a
marker of colonial conquest, resource assimilation, and cultural appropriation—but the collective visualization of the Rocky Mountain West as hunter's paradise conveniently glossed over issues of landscape politics and power
to focus on an imagined landscape of bucolic nature, faunal plenitude, and
strenuous exploring. Few wanted to go live in a cabin in the woods for a year
in the fashion of Henry David Thoreau or possessed the collateral for a big
game hunt George Gore–style, but the fantasy landscape of the hunt could
be "lived" by the act of reading, looking, or watching. Ernest Thompson
Seton may have railed at the "spectatoritis" of a public more inclined to
observe rather than participate in sports, but the folkloric imprint was nonetheless important. Trans-media storytelling had crafted a liminal frontier of
hunting games and adventure through animation. The limits of history and
geography proved similarly elastic. The power of hunter's paradise, a folklore of "meaningful myth-historical design," to borrow the terminology of
Richard Slotkin, allowed the preservation of an idea even while its material
ecology was in the throes of transformation. Bison no longer wandered the
plains, but the performing hunter heroes and heroines of the frontier played
to packed audiences each night, thrilling audiences with the testimonies of
"wild and woolly days" and in the process serving as "romantic morticians,"
embalming the western myth for posterity. Epiphany in the wilderness had
been marked for history, badged with honor, and committed to collective
memory. Preservation had been assured through performance.[54]

NOTES

1. Frederic Remington, "Buffalo Bill in London," *Harper's Weekly*, September 3,
1892.

2. Charles Jenkins, "The Dance Drama of the American Indian and Its Relation to Folk Narrative," *Lambda Alpha Journal of Man* 1, no. 2 (1969): 25; Donald M. Hines, *Ghost Voices: Yakima Indian Myths, Legends, Humor, and Hunting Stories* (Issaquah, WA: Great Eagle, 1992), 242–45.

3. Roland Barthes, *Camera Lucida: Reflections on Photography* (London: Vintage), 31–32, 57.

4. Michael Steiner, "Parables of Stone and Steel: Architectural Images of Progress and Nostalgia at the Columbian Exposition and Disneyland," in *Mapping American Culture*, ed. Michael Steiner and Wayne Franklin (Iowa City: University of Iowa Press, 1992), 42.

5. Edward Strahan, *The Masterpieces of the Centennial International Exhibition* (Philadelphia: Gebbie and Barrie, 1876), cxxxix; "The Hunters Camp," *Forest and Stream*, June 29, 1876, 333–34.

6. Steiner, "Parables," 48; Herbert Howe Bancroft, *Book of the Fair* (Chicago: Bancroft Company, 1895), 449–50; George R. Davis, *The World's Columbian Exposition, Chicago, 1893* (Charleston, SC: Trumbull White, 1893), 70–71; Halsey C. Ives, *The Dream City, A Portfolio of Photographic Views of the World's Columbian Exposition* (St. Louis: N. D. Thompson, 1893).

7. Rosemarie K. Bank, "Representing History: Performing the Columbia Exposition," *Theatre Journal* 54 (2002): 589–606.

8. William Cody, *Buffalo Bill (Hon. Wm F. Cody) and His Wild West Companions* (Chicago: Henneberry Co., n.d.), 13; W. F. Cody, *An Autobiography of Buffalo Bill* (New York: Cosmopolitan Book Co., 1920), 314.

9. "Buffalo Bill's Wild West and Congress of Rough Riders of the World, 1893" (program), 4, in William F. "Buffalo Bill" Cody Collection, MS 6, McCracken Research Library, Buffalo Bill Center of the West, Cody, WY (hereafter cited as BBCW); *Liverpool Mercury*, July 7, 1883; Twain quoted in Alan Gallop, *Buffalo Bill's British Wild West* (Stroud: History Press, 2001), 38; *Illustrated London News*, April 16, 1883; *Il Corriere* quoted in Jefferson D. Slagle, "America Unscripted: Performing the Wild West," in Nicolas S. Witschi, ed., *A Companion to the Literature and Culture of the American West* (Chichester: Wiley-Blackwell, 2011), 428.

10. Buffalo Bill, "Famous Hunting Parties of the Plains," *Cosmopolitan* 17, no. 2 (June 1894): 137–40; *New York Herald*, January 14, 1872; W. F. Cody, *The Adventures of Buffalo Bill* (New York: Harper and Row, n.d.), 223; Henry Davies, *Ten Days on the Plains* (New York: Crocker and Co., 1871), 29.

11. Cody, *Autobiography*, 1, 124; E. G. Cattermole, *Famous Frontiersmen, Pioneers, and Scouts: The Vanguards of American Civilization* (Chicago: M. A. Donohue, 1880), 1; William Lightfoot Visscher, ed., *Buffalo Bill's Own Story of His Life and Deeds* (Chicago: John R. Stanton, 1917), especially the preface, i–x, and Visscher's poem "A

Knight of the West," 339; Cody, *Adventures*, vii–iii; Prentiss Ingraham, "The Adventures of Buffalo Bill, from Boyhood to Manhood," *Beadle's Boys Library of Sport, Story, and Adventure* 1, no. 1 (December 14, 1881). See also W. F. Cody, *The Life of Hon. William F. Cody, Known as Buffalo Bill: The Famous Hunter, Scout, and Guide* (Philadelphia: Theodore Bliss, 1879); John Burke, *Buffalo Bill: From Prairie to Palace* (Chicago: Rand McNally, 1893).

12. *Sidney Plaindealer-Telegraph*, May 3, 1883. For Cody and the Wild West show, see Joy S. Kasson, *Buffalo Bill's Wild West: Celebrity, Memory, and Popular History* (New York: Hill and Wang, 2000); L. Moses, *Wild West Shows and the Images of American Indians, 1883–1933* (Albuquerque: University of New Mexico Press, 1996); Paul Reddin, *Wild West Shows* (Chicago: University of Illinois Press, 1999); Robert Rydell and Rob Kroes, *Buffalo Bill in Bologna: The Americanization of the World, 1869–1922* (Chicago: University of Chicago Press, 2005); Richard Slotkin, *Gunfighter Nation: The Myth of the Frontier in Twentieth-Century America* (New York: Atheneum, 1992), 63–87; Louis S. Warren, *Buffalo Bill's America: William Cody and the Wild West Show* (New York: Vintage, 2005); Richard White, "Frederick Jackson Turner and Buffalo Bill," in *The Frontier in American Culture*, ed. James Grossman (Berkeley: University of California Press, 1994), 7–65; Cody, *Autobiography*, 239; "Buffalo Bill's Wild West and Congress of Rough Riders," 1–2; Gallop, *Buffalo Bill's British Wild West*, 48.

13. William A. Annin, "Bill Cody," poem included in Cody, *Buffalo Bill (Hon Wm. F. Cody)*, 202.; "Buffalo Bill's Wild West and Congress of Rough Riders," 4; Cody, *Buffalo Bill (Hon. Wm. F. Cody)*, 202. See also Louis S. Warren, "Cody's Last Stand: Masculine Anxiety, the Custer Myth, and the Frontier of Domesticity in Buffalo Bill's Wild West," *Western Historical Quarterly* 34, no. 1 (Spring 2003): 49–69.

14. "Buffalo Bill's Wild West and Congress of Rough Riders," 4; Grossman, *The Frontier*, 27.

15. "Buffalo Bill's Wild West and Congress of Rough Riders," 5, 14, 6, 9.

16. Ibid., 5, 14; Cody, *Autobiography*, 319; C. Westmore and Z. Grey, *The Last of the Great Scouts* (New York: Grosset and Dunlap, 1913 [1899]), 327.

17. London *Era* cited in Cody, *Buffalo Bill (Hon. Wm. F. Cody)*, 9.

18. Kasson, *Buffalo Bill's Wild West*, 24; Slagle, "America Unscripted," 433; "Buffalo Bill's Wild West and Congress of Rough Riders," 4; *New York Herald*, June 30, 1874; Visscher, *Buffalo Bill's Own Story*, 265; Larry McMurtry, *The Colonel and Little Missie: Buffalo Bill, Annie Oakley, and the Beginnings of Megastardom in America* (New York: Simon and Schuster, 2006); W. E. Webb, *Buffalo Land: An Authentic Account of Discoveries, Adventures, and Mishaps of a Scientific and Sporting Party in the Wild West.* (Cincinnati: E. Hannaford, 1873), 149.

19. Theodore H. Hittell, *The Adventures of James Capen Adams, Mountaineer and Grizzly Bear Hunter of California* (San Francisco: Towne and Bacon, 1860), 12. See

also Theodore H. Hittell's interviews with Grizzly Adams, 1857–59, BANC MSS 2002/135c, Bancroft Library, University of California, Berkeley (hereafter cited as Bancroft).

20. Hittell, *Adventures of James Capen Adams*, 12–15; Marryat quoted in Richard Dillon, *The Legend of Grizzly Adams: California's Greatest Mountain Man* (New York: Coward-McCann, 1966), 26.

21. Hittell, *Adventures of James Capen Adams*, 13, 1, 58, 18; James C. Adams, "Wild Sports in the Far West: Old Grizzly the Bear Tamer," *New York Weekly*, May–October 1860, Francis Farquhar Papers, MSS C-B 517, Carton 1, Folder California Grizzly Bear—"Grizzly Adams," Bancroft.

22. Hittell, *Adventures of James Capen Adams*, 28–29, 83, 69; Adams, "Wild Sports in the Far West"; James Adams, *Life of J. C. Adams, Known as Old Adams, Old Grizzly Adams, Containing a Truthful Account of His Bear Hunts, Fights with Grizzly Bears, Hairbreadth Escapes, in the Rocky and Nevada Mountains and the Wilds of the Pacific Coast* (New York: N.p., 1860), 23–24; William Wright, *The Grizzly Bear* (New York: Charles Scribner's, 1909), 38.

23. Hittell, *Adventures of James Capen Adams*, 206.

24. Ibid., 169–70, 145, 298–99, 94; Adams, "Wild Sports in the Far West."

25. "California Wild Animals," October 17, 1856, "Francis Farquhar California Grizzly Bear: 'Grizzly Adams' Notes on Hittell/Adams," Folder California Grizzly Bear—"Grizzly Adams," Francis Farquhar papers, MSS C-B 517, Carton 1, Bancroft.

26. *Daily Alta California*, October 21, 1856, and December 9, 1856.

27. Theodore Hittell, "Great Show of Animals: Mountaineer Museum," *San Francisco Daily Evening Bulletin*, October 1, 1856; Theodore Hittell, "California Wild Beasts," *San Francisco Daily Evening Bulletin*, October 11, 1856; Hittell, *Adventures of James Capen Adams*, 377–78; *Spirit of the Times*, June 23, 1860; James Madison Grover Diary and Papers, MSS C-F 93, Folder 2, "Memories of James M. Grover, 1905," Bancroft.

28. *Spirit of the Times*, May 5, 1860; *New York Weekly* 15, no. 27 (May 31, 1860), through 16, no. 14 (February 28, 1861); Adams, *Life of J. C. Adams*, preface, 30, 34.

29. P. Barnum, *The Humbugs of the World* (London: John Camden Hotten, 1860), 22–29.

30. Ibid., 29; Obituary in *Harper's Weekly*, November 10, 1856, cited in Richard Dillon, *The Legend of Grizzly Adams: California's Greatest Mountain Man* (New York: Coward-McCann, 1966), 222; gravestone photograph in Folder California Grizzly Bear—"Grizzly Adams," Francis Farquhar Papers, MSS C-B517, Carton 1, Bancroft.

31. Richard H. Dillon, *Grizzly Adams: A Memorable Mountain Man* (Davis: University of California, 1966), 11; Frank Powell, "Old Grizzly Adams: The Bear Tamer, or the Monarch of the Mountains," *Beadle's Boys Library of Sport, Story, and Adventure*

23, no. 11 (June 11, 1899); *Captain "Bruin" Adams, The Bear Tamer: Old Grizzly: Romances for the Million* (London: General Publishing Company, n.d.), Tp S1589 E3 B4 1880z, Bancroft; Dillon, *Legend of Grizzly Adams*, 160–61; *Ann Arbor Argus*, June 1, 1888; William Wright, *The Grizzly Bear* (New York: Charles Scribner's, 1909), 47; Charles Sellier, *The Life and Times of Grizzly Adams* (Los Angeles: Schick Sunn Books, 1977), back cover.

32. *New York Herald*, May 15, 1908; Walter McClintock, "Blackfeet Indians of the Plains and Rocky Mountains" and "My Life among the Indians," Walter McClintock Papers, MS533, Box 1, Folder 2: "3 Lecture Notes," and Box 3: "Misc. Articles," both held at the Braun Research Library, Autry National Center, Los Angeles (hereafter cited as Braun).

33. All periodicals from Walter McClintock Papers, MS533, Box 1 Scrapbook and Box 1, Folder 4: "lectures for review," both held at the Braun; Letter to McClintock from Wilhelm, ex-Crown Prince of Germany, Wieringen, November 5, 1923, Walter McClintock Papers, MS533, Box 1, Scrapbook, Braun; Letter to McClintock from Alfred Hayes, Secretary, Birmingham and Midland Institute, n.d., Walter McClintock Papers, MS533, Box 1, Folder 7: "McClintock Correspondence re. his lectures," Braun.

34. Clippings from periodicals found in Walter McClintock Papers, MS533, Box 1, Scrapbook; Letter to McClintock from Hayes; Letter to McClintock from Arthur Tait, Leeds Institute of Science, Art and Literature, February, 12 1925, Walter McClintock Papers, MS533, Box 2, Folder 11: "Copies of Letters," Braun.

35. Rosemarie Bank, "Representing History: Performing the Columbia Exposition" in *Critical Theory and Performance*, ed. J. Reinelt (Ann Arbor: University of Michigan Press, 1992), 598.

36. Martha Cannary Burke, *Life and Adventures of Calamity Jane, By Herself* (n.p., 1896), n.p.

37. Traveller quoted in James McLaird, *Calamity Jane: The Woman and the Legend* (Norman: University of Oklahoma Press, 2005), 30; Dodge quoted in Richard Etulain, "Calamity Jane: Independent Woman of the Wild West" in Glenda Riley and Richard Etulain, eds., *By Grit and Grace: Eleven Women Who Shaped the American West* (Golden, CO: Fulcrum, 1997), 80; Macmillan quoted in Chicago *Inter-Ocean*, July 3, 1875.

38. *Black Hills Pioneer*, July 15, 1876; Richard Hughes, *Pioneer Years in the Black Hills*, ed. Agnes Wright Spring (Glendale, CA: Arthur H. Clark Company, 1957), 159–61; William Secrest, *I Buried Hickok: The Memoirs of White Eye Anderson* (College Station, TX: Creative Publishing, 1980), 102, 93–95; *Cheyenne Daily Sun*, July 7, 1877.

39. Horatio Maguire, *The Black Hills and American Wonderland* (Chicago: Donnelley, Lloyd & Co., 1877), 304; Horatio Maguire, *The Coming Empire* (Sioux City, IA:

Watkins and Smead, 1878); Edward Wheeler, *Deadwood Dick: Prince of the Road*, Bea-dle's Half Dime Novel Library vol. 1, no. 1 (New York: Beadle and Adams, 1877), 4; Edward Wheeler, *Deadwood Dick on Deck, or Calamity Jane, the Heroine of Whoop-Up*, Beadle's Pocket Library vol. 5, no. 57 (New York: Beadle and Adams, 1885), 24, 2, 3.

40. *Black Hills Daily Times*, October 5, 1895; Dora Dufran, *Lowdown on Calamity Jane* (Deadwood, SD: Helen Rezatto, 1981), 16–17; *Rapid City Journal*, January 20, 1896; J. Leonard Jennewein, *Calamity Jane of the Western Trails* (Rapid City, SD: Dakota West Books, 1953), 6; Etulain, "Calamity Jane: Independent Woman of the Wild West," 88.

41. *Princeton Press*, August 13, 1908; William Allen, *Adventures with Indians and Game, or Twenty Years in the Rocky Mountains* (Chicago: A. W. Bowen, 1903), 32–34; *Buffalo Morning Express*, August 4, 1901; *Inter Ocean* (Chicago), January 28, 1896.

42. Duncan Aikman, *Calamity Jane and the Lady Wildcats* (New York: Henry Holt, 1927), 93; Jennewein, *Calamity Jane of the Western Trails*, 6; Edward Senn, *Deadwood Dick and Calamity Jane: A Thorough Sifting of Facts from Fiction* (Deadwood, SD: n.p., 1939), 10.

43. Larry McMurtry sees Oakley's squirrel stories as the functional equivalent of Cody's "first Indian." See McMurtry, *Colonel and Little Missie*, 4; *Nashville Barrier*, March 28, 1891; *The Rifle Queen: Annie Oakley* (London: General Publishing Co., 1884), 3. Oakley recounted her autobiography in *The Story of My Life* (NEA Service, 1926). Biographical treatments of Oakley include Courtney Ryley Cooper, *Annie Oakley: Woman at Arms* (London: Hurst and Blackett, 1927); Walter Havighurst, *Annie Oakley of the Wild West* (London: Robert Hale, 1955); Shirl Kasper, *Annie Oakley* (Norman: University of Oklahoma Press, 1992); Glenda Riley, *The Life and Legacy of Annie Oakley* (Norman: University of Oklahoma Press, 1994); Isabelle S. Sayers, *Annie Oakley and Buffalo Bill's Wild West* (New York: Dover Publications, 1981); Annie Swartout, *Missie: An Historical Biography of Annie Oakley* (Blanchester, OH: Brown Publishing Co., 1947).

44. Annie Oakley, *Powders I Have Used* (Wilmington, NC: DuPont Powder Co., 1914); Oakley quoted in *Dramatic Review* (London), June 10, 1887.

45. The billing for Butler and Baughman appeared in the Sells Brothers Circus Courier, 1881; reprinted in Sayers, *Annie Oakley*, 6; *Pittsburgh Dispatch*, February 4, 1903.

46. "Buffalo Bill's Wild West and Congress of Rough Riders," 21–22; Dexter Fel-lows and Andrew Freeman, *This Way to the Big Show: The Life of Dexter Fellows* (New York: Viking, 1936), 73; "The Woman Rifle Expert," *World*, January 8, 1888, clipping from the Annie Oakley scrapbooks, William F. "Buffalo Bill" Cody Collection, MS 6, McCracken Research Library, BBCW; *The Sportsman*, May 4, 1887.

47. *London Evening News*, May 10, 1884; "Buffalo Bill's Wild West Show: Amer-ica's National Entertainment 1886 Program," 1, 3, William F. "Buffalo Bill" Cody

Collection, MS 6, McCracken Research Library, BBCW; "Buffalo Bill's Wild West Show: America's National Entertainment Brief Program 1892," 1, William F. "Buffalo Bill" Cody Collection, MS 6, McCracken Research Library, BBCW; *New York Times*, April 7, 1901.

48. Sayers, *Annie Oakley*, 19; *Glasgow Evening News*, December 1, 1901.

49. "Buffalo Bill's Wild West: America's National Entertainment 1886 Program," 34, and "Buffalo Bill's Wild West: America's National Entertainment 1887 Program," 47, BBCW; *New York Tribune*, July 22, 1894; *Brighton Guardian*, October 14, 1891.

50. "Rifle Expert Talks of Women and Firearms," *Cincinnati Times*, ca. 1904, Annie Oakley scrapbooks; Riley, *Life and Legacy*, 126; Cooper, *Annie Oakley*, 31.

51. Cooper, *Annie Oakley*, 173; *Rifle Queen*, 3; *Springfield Republican*, May 22, 1897.

52. Tracey C. Davis, "Shotgun Wedlock: Annie Oakley's Power Politics in the Wild West," in *Gender and Performance: The Presentation of Difference in the Performing Arts*, ed. Lawrence Senelick (Hanover, NH: University Press of New England, 1992), 153–54; *Chicago Daily News*, May 5, 1893; Stone quoted in Sayers, *Annie Oakley*, 85; *Rifle Queen*, 3; Leslie quoted in Kasper, *Annie Oakley*, 59; See also Tracey Davis, "Annie Oakley and the Ideal Husband of No Importance" in *Critical Theory and Performance*, ed. Janelle Reinert and Joseph Roach (Ann Arbor: University of Michigan Press, 1992), 299–312.

53. Jean Baudrillard, *Simulacra and Simulation* (Ann Arbor: University of Michigan Press, 1994), 6.

54. Frederick Jackson Turner, "The Significance of the Frontier in American History," *Proceedings of the Forty-First Annual Meeting of the State Historical Society of Wisconsin* (Madison, WI: Democrat Printing Co., 1894), 81–82; Seton quoted in David Macleod, *Building Character in the American Boy: The Boy Scouts, YMCA, and Their Forerunners, 1870–1920* (Madison: University of Wisconsin Press, 1983), 49; Clyde Milner, "The View from Wisdom: Region and Identity in the Minds of Four Westerners," in *Under an Open Sky: Rethinking America's Western Past*, ed. William Cronon, George Miles, and Jay Gitlin (New York: W. W. Norton, 1992), 204; Richard Slotkin, *The Fatal Environment: The Myth of the Frontier in the Age of Industrialization, 1800–1900* (Middletown, CT: Wesleyan University Press, 1985), 11–16; F. W. Turner, *Beyond Geography: The Western Spirit against the Wilderness* (New York: Viking, 1980), 297.

CHAPTER 6

THE SOUL IN THE SKIN

Taxidermy and the Reanimated Animal

"Rowland Ward, Naturalists . . . The Jungle, Piccadilly. Practical and Artistic Taxidermists. Designer of Trophies of Natural History; Preservers and Adapters of all Specimens of Animal Life. Natural Features of Animals adapted in Original Designs for Decorative Purposes and Everyday Uses." So read an advertisement for the famous house of taxidermy in London, ca.1898. Its proprietor, James Rowland Ward, was an indefatigable trophy hunter, publicist of the sporting vocation, and skilled animal mortician. A leading publisher of sporting books, the Rowland Ward Company evinced a powerful contribution to the hunting vernacular in print through more than thirty titles, including Ward's autobiography, *A Naturalist's Life Study in the Art of Taxidermy* (1913). The famous taxidermy emporium, provocatively dubbed "the Jungle" for its menagerie of exotic faunal charges, meanwhile served up the material culture of the chase to an eager market of largely aristocratic gentlemen who were keen to preserve the spoils of their imperial hunting adventures in Africa, India, and, of course, the American West. Mounted deer heads, grizzly bear rugs, and Rowland Ward's other reanimations effected the memorialization of hunter's paradise in far-flung climes.[1]

DOI: 10.5876/9781607323983.c006

Trans-media storytelling provided a rich visual and textual record of sporting pursuits, a record of the sacred chase in image and word. Literature, art exhibits, and stage shows facilitated the translation of hunter's paradise to an eager national and international audience. And, as Kitty Hauser has noted, photographs fulfilled a "social function as trophies and souvenirs." Taxidermy, however, went one better in its articulation of "the visible proof of experience." Mounted animals arranged on the wall provided a new sense of reality, the vanquished foe, preserved in three-dimensional form, the actual animal seemingly without need of explanation or illustration. Stories and photographs allowed the hunt to live on as performed narrative, but the trophy offered an object, the material culture of hunting itself. In that sense, it allowed for the fixtures of the game trail—its stories and its animal capital—to cheat mortality. As eminent naturalist William Hornaday explained, "Perhaps you think that a wild animal has no soul, but let me tell you it has. Its skin is its soul, and when mounted by skillful hands, it becomes comparatively immortal." Taxidermy was, then, a perfect lesson in preservation, an embodied ecology of encounter. With its vernacular of engineered immortality, bringing wild things to life and allowing them to live on for eternity (hungry insects notwithstanding), it offered the possibility of suspending hunter's paradise in perpetual animation. Meanwhile, the framing of these specimens—where they were situated and what poses they assumed—was also significant. As cultural theorist Nicole Shukin points out, animal capital incorporates both material and symbolic transactions, the "semiotic currency of animal *sign* and the carnal traffic in animal substances." Mounted for posterity in the sanctuary of the great indoors, the animals of the West formed a powerful necrogeography, a landscape of death that communicated a series of motifs: nature red in tooth and claw, the power of the hunter hero, the romance of imperial adventuring, and the allure of the West (both real and imagined). Just as "Buffalo Bill" and "Grizzly" Adams broadcast the folklore of the frontier far and wide, so too did their four-legged namesakes serve as important performers of western mythology.[2]

Taxidermy: Art, Science, and Reanimation

The word taxidermy derives from the Greek *taxis*, or arrangement, and *derma*, or skin. Animals have long been part of human cultures of collecting and relic worship, from the practical use of hides for skin and furnishings in the Pleistocene to the elaborate mummification processes of ancient Egypt. Native Americans used the skins of animals as totemic devices, celebrations of hunter and hunted at the same time. Represented visually in the art of George Catlin, Lakota hunters donned the hides of wolves to creep up on bison herds, fooling the prey and also hoping to soak up lupine power through osmosis. In Euro-American cultures, exotic species and sporting animals could be found on display in royal palaces and hunting lodges (a dried crocodile hung unceremoniously in the "portal of the lizard" in Seville Cathedral, a gift from the Sultan of Egypt to Alfonso X in 1260) and were illuminated in manuscripts (the apothecary's shop in Shakespeare's *Romeo and Juliet* featured a stuffed alligator).

Inspired by scientific enquiry and the global expansion of Europe, taxidermy emerged as an elite artistic vocation in the seventeenth century. A burgeoning interest in natural history—both exotic and local—saw the emergence of private collectors who typically favored birds for their size, simplicity of facsimile, and ease of placement in cabinets of curiosities. *Natural History* (1687), published by the Royal Academy, contained a notation on dissection and merchants transporting animals from the Indies for mounting in Amsterdam, while Sir Hans Sloane's collection of exotic creatures, including an elephant, camel, zebra, and countless hummingbirds, when bequeathed to the nation on his death in 1753, formed the basis of the British Museum collection. Louis Dufresne was the first to use the term taxidermy in his *Novelle Dictionnaire d'histories Naturalle*, in which he attributed the practice to a desire to preserve nature's beauty. Published in 1803, Dufresne's work was contemporaneous with Lewis and Clark's foray westward, an activity likewise infused with aims of documenting, collecting, claiming, and transporting relics of the faunal West back to Thomas Jefferson for the purposes of natural history and nation building.[3]

The age of the hunter, the nineteenth century might also be labeled the age of the taxidermist. It was during this period that practitioners adopted technical processes, became more professionalized, created a community of shared expertise, and achieved mainstream exposure. The invention of new chemicals allowed taxidermists to regard long-term preservation of specimens as something more than mere aspiration. Before the development of arsenic soap, for instance, fur mounts succumbed to infestation or insect attack in little more than a decade. Meanwhile, fervent interest in the natural sciences, colonial exploration and exhibition, death and memorialization, consumption, and domestic adornment saw taxidermy emerge as a popular pastime and a lucrative profession. C. J. Maynard, writing in 1883, remarked that a generation earlier the taxidermist was seen as "a little cracked" but now was thoroughly modish. Published manuals abounded, offering instruction to a ready market of amateur reanimators, including *Art Recreations* (1873), *Taxidermy* (1894), *Taxidermy, or the Art of Collecting, Preparing and Mounting Objects of Natural History for the Use of Museums and Travelers* (1820), *Practical Taxidermy and Home Decoration* (1890), and *The Art of Taxidermy* (1898).[4]

At the same time, museum culture from the 1880s embraced taxidermy as a way of communicating colonial encounters, educating the public on natural history, engaging in civic display, and offering triumphalist and scientific commentary on conquered spaces and their species complement. Early works to depict animals in their natural environments had been pioneered by Charles Wilson Peale in the country's first natural history museum in Philadelphia (1786), set up for "rational amusement" and featuring birds with painted backgrounds alongside freak-show fare of five-legged cows and monkeys dressed as humans. A century on, exhibits in the Field Museum, Chicago, the American Museum of Natural History, New York, and the National Museum, Washington, DC—modern "cathedrals of science"—deployed taxidermy in the interests of taxonomic classification and science communication. Under the guidance of professional taxidermists, including William Hornaday and Carl Akeley, emphasis was placed on biological realism, principally applied through the medium of the habitat display or diorama. Hornaday's "Fight in the Treetops" (1879), a staged contest in the forests of Borneo between two orangutans and installed at the American Museum of Natural History in 1882, and Akeley's Muskrat Group (1889), commissioned by the Milwaukee Museum, exemplified the new style in foregrounding ecological setting and animal groups. That said, often the distinctions between taxidermy as trophy, theater, and teaching tool were blurred, both in terms of supply lines and architectures of display.

The new taxidermy of the nineteenth century asserted its purpose as mimetic. Practitioners identified their craft as one of depicting a true and natural likeness. As Davie noted, "The chief object of the taxidermist's art is to faithfully reproduce the forms, attitudes and expressions of living animals within the actual skin." In this sense, the taxidermist was akin to a faunal forger charged with the task of effecting a masterful deception by facsimile. Significantly, taxidermists asserted that their representations of the animal had more impact, poise, and presence than other iterations of the "afterlife" of the hunt in artistic, literary, and photographic forms. As Rowland Ward argued, the "perfect representation" of the animal in material form allowed the "noble trophy . . . to have more value than a paper description." The mounting of animals for display offered a unique opportunity—material, visual, tactile—of reanimating the inanimate. Occupied with the creation of the ultimate simulacra, the new taxidermists played consummate natural historians. More than that, these showmen morticians traded in the illusion of the eternal. They spoke consciously of bringing life back to wild things— in Hornaday's parlance, to "catch the spirit of your subject." Practicing necromancy through naturalism, taxidermists traded in a discourse that spoke of close study, mysticism, and performance. As Hornaday remarked, "There is supreme pleasure in crowning a well-made manikin with a handsome skin and seeing a specimen take on perfect form and permanent beauty as if by magic."[5]

Empirical observation, artistic training, and scientific knowledge were the three foundational principles on which this act depended. The vocabulary of reanimation was graced by references to scientific credulity, training, and technical acumen. Exponents issued sharp criticisms against those who traded in the "inartistically upholstering of a skin," specimens overfilled with sawdust or straw, a practice that lent animals a bloated and unnatural countenance suitable for a freak show or gothic novella (in fact, William Hornaday noted that the literature on the subject often made the same mistake: too much "padding"). The overstuffed walrus (mounted for the Great Colonial Exposition in 1886 and now installed in the Horniman Museum, London) and other examples of "botched taxidermy" owed more to the techniques of furniture making than natural history, with animals rudely sewn and filled like easy chairs. Hornaday railed that "there is no inferno too deep or too hot for a slovenly, slatternly taxidermist."[6]

In place of this "deformity, disproportion and distortion," the new taxidermists argued, their profession traded in erudition and empiricism. Devotion to "displaying its beauty truthfully to life" demanded technical knowledge and the adoption of new processes. Requiring training in sciences and the arts, the new taxidermy demanded a hybrid apprenticeship. Expertise in surgery, anatomy, chemistry, and the natural sciences aided the practitioner in the task at hand. Taxidermy manuals thus offered painstaking illustrations of surgical instruments and incision techniques, musculature and skeletal structures, and information on available preservatives and natural history practices. Such expertise, argued C. J. Maynard, allowed the taxidermist to reproduce the "exact poise, the swell of the muscle, the exact shape of the eye which will give life and beauty to the subject in hand." Allied to the scientific and the physiological was the artistic and the aesthetic. Taxidermists spoke of capturing the beauty and bounty of nature, of texture, color, and shape in the literal crafting (by paint, plaster cast, and clay modeling) of a living dead. What joined science and art together was a foregrounding of biological detail, a focus on the ways of the animal (both as living forms and as cadavers). As Rowland Ward noted of his vocation, "I determined to study nature and adapt it, in connection with modelling, to the taxidermists art."[7]

The frontier West played a prominent role in the taxidermic revolution of the nineteenth century. On a basic level, the codes of exploration, collection, and documentation implicit in the process of westward expansion encouraged such practice. Lewis and Clark shot and shipped examples of every species they saw back to Washington for perusal. The West was represented in Peale's museum by animal agents—a mule and a wolf—taken during Stephen Long's expedition (1819–20). By the time of James Audubon's expedition up the Missouri in 1843, John G. Bell, a professional taxidermist, was hired specifically to advance the cause of natural history cataloguing. When the National Museum opened its Hall of Mammals in 1888, the star attraction was Hornaday's bison group. In the animated ecology of trophy mounts, signature western animals—elk, deer, bison, and grizzly bears—emerged as prized pieces. The wild fauna of the West garnered top billing in various theaters of display. From the frontier house and hunting lodge to the "dens" and trophy rooms of elite sportsmen on both sides of the Atlantic, taxidermy mounts broadcast a message of frontier takeover and imperial provenance, the prowess of the hunter hero, and the charm of charismatic megafauna. Commercial venues (particularly hotels and saloons) also proved complicit in this communication, depicting for the cause of salesmanship and frontier performance the trophies of a landscape won and a western playground in the making. Taxidermy carried the afterlife of hunter's paradise (literally) to its natural zenith, presenting in material form the power of the triumphant Nimrod, the abundance of the faunal frontier, and a visual signifier, or prompt, for the story to be told. In common with photographs and literature, taxidermy—the material culture of the hunt—thereby served as a memento of touristic adventuring and "sold" hunter's paradise to a broader population. Akin to Buffalo Bill's Wild West Show, with its self-styled hunter heroes (and heroines) performing to a popular audience, a grand cast of reanimated western animals brought the savagery of the mythic West to life.

Taxidermy, Trophies, and the Hunting Trail

The relationship between the taxidermy profession and the hunter proved crucial. The sporting fraternity was a key supplier of animal products to the taxidermy industry. Hunters traded heads and skins for private mounting and also supplied the museum community, suggesting a commercial element to the process of trophy taking and a new turn in the category of market hunter. Prince Maximilian of Wied sold his accumulated tally of western hunting spoils—some 4,000 birds and 600 mammals—to the American Museum of Natural History on its establishment in 1869. Hunters also represented a critical market for the taxidermy industry, with sporting types eager to reanimate their first kills, biggest trophies, and cache of game species.

The taxidermy studio duly became a locus of exchange and a performative stage, a place not only for facilitating the transaction of animal capital but also for hunters to share stories about sporting adventure and impart trail advice. Theodore Roosevelt visited Rowland Ward's "Jungle" emporium in 1910 after traveling to East Africa on a game safari, while John G. Bell's shop at Broadway and Worth in New York City functioned in similar fashion for the hunting fraternity of the eastern seaboard. Such communications encouraged a culture of competition, display, and measurement, as articulated by Ward's *Horn Measurements and Weights of the Great Game of the World* (1892)—a catalogue of statistics and illustrations of mounts that celebrated the faunal heroes of the hunt and their victorious hunters and that is now in its twenty-eighth edition—while material displays of exotic beasts in shop windows caused more than a passing distraction to traffic. Conjuring a borrowed landscape of wilderness cornucopia in city streets, hunter Eugene P. Bicknell remembered visiting John Wallace's taxidermy shop on Upper William Street, New York

City, where "almost always there would be news of unusual local birds . . . and it might even befall, on good day, that I should be allowed to take into my hands some rarity not yet dispossessed of the fresh beauty of its natural forms and plumage." The popularity of taxidermy and the social esteem curried by elite practitioners brought kudos to hunting as an exercise in imperial adventuring, scientific collection, marksmanship, and honorable masculinity. William Hornaday's catalogue of the skills demanded of the museum collector conveyed a good impression of the hunter hero: a committed naturalist, a good shot, physically resilient and energetic in demeanor. Based around the codes of acquisition, knowledge transfer, and display, the imagined community of the hunt allowed taxidermist and hunter to participate in a reciprocal exchange of animal capital and sporting mythology. Locked together in a trade of capture and camaraderie, the hunter and the taxidermist were conjoined in the acts of killing, performance, and reanimation.[8]

Taxidermy offered a vibrant articulation of the afterlife of the hunt, but more than that, concerns about mounting even occupied the thoughts of hunters in the field. In that sense, taxidermy was not just an ending, a souvenir, but rather an object whose meaning was bound up with the phenomenology of hunting itself. Taxidermy concerns dictated practice on the hunt right from the start, the promise of a trophy and its capture and preservation, mediating the hunter's performance activity and mindset from the outset. Taxidermy and the "politics of reproduction," in the words of Donna Haraway, start at the game trail.[9]

Focus on the taxidermy totem, the material culture of the afterlife of the hunt, seeped into sporting practices and linguistics. Hunters chose what time of year to visit the hunting grounds of the West according to myriad factors—timetables imposed by business, ship passage, the availability of guides, the habits and movements of animal populations, and the potential of inclement weather to influence accessing prey, camp comforts, or ease of movement—but the quality of animal hide and its implications for mounted specimens was one consideration. In this sense, the animal exerted a form of agency on the game trail courtesy of the nature of its pelage. Once on the trail, hunters spent time surveying the habits of game for the purposes of reanimation after the kill. According to Rowland Ward, "The true sportsman-naturalist should esteem the record of an animals pose or habits in life as important as any other record, so that when the specimen comes to skilled treatment, the naturalness of it many be a feature that enhances its value in every way." That said, biological classifiers were often replaced by a essentialist discourse trading in "trophies" and "heads." Hunting in Wyoming in 1897, acclaimed big game hunter Frederick Selous remarked that "a few fair heads can still be got by hard work and perseverance, but for every head obtained, a good deal of hunting must now be done." Later on the trail he noted that "it was not until September the 29th that I saw a mule deer buck with a head worth keeping." Likewise, Lewis Wise, a British hunter arriving in the West in 1880 after an elongated trip to Australia, expressed delight in his journal when seeing compatriot Captain Ashton arrive back at the ranch on the Powder River from a trip to the mountains: "He has had some excellent sport. In the afternoon their outfit came in and the 'trophies' which made my mouth water!" Such phraseology suggested a hunter's gaze that figuratively decapitated and framed the head of the animal with a shield long before it reached the taxidermist's studio.[10]

Taxidermic concerns infused the quest for animal quarry. Heads belonging to particular species were especially prized. Often hunters arranged trips in search of one specific animal, usually to complete their own private reanimated anthology of western game animals. Selous, for instance, returned to the West in 1898 specifically to find "heads" of bighorn sheep for his collection. Prey selection also depended on size and stature: large animals or those with multiple pointed antlers or an impressive countenance were favored. For British sportsman William Baillie Grohman, "My chief aim in visiting the Rockies so repeatedly was to bag big heads."[11]

Fresh from admiring Captain Ashton's trophy haul, Lewis Wise expressed delight at bagging an eleven-point elk on his next hunt. William Hornaday recommended that hunters shoot animals of "strictly first-class" caliber for mounting, a nod to the hunter as an advocate of natural selection by the gun, a two-legged apex predator engaged in the struggle for survival (and hunting heroism) with suitably vigorous faunal foes. George Shields, a regular visitor to the Rocky Mountains for hunting and a profligate writer, offered direct commentary on the mentality of the hunter when trudging the game trail with William Allen and L. A. Huffman in 1883 in Montana. Hearing the "electric thrill" of bugling elk, Shields cogitated on the mechanics of taxidermy, capture, and aesthetics: "To me on this occasion it was particularly interesting, for I wanted above all things on this trip to secure a good head for mounting, and the questions that ran through my brain were: Is this an old-timer? Has he a fine, well-developed head and broad spreading perfect antlers? And shall I be able to get him?"[12]

With the trophy animal in the crosshairs and the metaphysics of bullet trajectory and terrain accounted for, the hunter too found the issue of taxidermy prescient. It mattered where the fatal hit was made: first, to stop the animal in its tracks and, second, to make as clean a shot as possible to allow for minimum damage to the skin. Taxidermy manuals stressed the importance of good marksmanship, to bring the animal down swiftly. According to Davie, the hunter should "shoot to kill, but not to mangle." Rowland Ward's *Sportsman's Handbook* offered illustrations of animal bodies and advice on where to aim. In addition to the clean shot, placement was essential to enable easy mounting. As Rowley expressed it, "The less the hide is mutilated the better for our purpose." After all, a skin full of bullet holes or blown to pieces with ammunition made the task of reanimation much harder. Hornaday elucidated: "What is a tiger worth with the top of his head blown off, or a deer with a great hole torn in his side by an explosive bullet?" Environmental variables also factored into this equation. If the quarry fell down a cliff or into water during the chase, the animal body could be damaged or rendered inaccessible. Selous recalled one lengthy chase of a bull elk that ended with a satisfying kill atop a ravine. Watching the animal tumble fifty feet down a rugged gully, trail companion W. M. exclaimed, "Well! I be doggoned, he won't have much horns on him when he gets to the bottom of that." One piece of horn broke off, which the two men looked for in vain, but still salvaged the skin, skull, horns, and meat for their trouble. Even after retrieval, packing out could create its own problems, as articulated by Edward Buxton on his Rocky Mountain trip in the 1890s: "It is nearly as easy to lead pack animals loaded with wapiti horns, through such timber, erect and prone, as lay behind us, as to drag a flight of books through a knitted stocking." Taxidermy thus directed and shaped the hunter's gaze, making demands on the object-subject relationship of the field.[13]

In order for wild things to submit a perfect performance in their afterlife, painstaking detail was needed at the point of the kill. Protecting the memory of the moment for the purposes of reanimation meant that once shot, the context and condition of the animal were comprehensively documented. Vectors of itemization and classification lent the kill site an almost forensic countenance, a de facto autopsy in the field. Hunters cataloged the animal body—vital statistics of height, width, length, as well as descriptive vectors of texture, muscle shape, color, placement of hair, and surrounding vegetation—in order to extract the essence of its living form for reassembly later. Calipers, casts, and labels aided the process of record, as did drawings and watercolors. Heeding Rowland Ward's advice that "it must be borne in mind before all things, that the value of any object secured and preserved depends on the completeness with which all its natural features are saved, as well as the condition in which they are kept," British hunter and correspondent for *The Field*, Grantley Berkeley, sketched his bison before transport to the "Jungle," careful to record "the exact position and look of the animal" as it fixed his eye for "a contemplated charge."[14]

Some hunters used the camera as an aid to capturing the moment, using the opportunity to capture the visual essence of the animal on film as a valuable precursor to its resurrection in three-dimensional reality. Rowland Ward proved an advocate of the camera, noting, "An animal may be photographed within its surroundings, just as it fell; the picture may be made a nucleus of interesting and most instructive memoranda, of obvious value because such details are too often forgotten, or the impression made by them effaced, just in proportion as we move from the spot." William Hornaday instead saw the addition of photographic equipment to the tools of the hunter actuary as problematic: "No man who has his hands full of shooting, preserving, and packing specimens can afford to waste time on a camera with which to take dead animals." The capacity of the camera, in Hornaday's estimation, failed to capture the essence of a deceased elk or grizzly in the way that taxidermy did.[15]

Such doubts notwithstanding, the use of notes, sketches, and photographs to fully flesh out the details of the reanimated animal showed the afterlife of the hunt to be an exercise in trans-media storytelling, the material culture of the hunt, the trophy given embellishment and the breath of life by word and picture. In fact, the *Guide to Taxidermy* (1914) pointed out the value to the sportsman of the hunting notebook not only as a practical referent for taxidermy, but also as an object of reflection in later years that will "recall to your mind, in after years, many interesting facts that you have forgotten." In the hands of the hunter hero then, the demands of trophy taking mandated empirical observation, marksmanship, measurement and description, and possibly camera work in order to preserve the meaning of the animal "in a state of nature." In that sense, the different narrative articulations of hunter's paradise supported one another. The detailed cataloguing of the animal victim constructed the area around the kill stood as a de facto crime scene, a site of investigation, record, and reconstruction. Such an analogy seemed particularly relevant when hunters carefully placed manila paper underneath the animal body and drew its outline in pencil or chalk, as advised by Davie in *Methods in the Art of Taxidermy* (1894). Meanwhile, just as animals tested the limits of their captors in fleeing from the bullet, the organic detail of the animal body (notably in the case of big game animals) conveyed a sense of animal resistance to the project of reanimation, the complexity of the subject mitigating the potential of full reproduction and conveying a vestigial sense of animal agency even in death.[16]

Beyond the process of catalogue and facsimile came preservation. After successfully stalking, shooting, and capturing their prey, western hunters frequently feared losing the trophy. As A. W. Dimock said of his recently vanquished grizzly bear, "The prize was mine and my only fear was losing it." George Shields was so concerned that grizzlies might devour a cow elk shot in 1883 that he refrained from returning to the hunting camp and instead spent a night of solitude on a mountainside, waking at four in the morning to roast and eat the elk's heart before protecting it from a band of bears that arrived in the morning "like a band of redskins assaulting an emigrant train." The grizzlies too fell to Shields's rifle, were laid out with the elk, and were photographed by Huffman "amid the plaudits of the admiring multitude." Less dramatic but equally destructive, trophy pieces also faced insidious attack by maggots and flies. Although less rapid than in tropical hunting climes, the insect life of the West could happily munch away at (and ruin) a prized skin. Skinning thus emerged as a critical part of the pretaxidermy process, dismemberment an essential practice for enabling successful immortalization later.[17]

Hunters typically skinned and dressed the carcass at the kill site, thereby avoiding the possibilities of it being eaten by bears or wolves, assisting removal from often difficult terrain (Batty noted in *Practical Taxidermy* that "elk antlers are 'elephants' at camp, in a wagon, or on a mule's back, and no little pluck is required in transporting them through a hunting campaign"), and enabling processes of chemical treatment to begin. Dimock skinned his grizzly, rolled the hide, and stashed it safely away. As night fell and he wandered back to camp, he ruminated that "this had to be done for nothing must be omitted which could add to the triumph of my return." Hunters separated the flesh from the skin carefully, removed the entrails, and cut incisions in places that would not "mar the beauty of a head." A. Henry Higginson, working at Staunton Lake in 1899 on a collecting survey for a museum, "worked over" his first whitetail deer "for some two hours before I finally got it in good shape."[18]

A variety of methods were then used to preserve the spoils—wet storage in barrels of brine or salt to stave off decomposition or the use of chemical treatments, including arsenic, sodium, turpentine, alum, or Rowland Ward's patented "Taxidermine," to rub into dry stored skins. The use of these chemicals not only dictated the terms of the hunt—only when fully equipped with the necessary preservatives, Higginson noted, could the chase "begin in earnest"—but also effectively embedded the hunter in a modern industrial context. Despite the wilderness fixings, the rigors of biological time (decomposition) and the rhythms of modernity (railroad timetables and chemical procedures) mediated the activity of the hunt. Such aspects—based on the needs of preservation of hide and horn—lent the game trail an air of mechanization. On one level, processes of butchery and disembodiment likened the campsite to the Chicago slaughterhouse, itself a locus of animal capital and an agent of transmission between western field and the demands (in this case, culinary) of an urban industrial market. Stripped of its innards, labeled up as parts (head and hide, skull and antlers), the choice cuts of the trophy animal were barreled or boxed up and shipped to the taxidermy studio for reassembly (see figure 6.1). Time was of the essence. Elizabeth Custer recalled a grand hunt hosted for Detroit sportsmen by her husband in which the spoils of the chase were hauled back to camp on wagons and dispatched to Detroit for "preservation" the same day. Moreover, the mechanics of transport, preservation, and logistics meant that the gateway cities of the West—Denver, St. Louis, Chicago—also emerged as principal hubs for the taxidermy trade.[19]

The Taxidermy Economy, Animal Capital, and the Marketing of the West

Once the animal had been packed out from the game trail, it fell to the taxidermist to perform its reanimation from fragmentary body parts, notes,

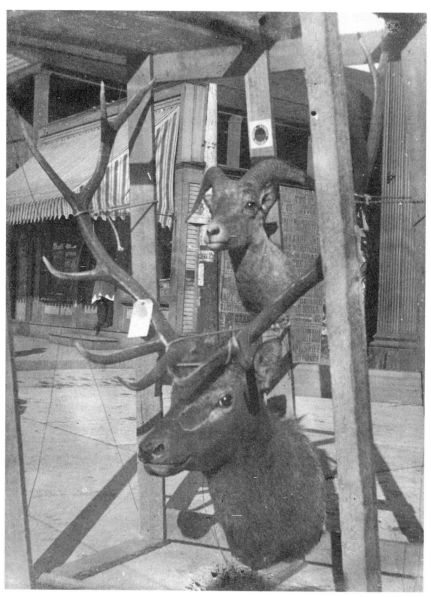

FIGURE 6.1. Elk and mountain sheep trophy heads, 1898. Photo by John S. McIntire. From "Photographic Album of a Rocky Mountain Hunting Trip, 1898," WA photos 37, Beinecke Rare Book and Manuscript Library, Yale University.

sketches, and labels to charismatic trophy haul. Some hunters chose to perform the task themselves, using popular instructional guides such as *Practical
Taxidermy* (1913) or *Hints to Sportsmen* (1851). The Northwestern School of
Taxidermy, established in 1903 in Omaha, Nebraska, even offered a "taxidermy by mail" course, advertised in the pages of *Hunter, Trader, Trapper*
and other sporting journals. Proprietor "Professor" J. W. Elwood claimed
40,000 enrollments by 1912. The possibilities of amateur practice allowed the
individual to participate fully in the construction of hunter's paradise from
trophy haul to hall, demonstrating fully his credentials as a polymath hunter
hero and scientific savant. Leon Luther Pray noted in his manual *Taxidermy*
(1913) that "the lover of field and gun may spend many fascinating hours at
the bench, preparing, setting up, and finishing specimens of his own taking"
with only a little "working out detail and a moderate amount of patience."
General Custer, for one, spoke enthusiastically of his devotion to the practice,
writing wife Elizabeth from the Yellowstone in September 1873 of his efforts
to preserve the animals of the chase for himself, his officers, and for a gift to
the Audubon Society (he also had a bison head set aside for his wife). As he
noted, long after the camp had retired for the night, he could be found in his
tent, sleeves rolled up "busily engaged preparing the head of some animal
killed in the chase." Custer boasted that an antelope head mount would take
him two hours, while his pride and joy was a whole grizzly, the "king of the
forest" in its entirety, depicted *"exactly as in life."*[20]

Typically, however, the hunting fraternity commissioned professionals to
mount their hunting trophies. For some the decision was logistical. Those
wandering game trails for several months at a time (which was a usual practice among the sport hunters) packed out as they shot, while the international fraternity favored a shipping out approach for obvious reasons. Those
in possession of, or aspiring to, upper-class status regarded themselves as first
and foremost hunters; taxidermy instead represented one of the auxiliary
services that supported the hunting experience. Ultimately, of course, the
task of mounting trophies of large game presented quite a challenge and
demanded expert skills best left to the profession community. Consequently,
the popularity of hunting in the nineteenth-century West ensured a steady
stream of traffic for the taxidermy trade. From Rowland Ward's London
"Jungle"—a trans-media, transnational hub of the sporting fraternity, dealing
with the exotic animals of the globe from grizzly bear to gnu—to the local

outfits that graced the towns of the frontier West, business was booming. Men such as Rudolph Borcherdt of Denver established a business in 1868 in a gun shop and soon moved to his own premises on Lawrence Street from where he shipped worldwide, and William Wright, who moved to Missouri in 1899, inspired by Grizzly Adams and P. T. Barnum to take up bear hunting in the summer and taxidermy in the winter, ran a brisk trade in the after-life of the hunt. German migrant Frank Schwartz left his job with Singer sewing machines (somewhat appropriately) to preside over a flourishing taxi-dermy business in St. Louis. By the early years of the twentieth century the Jonas Brothers and Jack C. Miles, both operating from Denver, ran successful trades in mail order taxidermy largely for the hunting community.

As Larry Borowsky notes, the taxidermy business successfully "marketed the 'life' in wildlife." As such, the taxidermist became a fervent (and largely uncredited) producer of frontier mythology. This variant of the skin trade, with animal heads strung up outside shops from Boulder, Colorado, to Birmingham, England, suggested money to be made from reanimated "ani-mals of enterprise" and provided fecund evidence of the selling of material and myth in the same trophy package. Taxidermy outfits effectively connected the western game trail to a global trade network in mounted specimens, helping craft a transnational nature's metropolis in which their position was pivotal. Products ranged from antlers and heads displayed on wooden shields, horn furniture, hat stands, and rugs to complete bodies and even bespoke items. A mark of the provenance of the West in mounted animal capital as well as interconnected processes of tourism and transport in their acquisi-tion and transport, Earl B. Wittich's Curiosity Store (est. 1880) stood opposite the Northern Pacific depot in Livingston, Montana, and invited visitors to Yellowstone Park to come in and select "Game Heads, Indian Curiosities Fur rugs, Fossils, Polished Agates, National Park Specimens, Buffalo, Steer and Mountain Sheep Horns in Novelties, Elk Antler Furniture and Hat Racks." Wittich, the ardent promoter, touted his collection of animate animal capital as "second to none throughout the Rocky Mountains" and his specimens as rare, cheap, and "moth-proof" and boasting a happy clientele all over North America and Europe.[21]

For the hide and subsistence hunter, the reasons for keeping animal quarry were obvious: money and food. For the sport hunter, a different kind of transaction predominated, one in which possession of the skin of the animal conveyed powerful motifs and served as valuable social capital. Sportsmen commissioned heraldic antlers, horn furniture, and head mounts for installation on walls and floors in private houses, hallways, and libraries. Some went as far as to create dedicated buildings for their faunal collections, as in the case of Major Powell Cotton at Quex Park, Kent, whose family seat is still roamed by exotic African beasts corralled in exquisite dioramas or Mr. Taylor, author of *Hunting Big Game in North America* (1919), who erected "a fire-proof building at his home in a little country town near Portsmouth for the purpose of preserving his trophies." In the home environment, the trophy was both decorative and demonstrative, and in fact taxidermists ran a brisk trade in hunting artifacts sold as commercial items for those who had never even graced the game trail but wanted to imbibe of western-themed ornamentation. Frank W. Calkins recalled meeting up with two hunters in Yellowstone who were "specimen hunting" for a curio shop in Chicago— one went out with "pack-sack, rifle and horn-hammer" while the other stayed in camp polishing horn already collected. Mounted heads, horn-embossed furnishings, and even elk-teeth watch chains proved popular as novelty items among a populace keen to participate in the modish charms of the Wild West. In that sense, the taxidermy economy offered a skin trade to rival the industrial processes of the beaver and bison fur market, simply one couched in pursuit of what historian Tina Loo dubs "commodity fetishes." As William Hornaday elucidated:

A naturally handsome mammal head which has been skillfully mounted is a thing of beauty and joy forever. Wearied with the survey of inane and meaningless pictures, stiff portraits, cheap statuettes and tawdry fancy decorations, the eye rests gladly and gratefully upon a fine head on a handsome shield, hanging in a good light, and blesses the hand that placed it there. Such an ornament calls forth endless admiration and query, even from those who know no other chase than that of the almighty dollar.

According to Pray's *Taxidermy*, "Antlered game heads that are mounted true to life in form and expression may go far to beautify many dining rooms, dens, and hallways, enhancing the artistic tone of the rooms in which they are placed." An advertisement for Rowland Ward concurred, emphasizing the fact that trophies "can be characteristically grouped and arranged to decorate Libraries and Smoking Rooms, or Special Rooms devoted to Trophies of Sport, with much unconventional and naturalistic effect that is very attractive."[22]

For the gentleman sport hunter, the display of trophies without having killed the animal struck as unbridled heresy. Theodore Roosevelt explained the qualification: "Nothing adds more to a hall or room than fine antlers when they have been shot by the owner, but there is always an element of the absurd in a room furnished with trophies of the chase which the owner has acquired by purchase." For the sport hunter, then, possession of the animal body proved crucial. It paid witness to a series of powerful cultural constructs signifying control over space, memory, selfhood, and authority over others. The trophy allowed for tales to be told and served as a visual prompt for an oral narrative that glorified the hunter hero, the winning of the West, and the sanctification of animal encounter. The politics of ownership featured highly in the cultural meanings of the sporting trophy. The trophy could not be purchased—it had to be earned to be fully possessed. In essence, it served as a totem for the performance of hunter's paradise itself. Without holding tenure over the spoils of the chase, the hunt was somehow devalued and contested. Even with the memory of the kill and the recollection of it, the lack of a material trophy left the metaphysics of capture unrequited. The trophy then offered abject proof, the animal body bringing a sense of authenticity and connection to reality. At the same time, its fundamental power came not only through its organic quality, but also from its role as a faunal vector, a carrier of the historical moment, of the hunter's victory and implied masculinity and of his mastery over space both wild and domestic.[23]

Bringing the Wild West Indoors: Reassembling the Story in the Hunter's "Den"

The trophy represented a powerful signifier of the hunting moment, a theatrical artifact around which the hunt could be extrapolated and experienced—in other words, performed once more. Both spectator and actor, the taxidermy head choreographed the story and "wilded" interior space with faunal authority. In a performance sense, it seemed to function rather like Buck the Animated Trophy Talking Deer, available in Walmart today, an animatronic subaltern whose mouth moves to the rhythms of song and speech delivered through a microphone. Of critical purchase was the way in which the mounted animal allowed the hunter to return to the trail and witness the trappings of frontier experience. As Rachel Poliquin has noted, physical encounters with taxidermy prompted "experiential readings," "knowledge gained in the recognition of the somatic presence of an animal." As such, the biotic fragments of wild things were invested with a vital performative function. Mesmerized by the magnetic presence of the trophy head of an 800-pound "monster elk" killed in Montana, George Shields described a powerful moment of encounter as follows:

> I got the entire head home in good condition, had it mounted and it now occupies the most conspicuous place in my "den." As I pause in the midst of this recital, and look up at it, it wears that same grand, majestic look it wore there on top of the Rocky Mountains in that cold crisp September morning, and I have but to give my imagination play, and I find myself surrounded by those same old snow-capped peaks . . . I can feel that fresh, frosty, invigorating atmosphere; I can hear those frozen leaves crush under my feet as I walk, and my blood dances through my veins as I climb from hilltop to hilltop in pursuit of the noble quarry.

The trophy represented a vector through which the entire hunting repertory—its trials and elations, sensory connections, contests and victories—could be revisited. As sportsman Edgar Randolph noted, "A fine trophy serves to identify most appropriately a hunting experience, and as the years roll by the memories of certain camps cluster about each head." Trophy value, then, was not simply determined by score, size, or stature, but by the specter of memory that conferred on it powerful social meanings and associations with frontier experience. In this regard, Ward's *Horn Measurements and Weights of the Great Game of the World* failed to encapsulate the full value of the "bag" in the way his taxidermy mounts did. Roosevelt noted of a favorite grizzly bear head that "the beauty of the trophy, and the memory of the circumstances under which I procured it, made me value it perhaps more highly than any other in my house." Reanimated animals represented powerful actors in the performance of the hunt as reenactment.[24]

The trophy conveyed a vital savagery that spoke to the reputation and the journey of the triumphant hunter. In that sense, it represented the final act in the quest narrative of the game trail. Sequestered in the masculine enclave of the trophy room, the victor confronted and confirmed his association with the wild—performing the hunt through a reunion of its critical actors. Often such spaces were referred to as "dens." Etymologically, the label is interesting in denoting the lair of a wild animal. Moreover, it also referenced the nomenclature of the frontier cabins where hunting fraternities gathered to shelter, carouse, hang skins, and tell tales. As James Mead noted of one such space at Salina, Kansas, owned by Tommy Thorn: "Some congenial spirits would gather in, hang a few quarters of fat buffalo in a cool place, and for a week or ten days 'the den' would be a place of joy, story, and song. It was not a disreputable resort, such as are found in cities, but a jolly hunters' club-house." Isabella Bird spent time in a hunter's cabin belonging to "Mountain Jim" Nugent near Estes Peak, which she called a den, for it "looked like the den of a wild beast." Everywhere she looked were signs of animal presence: the roof was covered with lynx and beaver furs, beaver pelts and antlers were pinned to the logs, offal was strewn about, and a deer carcass hung in the gloom beyond. In the postbellum industrial world, meanwhile, "the den" came to denote a masculine space where one might choose to take refuge for purposes of work or leisure, but the translation from frontier fixings to urban decor was fairly seamless. Frontier experience could be performed by the transport of an artifact culture. Surrounded by a "dead zoo" of animal foes—prancing birds, skulking coyotes, and watchful bighorn sheep—William Allen sat confidently in his lair, Winchester in hand, assuming for the camera the role of the all-conquering hero (see Figure 6.2). "Mr. Bobcat," shot by Allen in the Bighorn Mountains, stood "forever silent, yet alert," his eyes trained in arrested motion on a sandhill crane. The dramaturgy of the hunt and its central actors were reassembled in a new landscape of play. In this "biographical reading" of the trophy, namely of networks and narrative functions, the celebration of robust adventuring in the wilderness and the mastery of the hunter hero was paramount.[25]

The act of looking conjured a voyeuristic encounter with another world, offered an intimate peep into the realm of nature, and provided a lens through which the power of the animal and of the hunter could be witnessed. Trophies were repositories of memory that allowed for the retelling of the hunting story and, critically, its denouement: the passage of the hunter hero from greenhorn to seasoned creature of the frontier. As Roosevelt noted in *Hunting Trips of a Ranchman* (1885): "No sportsman can ever feel much keener pleasure and self-satisfaction than when, after a successful stalk and good

FIGURE 6.2. William Allen in his "den." From William Allen, *Adventures with Indians and Game* (Chicago: A. W. Bowen, 1903), 103.

shot, he walks up to a grand elk lying dead in the cool shade of the great evergreens, and looks at the massive and yet finely molded form, and at the mighty antlers which are to serve in the future as the trophy and proof of his successful skill." William Hornaday, too, noted the importance of mounting the first kill—a signal of rite of passage. The importance of possessing the trophy as a (usually) masculine signifier helped to explain the great lengths taken by hunters to haul their spoils out of the backwoods. This process, following on from the culture of display on the hunting trail, contained strong elements of performance. W. E. Webb concluded that "half the pleasure of hunting, if sportsmen would but confess it, consists of showing one's trophies to others."[26]

The trophy proved an important agent in communicating the story of masculine heroics common to various iterations of the hunting afterlife. A catalogue that accompanied an exhibit of American hunting trophies on loan to an exhibition in Britain remarked that "the fine series of heads . . . which adorn the walls tell a tale of many a successful stalk over difficult ground, many a glorious outwitting of this surprisingly active and keen-sighted animal." The trophy held purchase as a sacred relic of masculine rejuvenation and the enervating qualities of primal encounters in the West. The fetishistic significance of the gendered animal body was not lost on female companions and observers. As one member of a sporting party noted of a male counterpart, "Dear, enthusiastic, kind-hearted Bobbie, the role of conquering hero suited him so well, who will begrudge him that one trophy, meaning as it did the lure by which he gained a rich treasure of renewed health and energy." Moreover, once hung on the wall of the hunter's den, the trophy continued to radiate the revitalizing power of wilderness, as if the skin itself exuded the cathartic impulse of the trail experience long after its ending. For Edward Ruxton, a wall of trophies attested to "the authority and experience" of the sport and conjured "delightful memories" and "a stock of vigour from the most bracing climate in the world." Mounted heads allowed for the spirit of masculinity and sporting prowess to infuse and animate interior space and for the transformed hunter hero to stride confidently from the game trail to the world of urban industrialism (and back again). As Randolph pointed out, mounted heads "revive thrilling scenes which might otherwise become dimmed amid an uncongenial environment."[27]

Taxidermy confirmed the command of the hunter hero over past, personhood, and also place: the animal as article of frontier acquisition. Aldo Leopold noted that the power of a trophy came from "the seeking as well as in the getting," and served as a potent "certificate" that "its owner has been somewhere and done something—that he has exercised skill, persistence, or discrimination in the age-old feat of overcoming, outwitting, or reducing-to-possession." Read biographically, the trophy delivered a message of wilderness contested, conquered, and confined in a domestic setting. This not only confirmed the hunter as an "American native," as historian Daniel Herman has argued, but it served as an emblem of frontier tenure. Embedded in the mounted body was a narrative about the beauty of animal forms, the pleasure of apprehending them up close, the control of space, and the rightful appropriation of the resources of the West. The practical taking of trophies demonstrated Euro-American ownership over landscape and claims on a mythology. In *Buffalo Land* (1872), Webb made merry with tales of his hunting cronies—Dr. Pythagoras, Mr. Colon (with a son named, perhaps inevitably, Semi), and Professor Paleozoic—and issued a comment on the vanquishing of the bison. The "first victim of our prowess" was "to be skinned and horns used for a hat rack," raw nature conquered and reduced to decoration as an act of frontier takeover. Prior to shipping out, the animal skin had been propped up as an "impromptu throne" with horn armrests, on which had the professor composed a note to his students, "on a buffalo, in the year of my happiness, one." Although a satirical take on the eccentric world of the aristocratic game hunter, Webb's framing of the trophy was instructive. Taxidermy spoke of assumed sapient authority over nature and the rights to dictate access to territory and the ownership of the ecological resources of the West.[28]

The social functions of taxidermy were transnational in application. Reanimated by the colonial aristocrat in libraries and grand halls, the trophy was a heraldic signifier of power, prestige and pageant. Witnesses to a distantly claimed geography, trophies spoke of lands visited, explored and assimilated, nature wrestled with and wrested from savagery. Codes of masculine prowess, natural abundance, and geographical acquisition also held sway in a regional context, where local homes, civic buildings, and commercial spaces carried the faunal frontier forth as a demonstration of landscape politics and identity transformation. Horace Edwards related how the library of the Young Men's Association in Bozeman, Montana, was decorated with many antlers from deer, elk, and moose, which he found "very enticing" as an environment in which to read and smoke. Henry Helgeson from Missoula, writing of the 3,224 bison he "butchered" in 1870s Montana, mailed a photograph to a friend of himself standing in a pose of capture over one of the icons, the representative animals, of the West. On the back of the letter, Helgeson alluded to the powerful iconography of the trophy in writing his name as a triangle resembling a bison skull, evidence of his identity as a westerner and his mastery of its terrain. Helgeson's desire for commemoration also suggested that the desire to confirm provenance over the trophy was not only confined to sport hunters. Likewise, shots of hunters' cabins—such as that used by the Hilger brothers in Montana and marked by hanging skins, skulls, and trophies both inside and outside—articulated the prowess of the local hunting fraternity (in sport, subsistence, and market variants), their vocation and adopted homelands. Frontier cultures were keen to demonstrate their own affinity with the West (identified by its animal life) and also their command over ecological and storytelling milieus.[29]

Whether in the theater of West or just of it, taxidermy spoke thus not only of power over an environment but also of belonging: assuming a western identity through the parading of its symbols. Mary Ronan's "hall of death" at her Flathead Agency hostelry, so called by her children for its roster of trophy mounts of bear, mountain goat, elk, moose, deer, and caribou, served as both statement of ownership and pertinent advertisement of hunter's paradise for the sportsmen who stayed at the boardinghouse. Women as well as men were participants in this artifactual culture of the hunt. Evelyn Cameron demonstrated her credentials as hunter, naturalist, and frontierswoman by having heads mounted by a professional taxidermist in Mandan for display in the ranch house. The use of the trophy attested to the acquisition of local knowledge, the display of iconic western animals akin to local art prints of famous landmarks—signals too of aesthetic beauty or scientific interest. As much as it celebrated wild things, it also spoke of human ascendancy. Period photographs abound with examples of proud hunters standing before an array of taxidermy pieces that stand as material and symbolic evidence of their mastery over the frontier. John Mortimer Murphy's *Sporting Adventures in the Far West* (1879) offered a vivid example of imbedded gesture politics in the performance of the hunt, explaining how a group of hunters captured a grizzly that had seriously wounded one of their compatriots, cut off her head, and delivered it "as a trophy to the victim of her anger, and if he is not now dead it adorns his cabin in Humboldt county." This taxidermy bear, then, served as a tale of nature's savagery, human resilience, collective action, and the primacy of *Homo sapiens*. Like dead crows hung on a fence to ward off their living brethren, it issued a cautionary tale to the faunal residents of the West about questioning human authority.[30]

Masculine heroics, wilderness contest, and control over the socio-geography of the West represented the critical biographical readings of the sporting trophy. The aesthetics of display and the conventions of reanimation of the animal body meanwhile conveyed a set of descriptive messages about the animal and the West that spoke both to the environmental complement of the place and also to its mythological composition. The rationale of the modern taxidermist may have been to convey life in its accurate form, but its design schematics remained party to cultural constraints and tropes. In that fashion, taxidermy was, for all its sedentary quality, a stage and a performance, choreographed like the best Wild West show. The animal, after all, had to be consciously posed, often frozen into covenants of arrested motion as if paused in the midst of a leap or a glance. As Rowley noted, taxidermy involved the etiquette of display, the idea of a "front" or "point" to an arrangement.[31]

Hunting stories did not shy from their literary encounter with atavism. In trophy production, however, the violence of the hunt was sidestepped by production markers that emphasized the refurbished animal as unbloodied, pristine, and thus immortal. Just as in the storytelling and visual worlds, trophies stressed themes of regality, giganticism, or ferocity. Cervids were typically lordly and bison lumbering behemoths. Savage nature was expressed most starkly in the trophy tropes of the snarling wolf or mountain lion, and especially the wide-jawed grizzly bear. The reanimated West conjured a slice of primal life, carnality, and threat—the animal as brute creation. As Davie pointed out, 90 percent of carnivores were mounted with their mouths open, "trying to look fierce without having any adequate cause to do so." Hornaday too remarked on the tendency of taxidermists to depict animal life in the poses of "anger, rage or deviance," sometimes to counterproductive results, with jaws hyperextended so that "the animal seems to be yawning prodigiously."[32]

Along with the theme of nature red in tooth and claw, trophy taxidermy traded in discourses of the exceptional. Hunters preserved the best of their catches, hence the largest heads and most pointed antlers achieved public airing, a tendency that promoted a sense of the West as a place of charismatic megafauna, and its representative animals the mannequin artifacts of faunal master races. The Buckhorn Saloon in San Antonio, established in 1881 by Albert Friedrich, proved a case in point, with its mounted displays, including a seventy-eight-point buck above the bar counter that provoked great interest. As one visitor exclaimed, "We saw some horns *so big* at the Buckhorn, we just couldn't believe it and couldn't take our eyes off those fine horns." With the quality of heads and horns also came the predilection to display row upon row of mounts, alluding to the West as a veritable cornucopia of game. The Buckhorn, too, excelled in this regard. Billed as "a wonderland of mounted heads and horns," its walls and ceilings were crammed to full taxidermic carrying capacity, a reflection both of local game abundance, hunting traditions, and Friedrich's practice of trading antlers for whiskey. Postcards and souvenir brochures lent the saloon the look of a faunal catacomb, a canny example of the cornucopian West, the theatrical codes of the hunt, and the establishment's irrevocably western fixings.[33]

Of course, these descriptive valuations of the animal trophy relied on imagination. Heraldry shields, skins, or just antlers required the viewer to perform a cognitive leap, to fill the gaps in the faunal fabric and build a picture of the western landscape through fragments. Meanwhile, the craze for horn furnishings and the like spoke not only of the performance markers of the hunt but the politics of colonial appropriation and a fantasy architecture of the frontier. Perhaps the fullest articulation of the cult of the "domesticated wild" came from Rowland Ward's so-called "Wardian furniture" with its set pieces of alligator cigar boxes and elephant stools. Mounted on two legs and holding an electric light in his paw, Ward's grizzly bear standard lamp (displayed at the Philadelphia Centennial Exposition) conveyed a stark imprint of nature as tamed, the bruin taken from the wilds and incorporated as an anthropomorphic whimsical servant. Such pieces implied an inherent tension in taxidermy creations between the animal as code for the savage and its service as domestic subaltern. Describing his endeavors in the realm of wilding the living room, Ward noted, "Elephants do not at first glance seem to lend themselves as articles for household decoration, and yet I have found them most adaptable for that purpose." The trophy, then, served a dual purpose: a trinket of wilderness adulation and yet an artifact of its takeover.[34]

Corralled behind glass and nailed to shields, animal artifacts represented objects of veneration and of capture. Grantley Berkeley, fresh from a 1859 trip hunting bison at Fort Riley, enthused of the tail mounted on acorn that "now ornaments my rooms at Beacon lodge," a product well serviced to add "a sporting finish to the bells of drawing-room, dining-room and study." The politics of reproduction and the spatial and aesthetic codes of taxidermy thereby contained an implicit tension. Practitioners and customers idealized the materiality of the specimen, its lifelike countenance and promise of intimate encounter with the wild. At the same time, the prerogatives of design and allegory, not to mention the fragmentary nature of the animal body and the architecture of display, spoke of assimilation, appropriation, and artifice. Entirely removed from their landscape and often from their torso and limbs, taxidermy specimens represented biological fragments of the faunal frontier. Held together by wire, plaster, and clay, these artifacts were, in a sense, animatronic precursors to the mechanical puppets of fairgrounds, Disney parks, and arcades—robotic actors in a choreographed show. An ambiguous necrogeography, taxidermy both "wilded" the home and tamed the West by corralling wild things in the trappings of domestic space. Culturally constituted and reanimated by art and science, the cyborg ecology (at least underneath all the fur) of the trophy room spoke of civilization and wilderness in equal measure.[35]

Challenging the East-West Axis: Martha Maxwell and Taxidermy "From the Inside"

William Hornaday described his orangutan group in 1879 as "the beginning of an era in the progress of museum taxidermy in the United States." However, three years before he wowed the national scientific fraternity and the American Society of Taxidermists with his simian creation, a pioneer woman in Colorado was making her own innovations in taxidermy, display, and performance culture. Martha Maxwell, known as the "Colorado Huntress," emerged as a prominent taxidermist in Colorado during the 1870s, exhibiting her work in museums and shows and before a state and national audience. Maxwell's extraordinary collection of mounted animal life in the Rockies points to an important insider story of taxidermy, in other words, a story *in* the West as well as *of* it. Her work also serves to mediate the myth of female subservience on the frontier as well as highlighting (yet) another public outing of the hunter heroine. Women took up hunting as a vocation, embraced its connectivity to adventure, science, and personal renewal, and also emerged as expert witnesses to the hunting afterlife, both as writers and artists and also as natural historians and taxidermists. Significantly, as Maxwell's experience illuminated, the reanimation of the western frontier embroiled its practitioners in the politics of gender, scientific authority, and regional identity.[36]

Born in Pennsylvania in 1831, Martha Maxwell moved with her family to Wisconsin, where she grew up on a farm and learned to shoot. After an education at Oberlin College, she moved to Boulder, Colorado, in 1860 with her husband, twenty years her senior, who was lured by the promise of gold in the Pikes Peak area. For two years she ran a boardinghouse (and learned taxidermy from a German lodger) before returning to Wisconsin and employment under zoology professor E. F. Hobart at the local Baraboo Collegiate Institute. Moving back to Boulder in 1868, Maxwell and her extended family were living in a house a mile from town when taxidermy became a recreational pastime and gave purpose to her hankering for a wilderness landscape. As sister Mary recounted, "Having comparative leisure she was inspired with a desire to make a collection of its fauna." In common with other practitioners, Maxwell adhered to the aesthetic of realism, what her sister called a "desire for truthfulness in art," and saw it her responsibility to preserve representative and disappearing species. Initially reliant on specimens delivered by local men, Martha soon subscribed to Hornaday's ethic of complete immersion in the process, hunting for her own specimens on wagon and on packhorse through Colorado and Wyoming and noting the habits and characteristics of specimens in their own haunts. Alongside the typical homesteading activities of housekeeping, planting fruit trees, and tending a garden (the vocations of many western women), Maxwell "kept her gun at hand, and her eyes and ears open to the arrival of any living creature that could be appropriated to her enterprise." Such a comment invoked visions of a dyed-in-the-wool hunter heroine poised to tame the frontier, perfectly at home on the game trail and possessed with well-honed rifle skills and woodcraft. Like Isabella Bird, Maxwell claimed the landscape by appreciation and appropriation, staking ownership to the contours of the land by her own tread. Accordingly, Maxwell's pursuits situated taxidermy as a vocation that built an ecology of memory through collection and fostered the "knowing" of a new space.[37]

Significantly, Maxwell's experience as a taxidermist in Colorado illuminated a crossover between private and public, commercial, scientific, and theatrical aspects of the hide and horn trade. Taxidermy displays in her home literally brought the wild into the parlor, domesticating the fauna of the West for decorative purposes. One visitor recalled how "birds looked down in listening attitudes into the music book upon the organ [and] scolded each other from the corners of neighboring picture frames." Maxwell also produced specimens for the private market, making money from her reanimation of the West's natural plenitude in an entrepreneurial vein after the fashion of photographer Evelyn Cameron. In fall 1868, Martha placed the fruits of her forays into nature's laboratory before a public forum at the third Colorado Agricultural Society Fair. Her exhibit contained over a hundred avian varieties, from the smallest hummingbird to an impressive mountain eagle, each situated in their representative habitat. Judges at the fair commended the realistic representation, noting that the birds were "arranged in such natural position as almost to deceive the eye." Martha walked away with $50 and a diploma for her work, while the *Rocky Mountain News* commended her efforts: "The display of stuffed birds and small animals by Mrs. James A. Maxwell of Boulder, is probably the greatest attraction in the room. There are one hundred and ten varieties, consisting of eagles, hawks, [herons], cranes, ducks, snipes, squirrels, a young antelope, etc. etc.," each undertaken with "a great deal of taste" and "scientific attainments." Hunter's paradise was performed in all its wild glory.[38]

For Maxwell, good taxidermy was predicated on the idea of knowing every animal intimately, having, in the words of her sister, "a personal acquaintance" with it. Her sister described Martha's work as akin to "an artist painting the face of a friend." Yet this was not a labor of sentiment or abstraction, nor did it speak only of the amateur fixings of domestic hobby craft. In common with the new taxidermists of the East Coast, Maxwell regarded her vocation as a mixture of art and science, embedded in natural history pursuits and morally sanctioned for its taxonomic and classification value. True, her background spoke of an amateur tradition in natural history—and left her puzzled by the terminology of the profession at times—but she was eager to hone her skills and participate in a national professional discourse. After the success of her first agricultural fair exhibit, she wrote to the Smithsonian inquiring about the best books to study on botany. She also offered to supply western specimens for the institution. A conversation began with leading members of the museum—Joseph Henry, Spencer Baird, and Robert Ridgway—that lasted many years and involved the transmission of books and bodies between West and East for digest and cataloguing. Like the western hunter, Maxwell found herself enmeshed in a national exchange of biotic capital, part of a network of organic supply and information gathering. Although somewhat of a pariah in terms of her gender and scientific training, her local knowledge, long association with the West, and evident skills won kudos. As a testament to Maxwell's significance, a subspecies of screech owl found on her travels through the Rockies in 1877 now bears the label *Megascops asio maxwelliae* in her honor, while her sighting of the black-footed ferret offered final corroboration of Audubon's account. Meanwhile, her continuing thirst for collecting and mounting gained further commissions, financial gain, and a developing reputation for excellence. In 1869 she produced a 600-strong exhibit for the Colorado Agricultural Society fair, which she sold to Shaw's Garden in St. Louis for $600. The sale of the collection helped to finance the purchase of a new home at Boulder Creek, a salient indicator of the commercial value of taxidermy. As her daughter Mabel recalled, from this point Martha "regarded taxidermy as a profession rather than a mere hobby." From a specially designed shack near the main house—Martha's "den" (the name of which further complicated the masculine hegemony of the hunter)—works of "taxidermic immortality" took shape. Here Maxwell reanimated her creations using empiricism, science, and advanced modeling techniques. She studied animal anatomy, modeled in clay, and engaged the services of a local blacksmith to create an artificial skeleton on which to place the skin—cutting edge procedures akin to those used by William Hornaday and Carl Akeley and remarkable for their advanced levels, especially from a remote shack in Colorado and by a woman with no formal training.[39]

Maxwell saw her vocation as reformist, conservationist, scientific, preservationist, and moral. A strict vegetarian, Maxwell viewed the hunting of specimens as distinct from hunting for food. As she explained to friends who balked at her activities, "I never take life for such carnivorous purposes! All must die some time, I only shorten the period of consciousness that I may give their forms a perpetual memory; and I leave it to you, which is the more cruel? To kill to eat, or to kill to *immortalize*." In common with Hornaday and other exponents of the museum trade, Maxwell believed in the reanimation of the animal as endorsed by science. Vanishing species remained eternally secure in the exhibit culture of the museum, preserved for posterity in their true likenesses for all to see. Ritualistically claiming the animal as a scientific specimen successfully neutralized questions of killing, violence, and species decline in the material environment; while the power of the taxidermy elevated the animal body to a higher status than other valuations of animal capital. Moreover, Maxwell's commitment to her vocation also reflected a belief in female empowerment. An educated, independent woman, she nurtured the idea of her work as a visual signifier of female skills. She noted to sister Mary that "this revolutionizing the world with regard to women is what I am fighting for—working for—and determined to help accomplish." Hunting for specimens set Maxwell firmly in the mold of the frontierswoman and the lady adventurer, while her love for Turkish bloomer trousers paralleled that of Isabella Bird. For her, taxidermy and its public display represented conscious attempts to show that women could perform tasks as well as men. She regarded this calling as "work to do for the world" and thus more important that duties to husband and daughter. In fact, Maxwell's devotion to her arts led to hostility from daughter Mabel, who noted, "I was bitterly jealous of the animals that seemed to absorb all the affection for which I longed . . . Sometimes I wished that they were really alive so I could kill them myself."[40]

By spring 1873, the collection had outgrown the Maxwell household and Martha hit upon a new idea: build a museum to ignite interest in natural history and to preserve a record of disappearing fauna. This larger-scale venture would specialize in habitat displays illuminating "complete representation of the natural productions of Colorado"—a perfect and full record of western game, taxonomically complete. She envisaged it as "an academy of science," a forum for educating the young, with only a mere nod to "curiosities." The Rocky Mountain Museum opened on June 4, 1874, in rented rooms costing twenty-four dollars a month on the corner of 12th and Pearl Streets in downtown Boulder. A brass and string band heralded the grand public opening. The entrance fee was twenty-five cents. Maxwell's collection won eager support. The local paper saw it of "significant benefit to this country" and praised it "unexpectedly full and fine" with fauna "arranged with infinite patience and cunning art." "It is wonderful how much her tact and energy have accomplished," the editorial added. The collection included myriad species, described by one visitor as "everything in air, sea, earth, or under the earth, imaginable." Combining theatrical whimsy and educational device, the collection featured the standard fare of the "curiosity shop" and the natural history museum, including minerals and monkeys playing poker along with other novelties (sequoia bark and shark's jaw, Indian bones, and a 1560 edition of a German Bible). The museum's major contribution to the performance of natural history, however, lay in its animal groupings: a whole buffalo, birds gracefully posed on tree growth, a rocky escarpment featuring rocks, pine trees wandered by a bear, a family of deer, stag, doe, and fawns, a mountain lion pouncing on a deer, and ptarmigans in three coats of color. In one incident, the trapped cubs of a recently stuffed bear sow were introduced to their mother. The cubs displayed affection and joy at the reunion, suggesting to Maxwell the successful "life-like" illusion of her taxidermic creations, as well highlighting the impulse of taxidermists to create animals that conformed to gender norms of femininity and nurture as well as aggressive masculinity.[41]

Visitors attested to Maxwell's growing fame as a taxidermist as well as the crossover between the worlds of taxidermy as natural history and entertainment spectacle. P. T. Barnum came to view the establishment, although Martha did not meet him. Helen Hunt Jackson also attended as part of a sabbatical in Colorado to alleviate her tuberculosis in 1873–74. Written up as *Bits of Travel at Home* (1878), Jackson's testimony paid heed to the emergence of the western frontier travelogue as a vehicle for women's writing as well as highlighting the gender codes embedded in public scientific works connected to the afterlife of the hunt. While gun skills were somewhat expected of the western woman—the necessary defense of the homestead exuding an armed domesticity that Annie Oakley channeled so successfully in a performing context—the mastery of taxidermy spoke of a particularly scientific and professional vocation usually reserved for the eastern male scientific elite. As Jackson herself pondered, "That a pioneer women should shoot wild cats and grizzlies seemed not unnatural or improbable; but that the same woman who could fire a rifle so well could also stuff an animal with any sort of skill or artistic effect seemed very unlikely." Accordingly, she expected to see "grotesque" and "ungainly corpses," the work of a rank amateur. Instead, Jackson found herself pleasantly surprised by the realistic demeanor and artistry of the faunal complement. She applauded the collection's natural quality, notably the exhibit of a "great deer standing by the table, in as easy and natural position as if he had just walked in," and was totally fooled by a stuffed black and tan terrier lying on a rug that she thought was just resting, his eyes following her round the room. Other expert witnesses corroborated Maxwell's pioneering work. Ferdinand Hayden of the US Geological Survey felt the collection "excelled every other in the West," while Elliot Coues applauded its blend of "pleasure and instruction," finding it "far superior to ordinary museum work." Such plaudits confirmed Maxwell as a natural historian and architect of the new taxidermy.[42]

The Rocky Mountain Museum nonetheless struggled financially with a lack of tourist traffic. Maxwell showed her skills as a promoter, deploying animals as advertising symbols. Maxwell stuffed an eagle for the Boulder

Annual Fair that held a sign reading: "I am from Mrs. Maxwell's museum, don't fail to see her larger collection of curiosities." Contemporary use of animal mannequins as visual lures for commercial and theatrical outlets in the West was well established, so why not enact the same dramatic prompts for natural history museums? An advertisement also appeared in the *Women's Journal* of February 27, 1874, after correspondence with its editor, Julia Ward Howe. However, the museum continued to struggle, not least with Boulder harboring less than 1,200 residents by 1873. Maxwell moved the entire outfit to Denver's Lawrence Street and remodeled the museum for its new setting. Writing to sister Mary, Martha explained how she had reconstructed a habitat complete with a rocky cave through which visitors walked to the live exhibits, with the inventive use of a water pipe to craft a fountain: such devices suggested a precursory Disneyfication—the use of landscape as "weenies" to entertain visitors as they walked to focal exhibits. Meanwhile, the *Colorado Farmer* celebrated the "caves in miniature" as "a good representation of the Rocky Mountains." Realism and the vitality of animal display ruled spatial considerations. The family, meanwhile, was confined to a 25-by-45-foot basement under the museum, eating and sleeping surrounded by reanimations in progress. "A perfect Golgotha," quipped Martha.[43]

Aware of the opportunities for display at the Centennial Exposition in Philadelphia, Maxwell wrote to organizers in 1875, eager to have her work exhibited as part of the women's pavilion. She received no reply. However, as a signal of her importance in the national museum collecting enterprise, Spencer Baird contacted Maxwell and invited her to contribute a piece for the Smithsonian display in the government building. Maxwell responded enthusiastically, with an ambitious plan for several exhibits—a selection of small and large set pieces indicating various individual species as well as a "historical" series offering a grand display of patriotism and histrionics in the exposition tradition. Ditching the representation of animal groups for faunal metaphor, Maxwell here proposed a series of striking tableaux, the first involving an American eagle attacking the lion of the Old World in defense of the maiden Columbia, and the second with the lion vanquished and the victorious eagle shielding Columbia with its sturdy wing. Baird thought Maxwell's project too complicated (especially the cascading waterfall) and wanted to ditch the depiction of Old World faunal signifiers in favor of all-American wolves and deer or antelope. In the end, their collaboration came to nothing, and Maxwell designed a display for the Kansas-Colorado building. Her work spoke of female endeavor and of scientific classifiers, but most directly referenced the West in its most monumental and iconic style. Consisting of a naturalistic diorama of representative Rocky Mountain fauna, Maxwell's display contained some 100 animals and 400 birds, including elk, cougar, deer, bear, wolves, bison, plains, a rocky cave, and a running stream. The animals were arranged, according to her sister, "in an attitude of life-like action," a worthy display of the West as a superabundant animal paradise. Atop the fence that corralled the stuffed beasts from visitors hung a sign that read "woman's work"—a deliberate reference to Maxwell's emancipatory leanings.[44]

The exhibit certainly prompted many comments from some 10 million attendees. According to the *Boulder County News*, "The crowd is found waiting for the opening of the doors in the morning, and the place is thronged 'til night." The exhibit gained reportage in national media. The *Atlantic Monthly* said the most prominent feature of the Kansas building "is a mountain of rockwork covered with coniferous trees, mosses and lichens, down which trickles a stream; it might be mistaken for a cliff of Arafat, since here Noah's Ark seems to have discharged its freight. There are eagles, doves, owls, opossums, hedgehogs, rabbits on their hind legs, squirrels, goats, bears, panthers, deer, and so on, all a good deal occupied in preying upon each other, or being preyed upon." As with other public iterations of taxidermy, Maxwell's diorama offered a living montage via the medium of a dead zoo and gloried in invocations of the savagery and the cornucopia of the West. The scene was far more chaotic than the mainstream museum dioramas of the time, but its production of a monumental, mythic West was comparable. Some might argue that the biotic tumble of Maxwell's piece actually captured a more realistic scene. Ultimately, for the viewing public, the effect was palpable. Here was a slice of Rocky Mountain scenery reanimated, resplendent and thoroughly material. The art of taxidermy held firm to its aspirations of illusion as some prodded the animals to check if they were alive, while others marveled that the animals had been shot: "I've looked 'em over and I can't see any holes."[45]

Maxwell presided over the entire politics of reproduction from game trail to exhibition. She combined art, theater, education, and science in a fecund blend of western mythmaking of which she became a part. The *People's Journal* hailed her at once as "the living hero of the centennial exhibition," and the Colorado Centennial Committee presented her with a commemorative Evans rifle for her efforts, able to fire thirty-four cartridges in twenty seconds. Maxwell was valorized as a homegrown hunter heroine, an Annie Oakley of natural history. "In honoring her, you honor Colorado. She is a little woman, but she shoots," effused the presiding speaker. The politics of gender, ethnicity, science, and spatiality resonated as visitors issued forth comment not only on the exhibit, but also on its creator. The *Atlantic Monthly* marveled at "Mrs Maxwell, huntress and taxidermist, who not only stuffed, but also shot these animals" and who "stands before her own zoological show." The thrill of the West conjoined with the fact of female authorship. One group viewing the tableau was overheard saying, "Woman's work! What does that mean? Can it be possible any one wishes us to believe a *woman* did this?" Maxwell's sister was shot down with questions: "How could a woman do it?" "What did she do it for?" "Did she *kill* any of the animals" "How did she stuff 'em?" "Does she live in that cave?" "Is she married?" "Is she a half breed?" "Is she an Indian?" Interest gathered around the mystique of the "Colorado huntress" and her curious identity as a female taxidermist of the West. Some cast her as an Amazon, a "white Indian," a Nimrod in petticoats or a Calamity Jane–style eccentric. Many seemed surprised—and a sizeable number relieved—to find a slight, unassuming white woman, standing a little under five feet tall. The "armed woman as scientist" seemed much safer corralled in the trappings of a domestic countenance. *Harper's Bazaar* commented that "as a wife, mother and householder she holds a well-accredited and happy record."[46]

In the scientific community, Maxwell struck people as something of a maverick. She gained the admiration of leading exponents in the field and served as part of a network of expertise. From her "den" on Boulder Creek, she pioneered innovative techniques in modeling and articulated a "homegrown" perspective on western fauna. James Henderson, curator of the University of Colorado Museum, hailed her taxidermy work as "one of the earliest efforts in America to exhibit the animals of a large area in an imitation of their natural environment." As Glenda Riley points out, her dedication to the work of hunting, cataloguing, and collecting enmeshed her in a world typically considered the preserve of men. Her passion for taxidermy elicited an important exercise in highlighting "women's acceptance" of hunting cultures and countering "the oft-made statement that women brought a more compassionate philosophy to science." At the same time, Maxwell remained something of a pariah. In common with others in the hunter heroine tradition, she navigated difficult territory in challenging gender heterodoxy. Constraints of geography, gender, and professional elitism, meanwhile, ensured that her achievements remained largely under wraps. There is no evidence, for instance, to suggest that Hornaday was familiar with her work. In the end, Maxwell seemed to share more in common with her specimens than her peers—a vanished curiosity of the frontier West.[47]

From Preservation to Conservation: New Performance Readings of the Trophy

Taxidermy offered a powerful material culture of the hunt. As reanimated animals of enterprise, trophies represented objects of considerable social as well as economic capital, laden with what Rachel Poliquin has categorized as biographical, experiential, descriptive, and cautionary readings. Important in this transaction was the animal body, a powerful carrier for the story of hunter's paradise, malleable, instructive, and theatrical. Presenting a union of the faunal frontier with engineering design and the import of cultural memory, taxidermy represented a mesmerizing artifact. And despite its scripted and staged nature, the biological composition of the trophy did matter. Audiences were enthralled, entertained, amused, and humbled by animal actors and "their" West of abundance, savagery, amusement, and conquest: representatives of a landscape valorized and vanquished. The trophy required a story to furnish its being, its significance, its embodiment, but its organic quality and lifelike appearance still lent critical purchase. As Jonathan Burt reminds us, the "aesthetic of livingness" prompted a cognitive response as if "these images were living animals." In that sense, taxidermy kept the hunt alive.[48]

Preservation lay at the heart of the taxidermy project. Of the moment. Of the prowess of the hunter. Of the campfire story. Of the animal. With the "winning of the West," this well-established lexicon of immortality gained added significance and a new twist. That taxidermy carried the potential to bring the dead to life in the great indoors invested it with new social meanings as hunter's paradise faced up to its incipient demise. For institutions like the American Museum of Natural History, the Field Museum, and the National Museum as well as a swathe of regional collections, including Martha Maxwell's Rocky Mountain Museum, taxidermy presented an opportunity to preserve vanishing species and create a complete record of a frontier passing into history.

A keen example of the importance of the West as a critically located space in this emerging museum culture was William Hornaday's bison group at the National Museum. Promising nothing less than the reproduction of space, the "very soul of Nature all unchanged," the exhibit carried forth the codes of the new taxidermy with aplomb. Set within a glass case, the installation offered a window on nature, what Carl Akeley called a "peephole into the Jungle." Set in a prairie environment, complete with real sagebrush, six animals grazed besides an alkali lake, the imprints of their hooves evident in the soft mud. The *Washington Star* praised Hornaday's endeavor as "a perfectly picturesque group—a bit of the wild west reproduced . . . carefully cut out and brought to the museum." The bison *looked* authentic. They depicted the "facts" of natural history and western taxonomy in glorious 3-D. At the same time, however, the scene was just as scripted as the menagerie posed in the hunter's "den." A morality play on peaceful family life, a bull male stood at the center of the display as a dominant masculine archetype. Hornaday's description of him as a "giant of his race" not only referenced the scientific dogma of natural selection but also chose to celebrate the animal according to the ontology of the hunter hero and the performance mantra of the game trail. Two adult females and young animals gazed on in docile fashion. There were further constructions at play. Hornaday had collected some twenty-five animals from two different sites in Montana in the spring and fall of 1886. Eager to make his creations look their best, superior "trophy" specimens had been selected. Scruffy, emaciated, or wounded specimens need not apply.[49]

The message of the bison group was a conservationist one. An example of what Stephen Asma has called "the moral power of good taxidermy," Hornaday hoped to generate an experiential response among visitors in order to raise consciousness about the impending extinction of the bison. Stuffed beasts were deployed as inanimate ambassadors to save their animate brethren or, in the worst-case scenario, to immortalize their taxonomy for posterity. The incorporation of conservation into preservation was, on one level, effortless. After all, as Donna Haraway notes, taxidermy serviced the "production of permanence." In *The Story of Museum Groups* (1921), Frederic Lucas celebrated Hornaday's piece for telling the "whole story of the buffalo." That said, the scene was not exactly environmentally representative.

Here were a group of peaceful herbivores grazing happily forever on an undulating prairie—a forever West rather than a contemporary one. The bloated carcasses and bleached bones (recorded so starkly by frontier photographers) that graced the plains landscape in the 1870s and 1880s were scarcely to be seen. Moreover, Hornaday saw no contradiction in killing the animal to eternalize it for science. He killed the bison to save the genus. Intriguingly, he extended a similar transaction to sportsmen: "If you must go and kill things, save their heads and mount them as atonement for your deeds of blood. They will give pleasure to you and your friends long after you have hung up your rifle forever." The possibility of reading taxidermy as penitence offered a further complexity to the hunting afterlife. But, as Rachel Poliquin points out, "if taxidermied animals were easy to read, the process of looking at taxidermy would hardly be worth the effort." The reanimated animal represented a potent artifact around which gathered the axioms of death and life, the wild and the domestic, the scientific and the theatrical. In that, taxidermy represented a perfect example of the ecology of entanglement between hunters and wild things.[50]

NOTES

1. James Rowland Ward (1848–1912) gained an apprenticeship from his father, Henry, also an accomplished taxidermist and a member of the Audubon expedition. Rowland Ward established his own business, named J. Rowland Ward, in Harley Street in 1872 before moving to premises at 158 and, finally, 166 Piccadilly, also known as "The Jungle." He traded as Rowland Ward Limited from 1898. See James Rowland Ward, *The Sportsman's Handbook to Practical Collecting and Preserving Trophies* (London: Rowland Ward, 1891), 245; James Rowland Ward, *A Naturalist's Life Study in the Art of Taxidermy* (London: Rowland Ward, 1913).

2. Kitty Hauser, "Coming Apart at the Seams: Taxidermy and Contemporary Photography," *Make: The Magazine of Women's Art* 82 (December 1998–January 1999): 9; William Hornaday, "The Passing of the Buffalo," *Cosmopolitan* 4, no. 2 (October 1887): 9; Nicole Shukin, *Animal Capital: Rendering Life in Biopolitical Times* (Minneapolis: University of Minnesota Press, 2009), 7.

3. A developing scholarship exists in the history and practice of taxidermy, centered mostly on British colonial contexts and the museum and natural history trade. See Samuel J. M. M. Alberti, ed., "Constructing Nature behind Glass," *Museum & Society* 6 (2008): special issue, 73–98; Samuel J. M. M. Alberti, ed., *The Afterlives of*

Animals: A Museum Menagerie (Charlottesville: University of Virginia Press, 2011); Stephen T. Asma, *Stuffed Animals and Pickled Heads: The Culture and Evolution of Natural History Museums* (Oxford: Oxford University Press, 2001); John Mackenzie, *Museums and Empire: Natural History, Human Cultures and Colonial Identities* (Manchester: Manchester University Press, 2009); Stephen Quinn, *Windows on Nature: The Great Habitat Dioramas of the American Museum of Natural History* (New York: Abrams, 2006); Melissa Milgrom, *Still Life: Adventures in Taxidermy* (Boston: Houghton Mifflin Harcourt, 2010); Pat Morris, *A History of Taxidermy: Art, Science and Bad Taste* (Ascot: MPM, 2010); Sue Ann Prince, ed., *Stuffing Birds, Pressing Plants, Shaping Knowledge: Natural History in North America, 1730–1860* (Philadelphia: American Philosophical Society, 2003); Pauline Wakeham, *Taxidermic Signs: Reconstructing Aboriginality* (Minneapolis: University of Minnesota Press, 2008); Karen Wonders, *Habitat Dioramas: Illusions of Wilderness in Museums of Natural History* (Uppsala: Almqvist and Wiksells, 1993).

4. C. J. Maynard, *Manual of Taxidermy* (Boston: S. E. Cassino and Co., 1883), iii; L. B. Urbino et al., *Art Recreations* (Boston: Shepard and Gill, 1873); William Hornaday, *Taxidermy and Zoological Collecting* (New York: Charles Scribner's, 1894); R. Lee, *Taxidermy, or the Art of Collecting, Preparing and Mounting Objects of Natural History for the Use of Museums and Travellers* (London: Longman, 1820); Joseph Batty, *Practical Taxidermy and Home Decoration: Together with General Information for Sportsmen* (New York: Orange Judd, 1890); John Rowley, *The Art of Taxidermy* (New York: D. Appleton, 1898).

5. Oliver Davie, *Methods in the Art of Taxidermy* (Philadelphia: David McKay, 1894), 261; Ward, *Sportsman's Handbook*, 77; Hornaday, *Taxidermy*, 171, 149.

6. Rowley, *Art of Taxidermy*, v; Hornaday, *Taxidermy*, viii, 114. The phrase "botched taxidermy" is used by Steve Baker to describe contemporary taxidermy art by the likes of Damien Hurts and Bruce Nauman that offer hybrid forms with the following intention: "A botched taxidermy piece might be defined as referring to the human and to the animal, without itself being either human or animal, and without its being a direct representation of either. It is an attempt to think a new thing . . . Neither species, nor genus, nor individual, each one is open both to endless interpretation and, more compellingly still, to the refusal of interpretation . . . to prompt a moment of perplexity and non-recognition, of genuine thinking." The phrase is deployed here not as a marker of postmodern discourse but in a nineteenth-century context to describe the critique offered by the new-style taxidermist on older modes of practice. See Steve Baker, *The Postmodern Animal* (London: Reaktion, 2000), 55–61.

7. Montagu Browne, *Artistic and Scientific Taxidermy and Modelling* (London: Adam and Charles Black, 1896), 5; Ward, *Sportsman's Handbook*, x; Maynard, *Manual*, 94; Rowland Ward, *A Naturalist's Life Study*, 32.

8. Bicknell quoted in Mark Barrow, *A Passion for Birds: American Ornithology after Audubon* (Princeton, NJ: Princeton University Press, 1998), 31.

9. Donna Haraway, "Teddy Bear Patriarchy: Taxidermy in the Garden of Eden, New York City, 1908–1936," *Social Text* 11 (Winter 1984/5): 25.

10. Ward, *Sportsman's Handbook*, 87–88; Frederick Selous, *Sport and Travel: East and West* (London: Longmans, Green & Co., 1901), 184, 191; Diary of Lewis Wise (bound), Box 2, Folder 45, Garvan-Sheldon Collection MS232, Manuscripts and Archives, Yale University Library.

11. William A. Baillie Grohman, *Fifteen Years' Sport and Life in the Hunting Grounds of Western America and British Columbia* (London: Horace Cox, 1900), 44.

12. Hornaday, *Taxidermy*, 61; George O. Shields, *Rustlings in the Rockies* (Chicago: Belford, Clarke & Co., 1883), 38.

13. Davie, *Methods in the Art of Taxidermy*, 61; Rowley, *Art of Taxidermy*, 13; Hornaday, *Taxidermy*, 13; Selous, *Sport and Travel*, 203–4; Edward Buxton, *Short Stalks, or Hunting Camps, North, South, East, and West* (New York: G. P. Putnam's, 1892), 98.

14. Ward, *Sportsman's Handbook*, 18; Grantley Berkeley, *The English Sportsman in the Western Prairie* (London: Hurst and Blackett, 1861), 295.

15. Ward, *Sportsman's Handbook*, 18, 16; Hornaday, *Taxidermy*, 21.

16. C. K. Reed and C. A. Reed, *Guide to Taxidermy* (Worcester, MA: Chas. K. Reed, 1914), 33; Davie, *Methods in the Art of Taxidermy*, 56–57.

17. A. W. Dimock, *Wall Street and the Wilds* (New York: Outing Publishers, 1915), 432, 433–34; Shields, *Rustlings in the Rockies*, 34–38, 46–47.

18. Batty, *Practical Taxidermy*, 63, 65; A. Henry Higginson, "Montana Journal," Yale Collection of Western Americana, Beinecke Rare Book and Manuscript Library (hereafter cited as Beinecke).

19. Ward, *Sportsman's Handbook*, 23; Higginson, *Montana Journal*; Elizabeth Custer, *Boots and Saddles* (New York: Harper and Bros., 1885), 273.

20. Leon Luther Pray, *Taxidermy* (New York: Outing Publishers, 1913), 9; Elisha J. Lewis, *Hints to Sportsmen* (Philadelphia: Lea and Blanchard, 1851); Clipping for the Northwestern School of Taxidermy in *Hunter, Trader, Trapper*, February 1914, 21, Braun Research Library, Autry National Center, Los Angeles; Elizabeth Custer, *Boots and Saddles*, 292–93.

21. Larry Borowsky, "Filling Noah's Ark: Taxidermy, Exhibition, and Conservation in Nineteenth-Century Colorado," *Colorado Heritage*, May/June 2010, 15; Earl B. Wittich, "National Park Guide," (ca. 1889), four page pamphlet, Autry Library, Autry National Center, Los Angeles.

22. Henry Bannon to Charles Sheldon, December 31, 1919, Box 1, Folder 2, Garvan-Sheldon Collection, MS232, Yale University Library; Tina Loo, "Of Moose and Men: Hunting for Masculinities in British Columbia, 1880–1939." *Western Historical Quarterly*, 32, no. 3 (Autumn 2001): 306; Hornaday, *Taxidermy*, 158; Frank W. Calkins, *Frontier Sketches, Indian Tales, Hunting Stories* (Chicago: Donahue, Henneberry & Co., 1893), 20; Pray, *Taxidermy*, 87; Ward, *Sportsman's Handbook*, 253.

23. Theodore Roosevelt, introduction to Allen Grant Wallihan and Mary August Wallihan, *Camera Shots at Big Game* (New York: Doubleday, Page & Co., 1901), 8.

24. Rachel Poliquin, "The Matter and Meaning of Museum Taxidermy," *Museum and Society 6*, no. 2 (July 2008): 129; Shields, *Rustlings in the Rockies*, 42; Edgar Randolph, *Inter-Ocean Hunting Tales* (New York: Forest and Stream, 1908), 90; Theodore Roosevelt, *Hunting the Grisly and Other Sketches* (New York: G. P. Putnam's, 1900), 101.

25. James R. Mead, *Hunting and Trading on the Great Plains, 1859–1875*, ed. Schuyler Jones (Norman: University of Oklahoma Press, 1986), 100; Isabella Bird, *A Lady's Life in the Rocky Mountains* (Norman: University of Oklahoma Press, 1976 [1879]), 78; William Allen, *Adventures with Indians and Game, or Twenty Years in the Rocky Mountains* (Chicago: A W. Bowen, 1903), 103, 105.

26. Hornaday, *Taxidermy*, 20; Theodore Roosevelt, *Hunting Trips of a Ranchman* (New York: G. P. Putnam's, 1885), 317; W. E. Webb, *Buffalo Land: An Authentic Account of Discoveries, Adventures, and Mishaps of a Scientific and Sporting Party in the Wild West* (Chicago: Hannaford, 1872), 381.

27. *American Hunting Trophies: Catalogue and Notes* (New York: B. W. Dinsmore, n.d.), 15, Beinecke; Grace Gallatin Seton Thompson, *Nimrod's Wife* (London: Archibald, Constable & Co., 1907), 132; Randolph, *Inter-Ocean Hunting Tales*, 90; Buxton, *Short Stalks*, 73.

28. Aldo Leopold, *A Sand County Almanac* (New York: Ballantine Books, 1966), 284; Daniel Herman, *Hunting and the American Imagination* (Washington, DC: Smithsonian Institution Press, 2001); Webb, *Buffalo Land*, 261–62.

29. Horace Edwards to My Dear Friend Henry, May 23, 1873, Horace Edwards Letters: WA MSS S-1634:2, Beinecke; for photographs of Helgeson and Williams, see 948-558 and 945-623, Photographic Collection, Montana Historical Society Research Center Photograph Archives, Helena, MT; for Hilger hunting cabin, see *Helena Daily Record*, October 26, 1896.

30. Mary Margaret Ronan, "Memoirs of a Frontierswoman: Mary C. Ronan," master's thesis, Montana State University, Bozeman, 1932, 248; John Mortimer Murphy, *Sporting Adventures in the Far West* (New York: Harper and Bros., 1879), 26–27.

31. Rowley, *Art of Taxidermy*, 231.

32. Davie, *Methods in the Art of Taxidermy*, 262; Hornaday, *Taxidermy*, 171.

33. Ed Fritz Toepperwein, *Footnotes of the Buckhorn* (Texas: Highroad Press, 1960), 9; Clippings Folder: Historic Sites, Buckhorn Saloon; Albert Friedrich, "The Buckhorn Saloon"; Clippings and ephemera, courtesy of Bevin Henges, Buckhorn Museum, San Antonio.

34. Ward quoted in "Top Hat Taxidermy," http://www.tophattaxidermy.com/archive/rowland-ward-taxidermist.htm.

35. Berkeley, *English Sportsman*, 245–46.

36. Hornaday, *Taxidermy*, 231.

37. Mary Dartt, *On the Plains and Among the Peaks, or How Mrs. Maxwell Made Her Natural History Collection* (Philadelphia: Caxton, Remsen & Haffelfinger, 1879), 23, 34, 113.

38. Maxine Benson, *Martha Maxwell: Rocky Mountain Naturalist* (Lincoln: University of Nebraska Press, 1986), 82–83; Gayle C. Shirley, *More Than Petticoats: Remarkable Colorado Women* (Guildford, CT: Two Dot, 2002), 63; Borowsky, "Filling Noah's Ark," 14.

39. Dartt, *On the Plains*, 33, 118; Benson, *Martha Maxwell*, 89, 105.

40. Dartt, *On the Plains*, 119; Duane A. Smith, ed., *A Taste of the West* (Boulder, CO: Pruett Publishing Co., 1983), 24, 28; Mabel Maxwell Brace, *Thanks to Abigail: A Family Chronicle* (Printed privately, 1948), 60.

41. Smith, *Taste of the West*, 20–21; Dartt, *On the Plains*, 177; Benson, *Martha Maxwell*, 97, 99.

42. Helen Hunt Jackson, "Bits of Travel at Home," *Boulder County News* October 15, 1875; and *Bits of Travel at Home* (Boston: Little, Brown, 1906 [1878]); Hayden quoted in Smith, *Taste of the West*, 21; Coues quoted in Dartt, *On the Plains*, 217.

43. Benson, *Martha Maxwell*, 111–12, 113–15.

44. Benson, *Martha Maxwell*, 130; Dartt, *On the Plains*, 6–8.

45. Borowsky, "Filling Noah's Ark," 17; "Characteristics of the International Fair: IV," *Atlantic Monthly* 38 (October 1876): 500; Joan Swallow Reiter, *The Women* (Alexandria, VA: Time Life Books, 1978), 182–83.

46. "Characteristics of the International Fair," 500; *People's Journal*, October 2, 1876; Dartt, *On the Plains*, 5, 8–9; Laura Browder, *Her Best Shot: Women and Guns in America* (Chapel Hill: University of North Carolina Press, 2006), 65; *Harper's Bazaar* quoted in Smith, *Taste of the West*, 28.

47. Henderson quoted in J. S. Ingram, *The Centennial Exposition* (New York: Arno Press, 1976 [1876]), 648; Glenda Riley, *Women and Nature: Saving the "Wild" West* (Lincoln: University of Nebraska Press, 1999), 55.

48. Jonathan Burt, *Animals in Film* (London: Reaktion, 2008), 11.

49. Hornaday, *Taxidermy*, 249, 111, 238–44; Akeley quoted in Wonders, *Habitat Dioramas*, 125; *Washington Star*, March 10, 1888; Hornaday, *Taxidermy*, 140, 244. See

also Hanna Rose Shell, "Skin Deep: Taxidermy, Embodiment, and Extinction in W. T. Hornaday's Buffalo Group," *Proceedings of the California Academy of Sciences* 55, suppl. 1, no. 5 (2004): 102–3.

   50. Stephen T. Asma, *Stuffed Animals and Pickled Heads: The Culture and Evolution of Natural History Museums* (Oxford: Oxford University Press, 2001), 43; Haraway, "Teddy Bear Patriarchy," 21; Frederic Lucas, *The Story of Museum Groups*, Guide Leaflet Series no. 53 (New York: American Museum of Natural History, 1921), 26–27; Hornaday, *Taxidermy*, 158; Poliquin, "Matter and Meaning of Museum Taxidermy," 133.

ACT 3

SAVING THE HUNTING FRONTIER

CHAPTER 7

CONSERVATION, WILD THINGS, AND THE
END OF THE HUNTING TRAIL

Taxidermy was not the only project with preservation in mind in the late 1800s. While taxidermists were busily keeping "alive" their animal mounts, a number of communities turned to address issues of preservation and sustainability in the material environment. Central to this emerging consciousness was an awareness of the decline of game populations and the loss of habitat. In short, the foreseen end of hunter's paradise. This conservationist vernacular spoke of vanishing species and of encroachment, of processes of settlement, resource use, and environmental change. When the US Census Bureau declared the frontier closed in 1890, it formalized a figurative boundary and alluded to a new locution in the discursive landscape of hunter's paradise, that of imperilment. It also heralded a new epiphany in the wilderness that spoke of redress, renewal, and rights to access—in other words, a new performance of the hunt in which sportsmen and conservationists organized into associations, lobbied for game laws, and campaigned to preserve wildlife and wild landscapes. Accordingly, the terms of hunter's paradise encountered, invented, and claimed in previous years was renegotiated. Loss

DOI: 10.5876/9781607323983.c007

and butchery, ethics and conservation—a new epiphany in the wilderness—entered the lexicon of hunting performance.

Sport Hunters and the Saving of Hunter's Paradise

The dominant rhetorical paradigm for the majority of the nineteenth century was one of cornucopian bounty, superabundance, and inexhaustibility. Configured in various ways—as resources for sustenance, profit, sport, or symbolism—western game species represented animals of enterprise in a landscape of exploration, acquisition, and encounter. In the storied environment of hunter's paradise, wild things played a critical role. Folktales of the hunt, from Comanche stories of subterranean bison herds emerging to stock the plains to Sir George Gore's tin can alley trail across the West suggested a faunal resource seemingly without end. The West was, put simply, a provident landscape of biotic wonder. By the latter years of the 1800s, however, narratives began to change as commentators apprehended the rapid pace of expansion courtesy of modern industrialism. The carrier animal, or canary in the mine, in this regard was the America bison, suggestive of a new form of agency in historical narratives resting not on the presence of animals, as before, but on their impending disappearance.

From an estimated 60 million wild bison in 1492, only a few hundred remained by the 1880s. The representative animal of the West, recorded in petroglyphs, the journals of Lewis and Clark, and the artistic depictions of George Catlin, was now confined to straggler herds, a sorrowful remnant of the frontier. The causes of decline (both of the bison and other species equally beset by population crashes) were multifarious: habitat appropriation and settlement, the impact of mining and ranching economies, the harvesting of animals for profit, subsistence, and sport on an industrial scale, the incursions of the railroad, and improvements in technology from tanning processes to more powerful rifles. The dominant zeitgeist saw this as part of the triumphal march of an ascendant republic as expressed in works such as John Gast's histrionic *American Progress* (1872), a painting that colorfully depicted fleeing bison herds seeking respite beyond the canvas. Some viewed the demise of wildlife as tragic but inevitable. In *Montana As It Is* (1865), Granville Stuart mused: "It seems to be the destiny of the buffalo as well as of the Indians, to become extinct." Others, of course, read the destruction of the bison as necessary and desirable, the martyrdom of the animal a prerequisite for frontier pacification. Such sentiments informed Sheridan's criticism of the Texas legislature for considering measures to protect the bison in 1875 and prompted a War Department veto on a joint congressional bill the previous year. There was, however, an element of unease about the implications of this transaction among a growing number of people, a sense of the West lost as well as that won. Granville Stuart, himself a stock raiser, lamented how "swarms" of cattle had left a "dismal waste where once a beautiful landscape made glad the heart of the wandering trapper and hunter." The industrial decimation of the bison, in particular, marked a pivotal moment for many. According to William Hornaday, the practical destruction of the bison in 1884 augured the beginning of a "period of Extermination."[1]

The demise of game populations in the West prompted concerns from various quarters, of which the sporting community proved vocal. They were, after all, prime consumers of hunter's paradise in both material and cultural iterations. Rod and gun clubs, which, by the late 1870s, numbered more than 300 groups nationwide, presented the collective voice of a fraternity that was both growing in popularity and emerging as a powerful interest group in matters of environmental management. Established in 1887, the Boone and Crockett Club represented the most prominent of the game advocacy organizations nationally. Named after two of the nation's iconic hunter heroes who were not especially renowned for their measured approach to shooting, the club admitted members who had bagged an animal from three different species of North American charismatic megafauna, thereby looking more like part of the problem of wildlife decline than the architect of its salvation. An exercise in the pursuit of the strenuous life, the principal mandate of the club lay in promoting "manly sport with the rifle" and "travel and exploration in the wild and unknown, or but partially known, portions of the country." With membership limited to about 100 members, the club was decidedly elitist and eastern in nature, consisting largely of upper- and middle-class men from New York, Boston, Washington, DC, and Philadelphia. William Pickett (Wyoming), T. S. Van Dyke (San Diego), H. Pierce (St. Louis), Frank Crocker (Santa Barbara), and George Gould (South Dakota) completed the roster of named westerners. However, the club emerged as a more complex entity than its front as a well-heeled shooting fraternity suggests. Alongside aims of promoting masculine adventuring, the constitution of the Boone and Crockett Club vowed to work for the preservation of game and for the encouragement of natural history inquiry and observation. In *Hunting and Conservation* (1925) proponents George Grinnell and Charles Sheldon explained how "two aspects of outdoor life, which, to the uninformed, may seem opposed to one another" could be comfortably reconciled in the character of the naturalist hunter hero and the pursuit of "wholesome" recreation. The implicit requirements of the trail to "read" the animal and study its habits, they argued, encouraged an ethos of appreciation and preservationist instinct. As Grinnell observed, very soon in its existence, the club became more interested in "protection" over "destruction." Moreover, and specifically of interest here, the western theater loomed large in this equation—not only as a prime locus for the exercising of hunting credentials, but also as a threatened geography.[2]

Equally important were sporting clubs in the West, suggestive of an important regional dimension to the saving of hunter's paradise that not only challenged assumptions that residents of the frontier were irrevocably caught up in the mythology of superabundance but also finessed the idea of the early conservation movement as a core-periphery phenomenon in which eastern elites exercised control over the trans-Mississippi states in a quasi-colonial relationship. By 1910 Utah boasted eleven game protective associations, including the Salt Lake Hot Air Club. In Montana, rod and gun clubs prospered in Helena, Deer Lodge, Butte, Billings, and Missoula by the early 1880s. Bozeman established a gun club in 1883 under the inspiration of sporting outfitter and prominent civic figure Walter Cooper. These clubs allowed for camaraderie on and off the game trail and facilitated the rise of a local sporting-naturalist constituency able to shape game protection agendas in the western legislatures and also dedicate private spaces for game harvesting. Founded in southern California in 1900, the Bolsa Chica Gun Club assigned 2,500 acres of dammed wetlands at a cost of $80,000 near Long Beach for the encouragement of waterfowl, the centerpiece of which was a $12,000 "English Inn" for its forty members. A conservationist vernacular was evident in the foundational tenets of many clubs. The Deer Lodge Rod and Gun Club, established in 1880, ventured the aim "to protect game and fish under the laws as they exist" and to lobby for additional legislation. A second precept promised "to encourage healthful and honest shooting and fishing, and repress destructiveness" alongside the promotion of "sporting pleasures as pertain to such organizations generally." Fund-raising was also established to restore an effective salmon run in the Upper Columbia at Clarke's Fort Falls. Signed by twenty-four founding members, derived largely from local businesses and stock-raising communities, the *New Northwest* saw such citizen action as "timely" as well as imperative. It was, the paper contended, "through failure of associations of this character that the fish and game disappeared so rapidly from many of the older settled counties and are exhausting here."[3]

A central aspect of the emergence of what John Reiger dubs a "group identity" of sporting conservationists in the late 1800s was the articulation of an ethical code. The "true" sport allowed his quarry a fighting chance, minimized the killing of female or young animals, conducted the kill with honor and respect, and exercised restraint with the rifle. Promoting gallant behavior and "modest bags" over harvesting with abandon and cultures of commodification, sporting naturalists situated their ethical code as a conscious (and some might say conscience-easing) response to the demise of hunter's paradise in the West. They also drew on a number of antecedents, including codes of "fair chase" from European aristocratic tradition—in fact, the first American sporting manual, *The Sportsman's Companion* (1783), had been written by a British officer who signed himself "a gentleman"—and the developing ethical persuasion of antebellum sporting literatures such as *American Turf Register and Sporting Magazine* (1829) and the writings of "Frank Forester" in *Field Sports* (1848). An ethos of appreciation, respect, and self-regulation on the game trail was paramount. Article X of the Boone and Crockett Club's constitution proscribed "the use of steel traps; the making of 'large bags'; the killing of game while swimming in water, or helpless in deep snow, and the killing of the females of any species of ruminant (except the musk-ox or white goat)." Such testimony spoke not quite of the rights of animals, but certainly of reconfigured rites of the hunt.[4]

John Dean Caton commented favorably on the "new sportsman"—an evolving element in the performance genealogy of the hunter hero—in *The Antelope and Deer of America* (1877): "I am gratified to observe among modern sportsmen a more elevated tone, a higher culture, by which they understand the natural history of the various objects which they pursue." For C. W. Webber, this "hunter naturalist" was irrevocably western in garb, a fusion of "pioneer hunter" and "field naturalist" whose education came, in true

Turnerian style, from experiencing the frontier up front. Unlike a philosophical savant or urbane scientist, the hunter naturalist pushed "his way, rifle
in hand, into the secret places and confidences of nature," experiencing the
full gamut of the hunting economy and imbibing of its embodied expertise.
Whereas George Gore and his ilk had built masculine and heroic personas
on the strength of their soaring game tally as well as manly trail swagger,
the sportsman naturalist ventured a new iteration of the hunter hero, one
founded on wise use, conservation, and animal study. As Theodore Roosevelt
vociferated, "All hunters should be nature lovers. It is to be hoped that the
days of more wasteful, boastful slaughter are past and that from now on the
hunter will stand foremost in working for the preservation and perpetuation of wild life." These new codes of conduct, of ethics and fair chase, set
the hunter naturalist against (at least in their estimation) those who hunted
for "less honorable" means. As "The Western Outlook for Sportsmen" (1889)
explained, the "practical and observant sportsman" stood apart from (and
superior to) the "fashionable hunter" who "simply kill[s] for the sake of killing" and "wantonly destroy[s] that he might show on his return the trophies
torn from his victims" and the skin hunter and settler who kill "just for the
fun of it." An important bifurcation emerged between those judged respon-
sible for the demise of hunter's paradise—market hunters, subsistence hunters, wanton adventurers, and Indians—and the "true" sportsman. Practiced
in repertory, these distinctions proved of vital significance in determining
rights of access to hunter's paradise in an age of scarcity.[5]

Armed with ethics and socioeconomic clout, the ennobled conservationist
sportsman presented himself as a legitimate savior of hunter's paradise, an
honorable western knight in buckskin. Sportsmen performed their conservation advocacy through specialist journals such as *Forest and Stream* (1873), *Field
and Stream* (1874), and *American Sportsman* (1871). The (somewhat unwieldy)
subtitle to Charles Hallock's *Forest and Stream—A Weekly Journal of the Rod
and Gun, Angling, Shooting, the Kennel, Practical Natural History, Fish Culture,
Protection of Game, and the Inculcation in Men and Women of a Healthy Interest
in Out-Door Recreation and Study* ably highlighted the emerging rubric of the
conservationist hunter hero. As Hallock asserted, his journal was designed
for the true lover of nature and would never "pander to those in possession of depraved tastes." George Shields devoted a column in *Recreation* to
outing "the game hogs" caught literally red-handed in slaughtering game in

ungentlemanly fashion. Such articulations helped galvanize a group identity around the character of the reframed, and reformed, hunter hero. They also served purposes of political economy in conferring absolution, legitimacy, and enfranchisement on the sporting fraternity while removing rights from other typologies of the chase branded as wasteful, dishonest, and errant. Hunting for the purpose of renewal rather than meat lent the sports a higher cause, allowing sportsmen to claim authority to speak for game while still preserving the integrity of their vocation. Writing in *Harper's Monthly*, Shields lambasted skin hunters, Indians, and "foreign noblemen" for their deleterious take on western wildlife, while advising his fellow patrician "who desires to preserve a skin or head of any item must procure it very soon"—a stark juxtaposition of the rights of the included and excluded as well as a testament to the compatibility of conservation and taxidermy as practice, performance, and preservation code.[6]

Autobiographical articulation seemed an important part of the identity of the naturalist hunter hero, as Thomas Altherr notes, manifesting "the code by written word as well as example" and, in the process, illuminating another turn in the storytelling codes of the hunt. John Mortimer Murphy's *Sporting Adventures in the Far West* (1870) foregrounded conservationist credentials in his preface: "Having no desire to pose as a Nimrod, I may say that some of my hunting was as much for the purpose of studying the *ferae naturae* as for killing them, and that their life was frequently more pleasing to me than their death." Emphasis was placed on aesthetics, self-discipline, firearms protocol and environmental etiquette in the rhetorical narrative of the sporting-conservationist. Shields wrote in *Cruising in the Cascades: And Other Hunting Adventures* (1889) that "game of any land should always be pursued in a fair, manly manner, and given due chance to preserve its life if it is skillful enough to do so." A dominant theme of this sporting literature on the West spoke of loss, decline, and nostalgia for the old days, of a golden age of the frontier and the gloriously autobiographical purity of sporting pursuits both gentle *and* manly. Writing in *Forest and Stream*, George Grinnell noted that when a man from London came to his office asking for good bison hunting, "he was told to go back five years, which was another way of saying that the days of buffalo hunting—good or bad—have gone by." Such storytelling was consciously retrospective, antimodernist, and declensionist, trading in the discourse of vanished space and the loss of a halcyon era. As Frederick

Selous mused in 1901, "I can imagine no more perfect country in which to hunt than the Rocky Mountains must once have been."[7]

The demise of game populations in the West prompted performative flourishes of literary pathos, as exemplified by Allen's dedication in *Adventures with Indians and Game* (1903): "All of the wild life and all of its wild nature has passed from the earth. To them all I here say farewell." Also implicit in the storytelling rubric of the sporting naturalist was an activist mentality, a look forward as well as back, and a call to arms (or, more accurately, the tempering of their use by some, and their prohibition from others). If hunter's paradise was to be sustained as more than a landscape of taxidermy and literary memory, then action was needed to ensure the protection of animal capital. With a keen sense of American exceptionalism, the *Helena Weekly Independent* postulated, "At present we possess faculties for practising these sports that are unrivaled in any country. What folly then to destroy them?" Against the tide of resource exploitation, conservationists argued for the preservation of a fragment of hunter's paradise, a remnant slice of the once wild West for posterity and for the national good. At the very least, the very notion of sustainability—"wise use" in the vernacular of the day—was pretty radical in its tempered worship for the almighty dollar. George Grinnell witnessed sentiments of contrition in speaking of a need to restore "some of the beautiful things to nature which our selfishness has destroyed." Founder of the Audubon Society, Boone and Crockett Club, and editor of *Forest and Stream*, Grinnell was, in many ways, the visionary of the sporting conservationist movement. Setting out his manifesto in *Hunting and Conservation*, he spoke of the multiple constituencies of the conservation cause: sportsmen keen to furnish "abundant sport for themselves," those advocating a sentimental/nonconsumptive valuation of animals, and individuals for whom values of economics, community, and preservation for future generations carried sway. Grinnell's framework—a kind of social pyramid of conservation rationales—paid heed not only to the network of interests concerned about game decline, but in its considered deconstruction of preservationist constituencies pointed to the complexity of pigeonholing the sporting conservationist as either elitist mercenary or saintly savior of the wilds. Hunter-naturalists were not, as many pro-hunting writers would contend, calling for "the rights of nature," but neither were they categorical in their valuations of animals simply as moving targets for their exclusive use.[8]

Theodore Roosevelt alluded to the multiple strands of hunter-naturalist philosophy in *The Wilderness Hunter* (1893), in which he couched the importance of conservation in protecting "breeding grounds and nurseries for game" and "the grand beauty of the scenery" for the "community at large." He talked, moreover, of a sociological rubric: preserving the idealized frontier as a repository of masculinity and vigor. Lofting an idealized vision of nature and nation in perfect union on the western game trail, Roosevelt noted the importance of preserving the "free, self-reliant, adventurous life, with its rugged and stalwart democracy." When Frederick Jackson Turner crafted the historical mythology of the American West in his frontier thesis, he spoke of the contest between savagery and civilization, of "free land" and its contribution to the political, economic, and social cultures of the nation, of the West as a safety valve, and of stalwart Anglo-American men in possession of pioneer fortitude. Turner's narrative carried within it a fervent sense of the West as a restorative landscape, a space of energy and epiphany. Such an idea of the frontier as a heroic geography of portent spoke of many things—of commemorating the tautology of progress, of anxiety about the nation's post-frontier vigor, and of triumphant American idealism—but it importantly cast the West as a locus of national renewal and one for men in particular. For the likes of Turner and, indeed, Roosevelt, the loss of this conceptual and material space in which men could exercise their muscular ambitions was fundamental. Preservation, then, meant protecting the rites and the possibilities of performing the hunting frontier.[9]

The preservation of the hunter hero required the continued existence of the fearsome beasts that had animated the storytelling culture of hunter's paradise as vivid and instructional players in past years. The mandate of the sportsmen conservationist was multilayered and complex—altruistic, public-spirited, environmentally prescient, and also founded on the protection of resources for their own recreational use and according to an emerging (and specific) group code. Roosevelt was sanguine in this regard, advocating the protection of animal species "chiefly with the idea that there might be still good hunting that would last for generations." To cynical commentators, such remonstrations smacked of tokenism as well as a self-interested design to secure "bags" for the future and claim authority over the distribution of scarce environmental capital. Presenting game preservation as "for the people," sportsmen conservationists clothed their demands in a national democratic discourse that disengaged issues of wildlife protection from regional user rights and emphasized divisions in the typologies of the hunt. Specifically, the mantra of "wise use" emerged as a critical locus around which conservationist hunter heroes demonstrated their environmental efficacy. The sporting naturalist thus claimed ethical and environmental authority by killing not for ignoble desires for meat or profiteering but for his own restoration and the cause of passionate manhood. As Grinnell asserted, if it is morally right to kill to eat, then "it is morally right to kill it to preserve its head." Wise use, then, trumped use on its own: the higher value of the animal emanated from its ethereal connect—epiphany over calorific or dollar value. "Marksman," author of *The Dead Shot* (1882), duly castigated the market hunter as not only a poor aim "but more or less a poacher." Touting an ethical vantage (expressed via motions of conscience, natural history, and abstention), Colonel Dodge could, meanwhile, boast of killing 1,262 game animals and freely satiate his "appetite for murder." As an aside, Dodge admonished those commercial hunters who "think only of today." In rejecting the wanton killing of wildlife for pot or market, heretofore seen as frontier necessity and harbinger of forward progress in "taming" the savage West, such comments elucidated a new turn in the genealogy of the hunter hero. This new hierarchy of the chase contained implicit class and racial judgments that situated hunter's paradise as a social as well as environmental battleground.[10]

NATIONAL PARKS, BISON, AND THE POLITICAL ECOLOGY OF HUNTING

Setting land aside in dedicated reserves represented a critical strategy for the salvation of hunter's paradise, or at least its remnants. Windham Thomas Wyndham-Quin, the fourth Earl of Dunraven, established a hunting reserve in the Old World tradition at Estes Park in 1874. He had fallen in love with the Rockies on a series of hunting trips through the region in prior years, during which (guided by Bill Cody) he hardly struck a pose as incipient conservationist. In *Hunting in the Yellowstone* (1917), Dunraven gleefully reported riding after elk herds "like maniacs, cutting them off, till we can get in the midst of them, when we shoot all that we can." Buying up land under the terms of the Homestead Act, using a collection of reprobates and chancers who earned fifty dollars for signing their name to plots and passing land rights to the earl, Dunraven amassed somewhere between 6,000 and 15,000 acres. He built a lodge and the "English Hotel" for his guests (including Albert Bierstadt), who were hosted at the site for lavish hunting expeditions through the 1870s. Wrangles with settlers over legal rights, cattle disputes, and tax bills nonetheless soured the enterprise, and Dunraven sold the land owned by his Estes Park Company in 1907. Local users won out, again complicating a monolithic interpretation of western conservation. The flirtation with a wilderness hunting reserve cost the earl more than $200,000. A salient illustration of the interconnections between hunting, tourism, conservation, and contested user rights in the nineteenth-century West, Dunraven's stomping grounds now stand at the gateway to Rocky Mountains National Park, established in 1915.[11]

Inaugural measures in public territorial preservation were also firmly situated in the wild and heroic geography of the West. Credited with inventing the national park idea, western hunter and artist George Catlin recommended the establishment of "a nation's park containing man and beast in all the richness of their nature's beauty!" in 1832, following his travels in the Dakotas. The cornucopian West—hunter's paradise as depicted in his artistry—strongly informed the vision of a grasslands preserve, a picture of "pristine beauty and wildness" preserved for posterity and roamed by plains Indians and wildlife. Concern for the bison also loomed large in Catlin's manifesto, fearing that they "are rapidly wasting from the world." When protective status came to Yosemite, ceded to California as a state park in 1864, and Yellowstone, formally established as a national park in 1872 under federal control, priorities instead centered around the cause of scenic monumentalism and nature as a source of cultural pride. Arguments focused on preserving Yellowstone's geothermal curiosities from commercial ruin, a concern expressed by Cornelius Hedges to other members of the Washburn Expedition (1870) around the iconic (and possibly apocryphal) campfire at Madison Junction. Wildlife was scarcely an issue beyond the hunting and sustenance needs of western travelers. Instead, it was landscapes of rock and ice and nature's freakery—the Grand Canyon of the Yellowstone, Mammoth Hot Springs, and the Lower Geyser Basin—that framed protection (eased, it must be said, by the worthlessness of the Yellowstone Plateau for the purposes of mining or agriculture). Yellowstone's enabling act mandated the establishment of a "public park or pleasuring-ground for the benefit and enjoyment of the people," with stipulation "for the preservation . . . of all timber, mineral deposits, natural curiosities, or wonders within said park, and their retention in their natural condition." Tourist impulses carried the day. Canonizing Yellowstone as "our American wonderland—nay, the world's wonderland," the booster publication *Resources of Montana Territory* (1879) foresaw "a great central resort for the lovers of the grand, the beautiful and the sublime in nature from all parts of the inhabited universe."[12]

The national park presented clear evidence of the significance of the West in the birth of a modern conservation movement. It also demonstrated the salience of hunter's paradise as a philosophical and practical guide to environmental management. Land managers, sporting interest groups, and local boosters alike saw early on the value of national parks as breeding grounds for wildlife. In his inaugural annual report as superintendent of Yellowstone, Nathaniel Langford noted how "the wild game of all kinds with which the park abounds should be protected by law, and all hunting, trapping and fishing within its boundaries, except for purposes of recreation by visitors and tourists, or for use by actual residents of the park, should be prohibited under severe penalties." Successor Philetus Norris, who cut quite a presence as a hunter hero himself in fringed buckskin, nailed up posters in the park warning against "the wanton slaughter of rare and valuable animals." In his 1877 report, Norris couched the value of game in terms of aesthetics, rarity, and also economics: "Surely this might here prove a perpetual attraction to the eye, under proper regulations, to the chase, and their flesh judiciously slaughtered, to the palate of the countless health and pleasure seekers, when elsewhere unknown, save in the natural histories of extinct species. Within a decade the buffalo, the bison, and, in fact, the most of these larger animals, will be extinct or extremely rare elsewhere in the United States, and if our people are ever to preserve living specimens of our most beautiful, interesting, and valuable animals, *here*, in their native forest and glens of this lofty cliff and snow encircled 'wonder-land,' is the *place* and *now* the *time* to do it." He also suggested that a part of the park, a "waste corner," might be given over to the "practical rearing" and sale of young animals to zoologists, as well as the "sale of their flesh, pelts and furs"—conjuring Yellowstone national park as de facto fur farm and zoo supplier.[13]

According to George Grinnell, who traveled with the Ludlow Expedition to Yellowstone in 1875, it remained vital that the preserve in northwestern

Wyoming serve as a "last refuge" for game, a place where the essence of hunter's paradise could be preserved in perpetuity as a marker of the pre-frontier West and its glorious wildness, a sacred space where the "large game of the West may be preserved from extermination." In the context of charges of elitism, it remained significant that among the sporting naturalist community activist voices called for national parks rather than the private reserves favored by Dunraven (who, incidentally, was a vocal supporter of the Yellowstone project in his travelogue writing). As Daniel Herman notes, despite the problematic associations of elite conservation, the national park movement did forward a public "legacy of stewardship." Meanwhile, the multifarious applications of animal capital were not lost on Governor Crosby of Montana. In January 1883 he wrote to his counterparts in Wyoming, Idaho, and South Dakota asking for "cooperation and counsel" "to preserve the large game of Yellowstone "with a view that it shall be a refuge for the game driven from the neighboring Territories." Crosby also saw its value as a fecund supplier of animal produce: "The park, ere long, if preserved, might become stocked with game; and its overflow would furnish food for our own people, and for sportsmen who would be attracted to this Territory and spend annually large sums of money to the advantage of our citizens." Yellowstone preserved an opportunity for an animated tourist resort; a repository for species threatened elsewhere in the West; and a biotic spring that would feed game to surrounding areas.[14]

Protecting the integrity of Yellowstone National Park as a refuge nevertheless proved problematic. The dominant mentality favored development. As the *Butte Miner* put it, "civilization" was preferable to "game parks." Congress authorized park establishment but provided no funds for administration. Langford and Norris were absentee superintendents, discharging their responsibilities over the Wyoming preserve while holding down jobs elsewhere. The park received its first appropriation of $10,000 and a salaried staff in 1878, many of whom were political appointments and ill prepared for their charge to police Yellowstone's expanses. Punishment was limited to confiscating caches and ejecting wrongdoers. Gamekeeper Harry Yount faced an uphill task enforcing regulations from his remote cabin in the Soda Butte Valley from 1880. Park managers struggled with their dual mandate of winning a constituency for the "nation's pet"—by tourism and local trade—and managing its environmental resources from encroachment (particularly acute after the arrival of the Northern Pacific to Livingston in 1882). Visitors through the 1870s saw Yellowstone as freak show and shooting alley—delighting in the fun to be had stuffing trash in Old Faithful and facing down grizzlies with guns blazing. Infringements on game continued apace. As the editor of a Bozeman newspaper remarked of one set of visitors: "'fun' was their only thought from morn 'til night." In 1878, Superintendent Norris called for the imposition of restrictions on hunting from all but visitors and residents, fire prevention, the prohibition of timber cutting, and the removal of mineral specimens and other acts of "grossest vandalism." Envisaging Yellowstone as an imperiled fragment of frontier cornucopia, he noted how "hence in no other portion of the West or of the world was there such an abundance of elk, moose, deer, sheep," but he saw the tameness of park game as a problem—most would "stupidly gaze at man" and be "easily slaughtered."[15]

While early national park managers in Wyoming were reflecting on hunter's paradise under peril, arguments for the preservation of Glacier subscribed to a similar maxim. In common with Yellowstone, the slice of high Rocky Mountain scenery in northern Montana appealed foremost for its stunning topography. A prime mover in arguing the cause for protection was George Grinnell, who pitched the case for preserving the region in the pages of *Forest and Stream*. Grinnell had visited Blackfeet country with trapper James Willard Schultz in 1885, becoming enraptured by the scenic qualities of the area as well as its notable complement of wildlife. In "To the Walled in Lakes" (1885) and "Crown of the Continent" (1891) he broadcast the conventional tropes of scenic monumentalism, but spoke also of hunter's paradise lost, of bleached bison bones lying on the ground, a former utopia for wildlife: "once a great game country" but still of value, unique, as a remnant slice of western wilderness: "No words can describe the grandeur and majesty of these mountains . . . the beauty of its scenery, its varied and unusual fauna, and the opportunities it affords for hunting and fishing and for mountain climbing, [these] give the region a wonderful attraction for the lover of nature." Protection came for Glacier in the shape of a forest reserve in 1896 and a national park in 1910. Alpine topography carried the day, as well as the backing of the Great Northern Railroad, although game warranted as a high priority in animating the landscape of icy splendor. In a report entitled "To Establish Glacier National Park in Montana" (1908), Joseph Dixon explained how along with its topography and worthlessness for agricultural or mineral uses, the park could serve as a veritable hunter's paradise: "It is believed that these game animals and birds will increase in numbers, if protected by law from interference, to such an extent as to furnish in the overflow from the park a tempting supply to sportsmen for all time to come." The *Outlook* (1910), too, hoped that the preserve would "become in time an important game refuge," while, according to naturalist Ernest Thompson Seton, wildlife in Glacier represented "the best asset of the Park."[16]

Management precepts for Yellowstone and Glacier spoke of protection, natural conditions, and public trust, but the specifics of what a national park was for and how it should be maintained remained opaque. When Yellowstone was established in 1872, the 3,300-square-mile slice of Rocky Mountain terrain represented, in essence, an experimental landscape. The task for managers was sizeable—marshaling huge acreage, with little funds and precepts that were at once expansive and yet unrefined. As Roderick Nash notes, "We had a national park, in other words, before we realized its full significance." Enabling legislation in Glacier mandating its protection as a "public ground or pleasuring ground for the benefit and enjoyment of the people of the United States" proved similarly vague in its call for preservation "in a state of nature." It fell then to early managers and advocates to define the meaning and character of the reserves. Unsurprisingly perhaps, the language and codes of the chase exerted an important influence, with far-reaching consequences as to the salient definition of public good and the rights of particular constituencies to claim provenance over game. This new regimen of preservation, marked by the transfer of environmental authority from local commons to federally managed public land, allowed for the aesthetic culture and the political ecology of hunter's paradise to be effectively incorporated and redeployed. Using the language of science, preservation, and democratic national interest, national parks presented a complicated environmental bargain—they prospered, won constituents, and saved habitats and species, yet created a hierarchy of user rights that privileged sportsmen, tourists, and the abstract property of "the nation" in a newly demarcated frontier of conservation.[17]

Successful wildlife management in these early years meant a landscape teeming with large game. Under this mandate, managers sought to swell game herds, suppress fires, encourage vegetation favored by herbivores, and wage war on predatory animals. In Glacier's years as a forest reserve, wardens Frank Herrig and Frank Liebig patrolled the area, the former rarely seen without his Russian wolfhound. From the establishment of the national park in 1910, six rangers shepherded valuable game. Elk were imported from Yellowstone to increase the size of the herd, hay was planted, and salt licks were installed so that, in the words of Superintendent James Galen, elk "could be seen at most any time by tourists." This managed landscape, according to ecologists Dale Lott and Harry Greene, left the faunal victors in the conservation bargain akin to "bartered, domesticated captives" more than the free-roaming beasts of Catlin's commons. Such judgment strikes as rather harsh, but certainly the national park offered wilderness by design, one configured after the fashion of the European game park tradition and a faithful homage to the original "park" definition as "an enclosed piece of ground for beasts of the chase." Meanwhile, the storytelling codes of the West as hunter's paradise were effectively reprised and appropriated into park management strategy. Elk and deer earned kudos as noble, lordly, and attractive animals, while bears were afforded sanctuary for their comic anthropomorphism and appeal to park visitors as "quasi pets" in the words of the *Wonderland Museum* (1901). Wolves and coyotes—species that dined on the animals that managers, visitors, sportsmen, and conservationists appreciated—were instead configured as trespassers and came in for particular attack. In his 1880 report, Yellowstone's Superintendent Norris described elk as one of the "most beautiful, interesting and valuable of all those who inhabit this continent," wolves as "large" and "ferocious," and the coyote as "sneaking, snarling." Judged according to a biological morality, and sentenced, in the words of Roosevelt, as a "black-hearted criminal," wolves were subject to a consciously defined (and celebrated) program of extermination. Shooting, trapping, the use of poison, and clubbing pups in their dens were all authorized in pursuit of recalcitrant canines. In 1904, Yellowstone Superintendent John Pitcher related how wardens, scouts, and "certain good shots among the soldiers" were directed to kill them "whenever the opportunity is offered." In Glacier, settlers were awarded permits to hunt predators in the park in 1912, but the measure was revoked out of concern they might kill game species as well. Superintendents in northern Montana expressed perennial concern of a "gray peril" straying over from the Canadian border (and, interestingly, from the Blackfeet Reservation). Controlling a reserve he felt to be "overrun" by coyotes, Superintendent Galen in 1913 even considered infecting resident canines with mange. Five years on, Superintendent Payne feared for the efficacy of his preserve "surrounded by hundreds of miles of infested territory." In both parks, experts from the Bureau of Biological Survey were drafted to assist during the 1910s, aligning conservation management to a broader project of land-taming in the West for the purposes of animal husbandry. The last resident wolf pack was "cleaned" out from Yellowstone in 1923, with the five captured pups exhibited in a cage at Mammoth Hot Springs before being killed. Glacier's wolves had been largely eradicated by 1920.[18]

Historically, the Yellowstone Plateau was used by the Sheepeater, Crow, Blackfeet, Shoshone, Bannock, Nez Perce, and Snake for hunting and gathering and as a route across the Rockies to the bison plains. Campsites, well-worn trails, obsidian quarries, fired meadows, and fences used to funnel elk herds during the hunt attested to indigenous use of the region as a landscape of subsistence, ritual, and belonging. In Glacier, mountain trails had provided subsistence for the western Flathead, Kutenai, and Cree; while the Blackfeet peoples roved from the eastern plains to the "Backbone of the World" for hunting and gathering, shelter, and ritual. Stories of Old Man, Old-Man-of-the-Winds, and Thunder Man attested to the significance of the region in Blackfeet cosmology. However, in the new national park demarcation, native groups were reframed as outcasts, and ancestral influence was written out of the playground of pristine wilderness carved out of Rocky Mountain majesty for the nation at large. From reports of the Washburn-Doane Expedition (1870) to the inaugural park history written by Hiram Chittenden, a new story of Yellowstone was created in which indigenous peoples were fearful of the geothermal features and avoided the area. It was, argued reports, this borderland status that had allowed Yellowstone to prosper as a hunter's paradise. In Glacier, the writings of hunters James Willard Schultz and Hugh Monroe had confirmed Glacier as historic terrain for the Blackfeet, but the "Crown of the Continent" park as campaigned by George Grinnell stood for uninhabited wilderness. Walter McClintock had traveled extensively in Glacier in the late 1890s with the Blackfeet and placed it at "the heart of their game country." The political ecology of conservation thought otherwise.[19]

This "ideology of dispossession," as Karl Jacoby dubs it, witnessed the reframing of indigenous user rights as trespass on the basis of game preservation and tourist allure. Sporting magazines lambasted the Crow,

Shoshone, and Bannocks as salient enemies to Yellowstone's sacred purpose, insidious bands known for their "love of game butchery," while a 1889 Boone and Crockett Club resolution defined Indian incursions as a "serious evil." Yellowstone's Superintendent Norris complained bitterly about tribes roaming the park for "purposes of plunder, or concealment after bloody raids," and asked for military protection. In Glacier superintendents likewise complained about the transgression of boundaries, specifically incursions from the Blackfeet reservation, and the problems associated with elk migrating out of the park's eastern confines to be "ruthlessly slaughtered." Indigenous presence was allowed in a performative sense, in tourist dances on hotel lawns that broadcast a primitive exoticism of "Indian country" and in the brochures for the Great Northern railroad, which noted how the Blackfeet, "like the white man make it their summer playground. The Park abounds in mountains, lakes and waterfalls, hunting or warpaths." That said, the rubric of modern conservation firmly situated the Indian hunt rites firmly in the past. National park boundaries presented an inviolate frontier, a legislative border not to be crossed. In Yellowstone, Superintendent Norris offered pertinent commentary as to cultures of law, ethics, and the codes of the enfranchised and disenfranchised at play, castigating "those Indians [who] have no knowledge of the law, and submit to no restrictions, and it is hence believed that a single one of these hunting parties works more destruction during a summer's hunt than all the gentlemen sportsmen put together who annually visit this region." In Glacier, meanwhile, the issue of user rights witnessed a fierce contest over definitions of public land, with both sides invoking customary and legislative axioms. As Tail-Feathers-Coming-Over-the-Hill exclaimed to James Willard Schultz on seeing bighorn sheep and Rocky Mountain goats on the slopes of Rising Wolf Mountain in 1915, "There they are! Our meat, but the whites have taken them from us, even as they have taken everything that is ours!" Others claimed hunting prerogatives on the basis of legislative clauses written into the 1896 treaty in which they sold a strip of land to the federal government as forest reserve. Sources of game in Glacier had become increasingly vital in the absence of quarry elsewhere. As Little Plume wryly observed during treaty negotiations, "If we are hungry we go up to the mountains and get game." To the park managers, the establishment of Glacier National Park effectively removed this allowance, rebranding subsistence as sabotage in the process. The Blackfeet, however, read legislative precedent differently. Hunting parties continued to make forays into ancestral territory and cited their legal rights. The taking of game, a customary act, had become politicized and contested.[20]

Forays to Yellowstone and Glacier from indigenous hunters paid heed to ancestral practices. They also attested to the ecological and social collapse of hunter's paradise for the American Indian, specifically the decline of game across much of traditional terrain, and also to the imposed strictures of reservation life and the inadequacy of rations. In this context, the prohibition of indigenous hunting in national parks revealed more than the politics of recreation. Instead, restricting native access to landscapes of preservation spoke of far broader processes of assimilation, sustenance, mobility, and resistance as well as the emergence of federal organs in the West that assumed primacy over state and local powers. The parceling of land into national parks was just the latest example in the curtailment of indigenous rights to environmental resources in the West. The Blackfeet had been increasingly marginalized by settlement and federal appropriations since making their first treaty allowing railroad rights through ancestral land in 1855. Having seen their bison grounds in the Sweetgrass Hills destitute by the early 1880s, they conceded further land to the forest reserve in 1896 and finally to the national park in 1910. In Yellowstone, indigenous tenure had been relinquished tenure under the renegotiated Fort Laramie Treaty (1868), while Norris lobbied successfully for a slice of land in the north of the park to be ceded from the Crow and Blackfeet. The Sheepeater were relocated to the Wind River Reservation in 1871. With the demarcation of Yellowstone as federal parkland, conservation assumed a militarized countenance. In 1877–78, the Cavalry famously pursued Chief Joseph and the Nez Perce through the park as part of frontier skirmishes, while army control of Yellowstone between 1886 and 1918 signaled symbiotic processes of land conservation and pacification at work. The social mechanics of the hunt were also important considerations. Preventing indigenous forays was regarded as not only necessary for saving park wildlife but also as desirable from the perspective of cultural conditioning. Without the promise of game to pursue, the project of sedentary living, of making the Indian a farmer, was advanced. The removal of opportunities for hunting prevented the exercise of primal instincts, martial practices, or processes conducive to cultural renewal. As Montana's Governor Crosby elucidated:

"Hunting tempts him from his reservation and is mimic war. It excites the wild and crafty passions."[21]

If wolves represented biotic hazards to conserving hunter's paradise and American Indians represented a vestige of a primitive past unwanted and unwarranted in the new playground, then hide and pot hunters denoted a threat from the future—from industrialism, settlement, and unbridled commercialism. Criticism centered on waste and wanton destruction, usually committed by professional hunters who roamed in the park for pelts, tongues, hides, and teeth trinkets as well as the brazen criminality of locals who hunted trails and grazed livestock without concern for park boundaries. *Forest and Stream* bitterly complained about profit-driven skin hunters and urged its readers to refrain from saving up "all their indignation for Indians and half-breeds when white men, who understand the law and the real magnitude of such an offense, are guilty of the same misdemeanor." Illuminating antipathy toward faunal and human conservation miscreants, George Shields lambasted hide hunters camped twenty miles away from his sporting camp as "butchers" and "human coyotes" while William Hornaday derided residents of Gardiner, Montana, for their "gray-wolf quality of mercy" toward game, a pertinent reference to underlying tensions between sportsmen-naturalists and other resource users. In defense of the former, the issue was the inviolate status of the park itself, and the major culprits, as they saw it, were locals entering the park and taking game for profit. As Hornaday expressed somewhat exasperatedly, "Out West, there is said to be a 'feeling' that game and forest conservation 'has gone far enough' . . . Many men of the Great West,—the West beyond the Great Plains,—are afflicted with a desire to do as they please with the natural resources of that region." In the mantra of the sportsman-conservationist, the pursuit of game for pecuniary gain struck as both contemptible and derisory. Writing of the Yellowstone Improvement Company, which was literally munching its way through game while building a tourist resort, George Grinnell described a crime against the nation: "Every citizen shares with all the others the ownership in the wonders of our National pleasure ground, and when its natural features are defaced, its forests destroyed, and its game butchered, each one is injured by being robbed of so much that belongs to him." The public body of Yellowstone was being violated.[22]

According to John Reiger, Grinnell and other sporting conservationists helped "define the meaning of Yellowstone Park for the American people."

In this they drew on the nomenclature, codes of engagement, and value systems of the game trail. The national park went on to become an icon of global conservation, the crown jewel of environmental protection, and, in the words of Wallace Stegner, "America's best idea." The needs of the time required a regulatory framework, and species protection necessarily involved restrictions on hunting. As Daniel Herman notes, "Though conservation temporarily compromised hunting as a democratic practice, it saved wildlife." Accomplishing this goal involved altruism and biotic annuity and a fair degree of crisis management. Superintendent Captain Moses Harris complained how "the Park is surrounded by a class of old frontiersmen, hunters and trappers, and squaw-men . . . [who] As the game diminishes outside the Park, increase their efforts and resort to all sorts of expedients to get possession of that which receives protection of law." The sporting magazine *Forest and Stream* praised Harris for his martial efficiency: "He has relentlessly turned out of the Park the bad characters that at one time infested it, and has made his command a terror to evil-doers."[23]

From the other side of the fence, however, legitimate user rights were being disrespected by the machinations of heavy-handed federal authority. Conservation mandated a culture of exclusion that led to curtailed access to wildlife resources, the collision of hunting typologies, and the regulation of territory on behalf of a powerful cadre. According to Louis Warren, "By abstracting their constituency in this way, conservationists had a powerful foil to spatially bounded local prerogatives." Subsistence needs and opportunities for profit rated as legitimate recourses for the needs of the frontier region, not least with bison heads commanding $500 on the trophy market and twice as much for customers in London. Reading the conservationist ecology as unhelpful, illegitimate, and easy to circumvent, locals thus crafted a "shadow landscape" of game trails and hides beneath the scrutiny of managers. As an act of gesture politics, in 1915 a group of people cut holes in a perimeter fence (erected in 1903 to prevent elk from straying outside the northern boundary of Yellowstone) and stabbed several animals. In Glacier, where white hunters not only moved into the park but also operated from homestead claims within its boundaries, the situation proved enormously complicated. One settler from Belton saw hunting prohibitions as "depriving a person of his just rights as a citizen to forbid the having of game and the eating of it during the open season," while the overlapping of federal and state jurisdiction mitigated attempts at prosecution through the mid-1910s. Tempers flared over rights to and responsibilities for game, as in the case of the Yellowstone Valley Hunting Club, an enterprise set up in 1882 that gloried in the region's perennial wildness and guaranteed trophy kills for budding shots. To the conservationist contingent, it smacked of crass commercialism and contrivance. Grinnell fiercely satirized the "so-called sport" by asking if the Valley Club had burglar alarms and game "corralled in substantial enclosures, where the timid tourist could pop away with his repeating rifle" while President H. S. Beck riposted with claims of a superabundance West and Grinnell's lack of western experience. Competing voices of the hunter hero claimed rightful authority to speak for the region. In an age of scarcity, hunter's paradise had become acrimonious terrain.[24]

HUNTER HEROES, ANTIHEROES, AND THE POLITICS OF PERFORMANCE

Tales of fence cutting and insults hurled across the continent presented the tale of conservation as a continental binary, of eastern sportsmen-naturalists facing up against frontier-mentality pioneers. Such were features of the landscape of hunter's paradise and the competing codes of rites, rights, and ritual use in the West. At the same time, the issue of game consumption and protection was far more complex that John Reiger's judgment that eastern elites "saved the West from its own destructive inclinations" or Karl Jacoby's contention that local users bound by a "moral ecology" resisted the "compartmentalization of the countryside." Instead, the fissures and fixings of the hunt were intricate, fluid, and sometimes contradictory. Stake holding was not a simple case of elite altruism and local recalcitrance. Regional advocates couched environmental values in economic, aesthetic, sporting, and subsistence terms, integrating Yellowstone and Glacier into a local context of resource use and animal capital. Settlers resisted the bifurcation of their hunting practices based on custom, needs and wants, and localism. At the same time, many citizens agreed with Montana governor Crosby's criticism of hide hunters encamped at Henry's Lake, Idaho, and making deleterious inroads into elk migrating out of Yellowstone's western boundary as "trespass," and acted from a rubric of civic accountability and local pride in informing authorities of the whereabouts of poachers and the spiel of local taxidermists who claimed they could get any head for a price. The national park was

FIGURE 7.1. Wild buffalo grazing in Yellowstone National Park, 1904. Library of Congress.

an environmental and social good, and it was *theirs* to defend. In November 1886 the *Bozeman Avant Courier* weighed in on the issue of game resources and ownership in the West. Discussing the decline of hunter's paradise, the editorial castigated the "improvident Indian and the equally barbarous white man." Suggesting an element of regional pride as well as a frontier hunting code and a rubric of ownership, the paper related how the "old timers, who take a pride in these grand characteristics of our great Northwest, must feel indignant when they see two lazy hunters peddling 5,000 pounds of elk meat on our streets." But the picture here soon turned complicated. While the editorial recommended government action in the protection of game, it nonetheless balked at the national government "which takes such a fatherly interest in our national park," having proscribed the building of a railroad (and thus access to minerals) through "a small corner of it."[25]

Even the case of Edgar Howell, infamous hide hunter from Cooke City, who was caught red-handed by scout Felix Burgess in March 1894, presented a knotty story in the tale of saving hunter's paradise. Burgess found Howell skinning freshly killed bison near a cache of strung-up trophy heads and a makeshift lodge in the Pelican Valley. Conveniently roaming the park, *Forest and Stream* correspondent Emerson Hough wrote up the dastardly event in print as "A Premium on Crime," and a concerted lobbying campaign for better protection ensured. With only 200 bison left in Yellowstone, the timing was critical. The next month Congress approved "An Act to Protect Birds and Animals of Yellowstone National Park," finally giving game protection some teeth with a $1,000 fine and a two-year prison sentence for killing game. Howell, for his part, proved a complicated antihero. Personal testimony published in *Forest and Stream* paid heed to his credentials as a hunter hero, of gallantry and tenacity in the snowy wastes in pursuit of the bison, intimate knowledge of the terrain, skills as a manly provider on the frontier, and his indefatigable right to hunt. Howell presented to the sporting conservationist hunter hero a "rival masculine ideal," but one that was eminently translatable, despite the butchery motif. Some locals exhibited sympathy for Howell as a fellow pioneer trying to make his way, while others expressed outrage at his abuse of "their" park, a public space incorporated as object of regional identity. Livingston newspapers indicated the range of verdicts. While the *Post* saw Howell's actions as those undoubtedly born from frontier "necessities," the *Enterprise* called for the "remnant" park bison to be protected from those who valued them only for their "scalps and hides." Meanwhile, after his release, Howell ended up back in Yellowstone as a scout, a somewhat ironic reminder of Grinnell's recommendation in 1883 that park managers appoint seasoned westerners as wardens rather than "a lot of Eastern men who know nothing of the mountains and the habits of game." The story of poacher turned gamekeeper proved another turn in the narrative of hunter's paradise, a salient example of the complex genealogy of the hunter hero, and a canny example of the complicated archaeology of western conservation and hunting rights.[26]

Further complicating the narrative of conservation and, indeed, of the fixed identity of the hunter hero was the example of performing animals and preservation. While Hornaday and others were lobbying hard for the protection of the herds in national parks and bison reserves (see figure 7.1), the cadre of theatrical hunter heroes made their own inroads into consciousness-raising for the characteristic animal of the plains. Rocky Mountain Dick, scout for Custer and hunting guide, captured bear, bison, elk, and goat for display at his Elk Park Ranch near Henry's Lake, Idaho, to the delight of visiting guests in the early 1870s. A fierce critic of skin hunters and sports, Dick wrote for *Recreation* magazine, in which he championed the zoo as a preservationist organ and complained about game laws in Idaho, Montana, and Wyoming that prevented him from capturing live animals. "Is it not better," he contended "that a few animals should be confined in zoological gardens and parks, than that all should be killed?" Dick died in 1902, somewhat ironically, after being gored by one of his bison.[27]

Bill Cody's Wild West Show offered further elucidation on Dick's notion that "the catching of game tends to its preservation rather than extermination." The bison, of course, had lent Cody his famous nom de plume as a direct consequence of his skills as a hunter of more than 4,000 of them while working to supply the railroad teams of the Kansas Pacific. Just as Cody made the transition from market hunter hero to theatrical iteration, he also accomplished a shift from bison killer to conservationist (some might argue, inadvertently). With a flourish, "Buffalo Bill" stood center stage in the entertainment landscape of frontier experience, but, at the same time, his corralled bison were introduced to thrilled audiences on both sides of the Atlantic. Paraded in the show staple of the buffalo hunt, bison gathered round a water trough before cowboys firing blanks took them down. Visitors to the show grounds also had the opportunity to get up close and personal with Bill's charges in the back staging area, where a menagerie of beasts (as well as roaming Indian hunter heroes) delighted audiences. As the program for the 1887 show in Earls Court, London, elucidated, one of the "Fifteen Good Reasons to Visit Buffalo Bill's Wild West" was to "see buffalo, elk, wild horses and a multitude of curiosities." A necessary foil to the hunter hero was the animal, exposure to which bred awareness, an awareness that at times inspired interest in species protection. Rarity represented an important aspect of the herd's appeal. Reporting on Cody's show in 1884, the *Washington Post* noted how "the buffalo is fast becoming extinct." Even the advertisements for the show, complete with stock images of galloping bison (some of which were used as shaggy framing devices for headshots of Cody), drew attention to the form and wonder of the live animal. By 1893 the program was advertising the captive beasts (somewhat erroneously) as "the last of the only known native herd." Ultimately, the juxtaposition of bison killing and consciousness raising represented one of many tensions in the Wild West Show—from the use of electrical generators and lighting from the Edison company to illuminate the arena and manufacture a cyclone, to the opportunities for indigenous remuneration and cultural expression within what critics would describe as de facto prison camp. Like the "vanishing Indian" in Cody's frontier parade, the bison represented a complex artifact—part opponent, part destined to fail, but also party to a curious kind of advocacy, a salient reminder of the difficulties of a monolithic reading of audience response and social functions on the theatrical frontier.[28]

Meanwhile, the commercial value of performing bison introduced an economic rationale to their protection and a new take on the hide trade. Encouraged by the popularity of bison in many Wild West shows since P. T. Barnum's first documented performance using fifteen bedraggled animals for a show in Philadelphia in 1843, a number of enterprising ranchers had started rounding up animals for posterity and profit. From his youthful domestication of a squirrel named "Dick" in the woods of Illinois (which he sold for a princely $2.00), through a collection of curios (including "de-fanged" rattlesnakes), to his first capture of twelve bison on the plains (sold at $7.50 each) in 1872, Charles "Buffalo" Jones accrued a reputation as a trader of live animal capital. For Jones, alongside others, including cattleman Charles Goodnight, the bison promised a boom-time solution to the lot of the western rancher: resilient bovines to farm for meat, opportunities for crossbreeding to create the "cattalo" brand, and the prospect of trading in theatrical capital. The Miller Brothers 101 Ranch in Oklahoma, for instance, attracted 65,000 visitors to their "last buffalo hunt" Wild West show in 1905, which also billed Geronimo. Grinnell derided the performance as nothing more than a "Coney Island show," but, in a further turn in the complicated story of conserving hunter's paradise, animal collection served a conservationist agenda.[29]

Not only did the display of the "monarchs of the plains" make a good story, but bison corralled by ranchers Goodnight, Michel Pablo, and Charles

Allard were bought by the federal government in 1902 for $15,000 to boost numbers in Yellowstone (by then only twenty-three animals existed in the park's beleaguered wild herd), and they also formed the basis of the inaugural herd of the National Bison Reserve (1907). In fact, Goodnight's wife, Mary Ann Dyer, had played a critical role in the raising of orphan calves. Just as it had conspired in the construction and pursuit of hunter's paradise, now codes of performance aided its conservation. In Yellowstone, captive animals, numbering some seventeen animals, were corralled in Mammoth Valley and swiftly emerged as popular curiosities. Responsible for the animals' welfare was none other than Buffalo Jones. Jones, another reformed naturalist in buckskin and a complicated hunter hero (at least according to his biographer, Henry Inman, whose *Forty Years of Adventure* (1899) traced Jones's passage from a tenderfoot "paralysed" by gunfire and the "hideous monsters of the prairie," through sharpshooting days to a "close observer" of nature and conservationist hero), fed the herd with cut hay, hand-reared the young, and took to the park with dogs in pursuit of the mountain lions that predated on his precious charges. As Jones noted, the "destruction of our greatest game preserve" demanded action: He "could not sit still, and finaly [*sic*] be condemned for letting these animals perish." The fate of the bison demanded a new performance.[30]

NOTES

1. Granville Stuart, *Montana As It Is* (New York: Arno, 1865), 50, 52; William Hornaday, *Our Vanishing Wild Life: Its Extermination and Preservation* (New York: Charles Scribner's Sons, 1913), 387.

2. George Grinnell and Charles Sheldon, eds., *Hunting and Conservation* (New Haven: Yale University Press, 1925), xi; George Grinnell and Theodore Roosevelt, *Trail and Campfire: The Book of the Boone and Crockett Club* (New York: Forest and Stream, 1897), 343–44; George Grinnell, ed., *Hunting at High Altitudes* (New York: Harper and Bros., 1913), 490; "Constitution of the Boone and Crockett Club" and "Membership of the Boone and Crockett Club," Series II Subject Files, Boone and Crockett Club, 1901–1931, Box 31, Folder 151, HM223, George Bird Grinnell Papers, Yale University Library. For sympathetic scholarship on conservation and the role of sportsmen, see Thomas Altherr, "The American Hunter-Naturalist and the Development of the Code of Sportsmanship," *Journal of Sport History* 5 (1978): 7–22; Daniel Herman, *Hunting and the American Imagination* (Washington,

DC: Smithsonian Institution Press, 2003), 237–53; Michael Punke, *Last Stand: George Bird Grinnell and the Battle to Save the Buffalo* (Lincoln: University of Nebraska Press, 2007); John Reiger, *American Sportsmen and the Origins of Conservation* (Corvallis: Oregon State University Press, 2001 [1975]); Paul Schullery, "A Partnership in Conservation: Roosevelt in Yellowstone," *Montana: The Magazine of Western History* 28, no. 3 (Summer 1978): 2–15; James B. Trefethen, *An American Crusade for Wildlife* (New York: Winchester Press, 1975). A more critical appraisal of conservation initiatives and the input of sporting interests can be found in Thomas Dunlap, *Saving America's Wildlife: Ecology and the American Mind, 1850–1990* (Princeton, NJ: Princeton University Press, 1988); Thomas Dunlap, "Sport Hunting and Conservation," *Environmental Review* 12, no. 1 (Spring 1988): 51–59; Karl Jacoby, *Crimes against Nature: Squatters, Poachers, Thieves, and the Hidden History of American Conservation* (Berkeley: University of California Press, 2001); Louis S. Warren, *The Hunter's Game: Poachers and Conservationists in Twentieth-Century America* (New Haven: Yale University Press, 1997).

3. Matfield Collection Scrapbook, MS 645522, James Matfield Collection, Huntington Library, San Marino, CA; Dillon Wallace, *Saddle and Camp in the Rockies* (New York: Outing Press, 1911), 199; *New Northwest*, February 18, 1880.

4. John Reiger, *American Sportsmen*, 3; "Constitution of the Boone and Crockett Club."

5. John Dean Caton, *The Antelope and Deer of America* (New York: Hurd and Houghton, 1877), 345; C. W. Webber, *The Hunter Naturalist: Romance of Sporting, or Wild Scenes and Wild Hunters* (Philadelphia: J. B. Lippincott, 1859), 3–4, 31; Theodore Roosevelt, *Outdoor Pastimes of an American Hunter* (New York: Charles Scribner's Sons, 1908), 125; Franklin Satterthwaite, "The Western Outlook for Sportsmen," *Harper's New Monthly* 78, no. 468 (1889): 873–78.

6. Chris Hallock, "To Correspondents," *Forest and Stream*, August 14, 1873, 8; George Shields, "Antelope Hunting in Montana," *Harper's Monthly* 69 (August 1884): 369; George Shields, *Cruising in the Cascades: And Other Hunting Adventures* (Chicago: Rand McNally, 1889), 212.

7. George Grinnell, editorial, *Forest and Stream*, January 21, 1886; Frederick Selous, *Sport and Travel: East and West* (London: Longmans, Green & Co., 1901), 184; Altherr, "The American Hunter-Naturalist and the Development of the Code of Sportsmanship," 8; John Mortimer Murphy, *Sporting Adventures in the Far West* (London: Sampson Low, Marston, Searle & Rivington, 1870), 5; Shields, *Cruising*, 179

8. William Allen, *Adventures with Indians and Game, or Twenty Years in the Rocky Mountains* (Chicago: A. W. Bowen, 1903), 301; *Helena Weekly Independent*, January 20, 1876; George Bird Grinnell, "The Game Is Not for Us Alone," *Rod and Gun News*, clipping, n.d., George Bird Grinnell Papers, HM223, Box 35, Folder 198: Series

Subject files, West 1923–29, Yale University Library; George Grinnell, "American Game Protection: A Sketch," in *Hunting and Conservation*, ed. Grinnell and Sheldon, 201. See Paul Shepard, *The Tender Carnivore and the Sacred Game* (New York: Charles Scribner's Sons, 1972); Jose Oretega y Gasset, *Meditations on Hunting* (New York: Charles Scribner's Sons, 1972); and Jim Posevitz, *Inherit the Hunt* (Guilford, CT: Falcon, 1999), for the idea of the hunter as environmentalist incarnate. Lisa Mighetto, in *Wild Animals and American Environmental Ethics* (Tucson: University of Arizona Press, 1991), 41, argues the converse: that is, sportsmen were essentially mercenary in their thinking.

9. Theodore Roosevelt, *The Wilderness Hunter* (New York: G. P. Putnam's, 1893), 7, 270.

10. Theodore Roosevelt, *Ranch Life and the Hunting Trail* (New York: G. P. Putnam's, 1893), 1–6; Richard Irving Dodge, *The Hunting Grounds of the Great West* (London: Chatto and Windus, 1877), 61, 118, 117; Grinnell and Roosevelt, *Trail and Campfire*, 334; "Marksman," *The Dead Shot: The Sportsman's Complete Guide* (London: Longmans, Green, 1882), 126.

11. Earl of Dunraven, *Hunting in the Yellowstone: On the Trail of the Wapiti with Texas Jack in the Land of Geysers* (New York: Outing Publishing Co., 1917), 6.

12. George Catlin, *North American Indians* (Philadelphia: Leary, Stuart, and Company, 1913), 1:2–3, 1:294–95. Protection of the plains finally came with the establishment of the Tallgrass Prairie Reserve in 1996, while the National Park Service included indigenous subsistence rights under the Alaska National Interest Lands Conservation Act of 1980. The campfire story is related in Aubrey Haines, *The Yellowstone Story* (Boulder, CO: Associated University Press, 1977), 1:130; Nathaniel Langford, *The Discovery of Yellowstone Park: Diary of the Washburn Expedition to the Yellowstone and Firehole Rivers in the year 1870* (St. Paul, MN: Frank Jay Haynes, 1905), 117–18. Alfred Runte develops the "worthless lands" thesis in *National Parks: The American Experience* (Lincoln: University of Nebraska Press, 1979), 50–54; Robert Strahorn, *Resources of Montana Territory* (Helena, MT: N.p., 1879), 68.

13. Nathaniel Langford, *Annual Report of the Superintendent of the Yellowstone National Park to the Secretary of the Interior for the Year 1872* (Washington, DC: GPO, 1872), 4, Bancroft Library, University of California, Berkeley (hereafter cited as Bancroft); Philetus Norris, *Report upon the Yellowstone National Park to the Secretary of the Interior, 1878* (Washington, DC: GPO, 1878), 992–93, Yellowstone National Park Reports, 1877–1900,Bancroft; Philetus Norris, *Report upon the Yellowstone National Park to the Secretary of the Interior, 1877* (Washington, DC: GPO, 1877), 12–13, "Yellowstone National Park Reports, 1877–1900," Bancroft.

14. George Grinnell, "Their Last Refuge," *Forest and Stream*, December 14, 1882, 126; Crosby quoted in *Helena Independent*, January 26, 1883.

15. *Butte Miner* quoted in Helena *Independent*, March 15, 1893; *Bozeman Avant Courier*, July 31, 1874; *Bozeman Avant Courier*, September 12, 1873; Norris, *Report upon the Yellowstone National Park, 1877*, 11; Norris, *Report upon the Yellowstone National Park, 1878*, 992–93.

16. George Grinnell, "The Crown of the Continent," *Century* 62 (May 1901–October 1901): 660–63 (written in 1891); George Grinnell, "To the Walled in Lakes" Series, *Forest and Stream*, December 10, 1885, December 17, 1885, December 24, 1885, December 31, 1885; "To Establish Glacier National Park in Montana, 60th Congress, Report No. 580, Mr. Dixon from the Committee on Public Lands, April 29, 1908," Folder 1: Glacier National Park, Francis Farquhar Papers, MSS C-B 517, Carton 3, Bancroft; "The Proposed Glacier National Park," *Outlook* 94 (April 16, 1910): 826; Ernest Thompson Seton to Secretary to the Interior, November 23, 1916, RG 79, Records of the National Park Service, General Records, Central Files 1907–39, Box 23, Folder "Game Protection," National Archives and Records Administration, Washington, DC (hereafter cited as NARA).

17. Roderick Nash, "The American Invention of National Parks," *American Quarterly* 22, no. 3 (Autumn 1970): 731; *Laws, Regulations, and General Information Relating to Glacier National Park, Montana, 1910* (Washington, DC: GPO, 1911), 4–5.

18. James Galen to Secretary of Interior, February 12, 1913, RG 79, Folder "Game Protection," NARA; Dale F. Lott and Harry Greene, *American Bison: A Natural History* (Berkeley: University of California Press, 2003), 165; Lott quoted in Chris Magoc, *Yellowstone: The Creation and Selling of an American Landscape, 1870–1903* (Albuquerque: University of New Mexico Press,1999), 153; P. W. Norris, *Annual Report of the Superintendent of Yellowstone National Park to the Secretary of Interior for the Year 1880* (Washington, DC: Government Printing Office, 1880), 39–42, "Yellowstone National Park Reports, 1877–1900," Bancroft; Barry Lopez, *Of Wolves and Men* (New York: Touchstone Books, 1995), 142; John Pitcher, *Report of the Acting Superintendent of the Yellowstone National Park to the Secretary of the Interior for the Year 1904* (Washington, DC: GPO, 1904), 7–8, "Yellowstone National Park Reports, 1877–1900," Bancroft; Acting Superintendent of Glacier National Park to the Secretary of the Interior, February 19, 1912, Box 262, Folder 10, Glacier National Park Archives, Glacier National Park, MT (hereafter cited as GNPA); Assistant Secretary of the Interior to H. W. Hutchings, Acting Superintendent, February 24, 1912, Box 262, Folder 10, GNPA; J. L. Galen, *Report of the Superintendent of the Glacier National Park to the Secretary of the Interior, 1913* (Washington, DC: GPO, 1913), 11–12, Glacier National Park Library, Glacier National Park, MT (hereafter cited as GNPL); Superintendent to the State Veterinarian, Helena, MT, October 11, 1913, Box 262, Folder 10, GNPA; Walter Payne, *Report of the Superintendent of the Glacier National Park to the Secretary of the Interior, 1918* (Washington, DC: GPO, 1918), 16, GNPL; Superintendent's

1923 monthly report cited in John L. Weaver, *The Wolves of Yellowstone*, Natural Resources Reports, no. 14 (Washington, DC: GPO, 1978), 36.

19. Hiram Chittenden, *The Yellowstone National Park: Historical and Descriptive* (Cincinnati, 1915 [1895]), 9; Walter McClintock, "Hunting and Winter Customs of the Blackfoot," Series 2, no. 21, 2, Walter McClintock Papers, Beinecke Rare Book and Manuscript Library, Yale University; Walter McClintock, "My Life among the Indians" and "Old Indian Trails," Walter McClintock Papers, MS 533, Box 1, Folder 4: Lectures, Braun Research Library Collection, Autry National Center, Los Angeles; James Willard Schultz, *Blackfeet Tales of Glacier National Park* (Boston: Houghton Mifflin, 1916). For analysis of hunting rights and conflicts between the local communities and park authorities in Yellowstone and Glacier from their establishment through the twentieth century, see Jacoby, *Crimes against Nature*, 81–146; Robert Keller and Michael Turek, *American Indians and National Parks* (Tucson: University of Arizona Press, 1998); Mark David Spence, *Dispossessing the Wilderness: Indian Removal and the Making of the National Parks* (New York: Oxford University Press, 1999); Warren, *Hunter's Game*, 126–71.

20. Jacoby, *Crimes against Nature*, 85; "Protect the National Park," *Frank Leslie's Illustrated Newspaper* 68 (April 27, 1889): 182; "A Case for Prompt Action," *Forest and Stream* April 11, 1889, 234; Norris, *Annual Report, 1877*, 9; Galen, *Report, 1913*, 15; "Glacier National Park" (Great Northern Railway brochure) n.d., Folder 1: Glacier National Park, Francis Farquhar Papers, MSS C-B 517, Carton 3, Bancroft; Moses Harris, *Annual Report of the Acting Superintendent of Yellowstone National Park, 1889* (Washington, DC: GPO, 1889), 16, "Yellowstone National Park Reports, 1877–1900," Bancroft; Schultz, *Blackfeet Tales*, 1–2; "Letter from the Secretary of the Interior, Transmitting an Agreement Made and Concluded September 26, 1895, with the Indians of the Blackfeet Reservation," US Senate, Senate Document No.118, 54th Congress, first session, 13.

21. Crosby quoted in *Helena Independent*, January 26, 1883.

22. "Snap Shots," *Forest and Stream*, January 22, 1898, 61; George Shields, *Rustlings in the Rockies* (Chicago: Belford, Clarke & Co., 1883), 55; Shields, *Cruising*, 234; Hornaday, *Our Vanishing Wild Life*, 337, 335; "The People's Park," *Forest and Stream*, January 18, 1883, 481.

23. Reiger, *American Sportsmen*, 131; Herman, *Hunting and the American Imagination*, 12; Moses Harris, *Annual Report of the Acting Superintendent of Yellowstone National Park, 1886* (Washington DC: GPO, 1886), 7, "Yellowstone National Park Reports, 1877–1900," Bancroft; "A New Park Superintendent," *Forest and Stream*, May 30, 1889, 373.

24. Warren, *Hunter's Game*, 12; Jacoby, *Crimes Against Nature*, 108; Schoenberger to Secretary of the Interior, September 21, 1910, RG 79, Folder "Game Protection,"

NARA; "Where Some Game Goes To," *Forest and Stream*, March 17, 1881, 119; "The President Speaks," *Forest and Stream*, June 29, 1882, 423.

25. Reiger, *American Sportsmen*, 138; Jacoby, *Crimes against Nature*, 3, 87; *Bozeman Avant Courier*, November 25, 1886.

26. Emerson Hough, "A Premium on Crime," *Forest and Stream*, March 24, 1894, 243; "Park Poachers and Their Ways," *Forest and Stream*, May 26, 1894, 444; "The Capture of Howell," *Forest and Stream*, March 24, 1894, 378; *Livingston Post*, March 29, 1894; *Livingston Enterprise*, March 31, 1894.

27. Nolie Mumey, *Rocky Mountain Dick* (Denver: Range Press, 1953), 63–64.

28. 1998 Programme quoted in Alan Gallop, *Buffalo Bill's British Wild West* (Stroud: History Press, 2001), 48; *Washington Post*, June 1, 1896; "Buffalo Bill's Wild West Congress and Rough Riders of the World, 1893," in William F. "Buffalo Bill" Cody Collection, MS 6, McCracken Research Library, Buffalo Bill Center of the West, Cody, WY. For coverage of the complexities of Cody's show in relation to Indian affairs, see L. G. Moses, *Wild West Shows and the Images of American Indians, 1883–1933* (Albuquerque: University of New Mexico Press, 1996); and Louis S. Warren, *Buffalo Bill's America: William Cody and the Wild West Show* (New York: Vintage, 2005), 358–89. For a detailed appraisal of the fate of the bison in Cody's troupe, see David Nesheim, "How William F. Cody Helped Save the Buffalo without Really Trying," *Great Plains Quarterly* 27 (Summer 2007): 163–75.

29. George Grinnell quoted in Andrew C. Isenberg, *The Destruction of the Bison: An Environmental History, 1750-1920* (New York: Cambridge University Press, 2000), 175.

30. C. J. Jones to E. A. Hitchcock, May 16, 1905, Box 78, E-1, RG 70, NARA; Henry Inman, *Buffalo Jones' Forty Years of Adventure* (Topeka: Crane and Co., 1899), 22–23, 5, xi–xii.

HERETICAL VISIONS AND HUNTER'S PARADISE REDUX

Prescriptions for the salvation of hunter's paradise came from various constituencies and offered diverse takes on issues of environmental management, enfranchisement, and ethics. While the mainstream conservationist community spoke of regulation, restrictions on access, and the sanctification of sport as fair chase, others articulated different responses. Humanitarians and aesthetic preservationists pondered how conservation could be reconciled with the killing of animal life. Similar judgments came from reformed hunters who came to revoke the terms of the chase, often on the basis of a competing ethical code and a sense of personal guilt. Ideas of animal study and "hiker's paradise" as well as the practice of "camera hunting" promised a new version of the western game quest based on a nonconsumptive use of wildlife and the disaggregation of the hunting quest from the kill. Their performance of the hunt, in short, meant not doing it. Meanwhile, among American Indian communities in the Great Basin and across the plains, a formula for the restoration of hunting in ancestral lands came in the shape of the Ghost Dance, a movement that foretold a utopia of abundant game

DOI: 10.5876/9781607323983.c008

invoked by powerful ritual and one with far-reaching implications for settler and indigenous communities. Hunter's paradise redux spoke of radical nego-tiations and new codes of practice and performance.

HUMANITARIANS, PENITENT BUTCHERS, AND THE "FIERCE GREEN FIRE"

For the sporting naturalist, the game trail represented a place of personal renewal, spiritual engagement, and wilderness immersion. The idea of the hunter's gaze and its intimate connection to the animal—what Paul Shepard called "the traffic of energy"—animated stories of sport. Preserving hunter's paradise allowed for the sustaining of game stocks and the introspection of the chase. Competing discourses of sociological development and environmental philosophy in the latter 1800s adopted a different viewpoint. According to psy-chologist John Dewey, the "hunting psychosis" exerted a fundamental (and positive) impact over the economic and social structures of hunter-gather communities, but had limited application for modern life. Humanitarians went further, seeing the game trail not as a crucible of personal rejuvenation but as a place of biotic destruction and a landscape that encouraged the bru-talization of the human spirit. Exemplified by Henry Bergh's Society for the Prevention of Cruelty to Animals (SPCA) (1866), humanitarian philosophy centered on ideas of suffering and sentience and the moral implications of inflicting pain on animals. Where George Grinnell couched the importance of wildlife conservation in terms of the preservation of "living objects" for now and the future, humanitarians focused on the legal obligations and per-sonhood due to four-legged brethren based on their ability to "give forth the very indications of agony that we do."[1]

Significantly, as Lisa Mighetto has indicated, humanitarian sentiment and the incorporation of animals into rights-based discourses took place mostly in urban areas, where the majority of attention was focused on the welfare of domestic animals, animals of labor, and issues of vivisection. "Blood sports" did prompt some critical commentary, as did wildlife issues in the American West. From Henry Bergh and SPCA chapters came lament at the "useless and inhuman torture and destruction" of the bison as an "outrage . . . on man and beast." Colonel W. B. Hazen of the Sixth Infantry wrote to Bergh in defense of the "noble" and "harmless" animals being slaughtered by "so-called sportsmen" and hide hunters (incidentally pointing out that killing the herds was not necessary to subjugate the Indian—"the rule of justice" was ably equipped for such a purpose), while Mark Twain presented equally damning reportage of sportsmen, including what he saw as the affectations of masculine play iterated by Theodore Roosevelt. In his "Man's Place in the Animal World" (1896), under attack were British hunters who killed for "charming sport." Twain's narrative centered on ideas of waste, ethics (doctrines shared by the sportsmen-naturalists), and brutality. Comparing the aristocrats to snakes at the London Zoo, he remonstrated: "The Earl is cruel and the anaconda isn't, the earl wantonly destroys what he has no use for, but the anaconda doesn't." On another occasion he wrote how man is "the only creature that inflicts pain for sport, knowing it to be pain." Such a philosophy ventured a different solution to saving hunter's paradise and a radical reframing of the sport hunter as hero.[2]

The efficacy of conservation and sport hunting also prompted debate among the amateur or poetic naturalist community as exemplified by Henry David Thoreau, William Long, and John Muir. In common with the sporting conservationists, many among this constituency saw the spiritual and social value of communing with the wild and, indeed, recognized the value of hunting in terms of its engagement with material nature. At the same time, advocates favored an environmental philosophy based on a nonconsumptive interaction with wildlife. Thoreau accepted meat from hunters, saw them as "best men" (in comparison to farmers), and issued forth praise on the performance codes of the hunt—the stalk, the rhapsodic connection to gun and quarry, and the storytelling modus (as he noted of friend George Minott, "He loves to recall his hunting days and adventurers, and I willingly love to listen to the stories he has told a half a dozen times already"). At the same time, he described an evolution in his own practice from youthful hunting to a vocation of "naturalist or poet" marked by higher laws, restraint, and biocentrism. Thoreau's heretical dictum was "Now I go a-fishing and a-hunting everyday, but omit the fish and the game, which are the least important part." In *The Maine Woods* (1864) he issued forth a proto-biocentric manifesto situating hunting and the love of nature as oppositional: "Every creature is better alive than dead, men and moose and pine trees, and he who understands it right will rather preserve life than destroy it."[3]

For a growing community of aesthetic preservationists, the challenge of the West lay in preserving wild spaces and their faunal inhabitants for their own sake rather than for the utilitarian mantra touted by the sports-man-conservationist community. William Long railed at President Roosevelt because "every time he gets near the heart of a wild thing he invariably puts a bullet through it." The focus of John Muir and the Sierra Club (1892) was centered on preserving scenery and habitat as "cathedrals of nature," but wildlife still animated Muir's prose and environmental ethics. Notions of kin-ship underscored descriptions of the Douglas squirrel and the water ouzel in *The Mountains of California* (1894), while at times he sported a radical mis-anthropy. It was on the occasion of a deer hunt, which Muir described as "d—est work," that he issued what became one of his most quoted adages: "If a war of races should occur between the wild beasts and Lord man, I would be tempted to sympathize with the bears." Where Roosevelt spoke of a visceral exchange on the game trail with a nature red in tooth and claw, Muir conjured instead a landscape of harmony and beneficence and betrayed scant desire to indulge in a "murder business" that involved "no recognition of rights" for the four-legged.[4]

The first words of *Our National Parks* (1901) read: "The tendency nowadays to wander in wildernesses is delightful to see. Thousands of tired, nerve-shaken, over-civilized people are beginning to find out that going to the mountains is going home; that wildness is a necessity; and that mountain parks and reservations are useful not only as fountains of timber and irrigat-ing but as fountains of life." Muir's preservationist vision for the West con-jured not a hunter's paradise but a hiker's. Others venturing a fresh reading of the game trail based on a bloodless hunt included Enos Mills, who entitled one of the chapters of his *Wild Life on the Rockies* (1909) "The Wilds without Firearms," and Charlie Russell, who trudged the game trails of the Judith Basin with friend Jake Hoover but as a "harmless hunter." For Rowland Robinson, author of *Hunting without a Gun* (1905), a work dedicated to Muir, the promise of a woodland stalk without firearms brought a far richer visual "spoil" and left the "wild world no poorer for all he takes." Implicit in Robinson's treatise was a critique of the "savage blood thirst that we dignify by calling it love of sport."[5]

Similar renditions came from reformed hunters, so-called "penitent butch-ers," who came to revoke the terms of the chase on the basis of a competing moral code. Displays of contrition and motifs of redemption were common-place, suggestive of myriad varieties of epiphany at work in the theater of the hunt. Musing in his autobiography, sportsman Arthur Dugmore explained how hunting now struck him as inferior and unmanly—"a boy's sport"—a fierce rebuke to those hunter heroes enmeshed in manly posturing on the game trail. Dugmore's change of heart was founded on a sense of animal study and conservationist conscience: "As the years went by I became more and more deeply interested in natural history. The ideal of killing for the sake of killing lost its fascination. Further, it seemed wrong and foolish, inasmuch as it destroyed the creature that afforded the opportunity of study . . . The life of any animal, be it bird or beast, is far more interesting than the study of its dead body."[6]

Also common in the trope of the repentant hunter was the idea of reve-lation, often courtesy of a metaphysical connection with the animal quarry. Hunter Aldo Leopold represents the most cited example of hunting epiph-any, a man who famously reappraised his view of predatory animals while gazing into the piercing stare of a she-wolf through his gunsights in New Mexico in the 1920s. Leopold related the lupine encounter in "Thinking Like a Mountain" (1949):

> We reached the old wolf in time to watch a fierce green fire dying in her eyes.
> I realized then, and have known ever since, that there was something new
> to me in those eyes—something known only to her and to the mountain. I
> was young then, and full of trigger-itch; I thought that because fewer wolves
> meant more deer, that no wolves would mean hunters' paradise. But after see-
> ing the green fire die, I sensed that neither the wolf nor the mountain agreed
> with such a view.

Leopold did not abandon the hunt entirely (remaining a fervent supporter of bow hunting), but the precipitous engagement with the Sonoran wolf proved a foundational moment in his emerging "land ethic." In turn, the "fierce green fire" behind Leopold's ecological awakening became a canonical referent in modern environmental philosophy.[7]

There were nineteenth-century precedents to Leopold's "fierce green fire" in the form of actual or figurative conversions on the western game trail. Ernest Thompson Seton, the "Nimrod" husband of Grace, experienced a similar revelation while working as a wolf hunter in New Mexico during the 1890s. Drawn by a $1,000 bounty prize, Seton arrived at the Currampaw range and set about scattering poison bait and laying traps to trap a wolf the local stockmen had named "Old Lobo." Recounted as a short story in *Wild Animals I Have Known* (1898), the tale of "Lobo: King of Currampaw" conformed to the established tropes of the hunting story, with keen hunter pitted against a faunal outlaw possessed with "diabolic cunning." It was, moreover, a command performance of western mythology that spoke of a passing frontier, humanitarian sentiment, and, most significantly, an epiphany on the game trail. The pursuit of Old Lobo ended in January 1894, with the wolf lured to a trap by the howls of imprisoned mate Blanca (whom Seton had previously apprehended). As Lobo's "eyes glared green with hate and fury," the hunter equivocated and lay down his rifle: "Before the light had died from his fierce eyes. I cried, 'Stay, we will not kill him; let us take him alive to the camp.'" Taken to the ranch, Lobo was tethered and provided with meat and water, but died that night of a broken heart (a conclusion which aroused the ire of Roosevelt and other sporting naturalists who lambasted Seton for his sentimentalist and anthropomorphic presentation of animals). Valorized as a four-legged outlaw of the old frontier, doomed to fall before the sinuous forces of civilization, Lobo met a tragic and inevitable fate, but his penetrating gaze had prompted an ethical revelation. As Seton explained: "Ever since Lobo, my sincerest wish has been to impress upon people that each of our native wild creatures is in itself a precious heritage that we have no right to destroy or put beyond the reach of our children."[8]

Just as revelation came from direct engagement with the environment, the figurative journey to epiphany was frequently delineated in the storytelling landscape of the hunt. Autobiography, in this frame, served as confessional. The wilderness writings of Zane Grey elucidated such a process at work. In his essay "Roping Lions in the Grand Canyon," which appeared in *Forest and Stream* in January 1909, Grey gloried in the "savage sublimity" of the West as he recounted a hunting trek with Buffalo Jones in the Colorado Basin. Expressing the standard axioms of the hunter's yarn, Grey spoke of immersion in a "hunter's dream" where "men are still savage, still driven by a spirit to roam, to hunt and to slay." Skip to the final pages of the story—the literal and literary end of the game trail—and the reader found Grey apoplectic about the kill and its atavistic codes that now struck as irrational, dangerous, and foolhardy. "Colorado Trails," which appeared in *Outdoor Life* in March 1918, saw the author again enmeshed in a philosophical bind. Trailing with ranchers at the Stillwater River, he described the pursuit and treeing of a grizzly bear, the reluctance of his brother to make the kill, and his own uneasy dispatch of the animal. The historical moment of the kill sullied rather than defined the sacred encounter. As he vociferated: "The more I hunt the more I become convinced of something wrong about the game. All is exciting, hot-pressed, red. Hunting is magnificent up to the moment the shot is fired. After that it is another matter." Issuing a pointed barb at the sportsman-conservationist, he railed: "It is useless for sportsmen to tell me that they, in particular, hunt right, conserve the game, do not go beyond the limit, and all that sort of thing. A rifle is for killing."[9]

For settler A. J. Leach, the transformation from hunter to "penitent butcher" was directed by the shifting parameters of westward expansionism. When Leach arrived in Nebraska, he embraced the hunt wholeheartedly, heading to the game trail for months at a time. Also roaming across hunting typology, Leach sought animal capital for sport, subsistence, and, on a few occasions, for the market (the Kansas Nebraska railroad). In his estimation, the "frontier life" precluded any moralizing about the veracity of the hunt: in the survivalist crucible of the West, needs must. As he explained: "For five years after we settled in Antelope Country, if we had any meat at all in the family, it came from killing game." Over time, however, Leach reappraised his perspective to consider his behavior more critically, situating personal actions within a broader matrix of conquest, animal appreciation, and sense of ethical responsibility: "As I look back I almost wonder that I could have ever been hard-hearted enough to help destroy those beautiful and innocent wild animals . . . My conscience almost smites me even today, when there comes to my mind the thought of the time after time I have been guilty of taking advantage of those innocent animals when they were utterly unaware of danger."[10]

According to historian Stephen Fox, the repentant hunter proved a "familiar syndrome" in twentieth-century conservation and a fecund signal of "mature conservationism." Certainly, the imperilment of hunter's paradise and the complications of maintaining its integrity in a modern industrial nation indeed seemed to alter the perspective of even the most ardent sportsmen. Writing in his dotage, Teddy Roosevelt declared that "I am still something of a hunter, although a lover of wild nature first," while octogenarian William Pickett noted how "I have lost all desire to kill anything except for a housefly and a mosquitoe." At the same time, expressions of penitence often did not mean the rejection of the chase entirely. Mapping the contours of conscience in the hunting imagination thus involved a tricky navigation that resisted polemical readings of hunting epiphany.[11]

A man held up both as a standard-bearer of the "repentant hunter" and a model sportsman conservationist, William Hornaday proved a case in point. From keen hunting and natural history pursuits in his youth, Hornaday embraced the preservation of hunter's paradise first as a matter of taxidermic and taxonomic record before becoming captivated by the need to preserve wildlife in the material environment. In *The Extermination of the American Bison* (1889), he surveyed the biological habits of the species, set out the efforts made to capture specimens for the National Museum, and issued a fervent plea for the salvation of the genus. The narrative talked of loss, biotic vitality, and redemption through a moral conservation code. Significantly, alongside the science, Hornaday remained convinced of the power of literature as a consciousness raiser, that his treatise would "cause the public to fully realize the folly of allowing all our most valuable and interesting American mammals to be wantonly destroyed." Oratory was stark, evocative, and visually configured—a striking example not only of the trans-media culture of the hunt but also of the power of testimony to evoke environmental consciousness.[12]

Extermination paid heed to the credo of the sporting conservationist (Hornaday had, after all, joined the Boone and Crockett Club in 1896). But that was not the sum total of his hunting epiphany. In *Our Vanishing Wild Life* (1913), his second exposition on species conservation, Hornaday confessed:

> I have been a sportsman myself; but times have changed, and we must change also. When game was plentiful, I believed that it was right for men and boys to kill a limited amount of it for sport and for the table . . . Those were the days wherein no one foresaw the wholesale annihilation of species . . . In those days, gentlemen shot female hoofed game, trapped bears if they felt like it, killed ten times as much big game as they could use, and no one made any fuss whatever about the waste or extermination of wild life.

Faced with the threat of species extinction and the wholesale transformation of the West, Hornaday argued for a strident regime of protection and the obsolescence of the gun. Restrictions on bag limits and closed seasons, he contended, were not enough to stem the decline. The "army of destruction" raised against wildlife included "gentleman hunters," "gunners who kill to the limit," "game hogs," "meat shooters," "resident game butchers," and "hired laborers." Such comment was interesting in its use of martial language as well as its collapsing of hunting typology. Here Hornaday seemed to suggest that the salvation of wildlife in the West required not simply moderation but a disavowal of the chase. Readings of the hunt and its relation to ethics and epiphany were certainly complicated.[13]

"Hunting with the Camera": Consumption, Conservation, and the Transgressive Power of Photography

Both sportsman conservationists and reformed hunters articulated new discourses for hunter's paradise redux. Both of these visions were refracted through the camera lens. A combination of nature appreciation and concern for wildlife decline saw the conventions of photography as a tool of the game trail and a visual record of trophy taking challenged in the 1880s by the development of "hunting with the camera." From a modish device that framed the architecture of the chase, photography abetted conservation to offer a new visual incarnation of the West. With keen links to preservationist thinking, the camera became a way of documenting vanishing species, a signifier of sporting natural history, a marker of gentlemanly restraint, and a device of consciousness-raising for wildlife. For a small community of hunters, the implications of camera hunting were yet more radical, even rephrasing the terms of capture, consumption, and engagement with hunter's paradise itself. For such individuals, the attraction of a nonconsumptive use of wildlife while preserving the essence of the stalk, the taking of trophies by image alone, and the redundancy of the rifle entirely reconfigured the hunt as an entirely photographic one and abetted in the creation of natural history photography and film-making as a dedicated field. Technology facilitated the rise, then, of yet another hunter hero: a photographic one.

L. W. Brownell's instructional manual *Photography for the Sportsman Naturalist* (1904) highlighted an emerging discourse about conservation, natural history, sport, and the camera. As the author explained, the camera represented an essential tool of the conservation community, not least in its ability to "make animal life real to those who have never had the opportunity of seeing it in its natural state." It also had key purchase among hunters "who wish either to exchange their gun for a camera or to combine the pleasures of hunting with a camera with those of hunting with a gun." Laid out in a dedicated chapter on "photography and the sportsman," Brownell situated the camera as the tool of a "true" sportsman, someone who goes "to the wilds for the love of it and of the free, untrammelled life they can find there; who know their wild brethren and appreciate their right to life sufficiently to give them a fighting chance." The division lay not between hunters and nonhunters, but the ethical exponents of fair chase and those motivated only by wanton bloodlust or devotion to the dollar. Ethics of "wise use" thereby allowed the exercise of sporting ambitions and condoned the practice of hunting with the camera.[14]

In the conservationist mindset, a future hunter's paradise in the West meant legislation, limits to bags, and restrictions on access. Camera hunting also seemed a useful recourse to protect the wild things of the West (as well as the interests of the enfranchised hunter) in an age of ecological transformation. Teddy Roosevelt, preeminent frontier hunter hero, concluded, "More and more, as it becomes necessary to preserve the game, let us hope that the camera will largely supplant the rifle." Evelyn Cameron—equally a model of the hunter hero but in female guise—saw that "the great hunting days are over in Custer County and the ranchman and ranger will see to it that they never return. About all that is left to the sportswoman today is to hunt with the camera." For George Grinnell, too, the option of camera hunting represented an opportunity for sport in the woods in pursuit of a trophy, but with a reduced toll on wildlife. In a series of articles for *Forest and Stream*, he moved from a position of seeing the photograph as a supplement on the trail to a worthy vocation in its own right. At times, his editorials verged on the proto-ecological in their praise for the camera: "The wild world is not made the poorer by one life for his shot, nor nature's peace disturbed, nor her nicely adjusted balance jarred." Viewed through a conservation lens, hunter's paradise was reappraised and the camera was lofted as a modish device of capture more suited to the coming century than the Winchester '73.[15]

The swagger of elite sports(wo)manship could also be maintained in this new vocation. Hunting with the camera, argued Grinnell, demanded woodcraft and skill in needing to get "within closer range of his timid game than his brother of the gun." Armed only with camera, an encounter with a charging bruin was arguably far more dangerous, and presented far more of a manly adventure, than one orchestrated with a double-barreled shotgun. According to William Hornaday, "Any duffer with a good check book, a professional guide, and a high-powered repeating rifle can kill big game, but it takes good woodcraft, skill and endurance of a high order . . . to secure a really fine photograph." The prospect of stalking animals for the purposes of image capture thus confirmed the hunter's heroic mantle, requiring a cognate skill set of "hardihood, self-reliance and resolution" and favored a technological fetishism all its own (for Edward Buxton, the camera served as a worthy "alternative weapon" to "a mere tube of iron"). Just as the rifle had allowed for the flexing of frontier muscles in the nineteenth century, the camera offered a wilderness transaction for the twentieth. "It is an excellent thing to have a nation proficient in marksmanship, and it is highly undesirable that the rifle should be wholly laid by. But the shot is, after all, only a small part of the free life in the wilderness. The chief attractions lie in the physical hardihood for which the life calls, the sense of limitless freedom which it brings, and the remoteness and wild charm of primitive nature. All of these we get exactly as much in hunting with the camera as in hunting with the rifle," extrapolated Roosevelt. From the archetypal western hunter hero, such lines appeared to verge on the heretical, except when read through the lens of game scarcity and conservation consciousness.[16]

"Hunting with the camera" represented a deliberate response to the decline of hunter's paradise and offered a prescription for its salvation. While some hunters refused to see the synchronicity between rifle and camera—Edgar Randolph balked at the notion that the "platonic" impulses of "bloodless sport" could begin to give the same gratification—a sizeable number of hunters saw the utility of taking to the game trail armed with photographic equipment. Two of which were Colorado-based practitioners Allen Grant Wallihan and his wife Mary Augusta, whose work attested to an operational dialectic connecting camera, hunting, and conservation (as well as highlighting the important contribution played by women in cultures of nature preservation and sport). Both were enthusiastic hunters, a vocation they credited with inspiring interest in nature study. Mary recalled acquiring her first camera from a group of hunters in return for a pair of buckskin gloves she had made—a frontier transaction befitting the multifarious roles fulfilled by women on the "female frontier." The Wallihans' books, *Hoofs, Claws and Antlers of the Rocky Mountains, by the Camera* (1894) and *Camera Shots at Big Game* (1901) clearly displayed a hunting lineage in privileging the trophy qualities of animal capital and playing on the nomenclature of the chase. *Hoofs, Claws and Antlers* featured traditional shots of dead game, notably the classic trophy pose of Mary standing over two dead deer in "Doubles at One Shot." Moreover, the pursuit of a photographic bag frequently involved the hunting or trapping of animals and their killing. In a photograph captioned "Tree'd at Last" a harried cougar snarled at its camera captor. The animal had been driven to the branches by hounds. After the shot was taken, the cougar was, well, shot. Such activities confirmed the photograph and the gun as complicit tools of capture and signifiers of colonial dominion over nature.[17]

According to historian James Ryan, the camera hunters of the 1890s ventured a departure from the rifle in name only, a shift "in the terms of domination, away from a celebration of brute force over the natural world to a more subtle though no less powerful mastery of nature through colonial mastery and stewardship." Camera hunting enacted a process of visual capture that borrowed much from the imperial mechanics of the hunt. At the same time, Harry Johnston's description of this vocation as the "sportsmanship of the future" was not entirely disingenuous. The camera hunter offered an innovative gaze that apprehended wildlife as subjects for intimate encounter and visual capture. Trailing deer in the Black Mountains in October 1890, Allen Wallihan described tracking a herd using the typical language of the chase, seeking a "good head," and spying a target, he felt his "heart beat faster at the prospect of shooting game." However, armed with "a new 'gun'—the camera," this engagement with hunter's paradise spoke not of the kill but of the (continuing) vitality of nature, clandestine observation, and even of animal agency. Wallihan talked of his excitement at watching the deer undetected and how the shutter clicked "so faint that they did not hear it, and after a moment or two they passed on the trail, unaware of their proximity to mankind." Capturing and looking at the "authentic wild"—long the project of the hunter from the field to the taxidermy studio—remained at the essence of wildlife photography. But while trophy photographs and taxidermy offered the illusion of life, camera hunting witnessed its actuality. The product of a well-timed whistle and a camera clicking in tandem, several montages in *Hoofs, Claws and Antlers* even toyed with the animal's returning gaze. Beneath playful images of deer, captions read "What Did We Hear?," "Who Are You?," and "My Audience." Such images not only displayed the vitality of biotic life but also destabilized categories of seer and seen. Moreover, in committing the game of hunter's paradise to image, the camera hunter performed an important task of preservation advocacy.[18]

The activities of Mary and Allen Wallihan highlighted symbiotic links between hunting pursuits, the photo safari, and preservation imperatives in the West. Others, however, became so captivated by camera hunting that they rejected the rifle entirely in favor of a new interaction with hunter's paradise that foregrounded a nonconsumptive ethos of visual capture. This reframing of environmental engagement sprang from several factors, including concern at the demise of wildlife populations, direct encounter with nature, and the allure of the camera technology itself. Also frequent in the rationale of the camera hunter were considerations of ethics, sustainability, and environmental impact. As Carl Akeley adroitly put it, "When that game is over the animals are alive to play another day." On occasion, the camera itself delivered a form of epiphany. In the estimation of the *New York Times*, "Once one becomes a devotee of this form of bloodless hunting with its mainly pictorial rewards, he often loses interest in the sanguinary sport and takes up photography in the forest in earnest."[19]

A self-confessed "pioneer in this new sport" was George Shiras. Born in Pittsburgh in 1859, Shiras became an accomplished hunter and fisherman, acquiring an interest in natural history from time spent at Whitefish Lake, a "remote forest retreat" in Michigan. Experimenting with photography during the 1880s, Shiras effectively used customary tools of the hunter—canoe stalking, wires, bait, traps, and blinds—to shoot images of wild animals. The practice of jacklighting (using lanterns at night to effectively surprise game) proved of particular application to the photographic context. Shiras's techniques highlighted the mechanics of co-production between the gun and the camera safari, while his document of the visual capture of animals shared common descriptors. Making a canoe trip in 1889 armed with a canoe and a five-by-seven-inch camera, Shiras came across a buck with "striking attitude." Determined to bag the image, he ran the boat aground and seized his equipment: "Quickly I removed the cap from the lens and then replaced it. The deer, detecting this light movement, ran a short distance, then stopped, with head high in the air, and gazed anxiously in our direction." Shiras replaced the plate for a second exposure but in his haste spoiled both negatives. Reprising the hunting motifs of trigger itch and "the one that got away," he mused that the "'buck fever,' as in earlier days, had brought complete failure."[20]

Technology represented a vital aspect of Shiras's photographic enterprise. At a specially designed station at Whitefish Lake, he built tripods, remote control cameras, and automatic traps fired by wires and magnesium flash-guns. Cultures of experiment and object fetishism proved an essential aspect of camera hunting, positioning it at the intersection between wild nature and modern industrialism, a machine in the garden. After all, as Shiras mentioned, without "improved apparatus," photographic hunting would scarcely represent an interesting prospect. In this respect, the camera served as a device of technological communication, a way of speaking to nature in the fashion of the Winchester. Shiras talked about his own transition from a hunt "when the finger eagerly pulled the trigger" to one involving "the simple pressing of a button." Sometimes the synergy between photographic device and firearm was striking. The image "Doe," which Shiras submitted to a photography competition in *Forest and Stream* in 1891, was framed as if the viewer was looking down the sights of a gun barrel—an example of how the camera was commonly loaded with the provenance, metaphorical report, and technical reverence usually reserved for guns. Shiras duly spoke of the "graceful image of a hunted quarry . . . captured for all time."[21]

A friend of the sporting fraternity, paid-up member of the Boone and Crockett Club, and critic of the "misguided humanitarians who demand continuous protection for all things," Shiras appeared an archetypal sports-man conservationist. However, the photographic trail led him to challenge foundational terms of engagement with hunter's paradise. Increasingly con-vinced that the camera was "the winner over both rod and gun," Shiras set out a fresh manifesto that pointed toward new opportunities for wildlife cap-ture. This new "hunting creed" spoke of epiphany through practice, a rite of passage "from that of a keen sportsman, devoted to the use of a rifle, to that of a sportsman-naturalist, studying wild life with a camera." Shiras explained his attitude as "a particular mental evolution" accrued largely from direct engagement with Whitefish Lake. In the camera hunt, he argued, the logic of the ethical hunter hero reached its logical denouement (in common with the sporting naturalists, he believed the market hunter to be "incurable"). In a post-frontier condition, hunting struck as a needless relic; going to the woods was now to be embraced for the "delightful freedom of the wilderness" and not for the "pitiful death struggle of some wild thing." Preserving the chance to "pit his dexterity and resourcefulness against the experience, strategy, and inherent cunning of the game he pursues," camera hunting faced none of the problem of closed seasons and witnessed a much greater variety of species for the "photographic bag." Those clinging to the old mantas, Shiras railed, let "the peep-sights of a rifle" "circumscribe their vision."[22]

For many who heeded Shiras's advice, camera hunting was undertaken with a sense of conservation conscience. In fact, common among autobiographical narratives of the camera hunter was a sense of confession and catharsis. Rowland Robinson saw the camera as opening a whole new perspective on the game trail and, indeed, its memorialization: "Without it [the kill], and the gun that feeds it, we may get more than it could hold, and that which needs neither ice nor fire to preserve, not for the short space of a week, but for all our days." Viewing game through the photographic lens, many camera hunters reflected critically on past performances. Often, the semiotics of the camera hunt served as a locus of personal redemption in which advocates vociferated antipathy toward the demise of hunter's paradise and their own complicity in it. Perhaps unsurprisingly, the reformed hunter and the camera hunter were common bedfellows.[23]

A. W. Dimock, a New England hunter and the author of *Wall Street and the Wilds* (1915), came hunting in the West to renew his nerves in the fashion of the transformed man. He also indulged an interest in photography (first using a camera converted from a cigar box and then dry plates), a hobby that, by the 1880s, had advanced to a point where "the use of the camera had developed humanity in me until I couldn't bear to wantonly kill the beautiful creatures." Not the eyes of the prey, but the camera lens itself had prompted epiphany. Camera hunting indulged natural history, ethics, and a sense of atonement: "I like to forget the brutal bags of game I made in the long ago, but the thought of each camera shot brings pleasure. The life history of birds and animals as pictured by the camera contrast curiously with the game bag product of the fowling piece and the bloody trophies of the rifle." Dimock saw his photographic vocation as "pioneering" in its focus on live animals in their native haunts, while articles for the sporting press—he wrote "Camera versus Rifle" for *Mosaics* in 1890—struck him as "fugitive" in their ideological bent. These weapons of capture were, in his estimation, diametrically opposed: "One represents conservation and instruction, the other destruction alone." Similar themes graced the work of William Wright, author of *The Grizzly Bear* (1909). New Hampshire–born, Wright had migrated to Spokane and worked as a hunter and taxidermist. Musing on game pursuits, Wright chastised himself for studying the bruin simply to "better slay him" and explained how "interest in my opponent grew to over- shadow my interest in the game." Prey became animal. This realization led Wright to "lay aside" the rifle and switch to a new form of trail performance in the shape of a "photographic expedition" to Yellowstone National Park. Read not as co-producers on the game trail but fundamentally opposed, the storytelling code of the camera hunter cast the bullet and the photograph as very different mediums for appraising hunter's paradise.[24]

Camera hunting offered a radical approach to hunter's paradise that spoke of the enjoyment to be had without a gun and the nonconsumptive use of game resources. It also facilitated a new visual culture of the game trail. While the trophy shot focused overwhelmingly on the dead animal, the pho- tographic safari referenced the study and depiction of wild *life* and preserved the kudos of the hunter hero in the bargain. Shiras noted that "photographs of big game . . . were not only more beautiful than mounted heads or rugs but were far more impressive evidences of . . . prowess as a hunter." A recorder of live animals rather than strung-up corpses, the camera hunter offered a fresh version of game capture that prioritized life, movement, and continuity over mortal metaphysics. Paradise interrupted rather than paradise lost, this was less a necrogeography and more a photosensitive geography of the trail. Shiras's "Midnight Series" presented a remarkable body of work, startling in its portrayal of deer phantoms at night, biotic realism, sense of movement, and in the fact that the animals effectively "took" their own photographs by setting off trip wires. The series won gold and silver medals at the Paris Exposition in 1900 and the grand prize at the St. Louis World's Fair in 1904. Seventy-five of Shiras's images were published in a special edition of *National Geographic* in 1906, the first edition to feature the work of an animal photog- rapher. One French commentator hailed the images for their artistry: "The stag that is coming out of the reeds, how beautiful and majestic he is! And the doe! And the little family! I was quite stricken with amazement at them. This is not mere photography—it is high art." In broadcasting images of majestic and bounding live animals, Shiras introduced a fresh aesthetic to the "after- life" of the hunt. As the Frenchman added, "How happy I would be to place these splendid pieces in my hunting castle." Extending the visual culture of wildlife beyond the trophy shot, the camera hunter effectively bridged the gap between the community of nineteenth-century sportsmen interested in shots of capture and those who would develop the genre of wildlife film making in the twentieth century.[25]

For Susan Sontag the camera served as another "death weapon." According to Daniel Herman, it replaced the gun as a device for communicating with the wild. Debates about conserving hunter's paradise in the late 1800s revealed the photographic bind to be thoroughly ambiguous. A reaction to the demise of the animal complement of the West, "hunting with the camera" offered to remove, or at least reduce, the imprint of firearms on the landscape. Shiras, for instance, saw camera hunting as part of a wider imperative to restore "a proper ratio between hunter and hunted." For sportsmen conservationists, photography represented a way to continue wilderness adventuring without the wildlife toll—a suitable prescriptive for a modern industrial democracy with shrinking wild spaces and a growing population. Others, however, saw hunting with the camera as a landscape of redemption, atonement for delete-rious impacts on game, and evidence of a humanitarian agenda. As A. J. Leach mused, "How many times since have I thought, what a picture that would have made had I been armed with a camera instead of a rifle." The conver-sation between gun and camera raised issues of ethics, technology, species disappearance, resource use, and nature appreciation, but it was not mono-lithic in its prescription for salvation. Instead, it reprised broader discussions on American conservation discourse about preservation for wise use, aesthet-ics, and economics, and it inaugurated fresh debates about sporting codes and the essence of the hunt, what constituted a trophy, the value of alive over dead animals, and the environmental impact of hunting practices on the trail. Driven by a conservationist agenda, hunters traded rifled for cameras, devel-oped negatives, and considered the animal in its native haunts in a different way, in the process reframing the terms of hunter's paradise itself.[26]

VISIONS OF THE GHOST DANCE AND THE
RESTORATION OF HUNTER'S PARADISE

The saving of hunter's paradise prompted a diverse range of conservationist responses from Euro-American communities. American Indians, meanwhile, ventured their own solution to the crisis that looked to traditional forums for ritual restitution. Typically interpreted in the context of westward expansion—land seizure, treaty abrogation, assimilation, and environmental and social decline—the mechanics of the Ghost Dances that graced the West in the 1870s and, more prominently, a decade later were dominated by the issue of game decline and the ideology of hunter's paradise. Advocates spoke of a bygone age of plentitude, environmental transformation, respite and renewal, visions of apocalypse, and deliverance centered on the revitalization of game stocks and indigenous entitlements. As Bill Cody put it, "The old days of the West were to be restored. The ranges were to be restocked with elk, antelope, deer, and buffalo." In the vernacular of the Ghost Dance, the resurrection of hunter's paradise came not by adopting legislation, wise use practices, and land use management but by ritual practice and a different performance of the hunt.[27]

The stage for the initial Ghost Dance was Walker River, Nevada, home of the Northern Paiute. About 1869 a Paiute prophet named Wodziwob began to speak of a train coming from the east (a reference to the completion of the Transcontinental Railroad in 1869), an ethereal encounter with ancestors in the land of the dead, and a prescriptive strategy of community and environmental recovery. After falling into a deep trance, Wodziwob claimed he had met with elders in an abundant game paradise where he was told of their imminent return and the attendant overthrow of the whites. By participating in a circle dance, performed over five days with ritual face painting and bathing, this Elysium could be brought into being within three or four years. Here was another vision of hunter's paradise encountered, invented, and restored.

Wodziwob's prophesy of redemption paid heed to the environmental and social malaise suffered by the Paiute. Like other prescriptions to renew hunter's paradise in the West, his mandate sprang from a sense of game decline set within a broader framework of ecological and social collapse. The arrival of Argonauts seeking fortune in the Comstock Lode had brought deforestation and a decline in foraging supplies (notably pine nuts) on which the extended families of Paiute hunter-gatherers traditionally depended, while cattle and people had denuded native grasses and small game populations (also key sources of aboriginal subsistence). The political and cultural consequences of Euro-American arrival had brought land removal (Walker

River Reservation was established in 1860), epidemics, and subtle processes of acculturation. Droughts in 1863–64 and 1869 worsened the crisis, first in accentuating the scarcity of food supplies and also destabilizing the white economy which increasing numbers of Paiutes depended on as laborers. A strategic response to Euro-American expansion and attendant processes of ecological change, the 1870 Ghost Dance might well be described in terms of a conservationist vision enacted by a man whom ethnohistorian Michael Hittman calls a "crisis broker."[28]

Notions of hunter's paradise, destroyed and reconstituted, sat at the very center of Ghost Dance cosmology. Arriving at Walker River in May 1871, Indian agent C. A. Bateman recorded the popularity of "some unknown prophet who, in some way, had succeeded in advertising the farce that God was coming in the mountains beyond with a large supply for all their wants." Notable was the agent's identification of "game" as a critical marker, namely "what Indians most desire." Significantly, Bateman's description of a prophesy to "transform the sterility of Nevada to the fertility and beauty of Eden" presented an essentially conservationist vision. The agent agreed that such an idea was captivating—after all, attempts at the "glorious transformation" of alkali desert into agricultural utopia courtesy of hydraulic technology occupied the attentions of Euro-American boosters, bureaucrats, and engineers then and for years to come—but he remained cynical of the capacity of performed ritual to achieve results. Meanwhile, the means by which the Ghost Dance was disseminated ably illuminated the central role of the hunt to Paiute subsistence and cultural life. Wodziwob chose to broadcast his teachings at seasonal gatherings, including the pine nut festival and the rabbit drive, situating at once the important of the hunt as a sustaining force at Walker River and the Ghost Dance as an extension of traditional shamanic practices that paid heed to a distinguished history of hunting and performance in the West.[29]

The 1870 Ghost Dance found advocates among indigenous communities in Nevada, California, and Oregon but soon died out. Two decades later, another Ghost Dance emerged, again with an embedded vision of hunter's paradise lost and renewed and this time with broader purchase throughout the West. The architect of the 1890 dance, Wovoka, was a Paiute from Mason Valley, forty miles from the Walker River Reservation, with a reputation as a charismatic healer and weather prophet. On New Year's Day 1889, while out cutting wood, Wovoka fell to the floor unconscious. Brought back to his wikiup, he lay comatose with fever. To the surprise of those Paiutes gathered to observe a solar eclipse, the "dead" Wovoka woke up and offered the following testimony of his journey to the Spirit World, transcribed later by ethnologist James Mooney:

> Here he saw God, with all the people who had died long ago engaged in their oldtime sports and occupations, all happy and forever young. It was a pleasant land and full of game . . . God told him he must go back and tell his people they must be good and love one another, have no quarreling, and live in peace with the whites; that they must work, and not lie or steal; that they must put away all the old practices that savored of war; that if they faithfully obeyed his instructions they would at last be reunited with their friends in this other world, where there would be no more death or sickness or old age. He was then given the dance which he was commanded to bring back to his people.[30]

His vision too centered on a provident landscape of game. The importance of the hunt in the configuring of the 1890 Ghost Dance resounded in period testimony, with Indian agents and ethnographers alike foregrounding the notion of hunter's paradise, at least implicitly, as a critical element. A. I. Chapman recounted the story of Wovoka thus:

> One day while at work he heard a great noise which appeared to be above him on the mountain. He laid down his ax and started to go in the direction of the noise, when he fell down dead, and that God came and took him to heaven and showed him everything there; that it was the most beautiful country you could imagine; that he saw both Indians and whites, who were all young; that God told him that when the people died here on this earth, if they were good, they came to heaven, and he made them young again.

The markers of this utopian spirit world were various: dancing, gambling, and, notably, that "the country was nice and level and green all the time; that there were no rocks or mountains there, but all kinds of game and fish."[31]

The invocation to hunter's paradise in the 1890 Ghost Dance offered, like other conservationist philosophy, a look backward and a future prospect. In a world of environmental transformation, acculturation, and game decline, Wovoka harked back to an age of abundance in his descriptions of the people of "long ago" engaged in "oldtime sports and occupations" in a "pleasant land full of game." George Bird Grinnell in "Memories" (1915) had spoken in not dissimilar tones of his visit to the Black Hills with Custer in 1874, a country "full of game" in the shape of antelope and black-tailed deer, while his article "To the Walled in Lakes" had talked fondly of return to "the happy free life of the olden time." Meanwhile, judgments of ecocide and apocalyptic reckoning situated the philosophy of the Ghost Dance alongside modern environmental proselytizing after the fashion of Rachel Carson's *Silent Spring* (1962) or Paul Ehrlich's *Population Bomb* (1968). This idea of dramatic cataclysm, of a world literally drained of its capacity to survive and hence ripe for renewal or rebirth, also came through in James Mooney's writings. With the first chapter provocatively titled "Paradise Lost," Mooney went on to explain, "The doctrine that the world is old and worn out, and that the time for its renewal is near at hand, is an essential part of the teaching of the Ghost dance." In turn, visions of a restored landscape of plenty, and of game in particular, dominated the future envisaged by Wovoka. As Mooney observed, "The great underlying principle of the Ghost dance doctrine is that the time will come when the whole Indian race, living and dead, will be reunited upon a regenerated earth, to live a life of aboriginal happiness, forever free from death, disease, and misery."[32]

They may represent unlikely companions, but like Grinnell and Roosevelt, Wovoka offered a program of renewal and sustainability courtesy of environmental management. The mainstream conservation community sought solace in technocratic solutions, but Wovoka's answer lay in the ritual codes of the dance. This shamanic strategy, a performative invocation to inaugurate the return of hunter's paradise, pointed to the function of dance in indigenous society as a traditional device of environmental management and heroic storytelling. The Paiute round dance, with its antelope shamans and invocations to animal spirits, had long been used as a vector to encourage game stocks and good hunting. As ethnologist Willard Park recorded, "The ceremony was held for five consecutive all-night sessions and was presided over by a singer who stood inside of the circle of dancers, and by a dance leader who prayed for rain, wild seeds, fish, game, pine nuts, and good health." In Paiute cosmology the adoption of the Ghost Dance as an effective solution to environmental decay made total sense. It was, as anthropologist Thomas D. Overholt notes, "in terms of their culture, an essential 'rational' act."[33]

The Ghost Dance was to be performed every three months to usher in a new age of health and abundance. As one Paiute, "Captain Dick," related, "All Indians must dance, everywhere, keep on dancing. Pretty soon in next spring Big Man [Great Spirit] come. He bring back all game of every kind. The game be thick everywhere. All dead Indians come back and live again. They all be strong just like young men, be young again." According to Russell Thornton, the dance promised "demographic revitalization" through ethnic renewal. It also served as a provocative theatrical counter to Buffalo Bill's Wild West Show, a revue that carried the motif of hunter's paradise within the triumphal tale of wilderness exoticism and Euro-American bravado. Where Cody rode in to save the settlers' cabin from savagery, the performance of the Ghost Dance situated Wovoka as a different kind of hunter hero promising symbolic salvation.[34]

Conservation in the Euro-American tradition witnessed the control of natural resources under the auspices of a bureaucratic infrastructure informed by national prerogatives and scientific (read as objective) judgment. In the national park configuration of hunter's paradise, traditional user rights were often reframed as poaching, and access to game and territory (some would say necessarily) was curtailed. For Wovoka, on the other hand, the ecological crisis of the late nineteenth-century West prompted a different solution, one that inculcated the dance with the power of renewing an ancestral landscape of the two- and four-leggeds. His prescription of a future game utopia spoke of a place and time where the fruits of the West were abundant for all. Whereas conservationist visions in the Euro-American vernacular spoke of limited resources, wise use, and preserving fragments of a "wild West"—in the testimony of Montana pioneer David Hilger "sad remnants of their once former greatness"—the conservationist future augured by the Ghost Dance promised nothing short of hunter's paradise redux. Some of Wovoka's followers even advised the removal of the whites (who were variously turned to dust, caught in a flood, or transported to their homelands according to different renditions of the movement). Invoking the end of Euro-American presence in the West and the reclaiming of terrain by the indigene (human and nonhuman), these heretical visions broadcast a messianic message that effectively rolled back the frontier and promised the restoration of a "free land" of game for American Indians. As John Mayhugh, ex-agent from the Western Shoshone reservation, reported, "He tells them he has been to heaven and that the Messiah is coming to earth again and will put the Indians in possession of the country . . . he counsels the Indians not to disturb the White Folks saying that the blanket—or Rabbit skin that was put over the moon by the Indians long ago will soon fall off and then the moon which is now a fire will destroy the whites."[35]

White settlers had engaged Wovoka's services as a weather prophet. They were far less enamored with the militant millenarianism of his Ghost Dance. As the *Mohave County Miner* noted, "The Walapai are thoroughly imbued with the idea of the coming of Christ, and that it is not far distant when the Indians will have full possession and that all the dead Indians, deer, antelopes and other game will be back." The *Walker Lake Bulletin* was similarly uneasy, reading the ritual performance of the dance as tantamount to preparation "for war." Enigmatic and "unusual," the Ghost Dancers were "well armed and very saucy" and in possession of a liberation philosophy: "They say pretty soon they will own the stores and the ranches and houses." Taking refuge in the metaphorical fixings of a martial ecology, the paper exclaimed: "We are in the very heart of Indian Country. Within the radius of 40 miles there are over 1,000 able-bodied bucks."[36]

The 1890 Ghost Dance spread widely across the plains and the Rockies, duly becoming a conduit for resistance to westward expansionism. Kicking Horse of the Lakota related how "the Great Spirit told him that the earth was getting full of holes, and many places were rotten" and that "the Indian must keep dancing" to inaugurate a "wave of earth" that would move over the country, burying the whites, and "all the dead Indians would be restored to life again, and the buffaloes, horses, game, and their old hunting grounds would be as they were hundreds of years ago, and the Indians would for all time in the future own and occupy the earth." The decimation of an indigenous hunter's paradise, especially that of the bison, helped explain the pan-Indian appeal of Wovoka's vision. As Commissioner Morgan noted, "It is hard to overestimate the magnitude of the calamity, as they viewed it, which happened to these people by the sudden disappearance of the buffalo and the large diminution in the numbers of deer and other wild animals . . . the freedom of the chase was to be exchanged for the idleness of the camp . . . Under these circumstances it is not in human nature not to be discontented and restless, even turbulent and violent." The rapid decimation of the northern and southern herds by the mid-1880s had precipitated anxiety in the Euro-American conservationist vernacular. Among plains Indians, too, the rubric of the hunt infused the politics of conservation activism. After visiting Walker Lake in the winter of 1889–90, a Lakota delegation returned to the northern plains, with a song of human and animal renewal:

> The whole world is coming,
> A nation is coming, a nation is coming.
> The Eagle has brought the message to the tribe.
> The father says so, the father says so.
> Over the whole earth they are coming.
> The buffalo are coming, the buffalo are coming.
> The Crow has brought the message to the tribe.
> The father says so, the father says so.

The song of hunter's paradise redux offered an evocative demonstration of hunting as a motor not only of subsistence, but empowerment, cultural identity, and visionary thinking in the West. In common with conservationists, humanitarians, and camera enthusiasts, Wodziwob and Wovoka engaged in a consideration about game, ritual codes, and the transformation of wilderness to a modern industrial state. Translating ritual storytelling as "survivance," the Ghost Dance paid heed to a discourse on hunting and performance that had profoundly marked the nineteenth-century West.[37]

NOTES

1. John Dewey, "Interpretation of Savage Mind," *Psychological Review* 9 (1902): 217–30; Shepard quoted in John Mitchell, *The Hunt* (New York: Penguin, 1980), 30–31; Henry Bergh, "Extracts from Address of President Bergh, of New York," *Our Dumb Animals* 1 (June 1868): 6.

2. Lisa Mighetto, "Wildlife Protection and the New Humanitarianism," *Environmental Review* 12, no. 1 (Spring 1988): 37–40; Mark Twain, "Man's Place in the Animal World" (1896), in *Mark Twain's Book of Animals*, ed. Shirley Fishkin (Berkeley: University of California Press, 2010), 117–25.

3. Henry David Thoreau, *The Writings of Henry David Thoreau* (Boston: Houghton Mifflin, 1906), 5:304, 8:194, 11:424, 4:480; Henry David Thoreau, *The Maine Woods*, ed. Joseph Moldenhauser (Princeton: Princeton University Press, 1972 [1864]), 117–21. Also see Thomas Altherr, "'Chaplain to the Hunters': Henry David Thoreau's Ambivalence towards Hunting," *American Literature* 56, no. 3 (1984): 345–61.

4. William Long, "I Propose to Smoke Roosevelt Out," *New York Times*, June 2, 1907; John Burroughs, "Real and Sham Natural History," *Atlantic Monthly* 91 (March 1903): 298–309; Ralph Lutts, *The Nature Fakers: Wildlife, Science, and Sentiment* (Golden, CO: Fulcrum Publishing, 1990); John Muir, *The Mountains of California* (New York: Century, 1894), 226–43, 276–99; John Muir, *A Thousand-Mile Walk to the Gulf* (Boston: Houghton Mifflin, 1916), 121–22; for the aesthetic preservationist strand of conservation and wildlife policy, see Stephen Fox, *The American Conservation Movement: John Muir and His Legacy* (Madison: University of Wisconsin Press, 1981); and Lisa Mighetto, *Wild Animals and American Environmental Ethics* (Tucson: University of Arizona Press, 1991).

5. John Muir, *Our National Parks* (Boston: Houghton Mifflin, 1903), 1; Enos Mills, *Wild Life on the Rockies* (New York: Houghton Mifflin, 1909), 71–80; Charles M. Russell, *Good Medicine: Memories of the Real Hunt* (Garden City, NY: N.p., 1929), 90, 128; *Great Falls Tribune*, January 13, 1903; *Judith Basin Star* (ca.1920) and Dan Conway, "A Child of the Frontier," both in Jake Hoover Folder, Montana Historical Society Research Center (hereafter cited as MHS); Rowland Robinson, *Hunting without a Gun* (New York: Forest and Stream, 1905), 2, 348.

6. The idea of the "penitent butcher" was raised first in the British press surrounding the establishment of the Society for the Preservation of the Wild Fauna of the Empire (1903), a organ largely composed of aristocratic sportsmen. See Richard Fitter and Peter Scott, *The Penitent Butchers: The Fauna Preservation Society 1903–1978* (London: Collins, 1978); A. Radclyffe Dugmore, *Camera Adventures in the African Wilds* (New York: Doubleday, 1910), xvii–xviii.

7. Aldo Leopold, *A Sand County Almanac* (Oxford: Oxford University Press, 1949), 130.

8. Ernest Thompson Seton, *Wild Animals I Have Known* (New York: Charles Scribner's, 1898), 9; Seton quoted in Brian Leith Productions, *Lobo: The Wolf That Changed America*, directed by Steve Gooder (documentary for *Nature*, 2008).

9. George Reiger, ed., *The Best of Zane Grey, Outdoorsman* (Harrisburg, PA: Stockpole Press, 1972), 22–24, 42–47, 210, 217–20.

10. A. J. Leach, *Early Day Stories: The Overland Trail, Animals and Birds That Lived There, Hunting Stories, Looking Backward* (Norfolk, NE: Huse Publishing, 1916), 127.

11. Stephen Fox, *The American Conservation Movement* (Madison: University of Wisconsin Press, 1981), 336; William Pickett to George Grinnell, November 7, 1911, George Bird Grinnell Papers, HM223, Box 29, Folder 112: "Series II Corr Pickett, William D 1911–12, n.d.," Yale University Library; Roosevelt made the remark in *Wild Wings; Adventures of a Camera-Hunter among the Larger Wild Birds of North America on Sea and Land*, by Herbert Keightley Job with an introductory letter by

Theodore Roosevelt (New York: Houghton, Mifflin and Company, 1905) and is quoted in "Nature and Sport," *The Spectator*, December 30, 1905, 1129.

12. William Hornaday, *The Extermination of the American Bison* (Washington, DC: Smithsonian, 2002 [1889]), 371.

13. William Hornaday, *Our Vanishing Wild Life: Its Extermination and Preservation* (New York: Charles Scribner's, 1913), x, 59, 53–72.

14. L. W. Brownell, *Photography for the Sportsman Naturalist* (London: Macmillan, 1904), xvii–xviii, 8–9, 19–28.

15. George Grinnell, "Hunting with a Camera," *Forest and Stream*, May 5, 1892, 427; George Grinnell, "Shooting without a Gun," *Forest and Stream*, October 6, 1892, 287.

16. "Englishwoman's Life in West Brings Fame as Hunter of Game," *Washington Post*, November 4, 1906; Grinnell, "Shooting without a Gun"; William Hornaday, *A Wild Animal Round Up* (New York: Charles Scribner's, 1925), 331; Edward Buxton, *Short Stalks: or Hunting Camps, North, South, East, and West* (New York: G. P. Putnam's, 1892), 96; Theodore Roosevelt, *The Wilderness Hunter* (New York: G. P. Putnam's, 1893), 29.

17. Edgar Randolph, *Inter-Ocean Hunting Tales* (New York: Forest and Stream, 1908), iii, v; Allen Grant Wallihan and Mary Augusta Wallihan, *Camera Shots at Big Game* (New York: Doubleday, Page & Co., 1901), and *Hoofs, Claws, and Antlers of the Rocky Mountains, by the Camera* (Denver: Frank Thayer, 1894), 42, 31.

18. James Ryan, *Picturing Empire: Photography and the Visualization of the British Empire* (London: Reaktion, 1997), 136; Harry Johnston, introduction to C. G. Schillings, *With Flashlight and Rifle* (London: Hutchinson, 1906), xiv; Wallihan and Wallihan, *Hoofs, Claws, and Antlers*, 10–13, 16, 32, 48, 43; Wallihan and Wallihan, *Camera Shots*, 11. For camera hunting in the United States, as it developed particularly in the twentieth century and with reference to Africa, see Matthew Brower, *Developing Animals: Wildlife and Early American Photography* (Minneapolis: University of Minnesota Press, 2011), 25–82; Finnis Dunaway, "Hunting with the Camera: Nature Photography, Manliness, and Modern Memory, 1890–1930," *Journal of American Studies* 34 (2000): 207–30; Gregg Mitman, *Reel Nature: America's Romance with Wildlife on Film* (Seattle: University of Washington Press, 1999), 5–25.

19. Carl Akeley, *In Brightest Africa* (London: Heinemann, 1924), 45; "Hunting with the Camera," *New York Times*, June 18, 1916.

20. George Shiras, *Hunting Wild Life with Camera and Flashlight* (Washington, DC: National Geographic, 1936), vii, 25.

21. Ibid., 57–60; George Shiras, "Doe," *Forest and Stream*, September 8, 1892, 203; Grinnell, "Hunting with the Camera," 427.

22. Shiras, *Hunting Wild Life*, xx, 57, 25, 61, 64.

23. Robinson, *Hunting without a Gun*, 4.

24. A. W. Dimock, *Wall Street and the Wilds* (New York: Outing Publishers, 1915): 428, 444–46, 452, 453; William Wright, *The Grizzly Bear* (New York, Charles Scribner's, 1909), 11, 73, 142–45, 267.

25. Shiras, *Hunting Wild Life*, xix, viii, xcviii.

26. Susan Sontag, *On Photography* (New York: Penguin, 1977), 13–14; Daniel Herman, *Hunting and the American Imagination* (Washington, DC: Smithsonian Institution Press, 2003), 273; Shiras, *Hunting Wild Life*, xx; Leach, *Early Day Stories*, 189.

27. W. F. Cody, *An Autobiography of Buffalo Bill* (New York: Cosmopolitan Book Corp., 1920), 302.

28. Michael Hittman, "The 1870 Ghost Dance at the Walker River Reservation: A Reconstruction," *Ethnohistory* 20, no. 3 (Summer 1973): 256, 264.

29. Commissioner of Indian Affairs, *Annual Report of the Commissioner of Indian Affairs to the Secretary of the Interior, 1872* (Washington, DC: GPO, 1872), 558.

30. James Mooney, *The Ghost-Dance Religion and the Sioux Outbreak of 1890*, Fourteenth Annual Report of the Bureau of Ethnology, 1892–1893, part 2 (Washington, DC: GPO, 1896), 771–72.

31. A. I. Chapman to Gen. John Gibbon, December 6, 1890 (Exhibit B), in Thomas H. Ruger, "Operations Relative to the Sioux Indians in 1890 and 1801," *The Report of the Secretary of War, House Executive Documents, 1st Session, 52nd Congress, 1891–1892* (Washington, DC: GPO, 1892), 1:191–94.

32. George Grinnell, "Memories" (1915), 16, SC770, MHS; George Grinnell, "To the Walled in Lakes," *Forest and Stream*, March 18, 1886; Mooney, *Ghost-Dance*, 777, 661.

33. Willard Park, "Cultural Succession in the Great Basin," in Leslie Spier, A. Irving Hallowell, and Stanley Newman, eds., *Language, Culture, and Personality* (Menasha, WI: Sapir Memorial Publication, 1941), 183–84; Thomas D. Overholt, "The Ghost Dance of 1890 and the Nature of the Prophetic Process," *Ethnohistory* 21 (1974): 46.

34. Captain Dick cited in Mooney, *Ghost-Dance*, 784; Russell Thornton, *We Shall Live Again: The 1870 and 1890 Ghost Dance Movements as Demographic Revitalization* (Cambridge: Cambridge University Press, 1986).

35. David Hilger, "Overland Trail" (1907), 9, David Hilger Papers, SC854, Box 5, Folder 8: Writings (1907–1935), MHS; Mayhugh quoted in Brad Logan, "The Ghost Dance among the Paiute: An Ethnohistorical View of the Documentary Evidence 1889–1893," *Ethnohistory*, 27, no. 3 (Summer 1980): 273–74.

36. *Mohave County Miner* quoted in Henry F. Dobyns and Robert C. Euler, *The Ghost Dance of 1889 among the Pai Indians of Northwest Arizona* (Prescott: Prescott College, 1967), 19; *Walker Lake Bulletin*, November 12, 1890, and January 29, 1891.

37. Kicking Horse quoted in George Armstrong Custer, *Wild Life on the Plains* (St. Louis: Pease Taylor Publishing, 1891), 55–56; Commissioner Morgan's report and Lakota Song quoted in Mooney, *Ghost-Dance*, 829, 1072; Gerald Vizenor, *Survivance: Narratives of Native Presence* (Lincoln: University of Nebraska Press, 2008).

PRESERVATION AND PERFORMANCE

An Afterword to the Afterlife

On May 13, 1895, the inaugural Sportsman's Exposition opened at Madison Square Garden in New York. *Sporting Life* called the week-long exhibition a "Great show" that offered "articles and paraphernalia most dear" to the experienced sportsman as well as instruction to the newcomer as to "the benefits and use of that which gives health, strength, pleasure and profit to all who love the woods." The allure of the hunt in all its dimensions was laid out under one roof to create a borrowed landscape of frontier dramatics in the "great indoors." Stands advertised ammunition, firearms, kennel services, photographic materials (including a display from Scovill & Adams of New York, suppliers of Kilburn's gun camera), and a medley of sporting goods. To wash down the perfect consumer hunting experience were free cocktails from G. F. Heublein & Bros. from Hartford, purveyors of camping equipment. The array of objects on display pointed to the buoyancy of an outdoors economy of leisure and to the importance of the hunting frontier in the narrative discourse of the American West.[1]

DOI: 10.5876/9781607323983.c009

In the show arena were the full theatrical trappings of the hunt, "hunter's paradise" assembled for public digest and, indeed, purchase. Highly scripted and carefully staged, a combination of animal capital and mythological sign, the Sportsman's Expo offered an object lesson in the codes of recital and play that marked the performance of the hunt. Men peddling stories of heroic deeds, gleaming firearms, and resplendent trophies "red (and, indeed, read) in tooth and claw" communicated a repertory that spanned game trail and Wild West showground and connected the seasoned hunter and the armchair explorer together in a network of commerce, mythmaking, and dramatic purchase. Available in the arena was everything the budding sport hunter could wish for to achieve the perfect experience on the game trail: guns, cartridges, cameras, and all manner of outfitting ephemera—the mercantile culture of the hunt in its multiple iterations. Along with tools of enablement, the exhibition advertised the fulsome "afterlife" of the hunt in the form of hunting autobiographies, glossy photographs, evocative prints, and striking home décor in the form of taxidermy mounts. The rich material culture of the hunt—of interest to those wandering the tracks of the game trail and those preferring a more sedentary consumer experience of "the wild"—was clearly in evidence.

The appeal of the trans-Mississippi as an idealized landscape of game and gaming, likewise, was everywhere to be seen. As such, the Sportsman's Expo was just the latest in a distinguished genealogy of performances that gloried in the trans-Mississippi as hunter's paradise. Two exhibits in particular offered stark examples of the provenance of the West in the national imagination and of the key imprint of the hunting frontier in that mythology by century's end. Arranged in a series of cycloramas, hunter Frederick Webster told a canonical yarn in five montages, a primer on the narrative performance codes of the hunt that started with the first falls of snow in "At Last" and followed the game quest through to "A Lost Opportunity" as a fleeing bird escaped the bullet's flight. Webster's production pointed clearly to the importance of performance as a conceptual marker for understanding the material and semiotic dynamics of the hunt—a theme running throughout *Epiphany in the Wilderness*—and certainly paid heed to its implicit staging codes. The second, entitled "Recreation" and designed by notable western game hunter and conservationist George Shields, featured a hunter's cabin inside which was housed a collection of firearms, Indian artifacts, and a host of trophies including elk, antelope, Rocky Mountain goat, buffalo, and grizzlies. In one corner was draped a sleeping bag made of waterproof canvas and sheepskin, especially designed for use in the harsh frontier theater. Shield's arrangement illuminated the rich cultural ecology of the hunt in all its fabric, metal, biological, and reliquary details and, embedded within its curated objects and trinkets, the power of the West as a sacred site of personal and social memory.

As a whole, then, the Sportsman's Exhibition confirmed the hunting frontier as a richly textured terrain that was produced, played, and preserved by various actors over the span of a century. Acted and reenacted at fireside and festival hall, the performance of the hunt conjured a vibrant landscape of transformation, storytelling, and savage encounter—an epiphany in the wilderness. Standing preeminent in the process of narrative mythmaking was the masculine hunter hero: "leading man" of the game trail, curator of the hunting story in text and image, and "live action" frontier performer on the stage. Accordingly, alongside its assemblage of sporting goods, heads, and horns, the exhibition celebrated the hunter hero as adventurer, sharpshooter, and expert witness to the frontier experience. It was, after all, the Sportsman's Expo. Within the performance space of the exhibition, the hunter hero was not just producer and consumer but an artifact of the frontier himself. Hence, on the stand for the United States Cartridge Company were duly assembled several hunting guides installed in a "picturesque cabin," individuals who had facilitated the hunting experience for countless sport hunters seeking to play out their own performances of frontier experience. There to impart advice (and thereby enact once more their own expertise) were Jonathan Darling from Maine, who, *Sporting Life* noted, "has probably killed more big game than any other man in that State" and Wyoming's Ira Dodge, a champion grizzly hunter bearing the physical scars of bruin encounter. Giving floor space to archetypal hunter heroes in their typical fixings, the frontier drama playing out in Madison Square Garden gloried in the demonstrative flourish of the masculine frontiersman. Significantly, however, it also challenged his hegemonic status. As *Epiphany in the Wilderness* has highlighted, the imaginative contours of the hunting frontier served as a stage for the asserting of a heroic code that prized manly power as its heterodoxy. At the same time, however, the folkloric space of the game trail allowed room for alternative repertory in which performance served as a powerful vehicle for enacting a dissenting authority over story and space. As Rosemarie Bank reminds us, "This Wild West was a shared history and memory, a jointly occupied arena in which competing claims for authenticity could be presented and evaluated." At the Sportsman's Expo, the cast of hunter hero heretics were drawn from various quarters: Joe Francis, a Penobscot Indian, James Willard Schultz, published writer and ally of the Blackfeet, and "penitent butcher" William Wright. Such men provided alternative models of western masculinity and different templates for performing the hunt with pen, camera, or bow over shotgun and rifle. Providing incontrovertible proof that women as well as men were enticed by (and ably equipped for) the game trail and pointing to the hunter heroine as a popular stage attraction, Colorado's Mary Wallihan was on hand to articulate her skills with gun and camera and point to a "woman's way of knowing" on the game trail. Performance carried the day.[2]

By the time the exhibition opened in New York, the preservation of hunter's paradise had become not just a matter of personal remembrance and national mythology but an issue at play in the material landscape of the West. From sportsmen naturalists to Ghost Dancers, the imperilment of the game trail and its foreseen end prompted fresh approaches and new performance code. The dramatic narratives of hunting experience were vivid, diverse, and sometimes oppositional. What bound them together was a sense of the abiding importance of the hunt in individual and collective memory. The West had been firmly installed as a hunter's paradise in the popular imagination and equally exerted a powerful presence over the environmental and social lives of westerners. Animal capital exercised an important role in the dynamics of everyday existence, shaping the routines, livelihoods, identity politics, and environmental rites of multifarious communities. And now it was under threat. Epiphany in the wilderness, then, told of the impact of the environment on human socioeconomics and culture and also of the imprint of human society on the material world—an ecology of entanglement replete with animal and allegorical sign. Hunters revered, consumed, idealized, and reanimated the spaces they moved through, rendering the West a complicated landscape of subsistence, sport, profit, sacredness, belonging, and vitality. The centrality of the hunt to frontier experience, the fertile imagined landscape of hunter's paradise, and the pace of environmental change in the region thus conspired to make conservation irrevocably western in design. After all, the common denominator in the afterlife of the hunt was its preservation in text, image, and trophy. Both maintaining the memory of the hunt in story and protecting its material integrity via legislation and ethical code represented ways of keeping alive something that had proved so transformative. As the twentieth century dawned, the networks of performance and production that had made the game trail foundational to both biography and bioregion were carried forth in sacramental practice and social memory. Opened in 1904 near the eastern entrance to Yellowstone National Park, Pahaska Tepee—Bill Cody's hunting lodge and hotel—paid witness to the cultural ecology of hunter's paradise with its rough-hewn architecture of frontier theatrics and promise of campfire reverie and wilderness tonic. Evidently, the performing hunter hero needed down time as well and for that he went west. As Cody himself put it, when in need of rejuvenation, he took to Pahaska with a "bunch of congenial friends and a good cook . . . to hunt, play cards, relax and rest for three or four weeks, and it brings back my old self." This perhaps was the ultimate epiphany in the wilderness: the power of material nature to inspire and restore.[3]

Notes

1. "A Great Show: The Sportsman's Exhibition in New York," *Sporting Life* 25, no. 9 (May 25, 1895): 24–25.

2. Ibid.; Rosemarie Bank, "Representing History: Performing the Columbia Exposition," in *Critical Theory and Performance*, ed. J. Reinelt (Ann Arbor: University of Michigan Press, 1992), 605.

3. Hudson Kensel, *Pahaska Teepee: Buffalo Bill's Old Hunting Lodge and Hotel, A History, 1901–1946* (Cody, WY: Buffalo Bill Historical Center, 1987), 198.

SELECTED BIBLIOGRAPHY

Adams, James. *Life of J. C. Adams, Known as Old Adams, Old Grizzly Adams, Containing a Truthful Account of His Bear Hunts, Fights with Grizzly Bears, Hairbreadth Escapes, in the Rocky and Nevada Mountains and the Wilds of the Pacific Coast.* New York: N.p., 1860.

Adams, Kevin. *Class and Race in the Frontier Army: Military Life in the West, 1870–1890.* Norman: University of Oklahoma Press, 2009.

Aikman, Duncan. *Calamity Jane and the Lady Wildcats.* New York: Henry Holt, 1927.

Akeley, Carl. *In Brightest Africa.* London: Heinemann, 1924.

Alberti, Samuel J.M.M., ed. *The Afterlives of Animals: A Museum Menagerie.* Charlottesville: University of Virginia Press, 2011.

Alberti, Samuel J.M.M., ed. "Constructing Nature Behind Glass." *Museum and Society* 6 (2008): special issue, 73–98.

Alderson, Nannie, and Helena Huntington Smith. *A Bride Goes West.* New York: Farrar and Rinehart, 1942.

Allen, William A. *Adventures with Indians and Game, or Twenty Years in the Rocky Mountains.* Chicago: A. W. Bowen, 1903. http://dx.doi.org/10.5962/bhl.title .18606.

Altherr, Thomas. "The American Hunter-Naturalist and the Development of the Code of Sportsmanship." *Journal of Sport History* 5 (1978): 7–22.

Altherr, Thomas. "'Chaplain to the Hunters': Henry David Thoreau's Ambivalence towards Hunting." *American Literature* 56, no. 3 (1984): 345–61. http://dx.doi.org /10.2307/2926034.

Altherr, Thomas, and John Reiger. "Academic Historians and Hunting: A Call for More and Better Scholarship." *Environmental Review* 19 (1995): 39–56.

Animal Studies Group. *Killing Animals*. Chicago: University of Illinois Press, 2006.

Aquila, Richard. *Wanted Dead or Alive: The American West in Popular Culture*. Chicago: University of Illinois Press, 1998.

Aron, Stephen. *How the West Was Lost: The Transformation of Kentucky from Daniel Boone to Henry Clay*. Baltimore: Johns Hopkins University Press, 1996.

Asma, Stephen T. *Stuffed Animals and Pickled Heads: The Culture and Evolution of Natural History Museums*. Oxford: Oxford University Press, 2001.

Baker, Steve. *Picturing the Beast: Animals, Identity, and Representation*. Urbana: University of Illinois Press, 2001.

Baker, Steve. *The Postmodern Animal*. London: Reaktion, 2000.

Bank, Rosemarie. "Representing History: Performing the Columbia Exposition." In *Critical Theory and Performance*, ed. J. Reinelt, 223–44. Ann Arbor: University of Michigan Press, 1992.

Barr, Pat. *A Curious Life for a Lady: The Story of Isabella Bird, Traveller Extraordinary*. Middlesex: Penguin, 1970.

Barrow, Mark. *A Passion for Birds: American Ornithology after Audubon*. Princeton, NJ: Princeton University Press, 1998.

Barthes, Roland. *Camera Lucida: Reflections on Photography*. London: Vintage, 1993.

Basso, Matthew, Laura McCall, and Dee Garceau. *Across the Great Divide: Cultures of Manhood in the American West*. New York: Routledge, 2001.

Batty, Joseph. *Practical Taxidermy and Home Decoration: Together with General Information for Sportsmen*. New York: Orange Judd, 1890.

Bederman, Gail. *Manliness and Civilization: A Cultural History of Gender and Race in the United States, 1880–1917*. Chicago: University of Chicago Press, 1995. http:// dx.doi.org/10.7208/chicago/9780226041490.001.0001.

Bellesiles, Michael. *Arming America: The Origins of a National Gun Culture*. New York: Alfred A. Knopf, 2000.

Berger, John. *On Looking*. London: Bloomsbury, 1980.

Berkeley, Grantley. *The English Sportsman in the Western Prairie*. London: Hurst and Blackett, 1861.

Bird, Isabella. *A Lady's Life in the Rocky Mountains*. Norman: University of Oklahoma Press, 1960 (original work published 1879).

Boller, Henry. *Among the Indians: Eight Years in the Far West, 1858–1866*. Philadelphia: T. Ellwood Zell, 1868.

Bond, Jim. *America's Number One Trophy*. Portland: Metropolitan Printing Co., 1950.

Borowsky, Larry. "Filling Noah's Ark: Taxidermy, Exhibition, and Conservation in Nineteenth-Century Colorado." *Colorado Heritage* (May/June 2010): 12–21.

Branch, E. Douglas. *The Hunting of the Buffalo*. Lincoln: University of Nebraska Press, 1997.

Bronner, Simon. *Killing Tradition: Beyond Hunting and Animal Rights Controversies*. Lexington: University Press of Kentucky, 2008. http://dx.doi.org/10.5810/kentucky/9780813125282.001.0001.

Browder, Laura. *Her Best Shot: Women and Guns in America*. Chapel Hill: University of North Carolina Press, 2006.

Brower, Matthew. *Developing Animals: Wildlife and Early American Photography*. Minneapolis: University of Minnesota Press, 2011.

Brown, Richard Maxwell. *Strain of Violence: Historical Studies of American Violence and Vigilantism*. New York: Oxford University Press, 1975.

Brownell, L. W. *Photography for the Sportsman Naturalist*. New York: Macmillan, 1904. http://dx.doi.org/10.5962/bhl.title.55459.

Burgin, Victor, ed. *Thinking Photography*. London: Macmillan, 1982.

Burke, John. *Buffalo Bill: From Prairie to Palace*. Chicago: Rand McNally, 1893.

Burke, Martha Cannary. Life and Adventures of Calamity Jane, By Herself. N.p., 1896.

Burroughs, Raymond. *The Natural History of the Lewis and Clark Expedition*. East Lansing: Michigan State University Press, 1995.

Burt, Jonathan. *Animals in Film*. London: Reaktion, 2008.

Burt, Mary, ed. *The Boy General: Story of the Life of Major General George A. Custer as told by Elizabeth Custer*. New York: Charles Scribner's, 1901.

Butler, Judith. *Gender Trouble: Feminism and the Subversion of Identity*. New York: Routledge, 1999.

Buxton, Edward. *Short Stalks: or Hunting Camps, North, South, East, and West*. New York: G. P. Putnam's, 1892. http://dx.doi.org/10.5962/bhl.title.32102.

Calkins, Frank W. *Frontier Sketches, Indian Tales, and Hunting Stories*. Chicago: Donahue, Hennebery & Co., 1893.

Campion, J. S. *On the Frontier: Reminiscences of Wild Sports, Personal Adventures and Strange Scenes*. London: Chapman and Hall, 1878. http://dx.doi.org/10.5962/bhl.title.19401.

Carnes, Mark C., and Clyde Griffen. *Meanings for Manhood: Constructions of Masculinity in Victorian America*. Chicago: University of Chicago Press, 1990.

Cartmill, Matt. *A View to a Death in the Morning: Hunting and Nature through History*. Cambridge, MA: Harvard University Press, 1993.

Cartwright, David. *Natural History of Western Wild Animals and Guide for Hunters, Trappers, and Sportsmen*. Toledo: Blade Printing & Paper Co., 1875.

Catlin, George. *North American Indians*. Philadelphia: Leary, Stuart and Company, 1913.

Caton, John Dean. *The Antelope and Deer of America*. New York: Hurd and Houghton, 1877.

Cattermole, E. G. *Famous Frontiersmen, Pioneers, and Scouts: The Vanguards of American Civilization*. Chicago: M. A. Donohue and Co., 1880.

Cawelti, John. *The Six-Gun Mystique*. Bowling Green, OH: Bowling Green State University Popular Press, 1984 (original work published 1970).

Chittenden, Hiram Martin. *The American Fur Trade of the Far West: A History of the Pioneer Trading Posts and Early Fur Companies of the Missouri Valley and the Rocky Mountains and the Overland Commerce with Santa Fe*. 2 vols. Lincoln: University of Nebraska Press, 1986 (original work published 1902).

Chubbuck, Kay, ed. *Letters to Henrietta*. Boston: Northeastern, 2003.

Cody, W. F. *The Adventures of Buffalo Bill*. New York: Harper & Row, n.d.

Cody, W. F. *An Autobiography of Buffalo Bill*. New York: Cosmopolitan Book Corporation, 1920.

Cody, W. F. *Buffalo Bill (Hon. Wm. F. Cody) and His Wild West Companions*. Chicago: Henneberry Co., n.d.

Cody, W. F. "Famous Hunting Parties of the Plains." *Cosmopolitan* 17, no. 2 (June 1894): 137–40.

Cody, W. F. *The Life of Hon. William F. Cody, Known as Buffalo Bill: The Famous Hunter, Scout, and Guide, An Autobiography*. Hartford, CT: F. E. Bliss, 1879.

Coleman, Annie. "Rise of the House of Leisure: Outdoor Guides, Practical Knowledge, and Industrialization." *Western Historical Quarterly* 42, no. 4 (2011): 436–57. http://dx.doi.org/10.2307/westhistquar.42.4.0436.

Colpitts, George. *Game in the Garden: A Human History of Wildlife in Western Canada to 1940*. Vancouver: University of British Columbia Press, 2002.

Cook, John. *The Border and the Buffalo*. Topeka: Crane, 1907.

Cronon, William, George Miles, and Jay Gitlin, eds. *Under an Open Sky: Rethinking America's Western Past*. New York: W. W. Norton, 1992.

Custer, Elizabeth. *Boots and Saddles*. New York: Harper and Bros., 1885.

Custer, Elizabeth. *Following the Guidon*. New York: Harper and Bros., 1890.

Custer, George Armstrong. *My Life on the Plains*. New York: Sheldon and Co., 1874.

Custer, George Armstrong. *Wild Life on the Plains*. St. Louis: Pease Taylor Publishing, 1891.

Dary, David. *The Buffalo Book: The Saga of an American Symbol*. New York: Avon, 1974.

Davies, Henry. *Ten Days on the Plains*. New York: Crocker and Co., 1871.

Dee, D. *Lowdown on Calamity Jane*. Rapid City, SD: N.p., 1932.

DeVoto, Bernard, ed. *The Journals of Lewis and Clark*. Boston: Houghton Mifflin, 1953.

Dillon, Richard. *Grizzly Adams: A Memorable Mountain Man*. Davis: University of California, 1966.

Dillon, Richard. *The Legend of Grizzly Adams: California's Greatest Mountain Man*. New York: Coward-McCann, 1966.

Dimock, A. W. *Wall Street and the Wild*. New York: Outing Publishers, 1915. http://dx.doi.org/10.5962/bhl.title.26365.

Dizard, Jan. *Going Wild: Hunting, Animal Rights, and the Contested Meaning of Nature*. Amherst: University of Massachusetts Press, 1999.

Dizard, Jan. *Mortal Stakes: Hunters and Hunting in Contemporary America.* Amherst: University of Massachusetts Press, 2003.

Dobyns, Henry, and Robert C. Euler. *The Ghost Dance of 1889 among the Pai Indians of Northwest Arizona.* Prescott: Prescott College Press, 1967.

Dodge, Richard Irving. *The Hunting Grounds of the Great West.* London: Chatto and Windus, 1877.

Drannan, William F. *Thirty-One Years on the Plains and in the Mountains.* Chicago: Rhodes and McClure, 1900.

Dufran, Dora. *Lowdown on Calamity Jane*, revised edition. Deadwood: Helen Rezatto, 1981.

Dugmore, A. Radclyffe. *Camera Adventures in the African Wilds.* New York: Doubleday, 1910.

Dunaway, Finnis. "Hunting with the Camera: Nature Photography, Manliness, and Modern Memory, 1890–1930." *Journal of American Studies* 34, no. 2 (2000): 207–30. http://dx.doi.org/10.1017/S0021875899006349.

Dunlap, Thomas. *Nature and the English Diaspora: Environment and History in the United States, Canada, Australia, and New Zealand.* Cambridge: Cambridge University Press, 1999.

Dunlap, Thomas. *Saving America's Wildlife: Ecology and the American Mind, 1850–1990.* Princeton, NJ: Princeton University Press, 1988.

Dunlap, Thomas. "Sport Hunting and Conservation." *Environmental Review* 12, no. 1 (Spring 1988): 51–59.

Dunraven, Whindham Thomas Wyndham Quin, Earl of. *The Great Divide: Travels in the Upper Yellowstone in the Summer of 1874.* London: Chatto and Windus, 1876.

Dunraven, Whindham Thomas Wyndham Quin, Earl of. *Hunting in the Yellowstone: On the Trail of the Wapiti with Texas Jack in the Land of Geysers.* New York: Outing Publishing Co., 1917.

Dye, Job Francis. *Recollections of a Pioneer, 1830–1852: Rocky Mountains, New Mexico, California.* Los Angeles: Glen Dawson, 1951.

Dykstra, Robert. "Body Counts and Murder Rates: The Contested Statistics of Western Violence." *Reviews in American History* 31, no. 4 (December 2003): 554–63. http://dx.doi.org/10.1353/rah.2003.0068.

Dykstra, Robert. *The Cattle Towns.* New York: Alfred A. Knopf, 1968.

Ewers, John. *The Horse in Blackfoot Indian Culture.* Washington, DC: Smithsonian Institution Press, 1953.

Fishkin, Shelly Fisher, ed. *Mark Twain's Book of Animals.* Berkeley: University of California Press, 2011.

Fitter, Richard, and Peter Scott. *The Penitent Butchers: The Fauna Preservation Society, 1903–1978.* London: Collins, 1978.

Flores, Dan. "Bison Ecology and Bison Diplomacy: The Southern Plains from 1800 to 1850." *Journal of American History* 78, no. 2 (September 1991): 465–85. http://dx.doi.org/10.2307/2079530.

Floyd, Janet. *Writing: The Pioneer Women*. Columbia: University of Missouri Press, 2002.

Fox, Stephen. *The American Conservation Movement*. Madison: University of Wisconsin Press, 1981.

Francis, Charles. *Sport among the Rockies*. New York: Troy Daily Times Job Printing Establishment, 1889.

Frost, John. *Heroes and Hunters of the West*. Philadelphia: H. C. Peck and Theo. Bliss, 1860.

Frost, Lawrence A., ed. *With Custer in '74: James Calhoun's Diary*. Provo, UT: Brigham Young University Press, 1979.

Gallop, Alan. *Buffalo Bill's British Wild West*. Stroud: History Press, 2001.

Garraty, John A. *Theodore Roosevelt: The Strenuous Life*. New York: Harper and Row, 1987.

Gasper, Howland. *The Complete Sportsman*. New York: Forest and Stream, 1893.

Geist, Valerious. *Buffalo Nation: History and Legend of the North American Bison*. Stillwater, MN: Voyageur Press, 1996.

George, Susanne K. *The Adventures of the Woman Homesteader: The Life and Letters of Elinore Pruitt Stewart*. Lincoln: University of Nebraska Press, 1992.

Gillespie, Greg. *Hunting for Empire: Narratives of Sport in Rupert's Land, 1840–1870*. Vancouver: University of British Columbia Press, 2007.

Gillespie, Greg. "'I Was Well Pleased with Our Sport among the Buffalo': Big-Game Hunters, Travel Writing, and Cultural Imperialism in the British North American West, 1847–72." *Canadian Historical Review* 83, no. 4 (2002): 555–84. http://dx.doi.org/10.3138/CHR.83.4.555.

Gillmore, Parker. *Accessible Field Sports: The Experiences of a Sportsman in North America*. London: Chapman and Hall, 1869.

Gillmore, Parker. *Prairie and Forest*. New York: Harper's, 1874.

Giltner, Scott E. *Hunting and Fishing in the New South*. Baltimore: Johns Hopkins University Press, 2008.

Goetzmann, William H., and William N. Goetzmann. *The West of the Imagination*. New York: Norton, 1988.

Greville, Lady Violet. *Ladies in the Field*. New York: D. Appleton, 1894.

Grinnell, George, and Theodore Roosevelt. *Trail and Campfire: The Book of the Boone and Crockett Club*. New York: Forest and Stream, 1897.

Grinnell, George, and Theodore Roosevelt, eds. *Hunting at High Altitudes*. New York: Harper and Bros., 1913.

Grinnell, George, Theodore Roosevelt, and Charles Sheldon, eds. *Hunting and Conservation*. New Haven: Yale University Press, 1925.

Grohman, William Baillie. *Camps in the Rockies*. London: Sampson, Low, Marston, Searle & Rivington, 1882.

Grohman, William Baillie. *Fifteen Years' Sport and Life in the Hunting Grounds of Western America and British Columbia*. London: Horace Cox, 1900.

Grossman, James, ed. *The Frontier in American Culture.* Berkeley: University of California Press, 1994.

Haines, Aubrey. *The Yellowstone Story.* Boulder, CO: Associated University Press, 1977.

Halberstam, Judith. *Female Masculinity.* Durham, NC: Duke University Press, 1998.

Hall, Roger. *Performing the American Frontier, 1870–1906.* Cambridge: Cambridge University Press, 2001.

Hamilton, W. T. *My Sixty Years on the Plains.* New York: Forest and Stream, 1905.

Haraway, Donna. "Teddy Bear Patriarchy: Taxidermy in the Garden of Eden, New York City, 1908–1936." *Social Text* 11 (Winter 1984–85): 19–64.

Harding, A. R., ed. *Fifty Years a Hunter and Trapper.* St. Louis: A. R. Harding, 1913.

Hartley, Cecil B. *Hunting Sports of the West, Adventures of the Most Celebrated Hunters and Trappers.* Philadelphia: Bradley and Co., 1865. http://dx.doi.org/10.5962/bhl.title.18536.

Hastings, Lansford. *The Emigrants' Guide to Oregon and California.* Cincinnati: George Conclin, 1845.

Hauser, Kitty. "Coming Apart at the Seams: Taxidermy and Contemporary Photography." *Make: The Magazine of Women's Art* 82 (1998–99): 8–11.

Heclawa. *In the Heart of the Bitter-Root Mountains: The Story of the Carlin Hunting Party.* New York, G. P. Putnam's, 1895.

Herbert, Henry William. *Frank Forester's Field Sports of the United States and British Provinces of North America.* New York: W. A. Townsend, 1864.

Herman, Daniel. *Hunting and the American Imagination.* Washington, DC: Smithsonian Institution Press, 2003.

Herne, Peregrine. *Perils and Pleasures of a Hunter's Life, or the Romance of Hunting.* New York: Evans and Co., 1858.

Hines, Donald M. *Ghost Voices: Yakima Indian Myths, Legends, Humor, and Hunting Stories.* Issaquah, WA: Great Eagle, 1992.

Hittell, Theodore H. *The Adventures of James Capen Adams, Mountaineer and Grizzly Bear Hunter of California.* San Francisco: Towne and Bacon, 1860.

Hittman, Michael. "The 1870 Ghost Dance at the Walker River Reservation: A Reconstruction." *Ethnohistory* 20, no. 3 (Summer 1973): 247–78. http://dx.doi.org/10.2307/481446.

Hooper, Jonathan J. *Rod and Gun.* Tuscaloosa: University of Alabama Press, 1992.

Hornaday, William. *Our Vanishing Wild Life: Its Extermination and Preservation.* New York: Charles Scribner's, 1913.

Hornaday, William. *Taxidermy and Zoological Collecting.* New York: Charles Scribner's, 1894.

Hornaday, William. *A Wild Animal Round Up.* New York: Charles Scribner's, 1925.

Hornaday, William. *The Extermination of the American Bison.* Washington, DC: Smithsonian, 2002 (original work published 1889).

Hornecker, Martin. *Buffalo Hunting on the Texas Plains in 1877.* Geneseo, IL: Republic, 1929.

Hough, Emerson. *Let Us Go Afield*. New York: D. Appleton and Co., 1916.

Houze, Herbert G., Carolyn C. Cooper, and Elizabeth Mankin Kornhauser. *Samuel Colt: Arms, Art, and Invention*. New Haven: Yale University Press, 2006.

Howe, Henry. *Historical Collections of the Great West: Containing Narratives of the Most Important and Interesting Events in Western History—Remarkable Individual Adventures—Sketches of Frontier Life—Descriptions of Natural Curiosities*. New York: George Tuttle, 1857.

Hughes, J. Donald. *American Indian Ecology*. El Paso: Texas Western Press, 1983.

Hughes, Richard. *Pioneer Years in the Black Hills*. Ed. Agnes Wright Spring. Glendale, CA: Arthur H. Clark Company, 1957.

Hungry Wolf, Adolf. *Charlo's People: The Flathead Tribe of Montana*. Invermere, BC: Good Medicine Books, 1974.

Hutchinson, Horace, ed. *Big Game Shooting*. New York: Charles Scribner's, 1905.

Inman, Henry. *Buffalo Jones' Forty Years of Adventure*. Topeka: Crane and Co., 1899.

Isenberg, Andrew. *The Destruction of the Bison: An Environmental History, 1750–1920*. New York: Cambridge University Press, 2000. http://dx.doi.org/10.1017/CBO9780511549861.

Jacoby, Karl. *Crimes against Nature: Squatters, Poachers, Thieves, and the Hidden History of American Conservation*. Berkeley: University of California Press, 2001.

James, Edwin. *Account of an Expedition from Pittsburgh to the Rocky Mountains*. London: Longman, 1823.

Jeffrey, Julie Roy. *Frontier Women: The Trans-Mississippi West*. New York: Hill and Wang, 1979.

Jennewein, J. Leonard. *Calamity Jane of the Western Trails*. Rapid City, SD: Dakota West Books, 1953.

Jones, Allen Morris. *A Quiet Place of Violence: Hunting and Ethics on the Missouri River Breaks*. Bozeman, MT: Bangtail Press, 1997.

Kasson, Joy S. *Buffalo Bill's Wild West: Celebrity, Memory, and Popular History*. New York: Hill and Wang, 2000.

Keller, Robert, and Michael Turek. *American Indians and National Parks*. Tucson: University of Arizona Press, 1998.

Kelley, Joyce. "Increasingly 'Imaginative Geographies': Excursions into Otherness, Fantasy, and Modernism in Early Twentieth-Century Women's Travel Writing." *Journal of Narrative Technique* 35, no. 3 (2005): 357–72. http://dx.doi.org/10.1353/jnt.2006.0013.

Kensel, Hudson. *Pahaska Teepee: Buffalo Bill's Old Hunting Lodge and Hotel, A History, 1901–1946*. Cody, WY: Buffalo Bill Historical Center, 1987.

Kerasote, Ted. *Blood Ties: Nature, Culture, and the Hunt*. New York: Random House, 1983.

Kimmel, Michael S. *Manhood in America: A Cultural History*. Oxford: Oxford University Press, 2006.

Kingston, William. *Adventures in the Far West*. London: Routledge, n.d.

Kolodny, Annette. *The Land before Her: Fantasy and Experience of the American Frontiers, 1630–1860.* Chapel Hill: University of North Carolina Press, 1984.

Kolodny, Annette. *The Lay of the Land: Metaphor as Experience and History in American Life and Letters.* Chapel Hill: University of North Carolina Press, 1975.

Knoepflmacher, U. C., and G. B. Tennyson, eds. *Nature and the Victorian Imagination.* Berkeley: University of California Press, 1977.

Krech, Shepard, III, ed. *Indians, Animals, and the Fur Trade: A Critique of Keepers of the Game.* Athens: University of Georgia Press, 1981.

Lang, Lincoln. *Ranching with Roosevelt.* Philadelphia: J. B. Lippincott, 1926.

Latour, Bruno. *Reassembling the Social: An Introduction to Actor-Network-Theory.* Oxford: Oxford University Press, 2005.

Leach, A. J. *Early Day Stories: The Overland Trail, Animals and Birds That Lived There, Hunting Stories, Looking Backward.* Norfolk, NE: Huse Publishing, 1916. http://dx .doi.org/10.5962/bhl.title.18725.

Lee, R. *Taxidermy, or the Art of Collecting, Preparing and Mounting Objects of Natural History for the Use of Museums and Travellers.* London: Longman, 1820. http://dx.doi.org /10.5962/bhl.title.29582.

Leopold, Aldo. *A Sand County Almanac.* New York: Ballantine Books, 1966.

Leveson, H. A. *Sport in Many Lands.* London: Chapman and Hall, 1877.

Lewis, Elisha J. *The American Sportsman.* Philadelphia: J. B. Lippincott, 1906.

Li, Judith. *To Harvest, To Hunt: Stories of Resource Use in the American West.* Corvallis: Oregon State University Press, 2007.

Logan, Brad. "The Ghost Dance among the Paiute: An Ethnohistorical View of the Documentary Evidence 1889–1893." *Ethnohistory* 27, no. 3 (Summer 1980): 267–88. http://dx.doi.org/10.2307/481271.

Loo, Tina. "Of Moose and Men: Hunting for Masculinities in British Columbia, 1880–1939." *Western Historical Quarterly* 32, no. 3 (Autumn 2001): 296–319. http://dx.doi .org/10.2307/3650737.

Lopez, Barry Holstun. *Of Wolves and Men.* New York: Touchstone Books, 1977.

Lott, Dale F., and Harry Greene. *American Bison: A Natural History.* Berkeley: University of California Press, 2003.

Lucey, Donna M. *Photographing Montana, 1894–1928: The Life and Work of Evelyn Cameron.* Missoula, MT: Mountain Press, 1990.

Lutts, Ralph. *The Nature Fakers: Wildlife, Science, and Sentiment.* Golden, CO: Fulcrum Publishing, 1990.

Mackay, Helen Raynor. "Good Medicine: A Gracious Lady Remembers CMR in Her New Jersey Home." *Montana: The Magazine of Western History* 7 (Winter 1957): 37–38.

Mackay, Malcolm. *Cow Range and Hunting Trail.* New York: G. P. Putnam's, 1925.

Mackenzie, John. *The Empire of Nature: Hunting, Conservation, and British Imperialism.* Manchester: Manchester University Press, 1988.

Mackenzie, John. *Museums and Empire: Natural History, Human Cultures and Colonial Identities.* Manchester: Manchester University Press, 2009.

MacKethan, Lucinda. "Grace Gallatin Thompson Seton: Excerpt from A Woman Tenderfoot." *Legacy: A Journal of American Women Writers* 27, no. 1 (2010): 195–97.

Macleod, David. *Building Character in The American Boy: The Boy Scouts, YMCA, and their Forerunners, 1870–1920.* Madison: University of Wisconsin Press, 1983.

Magoc, Chris. *Yellowstone: The Creation and Selling of an American Landscape, 1870–1903.* Albuquerque: University of New Mexico Press, 1999.

Maguire, Horatio. *The Black Hills and American Wonderland.* Chicago: Donnelley, Lloyd & Co., 1877.

Maguire, Horatio. *The Coming Empire.* Sioux City, IA: Watkins and Smead, 1878.

Mangan, J., and J. Wavin, eds. *Manliness and Morality: Middle-Class Masculinity in Britain and America.* Manchester: Manchester University Press, 1987.

Marcy, Randolph. *The Prairie Traveler, A Handbook for Overland Expeditions.* New York: Harper and Brothers, 1859.

Marcy, Randolph. *Thirty Years of Army Life on the Border.* New York: Harper and Bros., 1866.

Marks, Stuart A. *Southern Hunting in Black and White: Nature, History, and Ritual in a Carolina Community.* Princeton: Princeton University Press, 1992.

"Marksman." *The Dead Shot: The Sportsman's Complete Guide.* London: Longmans, Green, 1882.

Marsh, James B. *Four Years in the Rockies.* Newcastle, PA: W. B. Thomas, 1884.

Martin, Calvin. *Keepers of the Game: Indian-Animal Relations in the Fur Trade.* Berkeley: University of California Press, 1979.

Mattes, Merrill J., ed. *Indians, Infantry, and Infants: Andrew and Elizabeth Burt of the Frontier.* Denver: Old West Publishing Co., 1960.

Mayer, Alfred. *Sport with Gun and Rod.* New York: Century Co., 1883.

Maynard, C. J. *Manual of Taxidermy.* Boston: S. E. Cassino and Co., 1883.

McClintock, Walter. *The Old North Trail.* New York: Macmillan, 1910.

McConnell, H. H. *Five Years a Cavalryman, or Sketches of Regular Army Life on the Texas Frontier, 1866–1875.* Norman: University of Oklahoma Press, 1996.

McGrath, Roger D. *Gunfighters, Highwaymen & Vigilantes: Violence on the Frontier.* Berkeley: University of California Press, 1984.

McHugh, Tom. *The Time of the Buffalo.* New York: Alfred Knopf, 1972.

McLaird, James. *Calamity Jane: The Woman and the Legend.* Norman: University of Oklahoma Press, 2005.

McMurtry, Larry. *The Colonel and Little Missie: Buffalo Bill, Annie Oakley, and the Beginnings of Megastardom in America.* New York: Simon and Schuster, 2006.

McShane, Linda. *"When I Wanted the Sun to Shine": Kilburn and Other Littleton, New Hampshire Stereographers.* Littleton, NH: Sherwin Dodge Publisher, 1993.

Mead, James R. *Hunting and Trading on the Great Plains, 1859–1875.* Ed. Schuyler Jones. Norman: University of Oklahoma Press, 1986.

Meltzer, Milton. *Theodore Roosevelt and His America.* New York: Franklin Watts, 1994.

Menzies, Mrs. Stuart. *Women in the Hunting Field.* London: Vinton, 1913.

Merchant, Carolyn. "George Bird Grinnell's Audubon Society: Bridging the Gender Divide in Conservation." *Environmental History* 15, no. 1 (January 2010): 3–30. http://dx.doi.org/10.1093/envhis/emq015.

Merritt, John. *Baronets and Buffalo: The British Sportsman in the American West, 1833–1881*. Missoula, MT: Mountain Press, 1985.

Messiter, Charles. *Adventures among the North American Indians*. London: R. H. Porter, 1890. http://dx.doi.org/10.5962/bhl.title.23349.

Mighetto, Lisa. *Wild Animals and American Environmental Ethics*. Tucson: University of Arizona Press, 1991.

Mighetto, Lisa. "Wildlife Protection and the New Humanitarianism." *Environmental Review* 12, no. 1 (Spring 1988): 37–40.

Milgrom, Melissa. *Still Life: Adventures in Taxidermy*. Boston: Houghton Mifflin Harcourt, 2010.

Miller, Dorcas. *Adventurous Women: The Inspiring Lives of Nine Early Outdoorswomen*. Boulder, CO: Pruett Publishing, 2000.

Mills, Enos. *Wild Life on the Rockies*. New York: Houghton Mifflin, 1909.

Milner, Clyde. "The Shared Memory of Montana Pioneers." *Montana: The Magazine of Western History* 37 (1973): 2–13.

Milner, Clyde, ed. *A New Significance: Re-envisioning the History of the American West*. New York: Oxford University Press, 1996.

Milner, Clyde, Carol A. O'Connor, and Martha A. Sandweiss, eds. *The Oxford History of the American West*. New York: Oxford University Press, 1994.

Mitchell, John. *The Hunt*. New York: Penguin, 1980.

Mitman, Gregg. *Reel Nature: America's Romance with Wildlife on Film*. Seattle: University of Washington Press, 1999.

Mooney, James. *The Ghost-Dance Religion and the Sioux Outbreak of 1890*. Fourteenth Annual Report of the Bureau of Ethnology, 1892–1983, part 2. Washington, DC: GPO, 1896.

Morris, Pat. *A History of Taxidermy: Art, Science and Bad Taste*. Ascot: MPM, 2010.

Moses, L. G. "'The Father Tells Me So!' Wovoka: The Ghost Dance Prophet." *American Indian Quarterly* 9, no. 3 (Summer 1985): 335–51. http://dx.doi.org/10.2307/1183834.

Moses, L. G. *Wild West Shows and the Images of American Indians, 1883–1933*. Albuquerque: University of New Mexico Press, 1996.

Muir, John. *The Mountains of California*. New York: Century, 1894.

Muir, John. *Our National Parks*. Boston: Houghton Mifflin, 1903.

Muir, John. *A Thousand-Mile Walk to the Gulf*. Boston: Houghton Mifflin, 1916.

Mulford, A. F. *Fighting Indians in the 7th United States Cavalry*. Corning, NY: Paul Lindsley Mulford, 1878.

Murphy, John Mortimer. *Sporting Adventures in the Far West*. London: Sampson Low, Marston, Searle & Rivington, 1870.

Myers, Charles E. *Memoirs of a Hunter: Fifty-Eight Years of Hunting and Fishing*. Davenport, WA: Shaw and Borden, 1948.

Nash, Roderick. "The American Invention of National Parks." *American Quarterly* 22, no. 3 (Autumn 1970): 726–35. http://dx.doi.org/10.2307/2711623.

Nash, Roderick. *Wilderness and the American Mind*. New Haven: Yale University Press, 1967.

Naylor, Natalie A., Douglas Brinkley, and John Allen Gable. *Theodore Roosevelt: Many-Sided American*. Interlaken, NY: Heart of the Lakes Publishing, 1992.

Nesheim, David. "How William F. Cody Helped Save the Buffalo without Really Trying." *Great Plains Quarterly* 27 (Summer 2007): 163–75.

Ormond, Clyde. *Hunting in the Northwest*. New York: Alfred A. Knopf, 1948.

Ortega y Gasset, Jose. *Meditations on Hunting*. New York: Charles Scribner's, 1972.

Overholt, Thomas D. "The Ghost Dance of 1890 and the Nature of the Prophetic Process." *Ethnohistory* 21, no. 1 (1974): 37–63. http://dx.doi.org/10.2307/481129.

Palliser, John. *The Solitary Hunter or Sporting Adventures in the Prairies*. London: George Routledge, 1856.

Pearson, Jeffrey V. "Nelson A. Miles, Crazy Horse, and the Battle of Wolf Mountains." *Montana: The Magazine of Western History* 51 (Winter 2001): 53–67.

Pearson, Mike, and Michael Slater. *Theatre/Archaeology*. London: Routledge, 2001.

Petersen, David. *Heartsblood: Hunting, Spirituality, and Wildness in America*. Washington, DC: Island Press, 2000.

Petersen, David, ed. *A Hunter's Heart: Honest Essays on Blood Sport*. New York: Henry Holt, 1996.

Peterson, Larry Len. *L. A. Huffman: Photographer of the American West*. Missoula, MT: Mountain Press, 2003.

Philo, Chris, and Chris Wilbert, eds. *Animal Spaces, Beastly Places: New Geographies of Human-Animal Relations*. London: Routledge, 2000.

Poliquin, Rachel. "The Matter and Meaning of Museum Taxidermy." *Museum and Society* 6, no. 2 (July 2008): 123–34.

Posewitz, Jim. *Inherit the Hunt*. Guilford, CT: Falcon, 1999.

Pratt, Annis. "Women and Nature in Modern Fiction." *Contemporary Literature* 13, no. 4 (Autumn 1972): 476–90. http://dx.doi.org/10.2307/1207443.

Pray, Leon Luther. *Taxidermy*. New York: Outing Publishers, 1913.

Prince, Sue Ann, ed. *Stuffing Birds, Pressing Plants, Shaping Knowledge: Natural History in North America, 1730–1860*. Philadelphia: American Philosophical Society, 2003.

Proctor, Nicholas. *Bathed in Blood: Hunting and Mastery in the Old South*. Charlottesville: University of Virginian Press, 2002.

Punke, Michael. *Last Stand: George Bird Grinnell and the Battle to Save the Buffalo*. Lincoln: University of Nebraska Press, 2007.

Quinn, Stephen. *Windows on Nature: The Great Habitat Dioramas of the American Museum of Natural History*. New York: Abrams, 2006.

Rabb, Jane, ed. *Literature and Photography: Interactions, 1840–1990*. Albuquerque: New Mexico University Press, 1995.

Randolph, Edgar. *Inter-Ocean Hunting Tales*. New York: Forest and Stream, 1908. http://dx.doi.org/10.5962/bhl.title.18539.

Rattenbury, Richard. *The Art of American Arms Makers*. Oklahoma City: National Cowboy and Western Heritage Museum, 2004.

Rattenbury, Richard. *Hunting the American West: The Pursuit of Big Game for Life, Profit, and Sport, 1800–1900*. Missoula, MT: Boone and Crockett Club, 2008.

Reddin, Paul. *Wild West Shows*. Chicago: University of Illinois Press, 1999.

Reiger, George, ed. *The Best of Zane Grey, Outdoorsman*. Harrisburg, PA: Stackpole Press, 1972.

Reiger, John. *American Sportsmen and the Origins of Conservation*. Corvallis: Oregon State University Press, 2001 (original work published 1975).

Rico, Monica. *Nature's Noblemen: Transatlantic Masculinities and the Nineteenth-Century American West*. New Haven: Yale University Press, 2013.

Riley, Glenda. *Confronting Race: Women and Indians on the Frontier*. Albuquerque: University of New Mexico Press, 2004.

Riley, Glenda. *The Female Frontier: A Comparative View of Women on the Prairie and the Plains*. Lawrence: University Press of Kansas, 1988.

Riley, Glenda. "Images of the Frontierswoman: Iowa as a Case Study." *Western Historical Quarterly* 8, no. 2 (April 1977): 189–202. http://dx.doi.org/10.2307/967250.

Riley, Glenda, and Richard Etulain, eds. *By Grit and Grace: Eleven Women Who Shaped the American West*. Golden, CO: Fulcrum, 1997.

Ritvo, Harriet. *The Animal Estate: The English and Other Creatures in the Victorian Age*. Cambridge, MA: Harvard University Press, 1987.

Robinson, Charles, ed. *The Diaries of John Gregory Bourke. Vol. 1, November 20, 1872–July 28, 1873*. Denton: University of North Texas Press, 2003.

Robinson, Rowland. *Hunting without a Gun*. New York: Forest and Stream, 1905.

Roe, Frank. *The North American Buffalo: A Critical Study of the Species in Its Wild State*. Toronto: University of Toronto Press, 1951.

Roosevelt, Theodore. *From the Alleghenies to the Mississippi, 1769–1776. Vol. 1, The Winning of the West*. New York: G. P. Putnam's, 1889.

Roosevelt, Theodore. *Good Hunting in Pursuit of Big Game*. New York: Harper's, 1907.

Roosevelt, Theodore. *Hunting the Grisly and Other Sketches*. New York: G. P. Putnam's, 1900.

Roosevelt, Theodore. *Hunting Trips of a Ranchman*. New York: G. P. Putnam's, 1885.

Roosevelt, Theodore. *Outdoor Pastimes of an American Hunter*. New York: Charles Scribner's Sons, 1908.

Roosevelt, Theodore. *Ranch Life and the Hunting Trail*. New York: G. P. Putnam's, 1893.

Roosevelt, Theodore. *The Wilderness Hunter*. New York: G. P. Putnam's, 1893.

Rothfels, Nigel, ed. *Representing Animals*. Bloomington: Indiana University Press, 2002.

Rotundo, Anthony. *American Manhood: Transformations on Masculinity from the Revolution to the Modern Era*. New York: Basic Books, 1993.

Rowley, John. *The Art of Taxidermy*. New York: D. Appleton, 1898.

Runte, Alfred. *National Parks: The American Experience*. Lincoln: University of Nebraska Press, 1979.

Russell, Charles M. *Good Medicine: Memories of the Real Hunt*. Garden City, NY: n.p., 1929.

Ruxton, Edward. *Ruxton of the Rockies*. Norman: University of Oklahoma Press, 1950.

Ryan, James. *Picturing Empire: Photography and the Visualization of the British Empire*. London: Reaktion, 1997.

Rydell, Robert, and Rob Kroes. *Buffalo Bill in Bologna: The Americanization of the World, 1869–1922*. Chicago: University of Chicago Press, 2005. http://dx.doi.org/10.7208 /chicago/9780226732343.001.0001.

Sage, Rufus B. *Rocky Mountain Life, or Startling Scenes and Perilous Adventures in the Far West*. Boston: Wentworth, 1857.

Sage, Rufus B. *Rufus B. Sage: His Letters and Papers, 1836–1847 and Scenes in the Rocky Mountains; with an annotated reprint of his "Scenes in the Rocky Mountains, and in Oregon, California, New Mexico, Texas, and the grand prairies"* vol. 1. Glendale, CA: Arthur Clark, 1956.

Salt, Henry. *Animals' Rights Considered in Relation to Social Progress*. New York: Macmillan, 1894.

Sandoz, Mari. *The Buffalo Hunters: The Story of the Hide Men*. New York: Hastings, 1954.

Sandweiss, Martha. *Print the Legend: Photography and the American West*. New Haven: Yale University Press, 2002.

Schechner, Richard. *Performance Studies: An Introduction*. New York: Routledge, 2002.

Schillings, C. G. *With Flashlight and Rifle*. London: Hutchinson, 1906.

Schullery, Paul. "A Partnership in Conservation: Roosevelt in Yellowstone." *Montana: The Magazine of Western History* 28, no. 3 (Summer 1978): 2–15.

Schultz, James Willard. *Blackfeet Tales of Glacier National Park*. Cambridge, MA: Riverside Press, 1916.

Selous, Frederick. *Sport and Travel: East and West*. London: Longmans, Green & Co., 1901.

Sellier, Charles. *The Life and Times of Grizzly Adams*. Los Angeles: Schick Sunn Books, 1977.

Senn, Edward. *Deadwood Dick and Calamity Jane: A Thorough Sifting of Facts from Fiction*. Deadwood, SD: n.p., 1939.

Seton, Ernest Thompson. *Trail of an Artist-Naturalist: The Autobiography of Ernest Thompson Seton*. New York: Charles Scribner's Sons, 1940.

Seton, Ernest Thompson. *Wild Animals I Have Known*. New York: Charles Scribner's, 1898. http://dx.doi.org/10.5962/bhl.title.60103.

Seton, Grace Gallatin Thompson. *The Log of the "Look See": A Half-Year in the Wilds of Matto Grosso and the Paraguayan Forest, over the Andes to Peru*. London: Hurst and Blackett, 1932.

Seton, Grace Gallatin Thompson. *Nimrod's Wife*. New York: Doubleday, Page & Co., 1907.

Seton, Grace Gallatin Thompson. *A Woman Tenderfoot*. New York: Doubleday, Page & Co., 1905 (original work published 1900).

Shell, Hanna Rose. "Skin Deep: Taxidermy, Embodiment, and Extinction in W. T. Hornaday's Buffalo Group." In *The Past, Present, and Future of Natural History: Proceedings of the California Academy of Sciences*, ed. A. Leviton, 88–112. San Francisco: California Academy of Sciences, 2004.

Shepard, Paul. *The Tender Carnivore and the Sacred Game*. Athens: University of Georgia Press, 1974.

Shields, George. *Cruising in the Cascades: And Other Hunting Adventures*. Chicago: Rand McNally, 1889.

Shields, George. *Rustlings in the Rockies*. Chicago: Belford, Clarke & Co., 1883.

Shiras, George. *Hunting Wild Life with Camera and Flashlight*. Washington, DC: National Geographic, 1936.

Shukin, Nicole. *Animal Capital: Rendering Life in Biopolitical Times*. Minneapolis: University of Minnesota Press, 2009.

Slagle, Jefferson D. "America Unscripted: Performing the Wild West." In *A Companion to the Literature and Culture of the American West*, ed. Nicolas S. Witschi, 427–42. Chichester: Wiley-Blackwell, 2011. http://dx.doi.org/10.1002/9781444396591.ch27.

Slotkin, Richard. *The Fatal Environment: The Myth of the Frontier in the Age of Industrialization, 1800–1890*. New York: Atheneum, 1985.

Slotkin, Richard. *Gunfighter Nation: The Myth of the Frontier in Twentieth-Century America*. Norman: University of Oklahoma Press, 1998.

Slotkin, Richard. *Regeneration through Violence: The Myth of the American Frontier, 1600–1800*. Middletown: Wesleyan University Press, 1973.

Smalley, Andrea L. "'Our Lady Sportsmen': Gender, Class, and Conservation in Sport Hunting Magazines, 1873–1920." *Journal of the Gilded Age and Progressive Era* 4, no. 04 (October 2005): 355–80. http://dx.doi.org/10.1017/S1537781400002759.

Smith, Henry Nash. *Virgin Land: The American West as Symbol and Myth*. Cambridge, MA: Harvard University Press, 1950.

Smits, David D. "The Frontier Army and the Destruction of the Buffalo: 1865–1883." *Western Historical Quarterly* 25, no. 3 (Autumn 1994): 313–39.

Sontag, Susan. *On Photography*. New York: Penguin, 1977.

Spence, Mark David. *Dispossessing the Wilderness: Indian Removal and the Making of the National Parks*. New York: Oxford University Press, 1999.

Spencer, George. *Calamity Jane: A Story of the Black Hills*. New York: Cassell, 1887.

Spotts, David L. *Campaigning with Custer and the Nineteenth Kansas Volunteer Cavalry*. Ed. E. A. Brininstool. Los Angeles: Wetzel, 1928.

Stange, Mary Zeiss. *Woman the Hunter*. Boston: Beacon Press, 1997.

Stange, Mary Zeiss. ""Women and Hunting in the West." Montana." *Magazine of Western History* 55, no. 3 (Fall 2005): 14–21.

Steiner, Michael, and Wayne Franklin, eds. *Mapping American Culture*. Iowa City: University of Iowa Press, 1992.

Stevens, Montague. *Meet Mr. Grizzly: A Saga on the Passing of the Grizzly*. Albuquerque: University of New Mexico Press, 1943.

Stewart, Elinore Pruitt. *Letters of a Woman Homesteader*. Boston: Houghton Mifflin, 1914.

Stewart, Elinore Pruitt. *Letters on an Elk Hunt by a Woman Homesteader*. Lincoln: University of Nebraska Press, 1979 (original work published 1915).

St. Maur, Susan Margaret McKinnon. *Impressions of a Tenderfoot during a Journey in Search of Sport in the Far West*. London: J. Murray, 1890.

Stockmesser, Kent. *The Western Hero in History and Legend*. Norman: University of Oklahoma Press, 1965.

Storer, Tracy, and Lloyd Tevis. *California Grizzly*. Lincoln: University of Nebraska Press, 1955.

Stuart, Granville. *Forty Years on the Frontier*. Cleveland: Arthur Clark Co., 1925.

Stuart, Granville. *Montana As It Is*. New York: Arno, 1865.

Sundstrom, Linea. *Storied Stone: Indian Rock Art in the Black Hills*. Norman: University of Oklahoma Press, 2004.

Swan, James. *In Defense of Hunting: Yesterday and Today*. New York: HarperOne, 1995.

Thoreau, Henry David. *The Maine Woods*. Ed. Joseph Moldenhauer. Princeton: Princeton University Press, 1972 (original work published 1864).

Thoreau, Henry David. *The Writings of Henry David Thoreau*. Boston: Houghton Mifflin, 1906.

Thornton, Russell. *We Shall Live Again: The 1870 and 1890 Ghost Dance Movements as Demographic Revitalization*. Cambridge: Cambridge University Press, 1986. http://dx.doi.org/10.1017/CBO9780511752735.

Thorp, Raymond W. *Spirit Gun of the West: The Story of Doc. F. Carver*. Glendale: Arthur H. Clark Co., 1957.

Toepperwein, Fritz Arnold. *Footnotes of the Buckhorn*. Boerne, TX: Highland Press, 1960.

Trefethen, James B. *An American Crusade for Wildlife*. New York: Winchester Press, 1975.

Turner, Frederick Jackson. *The Frontier in American History*. New York: Henry Holt, 1920.

Turner, F. W. *Beyond Geography: The Western Spirit against the Wilderness*. New York: Viking, 1980.

Urbino, L. B., et al. *Art Recreations*. Boston: Shepard and Gill, 1873.

Utley, Robert. *A Life Wild and Perilous: Mountain Men and the Paths to the Pacific*. New York: Henry Holt and Co., 1997.

Van Dyke, Theodore S. *Flirtation Camp, or, The Rifle, Rod, and Gun in California*. New York: Fords, Howard & Hulbert, 1881.

Vecsay, Christopher, and Robert W. Venables, eds. *American Indian Environments: Ecological Issues in Native American History*. Syracuse: Syracuse University Press, 1980.

Vibert, Elizabeth. *Trader's Tales: Narratives of Cultural Encounters in the Columbia Plateau, 1807–1846*. Norman: University of Oklahoma Press, 1997.

Visscher, William Lightfoot, ed. *Buffalo Bill's Own Story of His Life and Deeds*. Chicago: John R. Stanton, 1917.

Vivian, A. Pendarves. *Wanderings in the Western Land*. London: Sampson, Low, 1879.

Wakeham, Pauline. *Taxidermic Signs: Reconstructing Aboriginality*. Minneapolis: University of Minnesota Press, 2008.

Wallace, Dillon. *Saddle and Camp in the Rockies*. New York: Outing Publishers, 1911.

Wallihan, Allen Grant, and Mary Augusta Wallihan. *Camera Shots at Big Game*. New York: Doubleday, Page & Co., 1901. http://dx.doi.org/10.5962/bhl.title.40637.

Wallihan, Allen Grant, and Mary Augusta Wallihan. *Hoofs, Claws, and Antlers of the Rocky Mountains, by the Camera*. Denver: Frank Thayer, 1894.

Ward, James Rowland. *The Sportsman's Handbook to Practical Collecting, Preserving and Artistically Setting up of Trophies and Specimens*. London: Simpkin, Marshall, Hamilton, Kent & Co., 1891.

Ward, James Rowland. *Horn Measurements and Weights of the Great Game of the World: Being a Record for the Use of Sportsmen and Naturalists*. London: The Jungle, 1892.

Ward, James Rowland. *A Naturalist's Life Study in the Art of Taxidermy*. London: Rowland Ward, 1913.

Warren, Louis S. *Buffalo Bill's America: William Cody and the Wild West Show*. New York: Alfred Knopf, 2005.

Warren, Louis S. "Cody's Last Stand: Masculine Anxiety, the Custer Myth, and the Frontier of Domesticity in Buffalo Bill's Wild West." *Western Historical Quarterly* 34, no. 1 (Spring 2003): 49–69. http://dx.doi.org/10.2307/25047208.

Warren, Louis S. *The Hunter's Game: Poachers and Conservationists in Twentieth-Century America*. New Haven: Yale University Press, 1997.

Watts, Sarah. *Rough Rider in the White House*. Chicago: University of Chicago Press, 2003.

Webb, James Josiah. *Adventures in the Santa Fe Trade, 1844–47*. Philadelphia: Ralph Biber, 1974.

Webb, W. E. *Buffalo Land: An Authentic Account of Discoveries, Adventures, and Mishaps of a Scientific and Sporting Party in the Wild West*. Chicago: Hannaford, 1872.

Webber, C. W. *The Hunter Naturalist: Romance of Sporting, or Wild Scenes and Wild Hunters*. Philadelphia: J. B. Lippincott, 1859.

Westmore, C., and Z. Grey. *The Last of the Great Scouts*. New York: Grosset and Dunlap, 1913 (original work published 1899).

White, G. Edward. *The Eastern Establishment and the Western Experience*. New Haven: Yale University Press, 1968.

White, Richard. *The Roots of Dependency: Subsistence, Environment, and Social Change among the Choctaws, Pawnees, and Navajos*. Lincoln: University of Nebraska Press, 1983.

Williams, Megan Rowley. *Through the Negative: The Photographic Image and the Written Word in Nineteenth-Century America*. New York: Routledge, 2003.

Williamson, Andrew. *Sport and Photography in the Rocky Mountains*. Edinburgh: David Douglas, 1880.

Wishart, David. *The Fur Trade of the American West, 1807–1840: A Geographical Synthesis*. Lincoln: University of Nebraska Press, 1979.

Wislizenus, F.A. *A Journey to the Rocky Mountains in the Year 1839*. St. Louis: Missouri Historical Society, 1912.

Wister, Owen. *Red Man and White*. New York: Harper and Bros., 1895.

Wonders, Karen. *Habitat Dioramas: Illusions of Wilderness in Museums of Natural History*. Uppsala: Almqvist and Wiksells, 1993.

Wonders, Karen. "Hunting Narratives of the Age of Empire: A Gender Reading of Their Iconography." *Environmental History* 11, no. 3 (2005): 269–91. http://dx.doi.org/10.3197/096734005774434511.

Woodcock, Eldred. *Fifty Years a Hunter and Trapper*. St Louis: A. R. Harding, 1913.

Woodward, Arthur, ed. *The Journal of Lt. Thomas W. Sweeny, 1849–1853*. Los Angeles: Westernlake Press, 1956.

Worman, Charles G. *Gunsmoke and Saddle Leather: Firearms in the Nineteenth-Century American West*. Albuquerque: University of New Mexico Press, 2005.

Worster, Donald. *An Unsettled Country: Changing Landscapes of the American West*. Albuquerque: University of New Mexico Press, 1994.

Worthen, W. B. "Disciplines of the Text/Sites of Performance." *TDR* 39, no. 1 (Spring 1995): 13–28. http://dx.doi.org/10.2307/1146399.

Wright, William. *The Grizzly Bear*. New York: Charles Scribner's, 1909.

Ziter, Cary. *The Moon of Falling Leaves*. New York: Franklin Watts, 1988.

INDEX